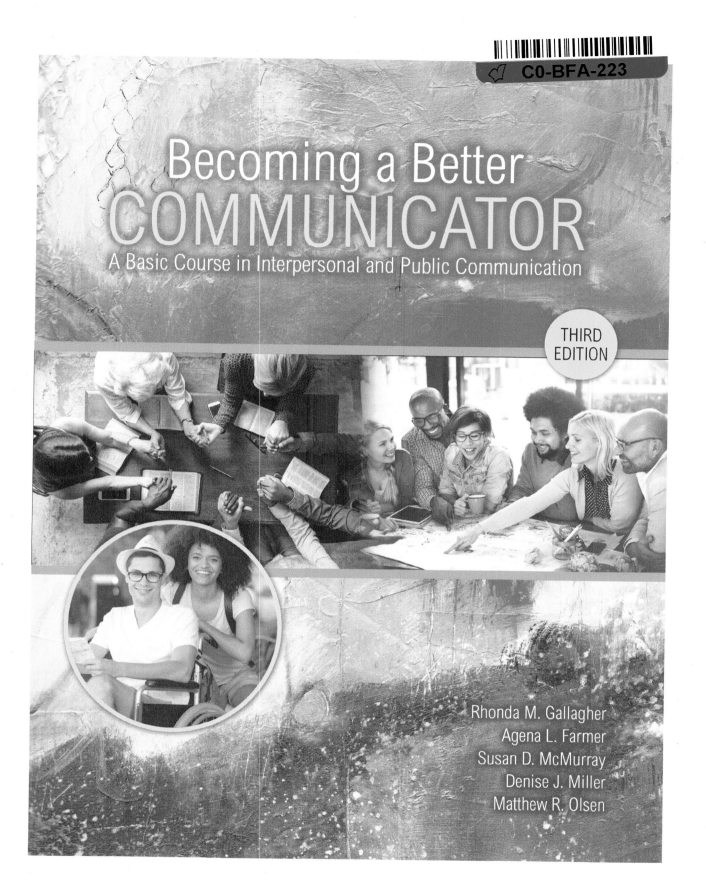

Becoming a Better
COMMUNICATOR

A Basic Course in Interpersonal and Public Communication

THIRD
EDITION

Rhonda M. Gallagher
Agena L. Farmer
Susan D. McMurray
Denise J. Miller
Matthew R. Olsen

Kendall Hunt
publishing company

First edition previously self-published by the authors.

Cover images © Shutterstock.com

Kendall Hunt
publishing company

www.kendallhunt.com
Send all inquiries to:
4050 Westmark Drive
Dubuque, IA 52004-1840

Copyright © 2017, 2018 by Kendall Hunt Publishing Company

ISBN: 978-1-5249-6719-2

Published in the United States of America

Contents

Contributors

We want to give a special thank you for the following contributors.

Marinell Scott-Hall, M.A.

Two contributing editors:

Katherine M. Kelley, Ph.D.

Marcela Chavan, Ph. D.

Introduction

Nearly a decade ago, I attended a lunch seminar about implementing a Christian worldview into classes, and it changed my life. The concept made perfect sense to me. I thought that of all the topics that lend themselves to that, surely communication was an obvious choice. It is no accident that the words "communication," "communion," and "community" all come from the same root. It is by communication that we commune with another soul and build our communities. Figuratively speaking, it felt as if a beam of light came through the ceiling to my brain when I saw how to do it. This book is an outgrowth of that experience.

The book is constructed as it is for two reasons. First, most college textbooks attempt to take an "objective, neutral" approach to content that expresses no moral or ethical perspective on how the material can be applied to real life. That just seems wrong to me. I'm not trying to indoctrinate my students, but applying the Golden Rule to how we deal with people seems pretty important for communication instructors. This is especially true since I see more and more students for whom there is a disconnect between "Christian belief" practiced in church services and how they behave in everyday life. In addition, I see more and more students dealing with anxiety, depression, abuse, and damaged psyches, so knowing that God thinks they are precious also seems increasingly important.

Secondly, most communication texts are written by academics as if the readers are academics, not college freshmen being forced to read something as dull as dishwater. Communication is exciting, and dare I say, fun! The text ought to reflect that, so we have adopted a very casual writing style in hopes that the text might be fun to read, and students might *actually* read it.

I started this book singlehandedly, but soon realized I wanted some help from other people who could bring different expertise, perspectives, and voices to it. I am so grateful to the other authors. Words cannot express how I feel about them.

When we first began to write together and word got out to other faculty members, we were told that before it was over, we would all hate each other. I am so happy to say those naysayers could not have been more wrong. We have disagreed with each other about content and methods, of course, but these people have become like siblings to me. We have met most weeks for 2-3 hours for about five years, and we have only become closer and learned from each other. I hope and pray that anyone who reads this has the privilege of working in a group like that at some time in their life.

Now, after a careful reworking of the book, we offer you the 3rd edition. It has been a labor of love with and for each other, and for you, dear reader. At any rate, this is our humble offering in hopes of helping students of life learn, grow, and become better communicators, and one by one, change their world.

Blessings,

Rhonda M. Gallagher, M.S.

Better Communicator's Overview

By Rhonda Gallagher, M.S.

1

Welcome to the study of communication! You are probably reading this book because you were required to for a foundational class in communication, and you probably thought you'd be required to give a speech, which prompted either dread or excitement. You may have felt like it was a waste of your time/money/energy to have to study something that you have been doing all your life, or you may have felt like the class would be so specific and deep that you wouldn't understand any of it. Well, if you're one of the people who found the idea of the class intimidating, you should know that communication is something you've been doing your entire life, so you already know some stuff. You just don't *know* that you know, and before the class is over, you'll know more! If, on the other hand, you're one of the folks who sees no reason to study communication, let me tell you why we need to study it. Even though we may have been doing it all our lives, we all have gaps in our communication skills such as listening, speaking, understanding others, building relationships, working with others, and public speaking. In fact, even within the communication faculty, we find areas in which we are weak. Furthermore, we need to be good at this because it connects with every area of our lives, whether our professional lives (Cope, 2015; Doloi, 2009), our friendships (Baxter & Phillpot, 1982; Berndt, 1986), our romantic connections (Egeci & Gencoz, 2006; Meeks, Hendricck, & Hendrick, 1998), our educational opportunities (Bainbridge Frymier, & Houser, 2000; Ortiz-Rodriguez, Telg, Irani, Roberts, & Rhoades, 2005), even our relationships with ourselves (Unal,

© Monkey Business Images/Shutterstock.com

Communication
the process of creating and sharing one's thoughts, emotions, or concepts with another person

2012; Joinson, 2001) and God. It is not accidental that the words communication, community, and communion all come from the same root. It is through our communication that we commune with others and build our communities. This is powerful stuff, so we need to become aware of it.

Communication is the process of creating and sharing one's thoughts, emotions, or concepts with another person. It's exchanging information through the use of symbols like words, actions, or facial expressions. It creates shared meaning and can be as complex as an abstract thought (Einstein's Theory of Relativity, for example) or as simple as your reaction to the weather. Sometimes, we communicate complex thoughts, and at other times just pure emotion. In any case, some basic principles of communication apply.

Principles of Communication: Basic Stuff You Need to Know

Communication must be received.

For communication to happen, at the bare minimum, you need communicators and a message to share. Someone has to receive the message. You can't create shared meaning without something to share and someone to share it with. But it doesn't have to be intentional to be communication. If you sneeze, it's not intentional, but it still communicates. Maybe you have allergies or are coming down with a cold. (You should know that there is a debate among communication scholars about this [Motley, 2009], but in my opinion, lots of communication takes place that isn't intended to occur.) If you see someone on the street coming toward you that you don't want to talk to, you may show it on your face by frowning. You didn't intend to share that thought, but you communicated it anyway. However, if you think of that person and frown but no one sees you, then the frown is not communication because no one received the message.

Communication uses symbols.

Symbol
something that represents something else

Basically, a **symbol** is something that represents something else. Symbols stand in for other things (Langer, 1942). There are different types of symbols, either verbal or non-verbal (Hybels & Weaver, 2001).

Verbal ⟷ Nonverbal

Sidebar 1A Symbols can be verbal or non-verbal

Words are verbal symbols, whether spoken or written. Whether you speak the words "ice cream cone" or I write them, they stand in for the thing you eat. But the ice cream cone can also be represented with a nonverbal symbol, specifically a picture of an ice cream cone or even a gesture, like licking the air over a clenched fist as if to eat it.

Communication is a continuous transaction.

By that, I mean that it is an ongoing process, not a single event. Multiple events happen that form the interchange between people. It is ongoing, and simultaneous, and unfolds over time (Hybels, & Weaver, 2001). We tend to think that each communication event existes independently from other communications, but that is not true. First of all, communication exists on a timeline. It has a past, present, and future. When you meet a member of the opposite sex, you bring to that interchange your past experiences. If you're a man meeting a woman, you subconsciously reference in your mind all the things you know about women from your past and you make predictions about how she will behave based on those things, so the past affects the interaction. Your mood, physical state, or distractions in the present may also affect how you interpret her behavior, so the present is affecting how you interpret her communication. Of course, if you think she is attractive, you may be thinking about whether or not you want to try to develop a possible relationship into a friendship or more. That's the future playing into the event. Furthermore, both parties give and take meaning from each other. We already know that we expect to contribute something to the conversation or interaction, and we expect a response. If no response is received, the interchange will languish and die. Both parties must engage in giving and receiving.

Communication is irreversible.

Because it exists on a timeline, you don't get to go back and undo it (DeVito, 2016; Wood, 2002). If you goofed and said something stupid or hurtful, or culturally insensitive, you have to work to overcome that. As much as you might want to smack yourself, you have to work with what you have created. You can't (as I once saw a woman do) say, "Oops! That wasn't very nice; let me take my spiritual eraser out and remove that right out of the air. Erase, erase, erase." Let me tell you, that did not make the message she sent go away!

Communication is inevitable.

Watzlawick, Bavelas, and Jackson (1962) said it best. "You cannot *not* communicate." Let me repeat that, because it's really important: you cannot not communicate. If you are alive and conscious, it is impossible not to send messages. You see, communication is continuous and simultaneous. Both parties send and receive messages constantly. If the person you spoke to stood perfectly still and showed no reaction while you were asking a question or making a comment, you'd think there was something wrong. We expect nonverbal feedback all the time to show that the

© Photographee.eu/Shutterstock.com

person we are communicating with is paying attention and listening, and we constantly give the same kind of feedback. We don't think about it; we just do it. If you're talking face to face, you expect eye contact. If you're talking on the phone, you expect to hear the odd "uh-huh" periodically to confirm the other person is still engaged. (I call that *ear contact*.) If you've ever had someone refuse to acknowledge you, they might *say* that they were "not communicating" with you, but you got the message, didn't you? They were angry and wanted you to know it!

Communication is affected by culture.

Culture
shared beliefs, values, symbols and knowledge of group history

Culture is made up of shared beliefs, values, symbols, and knowledge of group history. Culture is the sea in which all elements of communication swim. All words and actions are filtered through it, and someone from outside that culture may not know how to use or interpret those words and actions correctly. It changes meanings profoundly (Dobkin & Pace, 2003). It affects how we interpret everything: verbal and nonverbal symbols, relationships, behaviors . . . *everything*! Personal space varies widely between cultures (Hogh-Olesen, 2008), not to mention how you use eye contact or facial expressions, how you perceive power, or what are the expected behaviors for your gender. From one culture to another, nonverbal symbols can be very different. Looking someone in the eye in the U.S. is a sign of honesty, but in some countries, it is failing to show respect or even looking for a fight. Speaking a different language is only one way that verbal communication differs. Voice tone, volume, who speaks first in a group, and the topics you can and cannot discuss all are affected by culture. Even in countries that speak the same language, a word can mean different things. It may be an elevator in the U.S., but it's a lift in the U.K. The geographic region can make a difference and symbolic meanings can change. By the way, anytime a culture exists inside a larger culture, we call that a co-culture. Co-cultures can be based on geography, but also on social, religious, or political groups. Whenever a group of people within a larger culture become so closely associated with each other that they have developed group characteristics, that group has its own co-culture.

Co-culture
a culture that exists inside a larger culture

Communication is multidimensional: There's a Lot of Stuff Going On Here.

That means that there are different layers of meaning going on when people communicate with each other. There is the content message (what the words mean) and the relationship message (subtext meaning based on who is talking to whom) (Watzlawick et al., 1962). For example, if your coworker says, "You were late this morning," you might think they were expressing concern, offering professional advice, or even trying to tell you what to do. But if your boss says it, you know she is telling you to shape up! You know that is what she means because of your relationship with her, not the meaning of the words. Furthermore, there can be issues involving establishing power or ongoing unresolved issues that affect how we interpret what is going on in a given interaction. For instance, many American teachers wear black the first day of a new semester because it's a "power color" and they want to nonverbally establish control in the classroom. But, if I wear black to a funeral, it has nothing to do with power; it's actually a sign of respect in that context. Make sense?

So let's think about this question: What do you need for communication to take place?

Elements of Communication: Let's Cook Up Some Meaning

© Tarek Khouxam/Shutterstock.com

First, you need people to communicate. We'll call them **communicators**. Let's see how that looks. Imagine a guy named Joe. Joe is a student in Oklahoma who is from Oklahoma. If Joe wants to give information to someone else, he is initiating a message, so let's call him the sender. A **sender** is the person sending a initiating message to someone else. Let's call her Fatima. She is also a student at the same university as Joe. She is from Jordan. She is going to receive Joe's message. A **receiver** is the person who receives the message. Joe wants to tell Fatima about climbing trees when he was growing up in Oklahoma. That's Joe's message. The **message** is the idea one communicator wants to give to another communicator. In his mind, Joe sees an oak tree. The idea Joe wants to share is climbing a tree. He has to pick symbols to send that image to Fatima. In his mind, he has cultural understandings and personal experiences that comprise his **frame of reference**. So, Joe chooses the words, "I climbed a tree" from his frame of reference. The words are the symbols he picked from his frame of reference to carry his message. When Joe makes his statement about climbing trees, the message is carried to Fatima by the sound waves made by his voice and light waves that show any facial expressions or gestures he might use. A **channel** is the sensory medium that delivers the message; in this case the sound waves and light waves are the channels. We usually think of the channel as some form of sensory experience, like sound or sight or touch, but technology can also serve as a channel. We'll talk more about that later. So, the message has been delivered to Fatima. That makes her the receiver.

When Fatima receives the message, she goes to her frame of reference to decide what his words/symbols mean. Now, Fatima may be confused. Growing up in Jordan, she saw people climb trees, but they were palm trees and she hasn't seen any palm trees in Oklahoma yet. She may think he's bragging because climbing a palm tree is hard. She has to get clarification because their frames of reference don't overlap, so she doesn't understand his meaning. She responds to Joe with a question to be sure they are talking about the same thing. A response to a message is called **feedback**. Feedback is really important if you want understanding. If you have ever gotten a message from someone that didn't make sense and you weren't able to get clarification, you have some idea how important feedback can be. Feedback also moves the conversation forward. It is *really* important. When

Communicators
people who communicate

Sender
the person sending a message to someone else

Receiver
the person who receives the message

Message
the idea one communicator wants to give to another communicator

Frame of reference
cultural understandings and our own personal experiences

Channel
the sensory medium that carries the message

Feedback
a response to a message

we send and receive messages, we may not get the intended meaning because we do not share the same life experiences, but often we don't get the meaning because something interrupts or damages the meaning. Anything that prevents or distorts the transfer of the meaning is called interference.

Something else that affects and contributes to the communication process is that it always takes place in a setting. The context is the setting where the communication takes place. If the conversation takes place on the street corner, the traffic creates interference that would not have been a problem indoors. Setting can be physical, emotional, relational, communicative, or cultural. We'll also look more closely at those later.

Okay, so those are the elements of communication: sender, receiver, message, symbols, feedback, frame of reference, interference, and context. As you can see, there's a lot involved in this, and you intuitively understand how it works (Littlejohn & Foss, 2011). By this point, you may be saying, "This isn't so tough. It's pretty much common sense." And, to a large degree, that's true. Like I said earlier, you know about this stuff. You just don't know you know. Let's go on and look at each element a little more deeply and learn some stuff you didn't know. That's why you have this handy dandy textbook!

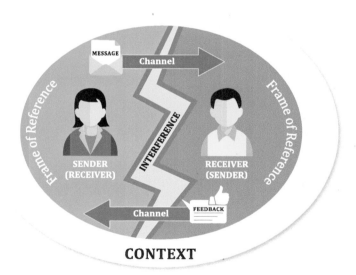

Sidebar 1B Communication model

© Kendall Hunt Publishing Company

Communicators

Communicators play two roles: senders and receivers. Senders send messages in multiple ways. They can use both verbal symbols (words) and nonverbal symbols (gestures, facial expressions, objects, time, voice tone, and more) to communicate. Senders broadcast the message but often are playing the receiver role at the same time. The receiver accepts the message while simultaneously sending feedback to indicate reception. It's a complex dynamic. When we communicate, we put ideas into symbols to send and translate the symbols back into ideas when we receive. The process of choosing symbols to represent the message is called encoding. The words are a form of symbol and carry the message. When we receive a message, the process of encoding must be reversed. We must translate the symbols to get the meaning. Decoding is the process of turning a symbol back into meaning. When we decode, we choose meanings for symbols from our frame of reference, which is made up of our cultural and personal experiences.

Encoding
process of choosing symbols to represent the message

Decoding
the process of turning a symbol back into meaning

Frame of Reference

When we receive a message from someone and decode the message, we must access our database of ideas and past experiences in order to translate the symbol and rebuild the meaning in our own heads. That database of experiences is made up of our cultural understandings and our own personal experiences and is called our frame of reference (Sherif, 1936; Syngg & Combs, 1949). Our lives to this point have given us many experiences. Those experiences create the lens through which we see the world and they affect the way we understand and interpret the meaning of events, actions, words, etc. (Moriarty, 1996). A shared frame of reference is essential for good communication. We need the same symbols to mean the same things to the communicators in order for clear communication to take place. Most of the time, our frames of reference are close enough that we can get the meaning without even thinking about it. But, sometimes they are different enough that misunderstanding can result. Think back on Joe and Fatima having a different understanding of "tree" and how the meaning of climbing the tree has different meanings. Culture also plays a role. If you are from the United States, you might gesture by putting your thumb and index finger together and spreading the other fingers to indicate that everything is okay. But in some South American cultures, that is considered a vulgar gesture, tantamount to the raised middle finger so common in American culture. How about a verbal example? If a person from England says "I need a lift," an American may assume that the English person is asking for a ride, but the actual need referred to was what the American would have called an elevator. You can see how having a different frame of reference can change the meaning. Differences in frame of reference are a cause of poor communication or misunderstanding. Our personal experiences also play into our frame of reference. An individual who has been mugged will have a very different reaction to someone grabbing their arm than an individual who has only been grabbed by loving family and friends for the purpose of playful wrestling.

Message

This is pretty self-explanatory, isn't it? The message is what one communicator is sharing with another communicator. It can be an idea, or our emotions, or whatever we want the other person to know (sometimes, we don't want them to know, but they get it anyway!) It's simple enough.

Feedback

g-stockstudio/Shutterstock.com

Feedback is such a commonly used term in our society that it's almost like "message" in that we all pretty much know what it means. Feedback is the expressed response to the message. Feedback can be spoken (verbal) or unspoken (nonverbal), like when you sigh, gesture, shrug, or show a facial expression. Even making eye contact can be feedback. The reason for this is that feedback must be *expressed*. You can have an internal response that you don't show, but it isn't feedback unless it is expressed. Imagine the head resident assistant of your dorm tells you that the entire floor has been so rowdy someone has complained to the administration, so everyone on your floor has to be in their own dorm room by midnight for the next week. If you groan or roll your eyes or complain, that's feedback. But if you keep a totally stoic expression, say nothing and act entirely normal even though you are upset, that is an internal response and no feedback was given. That's highly unlikely, by the way. Our emotions tend to leak out in our nonverbal communication without our consent (Ekaman & Friesen, 1975). Our nonverbal communication comes out of our feelings and attitudes, so very often we give feedback without even realizing it. It is possible to mask your reactions and send misleading feedback, but it's pretty tough to send absolutely *no* feedback.

Channel

The channel is the sensory medium that carries the message. If the message is spoken, the channel is the sound; if the message is written or shown through non-verbal communication, the channel is sight. When you shake hands with a friend or kiss your significant other, the channel is touch. All the senses can serve as the channel or medium. Why do you think people wear cologne? You can even send a message through taste. When your grandmother makes your favorite food, or your significant other gives you chocolates, they are telling you that they love you with every bite. So, the message is detected by our senses regardless of the channel.

Technology can also be considered a channel. Phone calls, text messages, email, video chat, and other forms of electronic messages are all ways we use technology as a channel. Even mass communication, like books, movies, magazines, or sale flyers from the local grocery store, is technology used to carry the message.

Channels work with varying degrees of effectiveness based on three things: richness, interactivity, and specificity. *Richness* refers to the number of channels used to carry the same message at the same time. As a rule of thumb, the more important the message, the more channels you want to carry the message. If you are in trouble at work, the boss may call you into his office to talk to you about it. He will almost certainly use sound to give the message to you, but he is also likely to make eye contact and may shake your hand or pat you on the back. He may give you a list of infractions. So, he will use sound, sight, touch, and technology to reinforce his idea. I have a friend who was a soldier stationed in Iraq. While he was gone, his wife sent him a message on Facebook to ask for a divorce. "Cold," you say? Yes, you are right. That was an important message and should have been delivered in some method using more channels to make it easier to take. But that woman was probably trying to avoid the second consideration in use of channels: interactivity.

Interactivity is the characteristic that allows the receiver to give feedback to the message. Feedback increases understanding, remember? So interactivity gives us the chance to be certain we understand. If you are talking with your college roommate about expectations regarding keeping the room clean, you can ask questions, reject an idea, and even argue if you want. You can give feedback and increase understanding between the two of you. If you get a letter from your little brother at boarding school, you might wish you could ask questions or encourage him or comfort him, but you can't because the channel (a letter) provides no opportunity for immediate feedback. It can be a problem.

The last aspect of channel is specificity. *Specificity* refers to how exactly a message can be aimed. A text message from your mom or a phone call from your grandfather or letter from Student Accounts concerning your last tuition payment all have very high specificity. They are specifically *for you*. But a mass email from the university may have very low

© Andrey_Popov/Shutterstock.com

specificity. The message was sent to you, but might not even apply to you. If the email has to do with veterans' benefits and you are not a veteran, the low specificity made the message meaningless for you.

Interference

Interference is anything that interrupts the delivery of the message. As you might expect, it can be sound, like loud music from a passing car, people talking at the movies, or static when your cell phone connection is breaking up. I have seen textbooks that called it noise instead for that very reason. But it can come through any of the same channels we have already identified. If your classroom has a fluorescent light bulb that flickers, that's distracting, and therefore, interference. If you've been talking with your mom on the phone and your roommate brings a pizza into the room, the smell may drive you crazy and make it impossible for you to concentrate on the phone call. See what I mean? Technology has its own variety of interference. If you are video chatting with a friend and the picture keeps freezing up, it may distract you from what the friend is saying, and it certainly diminishes your understanding of the message because you can't see the facial expressions in sync with the words that make that form of communication so appealing in the first place.

"We are communicating better but we are still not out of the woods."
© Cartoon Resource/Shutterstock.com

There are two basic types of interference: external and internal. Telling the difference is pretty simple. If it happens outside your own skin, it's external: if it's within your skin, it's internal. External interference might be any of the examples I mentioned in the previous paragraph. If you can't hear because of noise in the room, or can't see because something is in the way, or it's too hot, or too cold, too dark, too bright; if there are distracting smells, all these are external interference.

Internal interference takes place inside your skin, and it includes both physiological and psychological distractions. If you are hungry or sleepy or sick, those create internal interference. If you had a fight with your roommate, or your car has broken down, or you don't know how you will make this month's tuition payment, all those can be internal distractions. Good things can be distracting, as well. I promise you, if you win a million dollars, you will have trouble focusing on anything else for a while, and that will be internal interference for you. (God grant us all that sort of distraction!)

Semantic interference
a psychological distraction that comes from your emotional reaction to a symbol that has been used in your presence

Semantic interference is a specific kind of internal interference. It is a psychological distraction that comes from your emotional reaction to a symbol that has been used in your presence. My friend Matt can't stand to hear the word "literally" used inaccurately because people often use the word when they mean "figuratively." It produces so much semantic interference that he has trouble hearing the rest of what was said in the sentence. This is one reason we must avoid derogatory terms based on race, religion, gender, sexual preference, or anything else that gives rise to offense. True, it's unkind, and most religions have something to say about putting other people down, but it is also just bad communication. It gets in the way of understanding others and their understanding of us.

Context

The context is the setting where the communication takes place. It can be physical, relational, communicative, or cultural, but all contexts set the boundaries around the communication and how it happens.

I'm sure you can figure out that physical context is the actual place where the communication happens. If your communication class takes place in a small classroom, with desks arranged in a circle where you can make eye contact with everyone in the room, it is likely to feel relaxed and casual. It might make you more comfortable and therefore more willing to engage in the conversation, though some people prefer the anonymity of a large lecture hall. For many people, though, that casual setting says to you, "We're all here together, and we're all equal. It's safe to talk." If, on the other hand, your class meets in one of those big lecture halls, it is likely to be intimidating. It only has room for one speaker down front, which sends a very clear message: "You are not as important as the speaker, so sit down and be quiet!" Here's another example of how context can affect how a message is received. Imagine you wanted to skip your first year of college and hitchhike across Europe. Most mothers would think that was a bad idea. If you were going to talk to your mom about this, you'd need to pick nice, friendly, safe surroundings to break it to her, like the living room at home or during a walk in the park. You would not do this on a rollercoaster.

© Voyagerix/Shutterstock.com

© Matej Kastelic/Shutterstock.com

How would the two different settings affect your willingness to contribute to the conversation?

Another type of context is the relational context. Within a relationship, the relationship between the communicators itself defines the parameters of what you can talk about and how messages will be received. We have history in our families and those histories dictate how we will interpret something that has been said or done. For example, imagine Jonah, a young man whose father has been very critical of his behavior in the past. Jonah will be less likely to reveal sensitive information to his father if it shows him in a bad light, and any comment made by his father that reflects on his behavior is more likely to be perceived as criticism, even if that is not how it was intended. The relationship is what makes the difference. You should be able to have a confidential conversation with a pastor or priest because the relationship identifies that person as a spiritual mentor. In the same way, you shouldn't talk back to the police or a judge because the power they hold clearly defines the relationship and how you should behave. The nature of a relationship defines how a message will be understood, so we instinctively filter how we communicate based on that anticipated response.

Communicative context is a little different because it indicates the audience and purpose you are addressing. It is just the type of communication that is taking place. **Intrapersonal communication** refers to communication within yourself, your internal dialogue. When you try to decide what to wear, or who to vote for,

Intrapersonal communication
communication within yourself

Interpersonal communication
communication that happens between people in a relationship

Small group communication
three to seven participants that meet for some specific reason

Public communication
public speaking

Mediated communication
Communication that takes place between two communicators who are separated from each other and that uses some form of technology to deliver the message

or what someone meant, you are having an intrapersonal conversation. When you question your beliefs, or criticize yourself, or simply remind yourself to hurry and get to class, you are having conversations within yourself. **Interpersonal communication** is communication that happens between people in a relationship. It requires two or more people, and it doesn't have to be a very developed relationship to be interpersonal. If you have spoken to the person sitting next to you in class and shared even one thought, you have revealed something about yourself. You have begun a baby relationship. **Small group communication** involves three to seven participants who meet for some specific reason. That's key. You have to get together *for a purpose*. It may be as serious as deciding the fate of a court case, or as simple as meeting with friends just to hang out, but the people involved intend to get together. **Public communication** has a more common name: public speaking. Public speaking allows one person to do most, if not all, the talking while the audience mostly listens. The feedback from the audience is almost exclusively limited to nonverbal responses, like making eye contact, nodding, facial expressions, applause, etc. The speaker takes the bulk of the responsibility for establishing understanding and is separated from the audience by some space. When it is necessary for receivers to be separated from the communicator who is sending the message and some form of technology must be used as the channel for the message, we call it **mediated communication**. The technology used to deliver the message could be as developed as video chatting on your smartphone, or as simple as the paper your teacher gives you to explain the guidelines of an assignment. Now, it's a funny thing: if the teacher discusses the handout in your presence, the communication is public communication and the handout becomes a visual aid. If the teacher sends it to you by a friend or posts it online, it becomes mediated communication and the handout is the channel. The key is that you have to be *present* for public communication and absent for mediated communication.

By the way, these types of communication are not mutually exclusive. A communication event can be two kinds at once. For example, a small group that meets using an online platform is both small group communication and mediated communication at the same time. If a speaker is televised, the event is public communication for the people present with the speaker and mediated for those who watch on TV.

Ethical Implications

Well, now that we've covered the basic overview of what communication is and how it works, along with some basic ideas about it, we need to look at the moral and ethical implications of our communication.

People matter.

Let me say that again. People matter. How we communicate with others has a profound effect on the world. Josh Rio-Ross, one of my past students, said it best. "Behavior *is* communication," he told me. Doubt that? Think about the last time you had a really bad day. Did you respond by slamming a door? Did you cut someone else off at the stop sign? You may say that doesn't matter, but if it makes someone kick the dog or shout at a child, it matters to the dog or the child. Or, God forbid, *you* were the one who shouted at the child or kicked the dog.

Sometimes, we just don't think about what we are doing, and we produce results we wouldn't really want if we thought it through. Life is like a room full of Ping-Pong balls bouncing around. The Ping-Pong balls represent our aggressive actions, words, and gestures. Often the balls hit a wall (us) and if we respond angrily, the balls just keep bouncing around. Some people will tell you to just ignore them, yell back, or forget about them, but the world doesn't need harder walls; it needs softer ones. People who recognize the dynamics of an interaction and are secure in themselves can make decisions about how they will respond, versus reacting thoughtlessly.

So what are the little things we can do? First, there is civility. **Civility** means treating others decently. Rabbi Hillel, a contemporary of Jesus, told us not to do to others what we wouldn't want done to us, and Jesus said it in an even more profound way: "Do unto others as you would have them do unto you." Regardless of our religious background, the idea that we all want to be treated well appeals to us. We need to apply that same standard of behavior to ourselves that we apply to others (a standard that is often referred to as the Golden Rule). That leads me to the next thing we can do.

Civility
treating others decently

We need to measure our own behavior by the same standards we would apply to anyone else. That's called integrity. It requires honesty and dedication, but it will make our relationships richer.

We really need to try to see situations as others see them. Try putting yourself in their position and seeing what the world looks like from where they stand. It may look markedly different. A little humility serves us well.

Finally, tact. Our word choices are powerful. A little thought in advance of speaking can save a lot of misunderstanding, conflict, and hurt. Tact is choosing words that state the truth in a kinder, more palatable way. Rather than telling a friend their new haircut doesn't look good on them, one might say, "I felt your previous haircut suited you better."

Summary

Communication is constructing and sharing one's thoughts, emotions, or concepts with oneself or another. It requires that communicators send and receive messages. Ideas are encoded into symbols from the sender's frame of reference that are carried by the channel to the receiver. The receiver decodes the message based on his or her frame of reference and sends feedback to the sender which can enable understanding. Sometimes, interference gets in the way and misunderstanding follows. The interpretation of the message is influenced by the setting, whether communicative, emotional, relational, or cultural.

Basic principles about communication include the following:

- Communication must be received.
- It uses symbols.
- It is a process.
- It is irreversible.
- It is inevitable.
- It is multidimensional.
- It is affected by culture.

Finally, there is an ethical aspect of our communication. It calls for civility, putting yourself in another's shoes, integrity, and tact. In order to be ethical communicators, we must apply the Golden Rule, "Do unto others as you would have them do unto you."

Vocabulary Words

Channel
Civility
Co-culture
Communication
Communicators
Context
Culture
Decoding

Encoding
Feedback
Frame of Reference
Interference
Interpersonal communication
Intrapersonal communication
Mediated communication
Message

Public communication
Receiver
Semantic interference
Sender
Small group
  communication
Symbol

Discussion Questions

1. Have you ever chosen the wrong symbol to carry your message or decoded a symbol incorrectly, resulting in confusion?
2. What words create semantic noise for you?
3. Have you ever used a low interactivity form of communication to avoid awkwardness or conflict?

4. Tell about a cross-cultural experience you've had that showed you had a different understanding about something. Why did that communication fail? What could you have done to fix it?
5. Which kind of communication technology do you use most?
6. Do you ever wonder if you spend too much time on social media? Does face-to-face interaction ever make you nervous?

References

Bainbridge Frymier, A., & Houser, M. L. (2000). The teacher-student relationship as an interpersonal relationship. *Communication Education, 49*, 207–219. doi:10.1080/03634520009379209

Baxter, L. A., & Philpott, J. (1982). Attribution-based strategies for initiating and terminating friendships. *Communication Quarterly, 30*, 217–224.

Berndt, T. J. (1986). Children's comments about their friendships. In M. Perlmutter (Ed.), *Cognitive perspectives on children's social and behavioral development: The Minnesota Symposia on Child Psychology* (Vol. 18, pp.189–212). Hillsdale, NJ: Lawrence Erlbaum.

Cope, D. G. (2015). Cultural competency in nursing research. *Oncology Nursing Forum, 42*(3), 305–307. doi:10.1188/15.ONF.305-307

DeVito, J. A. (2016). *The interpersonal communication book* (12th ed.). New York, NY: Pearson.

Dobkin, B. A., & Pace, R. C. (2003). *Communicating in a changing world.* New York, NY: McGraw-Hill.

Doloi, H. (2009). Relational partnerships: the importance of communication, trust and confidence and joint risk management in achieving project success. *Construction Management and Economics, 27*(11), 1099–1109. doi:10.1080/01446190903286564

Eğeci, İ.S., & Gençöz, T. (2006). Factors associated with relationship satisfaction: The importance of communication skills. *Contemporary Family Therapy, 28*, 383–391. doi:10.1007/s10591-006-9010-2

Ekman, P., & Friesen, W. V. (1975). *Unmasking the face. Englewood Cliffs*, NJ: Prentice Hall.

Hogh-Olesen, H. (2008). Human spatial behavior: The spacing of people, objects and animals in six cross-cultural samples. *Journal of Cognition and Culture, 8*(3), 245–280. doi:10.1163/156853708X358173

Hybels, S. & Weaver, R. L., II. (2001). *Communicating effectively* (6th ed.). New York, NY: McGraw-Hill.

Joinson, A. N. (2001). Self-disclosure in computer-mediated communication: The role of self-awareness and visual autonomy. *European Journal of Social Psychology, 31*(2), 177–192. doi:10.1002/ejsp.36

Langer, S. (1942). *Philosophy in a new key.* Cambridge, MA: Harvard University Press.

Levinson, W. (1994). Physician-patient communication: A key to malpractice prevention. *The Journal of the American Medical Association, 272*(20), 1619–1620. doi: 10.1001/jama.272.20.1619

Littlejohn, S. W., & Foss, K. A. (2011). *The theories of human communication* (10th ed.). Long Grove, IL: Waveland Press.

Meeks, B. S., Hendrick, S. S., & Hendrick, C. (1998). Communication, love, and relationship satisfaction. *Journal of Social and Personal Relationships, 15*(6), 755–773. doi:10.1177/0265407598156003

Moriarty, S. E. (1996). Abduction: A theory of visual interpretation. *Communication Theory, 6,* 167–187.

Motley, M. T. (2009). Consciousness and intentionality in communication: A preliminary model and methodological approach. *Western Journal of Speech Communication, 50*(1), 3–23. doi: 10.1080/10570318609374210.

Ortiz-Rodríguez, M., Telg, R. W., Irani, T., Roberts, T. G., & Rhoades, E. (2005). College students' perceptions of quality in distance education: The importance of communication. *Quarterly Review of Distance Education, 6*(2), 97–105.

Sherif, M. (1936). *The psychology of social norms.* Oxford, England: Harper.

Unal, S. (2012). Evaluating the effects of self-awareness and communication techniques on nurses' assertiveness and self-esteem. *Contemporary Nurse 43,* 90–98. doi:10.5172/conu.2012.43.1.90

Watzlawick, P., Beavelas, J. B., & Jackson D. D. (1967). *Pragmatics of human communication: A study of interaction patterns, pathologies and paradoxes.* New York: W. W. Norton.

Wood, J. T. (2002). *Interpersonal communication: Everyday encounters* (3rd ed.). Belmont, CA: Wadsworth.

Additional Readings

Everyone Communicates, Few Connect: What the Most Effective People Do Differently
by John C. Maxwell

Simply Said: Communicating Better at Work and Beyond

by Jay Sullivan

The Science of Communication: Develop Charisma and Learn How to Talk to Anyone

by Ian Tuhovsky

Better Communicators Are Self-Aware

By Rhonda Gallagher, M.S.

© syda Productions/Shutterstock.com

2

Socrates said, "Know thyself." Of all the commands I've heard, that is one of the toughest to obey. It requires hard work, honesty, and commitment. How we see ourselves colors everything in our communication. It frames how we view and hear everything around us, and it is shaped by our past communications with others (Kollock & O'Brien,1994).

How does our self-concept develop? In what ways do our self-awareness and self-concept affect our communication? How do we become more self-aware? These are some pretty important questions. There are things that we can do to become more self-aware, like becoming aware of what God says about us and making better choices in friendships, but be patient, we'll get to those.

Some Definitions: Know Myself? How?

To say that this chapter deals with self-awareness alone is actually incorrect. Self-awareness, self-concept, identity, and self-esteem are concepts that are related and used in our culture almost interchangeably, but they are different. How you think of yourself includes several elements. Let's begin by defining some terms.

Self-concept
the stable image you have of yourself over time

Your **self-concept** is the stable image you have of yourself over time (Kollack & O'Brien, 1994). It is relatively consistent and not easily subject to change. It includes what you know about yourself, as well as how you identify with groups to which you belong, among other things, and the parts that go into its construction interact. Of course, all those interlocking pieces—our self-awareness, group identities, and self-perceptions—are built into our self-concept very early as we learn how "cute" we are, whether or not we are outgoing, and those things for which we show aptitude, etc. Societal expectations also play a big role in how we see ourselves. (Collier, 2009) Our culture tells us what constitutes a "good" person. We learn our beliefs and values from our culture and home, and those things become a part of how we see ourselves. By comparing ourselves with those standards, we judge our own worth. For instance, in the U.S., people who are competent, confident, industrious, attractive, and intelligent are deemed valuable. From our earliest childhood, we judge our own ability to perform socially and academically and assign value to that.

© logoboom/Shutterstock.com

Self-awareness
what you know about yourself

One part of your self-concept is self-awareness. **Self-awareness** is what you know about yourself. Now that wasn't too hard, was it? What you know about yourself is central to self-concept. What you know about yourself can be deep or superficial, simple or complex. It can be as easy as the color of your eyes or as difficult as understanding why certain people make you feel insecure. For example, I am a sucker for stray animals, especially cats. I knew that about myself but didn't necessarily understand it. I used to think I loved little animals because I was a good, tenderhearted person, but in actuality, I get a rush from rescuing little, lost kitties. I had to learn that about myself. Our sense of self changes over time. How do we become self-aware? Through interpersonal interaction, role-playing, media consumption, and experience. More about that later.

Identity
the perception you have of yourself as a member of a group

Identity is the perception you have of yourself as a member of a group. A person looks at a group to which they belong and determines whether they are a "good" member of the group. Think about a group you belong to. Gentlemen, some of you may have been Eagle Scouts. Think about the characteristics of an Eagle Scout and what their organization says about them: "A Scout is trustworthy, loyal, helpful, friendly, courteous, kind, obedient, cheerful, thrifty, brave, clean, and reverent" (www.scouting.org). If you were an Eagle Scout, you may look at that list and say, "I'm all those things, except thrifty, and I'm helpful some of the time." You probably think you're a pretty good Eagle Scout. You've judged yourself as you identified the characteristics of group membership.

So, self-concept includes our self-awareness and our identity. Now that we have defined some terms and got some basic concepts out of the way, let's take a look at how they are formed.

Self-awareness: What Does It Mean to Be Self-aware?

Multiple things work together to help us develop self-awareness. They include: interpersonal interaction, social comparison, role-taking, self-perception, and life experience.

Reflected Appraisals: What Did You Say?

We are not born knowing ourselves; we get feedback from others that tells us who we are. Think about some things you've been told about yourself. **Reflected appraisals** are our perceptions about the messages others send us about ourselves, sometimes called the "looking-glass self" (Mead, 1934; Coley, 1964). These messages can be either verbal or nonverbal, but they all provide indications about our value in the eyes of others, and what they say tells us who we are. Little children are not born knowing about the world. They are as intelligent as you or I; they just haven't had the experience to know what things mean yet, so they believe what they are told. That can be good or bad. If your parent tells you that you are smart, beautiful, competent, and kind, you will incorporate that into what you know and believe about yourself. If your parent tells you bad things about yourself, you'll believe that, too. For a while, I volunteered at a women's minimum security prison and talked with several inmates about what they were told about themselves when they were children. Many of the women were told they were stupid, incompetent, ugly, useless, in the way, and that they would never amount to anything. When a woman is told these kinds of things about herself early in life, is it any surprise she believes she belongs in prison and acts accordingly? For anyone, but especially for children, these sorts of messages can have lifelong consequences (Vaches, 1994).

> **Reflected appraisals**
> our perceptions about the messages others send us about ourselves

Sidebar 2A   Consider this . . .

- When you were a child, what did people tell you about yourself?
- Do you think they were right?
- How big a role do you think those messages played in who you have become? Did you conform to them? Did you try to disprove them?

Another type of reflected appraisal that affects our self-concept is the generalized other. The **generalized other** is the composite projection of social values and approved behaviors that we believe others use to judge us (Holdsworth & Morgan, 2007; Mead, 1934). You know how you sometimes wonder what "other people" will think? Those "people" aren't real; they represent a made-up persona that cannot actually be tied to any one person. While this is not really feedback from other people, we *process* it as if it was. In my opinion, there is no slave to the generalized other like a 14-year-old girl who worries all the time about "what other people will think" about her. (The funny thing is that most people just don't think about us that often. They are too busy thinking about themselves! As my mother used to say, "If you knew how seldom others think about you, you wouldn't care so much what they thought." Wise woman, my mother.)

> **Generalized other**
> the composite projection of social values and approved behaviors that we believe others use to judge us

What people say about us, or what we *think* they say about us, can profoundly affect how we see ourselves. When we interact with people, that feedback can manifest in different ways in response to how we behave. **Facework** is presenting a particular side of yourself to people based on the setting (Goffman, 1967). Just like the sides of a jewel, you have many "faces"; the stone is consistent throughout, but it appears different from different angles. People are like that; you can show a different persona in different communication settings, and each one is still true (Goffman, 1959). For instance, you probably act differently and use different language with your friends than you do with your grandmother, and neither of these represent how you would act at work. You are *still being yourself* in each setting, but you are acting in a way that is appropriate in *that* communication setting. People can react to you in multiple ways, and that can affect how you will behave in the future. (Littlejohn & Foss, 2011). They can **confirm** you (react to your persona as if it is true), **reject** you (react as if your persona is not true), or **disconfirm** you (fail to notice the presentation of a persona at all) (Watzlawick, Beavenlas, & Jackson, 1967). Disconfirmation can be damaging to your self-concept because it sends the message that you matter so little you don't even register with other people. This feedback is one form of the interaction that shapes what we think of ourselves.

Facework
presenting a particular side of yourself to people based on the setting

© Nastya22/Shutterstock.com

Confirm
When others react to your persona as if it is true

Reject
When others react as if your persona is not true

Disconfirm
When others fail to notice the presentation of a persona at all

Self-fulfilling prophecies
statements about our future behavior that we hear and subconsciously make come true

This brings me to the related concept of **self-fulfilling prophecies**, which are statements about our future behavior that we hear and subconsciously make come true (Watzlawick, 1984/2011). Think of it as a kind of reaction to a reflected appraisal. For instance, if you've been told all your life that you're attractive, you may act more confidently than you otherwise would and present yourself in such a way that people also *see* you as an attractive person. Or maybe you have been told so often you are clumsy that you begin to believe it. When you are offered the opportunity to try out a sport, you may expect to play badly because you've been told and now believe that you are clumsy. You may actually subconsciously sabotage yourself and play badly, even if you have an aptitude for the sport. Now, why would you do that? The theory is that whenever we perform in a way that is inconsistent with our self-concept, it produces internal stress because those contradictions mean we will have to re-think who we are. That internal stress can be so profound you might subconsciously alter your performance to match your self-concept in order to avoid that stress. On the other hand, in teaching honors classes for several years, I have seen honors students work themselves to exhaustion in order to achieve "all A's". The idea of *not being* a "straight-A student" is so threatening that they may go to great lengths to preserve their self-concept. What we think about ourselves is extraordinarily powerful.

"Son, there's a world out there ripe for the taking. You better stay home with me."
© Cartoon Resource/Shutterstock.com

Social Comparison: Shall I Compare Me to a Summer's Day?

Another way of building our self-concept is through **social comparison**, which is learning about ourselves by comparing ourselves to other people (Festinger, 1954). Little children get their self-concept mostly from reflected appraisals, but as they grow they move on to social comparison. A little girl may not have much confidence in her ability to judge herself, but she can recognize "good" or "acceptable" attributes in others and compare herself to see if she is alright. It seems like girls around age eight or nine suddenly have to have the same jeans, the same dress, or the same backpack as all the other girls. That is because they have moved into social comparison, which they may continue using as a means of learning about and evaluating themselves for the rest of their lives. As we age, our dependence on social comparison decreases, but it never goes away.

While men and women both engage in social comparison, they tend to compare themselves in different areas (Schwalbe & Staples, 1991). Once again, these are generalizations, but they often hold true. Men tend to focus on areas of achievement (Joseph, Marcus, & Tarodi, 1992) and athleticism: who has the better job, fastest car, best sound system, prettiest girlfriend, or is the biggest professional/financial success. Women, on the other hand, are more likely to compare themselves to peers like girlfriends and other females of their own age in areas of beauty and connection (Joseph, et al., 1992). They look at how pretty they are or how well dressed and accessorized, or they consider how many friends they have and how popular the friend group is.

Mass media (publicly published forms of communication that are not addressed to individuals, like magazines, books, movies, websites, etc.) also play a role in our social comparison. When we consume mass media, we inevitably compare ourselves to what we see. We can see the areas in which we do or do not match up, and we tend to accept those ideals without too much thought. Celebrities like Jenifer Lawrence and Rihanna cast a long shadow for the rest of us women, and men like Chris Pine and Bradley Cooper set the bar for men. Think for a moment about what characteristics exemplify the "beautiful people" in our culture. They are attractive, fit, intelligent, socially sensitive, tolerant, witty, financially comfortable, and professionally and romantically successful. We compare ourselves to these public figures, even though very few of us can meet the same standard. Depending on what we see, our self-esteem may be either reinforced or damaged.

Social comparison
learning about ourselves by comparing ourselves to other people

Sidebar 2B Superman . . . .

Superman has changed—and not just out of his mild-mannered suit and horn-rimmed glasses. In the mid-1950's, the ideal look for a man was George Reeves in the TV series "Superman". Compare him to Henry Cavill in *Man of Steel* (2013). If poor George was trying to get the same role today, he'd have a tough time getting an audition. He just wouldn't be fit enough—no muscular definition.

© MeSamong/Shutterstock.com

In the 1950's, some men compared themselves to George Reeves. People struggled with body image then, too, but expectations of bodily perfection have changed. We still are struggling to achieve it, but higher standards decrease our likelihood of success, and failure to meet standards can still negatively affect our self-image.

Mass media
publicly published forms of communication that are not addressed to individuals

Role Taking: I'd Like to Audition for the Role of . . . .

Role-taking
trying on a new persona to see if it fits you

Think back on your early teens. Did you ever try to reinvent yourself? Maybe you did "Skater" or "Preppie" or "Emo" or "Band Geek" or "Brooding Artist." **Role-taking** is trying on a new persona to see if it fits you (Griffin, 2000). If it doesn't feel right or you don't like it, you may abandon the role immediately. But it if fits you and expresses who you really think of yourself as being, you may adopt it permanently. It could also become a part of you for a while and be dropped when it doesn't "fit" anymore. It's like shopping for a jacket. You see something you like, and you slip it on. If it fits, great; if it doesn't, you put it back on the rack and try another until something fits. When I was in middle school, I knew a lot of girls who really worked at their appearance, and I called them "girly girls." One week, I tried on "girly girl." That's how long it lasted—about a week. It just took too much time. That was when I figured out that I like low maintenance hair and make-up. Being a "girly girl" is just not who I am, but I had to try the role on to see if it worked, and I learned more about myself in the process. Role-taking is useful in learning about yourself, but another benefit of it is that it enables us to see the world from multiple perspectives. It broadens our horizons and builds empathy (Griffin, 2000).

Self-perception
how you judge yourself based on your own standards

© wavebreakmedia/Shutterstock.com

Self-perception Who Do I Think I Am?

We learn from reflected appraisals almost exclusively when we are young; we add social comparison and role-taking as we get older. **Self-perception** is how you judge yourself based on your own standards, and it comes after reflected appraisals and social comparison. After you live a while, you start to think for yourself about what makes a person or situation good or bad. You no longer need someone to tell you or to compare yourself to another to figure it out. For instance, an older woman may know that there are some styles that look good on others but will not work for them. They don't need to be told by anyone else or compare their reflection to another's to know the style won't work for them. They know from experience.

Sidebar 2C Discuss this with a friend . . .

- Find a friend you trust. You may have to call someone from home if you're new on campus.
- Share with them a life experience you had that taught you something about yourself.
- Listen to their story about learning about themselves through experience.

Life Experiences: Speaking of Experience . . . .

Life experiences also teach us about ourselves. Despite the fact that we are not usually seeking out experiences to help us learn about ourselves, life offers us lessons, anyway. You might think you would like a particular kind of foreign food, but when confronted with it, you are surprised to learn that you don't like it after all. My sister didn't think she would enjoy live theater, but once she attended a show, she loved it! Experience is valuable for building self-awareness and self-concept. Once we learn new things about ourselves, we incorporate them into our self-concept; we may or may not like what we have learned, so our self-esteem may benefit or suffer accordingly.

The Johari Window: Can I Measure My Self-awareness?

Yes, you can! There is a sort of psychological test for self-awareness. The Johari Window (See Sidebar 2D) is an instrument for measuring a person's degree of self-awareness, and it demonstrates the importance of our interaction with other people in understanding ourselves or situations (Luft, 1984). The Johari window has four squares, or panes.

Johari Window
an instrument for measuring a person's degree of self-awareness

The *open pane* reflects the area in which we are willing to share and also willing to receive others' feedback. Maybe you wear glasses, and it's not a big deal to you. As such, you readily discuss and receive the comments of others about your glasses and how they affect your appearance.

Known to...

	self	others
others	Open Pane	Blind Pane
self	Hidden Pane	Unknown Pane

Known to...

Sidebar 2D   The Johari Window
© Kendall Hunt Publishing Company

The *blind pane* illustrates the areas of communication in which other people are responding to us, but we are unable to perceive their responses. For instance, maybe you have bad breath in the morning but don't know it. Other people may be leaving bottles of mouthwash outside your dorm room door and telling you to go brush your teeth first thing in the morning, but you may still be oblivious. Our degree of self-esteem affects how much criticism we can receive as well as how we interpret positive feedback. So if bad breath seems the most embarrassing thing you can imagine, you will be predisposed not to receive the feedback.

The *hidden pane* deals with things that we know but are not willing to share with others, maybe because of shame, embarrassment, or fear of being vulnerable. Maybe during high school, you went through a period of role-taking the "bad kid" and were arrested a couple of times. That is information you will probably be hesitant to share with others until you know them.

The *unknown pane* contains the information that no one knows. We don't even know it because no situation has arisen enabling us or anyone else to learn it (Luft, 1984). One of the young men reading this now might have been a wonderful jouster in the 14th century, but nobody knows, because it has never come up. (You may need to join a Renaissance faire to find out!)

Self-monitoring
trying to see one's own actions as others would see them

Some people are very self-aware. They engage in what we call **self-monitoring**, which is trying to see one's own actions as others would see them. They are honest with themselves about themselves. People who are very attentive to what they are doing and why they are doing it are called *high self-monitors*. This requires some degree of empathy, since they must imagine what other people are feeling and how those people will respond to their actions or words. People who are not self-aware are referred to as *low self-monitors*. They are often clueless about how others perceive their actions. An example of a low self-monitor would be someone who talks about themselves all evening when they are out with friends. We all know that isn't cool, but a poor self-monitor does not realize what they are doing. If they do realize it, they might actually think no one else will notice.

Your values can influence whether or not you can see a particular thing about yourself. For instance, for years I didn't really like little children much. I found them boring, noisy, messy, and hard to manage. But I never would admit this to myself, because not liking little children just seemed sort of un-Christian, cold-hearted, and mean. Jesus liked little kids, so I had to like little kids, too. I told myself that I liked them and sort of refused to recognize it was not true. I thought good people liked children, and I was a good person, so I liked kids, even if I didn't have much fun with them. See? My values influenced what I was able to tolerate knowing about myself.

Looking at the Johari window, one can imagine the ways that self-awareness and self-concept can affect how much is shared or received. Obviously, people who are closed to feedback due to lack of self-knowledge or fragile self-concept cannot even recognize what others may be telling them about themselves, regardless of whether it is negative or positive. It will also cause them to have a bigger unknown pane and may prevent them learning through trying new things because they are closed to self-revealing experiences and feedback from others. By the same token, a poor self-concept may prevent us from sharing information that we know. Things in the hidden pane are our secrets. Though they can be good or bad, for some reason we have chosen to conceal them. Some people have poor boundaries and overshare. They tell you way more than is appropriate to the level of the relationship. They have huge open panes. That is psychologically dangerous territory, however, because not everyone will treat your secrets with respect!

Emotional Intelligence: Oh, I Am So Smart!!

Closely associated with self-monitoring is emotional intelligence. **Emotional intelligence** is the ability to recognize, understand, use, and control our emotions and those of others (Goleman, 1995; Salovey & Mayer, 1990). In the first stage, *recognizing emotions* means recognizing that butterfly feeling in your stomach as excitement, or shaking hands as rage, etc. In the second stage, *reasoning with emotions*, we engage with our emotions and harness the power they generate. When we can realize our feelings, it is possible to use that emotional power to drive our will to work on a problem or accept good things that have come to us. The third level is *understanding the emotion*. It means being able to see the connection between the emotion one is experiencing and the cause. You may feel butterflies in your stomach and realize that you are nervous because you have to give a presentation in class for which there is an important grade. You know what you are feeling and what caused it. Being able to step away from the emotion a little bit is helpful. It enables you to examine what you're feeling and why. That's why your mom told you to count to ten when you become upset; it gives you time to calm yourself and reflect on what your feelings are. The last level is *controlling emotion*. It is our responsibility to recognize, understand, harness the power of, and choose how we will respond to our emotions. At this level of maturity, we are able to choose when and where we will deal with what we are feeling. We intuitively know that there is an element of appropriateness to sane, mature behavior. You might receive a phone call from your boss offering you a coveted promotion while attending a post-funeral reception, but good taste dictates that you not share that good news at a time when others are dealing with loss.

Emotional intelligence
the ability to recognize, understand, use, and control our emotions and those of others

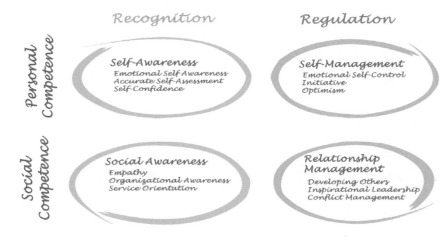

Personal Competence

Social Competence

Recognition

Regulation

Self-Awareness
Emotional Self-Awareness
Accurate Self-Assessment
Self-Confidence

Self-Management
Emotional Self-Control
Initiative
Optimism

Social Awareness
Empathy
Organizational Awareness
Service Orientation

Relationship Management
Developing Others
Inspirational Leadership
Conflict Management

Sidebar 2E Emotional Intelligence

© arka38/Shutterstock.com

Identity: "One of These Things Is Not Like the Other . . ."

Identity is the set of characteristics that make up a person. You explore your identity by figuring out the characteristics of the groups to which you belong and comparing yourself to those characteristics to see if you conform. You then incorporate those identities into your self-concept (Littlejohn & Foss, 2011). There are many elements of an individual's identity. The three most central identities are gender identity, social identity, and cultural identity. Each one plays a role in how we see ourselves, but they all contribute to who we think we are. Which identity is most important for an individual may vary. Sidebar F illustrates that.

Gender Identity

Gender identity is the recognition of ourselves as masculine or feminine, and relates to behaviors and personality traits that are culturally associated with one sex or the other (Dobkin & Pace, 2003). This is central to a person's identity, and it is the first to form. Little children can tell you if they are boys or girls pretty early, though their reasoning may be a bit fuzzy. They may say that girls have long hair and boys play with trucks, but they have a pretty good idea which they are. In the U.S. masculinity is associated with being strong, decisive, assertive, competitive, etc., and femininity equates to being kind, quiet, pretty, nurturing, accommodating, etc. Most of us have compared ourselves to gender characteristics and decided how masculine or feminine we are. If a woman can be nurturing and kind but is no good at the passive and quiet thing, she may feel fairly feminine, and give herself 7 out of 10 on the feminine scale. See how it works?

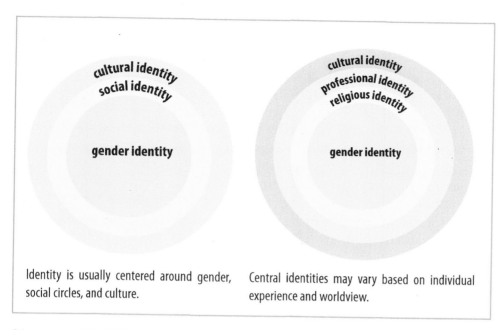

Identity is usually centered around gender, social circles, and culture.

Central identities may vary based on individual experience and worldview.

Sidebar 2F While a person may use the three most common identities as described above, other varieties and order of identity do exist.

© Kendall Hunt Publishing Company

Cultural Identity

Cultural identity is the way we identify with racial or ethnic groups to which we belong. Race is physical and based on skin, hair and eye color, bone structure, and body build, but ethnicity is psychological and focuses on the culture of a particular group. You probably already know the characteristics of your cultural group and how closely you conform to that. In the movie, *My Big Fat Greek Wedding*, the main character reveals what she thinks it means to be Greek: loud, outgoing, family-oriented, food-loving, and into each other's business. She identifies with her Greek heritage to some degree, but not fully. Her "Greekness" is part of her identity but not the whole thing. She is also American, which makes her Greek-American. When people belong to two cultural groups, they can identify with both of them, with either, or with neither, and this can be reflected in how they interact with other people (Ting-Toomey & Chung, 2012).

Social Identity

Social identity is more about the social group we choose to hang around with. It is actually more central to our sense of self than our cultural identity, but I think it is easier to understand if we first understand cultural identity. Maybe you're a musician or an engineering major or an athlete. You know the characteristics of that group. Imagine Blane, a freshman drama major. He identifies the characteristics of a drama major as outgoing, aware of all the current movie and stage productions, and active in most of the on-campus shows. However, he's somewhat shy. Since he is aware of the theater scene and volunteers for school productions, he thinks he's a "pretty good" drama major, even though he is shy.

Of course, there are other kinds of identity such as religion, profession, etc., and the interaction of one form of identity may mitigate another. Social Identity Theory (Abrams & Hogg, 1990) says that we belong to many groups and therefore have many identities. You can belong to multiple groups at the same time and have an identity for each of those groups, but some of those are more important in a given situation. Which elements of our identity are more important to us at a particular time depends on whether we feel the need to see our similarities with another group or are more concerned about the differences. Let's say Sasha is a musician with a Catholic background. If Sasha is having dinner with another musician who is Baptist, she may be focused on her religious identity in that moment because the differences are more important and/or interesting to her at that time in that setting, or she may choose to focus on the fact that they are both musicians.

Stereotypes
predictions about how people will behave based on the expected characteristics of the group they belong to

On a related note, let's talk about stereotypes. Stereotypes (predictions about how people will behave based on the expected characteristics of the group they belong to) can affect our self-concept as well as our identity. Stereotypes are not the same as identity; identity represents the real characteristics of the group to which we belong, but stereotypes may have no basis in reality. We know the stereotypes of the groups to which we belong, and we are often consciously aware that the expectation to conform to the stereotypes exists. The problem, however, arises when we subconsciously try to conform or disprove the stereotypes applied to us. Steele and Aaronson (1995) demonstrated that stereotypes seem to have more effect on the people who *are* stereotyped than people who *hold* the stereotype. In fact, when a person is called a racial slur, it can actually cause that person to act in ways that conform to the negative stereotype referenced by the slur (Calvert, 1997).

Getting Better

The fact is that few of us are really self-aware. We think we know ourselves, but we have blind spots about who we are, what we do, and why we do it. We may be aware that we do something but are deluded about our motives. So how do we get a more accurate self-concept?

Ask God to help you build a more accurate self-concept. We don't know ourselves, but He says in James 1:5, "If any of you lacks wisdom, let him ask of God, who gives to all liberally and without reproach, and it will be given to him." I am convinced that God wants us to know ourselves because we cannot deal with our failings until we know we have them, and we cannot assume we just know. We need His help.

Surround yourself with people who help you, not hurt you (Dobkin & Pace, 2001). Think about it for a minute. You need friends who will tell you the truth about yourself—the good and the bad. Occasionally, solicit their feedback. Proverbs 27:6 says, "Faithful are the wounds of a friend." Even if what they tell you is painful at the time, it can help you grow and improve, and a true friend is one who loves you enough to believe you can be better. Also, find some friends who have the characteristics and skills that you lack. If you're a procrastinator, make some friends who aren't. If you're prone to gossip, don't hang around with people who gossip. Get the picture? Their good habits will rub off on you over time.

Sidebar 2G Consider this . . .

- Who is a safe person you can share with?
- What areas of weakness do you have? Who do you know who is strong in that area?
- What area of yourself do you wish were different?
- What is a reasonable goal for dealing with that area?
- What scriptures do you know that reveal what God thinks about you?

Control your self-disclosure (Dobkin & Pace, 2001). **Self-disclosure** is revealing personal information about yourself to another (Jourard,1964; Dindia & Fitzpatrick, 1997). Be careful what you tell others about yourself. I'm not talking about telling someone else your favorite color; I'm talking about your deepest fears, failures, and insecurities. Be careful to surround yourself with people who are trustworthy. You should only share those deep things in trusted, intimate relationships. There are risks to self-disclosure, of course. The person can judge you, reject you, tell your secret to others, or use the information to manipulate or hurt you at a later time. But there are benefits of self-disclosure, too. You can often get another perspective on the issue; that friend may be able to tell you things about yourself that you didn't realize. Self-disclosure can also build the relationship (Jourard,1964; Dindia & Fitzpatrick, 1997); it helps to have someone to share your load, and there can be real healing in sharing your deep hurts with another. However, be careful how much you share and with whom. In Matthew 7:6, Jesus tells us, "Do not give what is holy to the dogs; nor cast your pearls before swine, lest they trample them under their feet, and turn and tear you in pieces." Do you know how to tell if it's safe to disclose? Give a small piece of information and see if the listener responds with a disclosure of their own. It should be about the same level of seriousness and about the same amount of disclosure. Watch how they respond and wait a while to see if they kept the confidence. If they were responsible with what you shared, you can share a little more. Take your time building a relationship of that level of intimacy. Those revelations are very powerful, and you don't want to give your pearls to those who will not respect them. As it says in Proverbs 4:23, "Above all else, guard your heart, for everything you do flows from it."

Self-disclosure
revealing personal information about yourself to another

Accept yourself (Dobkin & Pace, 2001). This can be difficult, especially if you are a perfectionist as so many of us are. So how do we do that? Realize that all human beings are flawed. It's the nature of the beast, as they say. Yes, there is bad in the human heart, but there is also good, and God can see that even if you can't. Recognize that you are a mix of good and bad; you're complex. You don't really know the depths of your own heart. Only God truly knows your heart, but He loves you anyway, so you're just going to have to trust His judgment. By accepting that all people are flawed, we can accept that we have value. If it's good enough for Him, it's going to have to be good enough for us.

Set reasonable goals (Dobkin & Pace, 2001). Unrealistic goals only set you up for failure and self-loathing. Try to be reasonable. If you know you struggle with procrastination, don't suddenly decide you'll never put anything off again; instead, begin with one single goal. Try just starting on your homework earlier than the night before it's due. Plan to study a little every day on a couple of subjects. Do that, and then you can move on to all your subjects, then to cleaning your room for a few minutes every day, etc. See what I mean? Be reasonable. Rome wasn't built in a day.

Finally, *remember what God said about you.* You are "fearfully and wonderfully made"(Psalm 139:14), "accepted in the Beloved" (Ephesians 1:6). You are His child (I John 3:1) and a conqueror (Romans 8:37). God saw something in you that He loved, and He loved you even in your messed-up-ness. Romans 5:8 says "But God demonstrates his own love for us in this: While we were still sinners, Christ died for us." If I could tell you only one thing in this chapter, it would be that you are *infinitely precious* to the Father. Let me say that again. You are *infinitely precious* to the Father; from that realization all other healing, love, and moral behavior flow. Don't forget what He thinks about you. Your identity is ultimately rooted in what God says about you, not what anyone else thinks, including yourself.

Ethical Implications

First of all, you are responsible for what you know. You don't fully know yourself, so seek feedback from reliable sources who will tell you the truth, and work on what they tell you. A little humility becomes us all. We all have flaws and issues. If you are a person with high emotional intelligence, don't use it to manipulate others. The temptation will be there, but don't. Instead, use it to challenge yourself.

Don't judge other people harshly, because their self-perception may be based on something you don't know. Recognize that you hold stereotypes about others and yourself. Just knowing you have them won't fix them, but at least the knowledge will bring those stereotypes into the light and you can begin to address them. Realize that we all have the tendency to be more generous with ourselves than we are with others. We tend to justify ourselves and judge others harshly. You need to be honest with yourself and apply those same standards you have for others to yourself. That's called integrity.

When you find a good, reliable soul to trust with information you don't often reveal to others, be appropriate in your level of self-disclosure. You can overwhelm others with too much information and make them really uncomfortable (Floyd, 2014). We all sort of subconsciously know that we should share in equal types and amounts to others' disclosures, and if you overshare, you're going to force your friend into a tight spot. Besides, if you're taking your time to see if they're safe, you should avoid this anyway.

Be careful what you say to other people about them, especially children! Remember that those little guys will believe you and internalize that into their self-concept. They are going to have to live with what you told them for a lifetime. Don't lie to them and tell them they are neat if they are really a slob, but don't call them a slob, either. Tell them you know they are working on being neater. Tell them they are smart, capable, and beautiful every day. Be kind in what you say to everybody. You know that "the power of life and death is in the tongue" (Prov. 18:21).

Summary

Self-concept is our view of ourselves that doesn't change easily, and is made up of self-awareness and identity. Self-awareness is what we know about ourselves, while identity is our sense of self in relation to groups to which we belong. Interaction with others greatly affects how we come to see ourselves, and reflected appraisal is our perception of what others say about us. Role-taking is trying on different personas to see if they fit us. In facework, we present ourselves differently in different settings, but all of our faces can still be part of our authentic selves, and how others respond to them affects our self-concept. As we believe what others say of us, those things may become self-fulfilling prophecies. Social comparison is another way to come to know ourselves. We compare ourselves to others around us, stereotypes, and media representations that represent cultural values. Identity requires a specific kind of social comparison. The three main types of identity are gender, social, and cultural, though other types do exist. Self-perception is judging yourself based on your own values, and we also learn about ourselves from life experiences. The Johari Window is a measurement of how self-aware we are. People who are very self-aware are high self-monitors, and those who are not are low-self monitors. Emotional intelligence deals with recognizing, using, understanding, and controlling one's emotions. Steps in improving your self-concept include asking God to help you know yourself, surrounding yourself with helpful people, controlling your self-disclosure, accepting yourself, setting reasonable goals for yourself, and remembering what God thinks of your worth.

Vocabulary Words

Confirm	Mass media	Self-disclosure
Disconfirm	Reflected appraisals	Self-fulfilling prophecy
Emotional intelligence	Reject	Self-monitoring
Facework	Role-taking	Self-perception
Generalized other	Self-awareness	Social comparison
Identity	Self-concept	Stereotypes
Johari Window		

Discussion Questions

1. What did people say to you about yourself when you were growing up?
2. Which groups do you most closely identify with?
3. What stereotypes have been applied to you? How did it affect how you acted?
4. How could you change your media consumption in a way that would help your self-esteem instead of hurting it?
5. What roles have you tried on in the past?
6. What have you learned about yourself from experience?

7. Who do you know that you think is really emotionally intelligent?
8. If there is an area of your self-concept you'd like to improve, what is it?

References

Abrams, D. & Hogg, M. (1990). *Social identity theory: Constructive and critical advances*. Hemel Hempstead, England: Harvester Wheatsheaf.

Calvert, C. (1997). Hate speech and its harms. *Journal of Communication, 47*, 4–19.

Cooley, C. H. (1964). *Human nature and the social order*. New York: Schocken Books.

Collier, M. J. (2009). Culture and communication. In S. W. Littlejohn & K. A. Foss (Eds.), *Encyclopedia of communication theory* (Vol. 1, pp. 279–285). Thousand Oaks, CA: Sage.

Dindia, K., & Fitzpatrick, M. A. (1997). Self-disclosure in spouse and stranger interaction. *Human Communication Research, 23*(3), 388–412.

Dobkin, B. A., & Pace, R. C. (2003). *Communication in a changing world*. New York: McGraw-Hill.

Floyd, K. (2014). *Communication matters* (2nd ed.). New York: McGraw-Hill.

Goffman, E. (1959). *The presentation of self in everyday life*. Garden City, NY: Doubleday Anchor Books.

Goffman, E. (1967). *Interaction ritual: Essays on face-to-face behavior*. Garden City, NY: Doubleday Anchor Books.

Griffin, E. (2000). *A first look at communication theory* (4th ed.). New York: McGraw-Hill.

Goleman, D. (1995). *Emotional intelligence*. New York: Bantam.

Holdsworth, C., & Morgan, D. (2007). Revisiting the generalized other: An exploration. *Sociology, 41*(3), 401–417. doi: 10.1177/0038038507076614

Joseph, R. A., Markus, H. R., & Tarodi, R. W. (1992). Gender and self-esteem. *Journal of Personality and Social Psychology, 63*(3), 391–402.

Jourard, S. M. (1964). *The transparent self*. Princeton, NJ: D Van Nostrand.

Kollac, P., & O'Brien, J. (1994). *The production of reality: Essays and readings in social psychology*. Thousand Oaks, CA: Pine Forge Press.

Littlejohn, S. W., & Foss, K. A. (2011). *Theories of human communication* (10th ed.). Long Grove, IL: Waveland Press.

Luft, J. (1984). *Group processes: An introduction to group dynamics* (3rd ed.). Palo Alto, CA: Mayfield.

Mead, G. H. (1934). *Mind, self, & society*. Chicago: University of Chicago Press.

Salovey, P., & Mayer, J. D. (1990). Emotional intelligence. *Imagination, Cognition, and Personality, 9*, 185–211.

Schwalbe, M. L., & Staples, C. (1991). Gender difference in self-esteem. *Social Psychology Quarterly, 51*(2), 158–168.

Steele, C. M.; Aaronson, J. (1995). Stereotype threat and the intellectual performance of African Americans. *Journal of Personality & Social Psychology, 69*(5), 797–811.

Ting-Toomey, S., & Chung, L. C. (2012). *Understanding intercultural communication*. New York: Oxford University Press.

Vaches, A. (1994, August 28). You carry the cure in your own heart. *Parade*. p. 4.

Watzlawick, P., Beavenlas, J. B., & Jackson, D. D. (1967). *Pragmatics of human communication: A study of interaction patterns, pathologies, and paradoxes*. New York: W. W. Norton.

Watzlawick, P. (1984/2011). Self-fulfilling prophecies. In J. O'Brien (Ed.), *Production of reality: Essays and readings on social interaction* (pp. 392–408). Los Angeles, CA: Pine Forge Press.

Additional Readings

The Gifts of Imperfection

by Brene Brown

Approval Addiction: Overcoming Your Need to Please Everyone

by Joyce Meyer

Emotional Intelligence

by Daniel Goleman

Stickman Theology

by Terry Ewing

Better Communicators Are Perceptive

By Rhonda Gallagher, M.S.

3

Have you ever thought you knew what was going on and later found out you missed it by a mile? There are so many subtle things involved in our process of perceiving our worlds that we can mess it up very easily. In fact, it's harder to get it right than to get it wrong, but before we can really understand how to be perceptive communicators, we need to understand the process of perception itself.

What Is Perception?

Perception
the process by which we gather information from our surroundings

Perception is the process by which we gather information from our surroundings (Dobkin & Pace, 2003; Floyd, 2014; Wood, 2002). This definition is dependent on two concepts we discussed in the first chapter that may not have seemed important at the time but which are very important in understanding perception. First, communication does not have to be intentional. We communicate information without intending to do so. If you sneeze, you broadcast the message that you may have a cold. You did not intend to share that, but you did so, nonetheless. Secondly, someone must receive the message for communication to happen. So people are communicating to us all the time, but we must be paying attention to get the message.

Perception uses all our senses and may or may not require awareness (Littlejohn & Foss, 2011). If you visit your sister who has a new baby and she seems distressed, you gather information from the surroundings and put together the story. If the house is hot, the baby is crying, and your sister is sweating, you may conclude that there is a problem with the air conditioning, and the baby is crying because he is hot. That would be a reasonable assumption. You perceived through your sense of sound that the baby is crying, through sight that your sister is sweating, and through the sense of touch that the room feels hot. All those senses helped you "get the message."

The Perceptual Process

The process by which we gather information involves three steps. The perceptual process begins with selection. **Selection** is the step in the perceptual process in which you focus your attention on one form of sensory stimuli. You are surrounded by sensory information all the time, and you can't pay attention to all of it (Goldstein, 2007). Right now, as I write, my computer fan is running, the ceiling fan blowing on my skin, and the traffic is passing on the street outside. But I don't *think* about all that. My attention is mostly on the letters on the screen, though I might notice a vehicle passing if it was extremely loud. For the most part, my attention is fixed on one item. When we select what we will attend to, we shut out the other sensations going on around us and put our full attention on that important thing, whatever it is. That is selection.

Selection
the step in the perceptual process in which you focus your attention on one form of sensory stimuli

The second step is organization. **Organization** is the brain's process of identifying what the sensory information is. We don't think about this at all. It happens in the background of our minds. Whatever bit of sensory stimuli you are focused on is stored in your short-term memory and your brain begins to search through the database of memories you possess. It is looking for a match. When it identifies whatever you're focused on, it has organized the stimulus. This business of organization is really powerful. Have you ever seen those optical illusions in which you look at a picture and can see either a young woman or an old one, a rabbit or a duck, faces or a vase? If you've ever wondered why people see different things, it's because of organization. We are all looking at the same stuff, but our brains organize it differently.

Organization
the brain's process of identifying what the sensory information is

Sidebar 3A Whether you see dogs or cats is the result of organization in your brain

© Veronika Kokurina/Shutterstock.com

The final step in the process is interpretation, which is the process of figuring out what the entity we just identified means to us. It takes place almost instantaneously. As soon as you identify the stimulus, your brain forms the links to your past experiences and makes a judgment about how it relates to you. Think about the smell of chocolate chip cookies; it probably evokes memories and past sensory experiences for you. Maybe you think of baking cookies with your grandmother or working at a cookie shop in the mall. (Who wants a cookie now?) Once we know what something is, we immediately begin to look for how it connects to us. Now that you have a brief overview of these stages and how they work, let's look at each one in much greater depth.

Interpretation
the process of figuring out what something means to us

Selection

As you recall, selection is focusing on one bit of sensory stimuli. We may do that for a number of reasons. We might notice an object or situation because of its **personal relevance**, which means that we notice it because it is connected to us in some way. Remember your first car? When you got it, suddenly you saw that kind of car everywhere, right? There were not immediately millions of cars identical to yours on the road at the same time you got one. You noticed those cars because they had personal relevance to you.

Personal relevance
personal connection

The second mechanism that causes us to notice something is novelty, which is the quality of standing out by being unusual or intense (Floyd, Ramirez, & Burgoon, 2008; Goldstein, 2007). (Some textbooks call this vividness, but that's going to

Novelty
the quality of being really unusual

be used as a vocabulary word in another chapter, so in order to avoid confusion, we'll just use novelty, OK?) A few years ago, the Tulsa Zoo had a fund raiser for the new penguin exhibit. Businesses and organizations all over town put out giant, custom-painted fiberglass penguins. If you drive past one of those penguins, you don't notice the buildings, or the traffic, or the pedestrians. You notice the penguin. You notice because it's unusual, because of its novelty.

Social learning

paying attention to specific actions or behaviors if we are trying to learn something

Social learning is paying attention to specific actions or behaviors if we are trying to learn something. This is another reason we select specific stimuli to attend to. Have you ever heard someone say, "Monkey see, monkey do"? Usually, the speaker is referring to a small child who has imitated someone else's behavior. The child learns by watching others and imitating them. This term social learning comes from Social Learning Theory (Bandura, 1977). If you've already had a psychology class in high school or college, you are familiar with B. F. Skinner's idea that humans learn from reinforcement of their personal behavior (Schacter, 2011). Social learning theory took that farther and said that people can learn not only from their own personal experiences, but also by observing what others (Bandura called them models) did and the results of their actions (Bandura & Walters, 1963; Bandura, 1977). Those models can be real people performing an action that we see the consequences of, or they can be verbal instructions given to; they can even be in media we consume. (Remember our discussion of media and social comparison in the self-awareness chapter? In part, our observation of personalities in media is both social comparison and social learning [Brown, 2002; Levine & Smolak, 1998] though we don't usually think about it in those terms.) We all engage in social learning in new circumstances. When you first arrived at college and you went to the school cafeteria, how did you know what to do with your tray when you finished? You probably didn't ask anyone. Instead, you just watched what other people dçid and followed their example. That was social learning.

Organization

The second step of perception is organization. We identify what the sensory stimulus is in this step. It's the part where your brain is scanning your past experiences for a match to the current one. There is a theory called constructivism that attempts to explain how we identify and organize memories and concepts. Constructivism (Delia, O'Keef, & O'Keefe, 1982) says that we create categories in our heads for like things (Littlejohn & Foss, 2011), and we go to those categories to store and locate information we need. Think of your mind as a warehouse full of shelves on which there are storage bins. Each storage bin is a construct. A construct is each single category of like things in which we hold memory. You have a construct for "home", "cat", "clown", "mom", "best friend", etc. When you need to retrieve information, you go to your storage area (constructs) and look in the appropriate bin. Have you ever wondered why you can know someone casually in one setting but may not recognize them in another? You might have a class with someone but not recognize them at church. Constructivism would say that you were looking in the wrong bin. At church, you are looking in "church friends." You are unlikely to find someone from the "classmate" group in there until you realize they belong to both groups and put their memory in both. Make sense?

Constructivism
theory that we create categories in our heads for like things, and we go to those categories to find information we need

Construct
a single category in which we hold memory

Basically, we can build our bins (constructs) in one of four ways: prototypes, stereotypes, personal constructs, and scripts (Wood, 2002). The first kind of construct is called a prototype. Many of us are familiar with the word "prototype" to refer to the first kind of a new invention, but in communication a prototype is a collection of informational bits that make up a culturally recognized type of person, object, or event. They are idealized image of a given category (Fehr, 1993). To help us understand, think for a moment of a doctor. If I say "doctor", what comes to mind? You probably see a male wearing a stethoscope, a white coat, maybe carrying a clipboard. Each piece of that picture (stethoscope, white coat, and scrubs) is a piece of the cognitive puzzle. That collection of information makes up the prototype for "doctor." Often our first experiences of an events, object, or group of people will become our prototype until a more powerful experience replaces it. We have prototypes for people, objects, and events. The prototypical restaurant has tables, chairs, napkins, silverware, servers running around, and food, of course. See what I mean?

© ESB Professional/Shutterstock.com

Prototype
a collection of informational bits that make up a culturally recognized type of person, object, or event

Now, if we take the prototype and attach a prediction about how a prototype will *behave*, we have moved into stereotypes. In chapter 2 we established that a stereotype is a predictive assumption about behavior based on assumed characteristics of people, objects, or events. For instance, if you see a woman in scrubs, you may assume she's a nurse. By the way, you are employing a stereotype, and you might be wrong. If you assume your Asian friend is good at math or that your Arabic neighbor is Muslim, you are engaging in stereotyping.

The third type of construct is the personal construct. If both prototypes and stereotypes belong to the culture as a whole, a personal construct pretty much belongs to you. A **personal construct** is your personal interpretation of a particular event, object, group of people, or relationship based on your personal observations and experience (Kelly, 1955). Let's consider the clown construct for a minute. For most of us, clowns go in the "happy" bin with the circus, birthday parties, and parades. But even as you read this, some of you are cringing because you find clowns creepy or weird. Why would an adult intentionally dress up in strange clothes, paint their face, go around making balloon animals, and ride a tiny tricycle? It doesn't make sense and is therefore sort of scary. Usually a personal construct is rooted in a past experience that makes a strong impression on you. Maybe you met your first clown as a very small child and got scared. When you created your "clown" construct, you put it in the bin marked "scary stuff". (Of course, the movie "It" ruined clowns for

Sidebar 3C Parents can teach all kinds of scripts, both good and bad.

a lot of people. Thank you, Stephen King.) Or take the example of someone who has always loved parks but then gets mugged in one; the experience may completely redefine the construct for "park" and move it from "safe place" to "dangerous place."

Personal construct
your personal interpretation of a particular construct based on your personal observation and experience

The last type of construct is the script. A script is a pattern for expected behavior (Hamilton & Sherman, 1989; James & Joneward, 1971). If someone says "Hi! How are you?" to you, you know the expected response is "Fine, thank you. How are you?" You have been doing this so long that you know what is expected of you and perform accordingly. You are playing out a script. You say "Congratulations!" at a wedding, "I'm sorry for your loss" at a funeral, and when you see a new baby, you say "Awww! How sweet!" You know what's expected. So, when you are prompted with the cue by someone else ("Hi! How are you?"), you reach into the appropriate bin (marked "greetings") and pull out the appropriate response ("Fine. How are you?").

Script
a pattern for expected behavior

Scripts can also play out in actions. You learn how to interact with the opposite gender from observing your parents in action. You learn their scripts. Then you grow up, and someone comes along you like, so you try out some of the behavior patterns you know to see how they react. If they know the "right" responses, the relationship may develop. If not, it will sort of fizzle. It's like you don't have the tools to move the relationship forward which, in fact, is exactly the case. If, on the other hand, you meet someone who knows the familiar behaviors, a relationship may develop even if that person didn't really knock you off your feet initially. Of course, this can backfire. Parental role models can teach the negative scripts of bad relationships. We can learn a destructive script just like a constructive one, and when we go shopping for our significant other, we utilize familiar communication patterns that may not be healthy.

Another thing that influences organization is closure. Closure is the ability of the brain to supply missing parts from a picture or situation. The idea comes from Gestalt Theory (Ehrenfels, 1937) which basically says that individuals look for patterns in bits of sensory stimuli, and if something is missing, try to supply the missing pieces to create a big picture that makes sense. It is the skill that enables us to look at some parts and see the whole, and we can apply it to visual images or behavior patterns. It plays a major role in learning to read. The brain doesn't have to identify all the letters in a word to know what the word is. You learn to pay attention to key letters and sort of "fill in" the rest of the word, like puzzle pieces. We have all seen license plates that have missing letters from words that make abbreviated messages. Closure is what lets you read them. You see the sensory information "SKKR MOM" and read "Soccer Mom" or "#1NTRN" and read "Number 1 Intern." It is also what enables us to fill in missing pieces from images. If you see the top half of someone's face and recognize them, your brain is filling in the missing parts.

Closure
the ability of the brain to supply missing parts from a picture or situation

© Joseph Sohm/Shutterstock.com

Closely associated with closure is another communication concept called perceptual constancy. Perceptual constancy is our tendency to continue to perceive something the same way over time (Pearson & Nelson, 1997). That means that

Perceptual constancy
the tendency to continue to perceive something the same way over time

when we have an established construct for a person, thing, or event, we are likely to perceive it the same way and not even notice changes unless they are glaring. If you have ever dieted for weeks and taken off 15 pounds, you keep hoping someone will notice and comment. People you see every day might not notice, but someone who has not seen you in a long time might notice immediately. This idea of perceptual constancy can have profound effects on individuals who want to change themselves. If you were rebellious throughout high school and then had a life-changing event (such as a religious experience, giving birth, the death of a friend, or serving time in prison), you may make radical changes in your lifestyle. This disorienting dilemma is necessary for change to take place (Olsen et al., 2015). But society doesn't make it easy for you. Even though you are working hard to change your behaviors, people will continue to treat you as if you have not changed. They will continue to expect you to be rebellious even when you haven't been like that for a long time. It's hard to change others' perceptions of who you are. It takes time and commitment. (If this is you, don't lose hope. Others' expectations of you will change. It's just going to take time. I have more to say about this later in the ethical implications section, but we're working on concepts here, so be patient.)

Interpretation

The final stage of perceiving is interpretation. Interpretation is determining what a particular bit of stimuli means to us. If we smelled cinnamon and made the leap to apple pie, and then to Christmas, we have determined that the smell means Christmas. Like organization, interpretation is influenced by our past experiences. If anything, interpretations may be even more individualized, and they take us one level deeper into our own past experiences.

Two things influence our interpretation. The first is context (Dobkin & Pace, 2003). By now you know that context is the setting in which the communication takes place and that the context can be physical, cultural, emotional, relational, or communicative. Any of those can influence what we think something means. For example, your mother may tell you that you've spilled soup on your shirt. If you are at home at the table with her, you will probably laugh, dab at it with the napkin, and wait until you finish eating to change because you are comfortable with her. But if she told you that you've spilled soup on your shirt in a fancy restaurant with the family of your significant other, it might be different. If she whispered it to you, it would be interpersonal communication. You would take it as a private comment and assume she was trying to keep you from being embarrassed. If she said it loudly and included everyone at the table (making the communicative setting a small group), you might feel she had been very insensitive to you, and you would probably feel betrayed, embarrassed, angry, or hurt. In essence, the volume of the comment changed the communicative context. See how the change of context altered the meaning? Ladies, if your sweetie kisses you on the cheek, you will probably think it's affectionate or romantic. But if your boss does it, it's sexual harassment. The action is the same; it's the relational context that changes the meaning. Cultural context also makes a lot of difference (Floyd, 2014). In most Western cultures, looking your teacher in the eye means that you are being attentive, but in some other cultures, it is considered disrespectful. See what a major role culture plays in establishing meaning? Culture is the sea in which the elements of communication float, or swim, or sometimes sink!

© Monkey Business Images/Shutterstock.com

Another way that we interpret information is through attribution (Kelley, 1967; Aronson, 1984). **Attribution** is drawing a conclusion about why we or someone else has acted in a particular way. Sometimes, we just get it wrong. Your best friend might buy you a small gift for no apparent reason, and you could interpret that many different ways. You might think they were trying to "butter you up" so they could ask a big favor, or that they really love you and want to make you happy, or they did something bad and feel guilty. Any of those things could be true, or it could be for another reason altogether. The bottom line is that we are just not very good at determining why people do things, so we need to be cautious in our judgments. There are multiple kinds of attribution mistakes, but we'll get into those more in the chapter 11 on being considerate.

Attribution
drawing a conclusion about why we or someone else has acted in a particular way

Implications of Perception

So far, we've examined several bits of information about how we perceive things, but not really how these elements work together to affect how we see our world. It's hard to separate the interplay of these perceptual steps. They run together like watercolors on a page, but we can talk about some of the ways they blend. I suppose a good place to start is by looking at our perceptual filters.

Filters
the pre-existing patterns in our minds that cause us to notice some things and not others

Filters: Straining the Facts

What you choose to pay attention to and how you identify what you are seeing or hearing can be altered by your own filters. **Filters** are the preexisting patterns in our minds that cause us to notice some things and not others. For instance, if you are an athlete you are probably interested in sports. If you meet a new person who is wearing the latest athletic shoes, you'll be more likely to notice that than another person who isn't an athlete. Okay, let's look at another example. Maybe you were unfairly fired from your job. You see a friend going through an experience at work similar to the one that led to your own firing. Because you have a filter for that, you are more likely to see your friend's job as being in jeopardy. So, our filters affect selection and what we pay

© paffy/Shutterstock.com

attention to. But they also play into our perceptual constancy, which affects our organization and interpretation.

Self-concept

One thing that strongly influences what we select, as well as how we organize or interpret stimuli, is our self-concept and self-perception. (I know, I know! We discussed this in the last chapter, but so many of these communication concepts weave in and out of the discussion, and keep resurfacing. They are like balls of yarn that have become hopelessly tangled. You can't talk about one without at least acknowledging the other.) If your self-concept is in any way inaccurate, it will distort your perceptions of other things. Many American women are focused on their physical appearance, specifically weight. When they meet other women, they immediately compare their own weight to those women and make judgments about themselves as well as the women to whom they have compared themselves. Or maybe they are so desperate for affirmation, they misinterpret what they've heard to meet that emotional need. We can even want to see something so badly that we see it when it isn't there. Ever thought that a job interview went better than it really did or that someone had a crush on you when they didn't? Unfortunately, we often don't even realize that we filter what we see.

© Anna Om/Shutterstock.com

Priming
the process by which the brain follows constructs recently used to organize new information

Priming

Recent events may also cause us to fail to recognize an object or event for what it is because that recent experience predisposes us to see things in the same way. That's called priming. **Priming** is the process by which the brain follows constructs recently used to organize new information (Tabossi, 1988; Tourangeau & Rasinski, 1988). Let me give you an example. Answer some questions (Play along. It will be fun!) What colors are on the pages of a newspaper? Got it? OK, next question: in what continent is Nigeria? Now, think of an animal. If you're like most people, you thought of a zebra. Why? Because you had just thought of the colors black and white, and also about Africa. The zebra is a black and white animal found in Africa. (Well, maybe the picture helped.)

© EcoPrint/Shutterstock.com

Narrative Paradigm Theory: Story Tellers Rule!

Narrative Paradigm Theory
humans look for stories and patterns in events in an effort to make sense of life

This next thing is HUGE! Are you ready? Here it is: Humans are always on the lookout for a good story. Walter Fisher came up with **Narrative Paradigm Theory**, which basically says that humans look for stories and patterns in events in an effort to make sense of life. We base our judgments of the truth of a story on whether the events make sense together, if the characters act in ways that are true to themselves, and whether events strike us as being plausible in the world as they know it. (We'll examine this testing a story for truth a little later, but be patient with me; we're not ready for that yet!) In fact, Fisher (1984) went so far as to say that pretty much all forms of communication besides greetings and those things we say to maintain relationships are processed in the mind like a story and we evaluate the persuasive messages in them by testing them as we would a story. The important thing I want you to see here is that our impulse to see the story affects how we perceive reality. For instance, let's say LaMont's birthday is just a few days away, and his roommate, Eric, is late getting home. If Eric says he was stuck in traffic because of an accident, LaMont may hear the story and conclude that Eric was actually late because he was buying LaMont a gift and wants to keep it a secret until the big day. LaMont has made a connection in his own mind between the two unrelated events because he is looking for a pattern that simply does not exist. While I hope LaMont has a great birthday, he still misinterpreted what actually happened.

Implicit Personality Theory

Implicit Personality Theory is a group of theories which collectively state that we associate certain characteristics together. If a person has one of the traits, we assume they will have others. For instance, if a person seems both intelligent and quiet, believing they are also friendly sort of goes with it. (Rosenberg & Sedlak, 1972) Or, if Manuel is a practical joker, people may assume he's irresponsible. But, there's a problem with these assumption: they are often wrong. For a real-life example, one of the authors, Denise Miller, is like that. She loves to tease and play jokes, but she's as responsible as any-one I ever met! By the same token, I am a chipper, upbeat person when I interact with others, so people assume I'm opti-

© espies/Shutterstock.com

Implicit Personality Theory
group of theories which collectively state that we associate certain characteristics together

mistic. I'm not; I'm a pessimist to the core. But most people assume that because I'm cheerful I must also be optimistic. Implicit Personality Theory is similar to stereotyping. It's basing a judgment about someone or something based on incomplete information, and could be wrong or right.

Ethical Implications

Be careful what you put before your eyes. What you expose yourself to repeatedly can cause you to perceive more than what is really there, or filter out important other information because of your expectations. Here's an example: Studies show that people who regularly view pornography have a warped perception of intimacy and sexuality. What we consume becomes part of us, so watch your mental "diet." Moreover, it's not just what we watch. It's what we think about too.

If you have unhealthy scripts in your family of origin, get some counseling, and learn some healthy communication patterns. If you don't, you're likely to repeat the mistakes your parents made. Check your baggage before you get on the plane!

About stereotypes, realize that you will probably use them some of the time, but try your best to see people as individuals. Be aware that you may make mistakes in your attribution sometimes. Apply the same standards to yourself that you apply to others; that's integrity. Be merciful in your judgments of others because you know that "with the same measure you use, it will be measured to you" (Matt. 7:2).

If you are that person trying to live down your past reputation and other's tendency to maintain that perceptual constancy about you, remember that it doesn't matter so much what people think about you. Check out Galatians 1:10. Your purpose is not to win the approval of men, but of God, so try not to let those folks get to you. The grace you received is from God, not men, and the scripture tells you that you are a new creation (II Corinthians 5:17). Of course, change in behavior takes time, but God's opinion defines truth, and He sees and loves you already.

Be aware of your filters, as well as your tendency to want to make the story make sense. You may need to ask some truthful friends to give you some feedback about how you react to new ideas and people. The very fact that people have filters distorts their own ability to get to the truth of situations. You may need some help to come to the valid conclusion.

You also need to be conscious of the assumptions you make about people before you know them well. It makes it easy to categorize people, but it doesn't serve anyone in the long run, either them or you.

Summary

Perception is how we gather information from the surrounding world. It has three steps: selection, organization, and interpretation. We select information based on personal relevance, novelty, and social learning.

Organization involves retaining and re-accessing information. One theory about organization is constructivism. Constructs are ways of building the structure for remembering. Four types of constructs are prototypes, stereotypes, personal constructs, and scripts. Closure also affects how we determine what something is or is not.

Interpretation depends upon context, and attribution to assign meaning. We can come to the wrong conclusions. Perceptual constancy is interpreting things the same way over time.

Other sorts of things can affect how we select what to attend to, like our personal filters which can be shaped by past experiences, or self-esteem. The impulse to make a story out of seemingly unrelated incidents, known as Narrative Paradigm Theory, may make us organize information incorrectly, as can priming. Implicit Personality Theory may cause us to misinterpret information and assign traits to people that they do not possess. Any of these can affect our perceptions

Vocabulary Words

Attribution	Narrative Paradigm	Personal relevance
Closure	Theory	Priming
Construct	Novelty	Prototype
Constructivism	Organization	Script
Filters	Perception	Selection
Implicit Personality Theory	Perceptual constancy	Social learning
Interpretation	Personal construct	

Discussion Questions

1. Share a time that you misinterpreted something really badly. How could you have possibly prevented the mistake?
2. When do you rely heavily on scripts?
3. When has cultural context interfered with your communication with someone else?
4. When have you attributed a particular motive to another person and been proven wrong?

5. What personality traits do you think go together?
6. Can you think of a time you have seen yourself or someone else let their self-concept affect what they perceived?
7. Has perceptual constancy ever caused you to fail to notice a change in someone you knew?

References

Aronson, E. (1984). *The social animal* (4th ed.). New York: W. H. Freeman.

Bandura, A. (1977). *Social learning theory*. Englewood Cliffs, NJ: Prentice Hall.

Bandura, A., & Walters, R.H. (1963). *Social learning and personality development.* Holt Rinehart and Winston: New York.

Brown, J. D. (2002) Mass media influences on sexuality. *Journal of Sex Research 39*(1), 42–45. doi:10.1080/00224490209552118

Delia, J., O'Keefe, B., & O'Keefe, D. (1982). The constructivist approach to Communication. In F. E. Dance (Ed.), *Human communication theory*. New York, NY: Harper and Row.

Dobkin, B. A., & Pace, R. C. (2003). *Communication in a changing world*. New York, NY: McGraw-Hill.

Ehrenfels, C. V. (1937). On Gestalt qualities. *Psychological Review, 44*(6), 521–524.

Fehr, B. (1993). How do I love thee; Let me consult my prototype. In S. W. Duck (Ed.), *Understanding relationship processes, 1: Individuals in relationships* (pp. 87–122). Newberry Park, CA: Sage.

Fisher, W. (1984). Narration as a human communication paradigm: The case of public moral argument. *Communication Monographs, 51*, 1–22.

Floyd, K. (2014). *Communication matters* (2nd ed.). New York, NY: McGraw-Hill.

Floyd, K., Ramirez, A., & Burgoon, J. K. (2008). Expectancy violations theory. In L. K. Guerrero, J. A. DeVito, & M. L. Hecht (Eds.), *The non-verbal communications reader: Classic and contemporary readings* (3rd ed., pp. 503–510). Prospect Heights, IL: Waveland.

Goldstein, E. B. (2007). *Sensation and perception* (7th ed.). Pacific Grove, CA: Wadsworth.

Grice, H. P. (1975). Logic and conversation. In P. Cole & J. L Morgan (Eds.), *Syntax and semantics: Speech acts.* (Vol. 3, pp. 41–58). New York: Seminar Press.

Hamilton D. L., & Sherman S. J. (1989). Illusory correlations: Implications for stereotype theory and research. In D. Bar-Tal, C. F. Graumann, A. W. Kruglanski, & W. Stroebe (Eds.), *Stereotyping and Prejudice*. Springer, New York, NY: Springer Series in Social Psychology.

James, M., & Joneward, D. (1971). *Born to win: Transactional analysis with Gestalt experiments*. Reading, MA: Addison-Wesley.

Kelley, H. H. (1967) Attribution theory in social psychology. In D. Levine (Ed.), *Nebraska Symposium on Motivation* (Vol. 15, pp. 192–238). Lincoln: University of Nebraska Press.

Kelly, G. (1955). *The psychology of personal constructs*. New York: North.

Levine, M. P., & Smolak, L. (1998). The mass media and disordered eating: Implications for primary prevention. In W. Vandereycken & G. Noordenbos (Eds.), *Studies in eating disorders: An international series. The prevention of eating disorders* (pp. 23–56). New York, NY, US: New York University Press.

Littlejohn, S. W., & Foss, K. A. (2011). *Theories of human communication* (10th ed.). Long Grove, IL: Waveland Press.

McCormack, S. A. (1992). Information manipulation theory. *Communication Monographs, 59*, 1–16.

Olsen, M. R. (2015). *Maturity and the Hispanic male: A grounded theory from the characteristics and experiences that lead to the maturation of the Hispanic male student*. Retrieved from ProQuest Dissertations Publishing.

Pearson, J. C., & Nelson, P. (1997). *An introduction to human communication: Understanding and sharing* (7th ed.). Madison, WI: Brown and Benchmark.

Rosenbert, S., & Sedlak, A. (1972) Structural representations of Implicit Personality Theory. In L. Berkowitz (Ed.), *Advances in experimental social psychology* (6th ed.). New York: Academic Press.

Schacter, D. (2011). *Psychology* (2nd ed.). New York, NY: Worth.

Tabossi, P. (1988). Effects of context on the immediate interpretation of unambiguous nouns. *Journal of Experimental Psychology: Learning, Memory, and Cognition, 14*(1), 153–162. doi:10.1037/0278-7393.14.1.153

Tourangeau, R., & Rasinski, K. A. (1988). Cognitive processes underlying context effects in attitude measurement. *Psychological Bulletin, 103*(3), 299–314.

Wood, J. W. (2002). *Interpersonal communication: Everyday encounters* (3rd ed.). Belmont, CA: Wadsworth.

Additional Readings

Visual Intelligence: Sharpen Your Perception, Change Your Life

By Amy E. Herman

4 Essential Keys to Effective Communication in Love, Life, Work—Anywhere!: A How-To Guide for Practicing the Empathetic Listening, Speaking, and Dialogue Skills to Achieve Relationship Success

by Bento C. Leal, III

Perception and Deception

by Joe Lurie

© Monkey Business Images/Shutterstock.com

Better Communicators Are Aware of Nonverbal Cues

By Rhonda Gallagher, M.S.

4

So far, we have discussed how self-concept and perceptiveness feed into our understanding of communication. But there is a lot more to understanding people's messages than just what they say; nonverbal communication plays a huge role in building shared meaning. **Nonverbal communication** includes all messages that are sent by other means than words. It includes gestures, body posture, voice tone, and meaningful use of the eyes, just to name a few. We send them both intentionally and unintentionally (Hickson, Stacks, & Moore, 2004), and we don't think about them much (Birdwhistle, 1974; Dobkin & Pace, 2003; Ekman & Friesen, 1968; Hickson et al., 2004; Wood, 2002).

Nowhere in your formal education are you taught much about nonverbal communication (Hickson, et al., 2004), and that is a real shame. Think how your life would have been changed if someone had taught you in eighth grade that you could tell if the bully was bluffing, or if your mom was dodging a question, or if your lab partner was mad at you. Most of us begin to learn the use and unspoken principles of non-verbal communication during childhood (Mayo & La France, 1978), and it becomes a part of our communication repertoire. You don't know how you know that your lab partner is angry, but you probably know. You have learned to read nonverbal messages without a lot of conscious thought.

Sometimes, though, we just don't seem to get it. In those settings, we are not very socially proficient, but often can't say why. Well, this may be why: we may not be reading or using nonverbal messages correctly. A large percentage (more than 2/3) of our communication is nonverbal (Birdwhistle, 1970; Mehrabian, 1981; Philpott, 1983). It's huge in our daily interactions! This chapter will deal with not only reading others' nonverbal cues, but also the non-verbal messages we are sending. So, if you are one of those folks who doesn't get it, or even if you do, this major gap in your education is about to be remedied. Rejoice!

Principles of Non-verbal Communication: Basic Stuff You Need to Know

Nonverbal Communication Is Continuous.

Remember when we first began discussing communication and one of the big ideas was that you cannot avoid communicating something? Well, that's because our non-verbal cues do that. We may not be aware of it, but we send and receive messages all the time by way of facial expressions, voice tone, gestures, and the way we use objects, among other things (Hybels & Weaver, 2001). Your choice of clothing or the emphasis you place on certain words reveals information about how you feel or think. Even when you aren't there to send a message, the tidiness or messiness of your car says things about you! More about that later.

© Selins/Shutterstock.com

Nonverbal Communication Is Not Language.

Scholars concur that nonverbal communication is not language (Burgoon & Saine, 1978; DeVito, 1989; Harrison, 1974; Hickson, 2004). To call it "body language" is misleading. Both language and non-verbals are learned, but language comes later (Mayo & La France, 1978). Language has syntax and grammar and uses time markers (verb tense) to establish a lot of the meaning; non-verbal communication function is based in the present, and with no particular grammar, syntax or rules of usage (Hickson, 2004). Verbal and non-verbal communication are handled predominately in different parts of the brain (Hickson, 2004; Bowers, Bauer, & Heilman, 1993). Babies have no language skills at all, but they are well able to make their feelings and wishes known by their nonverbal messages. The pitch and intensity of a cry may change, so that parents know a "hurt cry" from an "angry cry." Babies use eye contact, they point, they laugh. Furthermore, they derive comfort from loving touch and the sounds of a gentle voice so we know they receive non-verbal communication as well as sending it. They understand the message, even though they don't know the meanings of the words are that mom is crooning. None of that is verbal. These are all forms of non-verbal communication, and they clearly carry meaning, but they are not language.

Most Nonverbal Communication Is Unconscious.

As I said earlier, we don't think much about our non-verbal communication; our brains suppress a lot of the awareness (Ekman & Friesen, 1968), and we just do it. Our nonverbal messages express our emotions and attitudes (Bowers, Bauer, & Heilman, 1993). They sort of bypass our awareness and just jump out there on their own. If you have ever pulled a four-week-old box of strawberries out of your refrigerator, you didn't think to yourself, "These strawberries are bad. I will register my displeasure by turning my head, making a face, holding the fuzzy fruit at arm's length, and saying 'Phew!'" You didn't think about it; you just did it because it expressed how you were feeling.

Without Coaching, Your Body Doesn't Know How To Lie.

Our bodies want to tell the truth. If a person sends us one message verbally and contradictory information nonverbally, we'll usually believe the nonverbal message (Floyd, 2014). Our subconscious mind usually catches the contradiction and tells us what is true. You can consciously choose to try to mask the truth by forcing yourself to hold a relaxed posture or smile when you are angry, but most often, your body will give you away (Ekman & Friesen, 1982). For a fraction of a second, your face will register your true feelings in micro expressions (facial expressions that happen so fast most of us don't catch them; Yan et al., 2013). There is a whole field of science opening up in communication in which trained observers watch nonverbal indicators to determine if the truth is being told. If you've never treated yourself to an episode of *Lie to Me* or read Malcolm Gladwell's book *Blink*, you really should. It will be a revelation to you—also fun!

Micro expressions
facial expressions that happen so fast most of us don't catch them

The Meaning Of Nonverbal Communication Is Strongly Influenced By Context.

Different actions mean different things in different settings. Remember that context includes communicative, physical, relational, and cultural settings. A lot of the meaning is dependent on the setting. If you ruffle the hair of your best friend in a casual physical setting and your relationship is good at the time, your friend is likely to interpret the action as friendly play. On the other hand, if you do it with your professor in a formal setting, it's likely to be interpreted as an insult. In fact, the relationship context alone would cause it

Tim Roth starred in the TV show Lie to Me which dealt with recognizing deception through use of nonverbal communication.

Kevin Winter/Staff/Getty

to be an insult in most Western communities, because culturally, one is expected to show respect to one's teacher. The difference is not the gesture; it is the relationship context. By the same token, you would let your mom stand very close to you, but not most other people. Now, you might let a total stranger into that space in a crowded elevator, because the physical context has made it acceptable, but that is the only reason. In an elevator that is not crowded, people space themselves accordingly. This is also why you don't talk to or make eye contact with people in crowded elevators. You are already in their intimate space; it would be too much of an intrusion to interact with them by speaking or making eye contact. The setting makes the behavior intrusive, not the action itself.

Culture and Gender Also Strongly Influence Nonverbal Communication.

You'll hear that over and over throughout this textbook, primarily because culture and gender play into all elements of communication. They flavor everything we do. In relation to nonverbal communication and gender, men take up more personal space than women, for example, and women touch more (Anderson, 1999). In interpersonal interactions, women square off face to face and make more eye contact while men stand at oblique angles and play "eye tag" with each other (Tannen, 1990). We see this stuff all the time and probably don't even notice it, but it influences our communication in a big way. There are traditionally masculine and feminine ways to communicate, especially nonverbally. We recognize it, though we may not think of it in those terms.

Culture also plays into how we define nonverbal actions. In many Latin American countries, it is standard to greet another with a kiss on both cheeks, but in the U.S., that action is too personal. Making direct eye contact in the U.S. is considered a way of showing honesty and transparency, but in Egypt it is considered disrespectful or confrontational (Richmond & Gestrin, 1998). Male friends hold hands in China and the Middle East as a gesture of friendship, but in the U.S. heterosexual men would never do that. Spatial requirements for interaction vary from culture to culture. Let me give you an example from my own life. I was born and raised in the United States. When I was in college, I had a friend from Iran. Iranian personal space is much smaller than American personal space, so when he tried to initiate conversation he would move up to about 12" from me, but that was too close for my comfort. He had entered my intimate space, so I would back up. But then I was too far away for *him* to feel comfortable having a friendly conversation, so he would move forward until it felt right to him. You can probably guess what I did in response. I'd move, and he would chase me down the sidewalk backwards in an effort to be friendly! Our different understandings of what that nonverbal message meant made it difficult for us to communicate. One of the interesting things about cultural differences is that we tend not to notice them until they produce some kind of misunderstanding or conflict. Remember, nonverbal messages are mostly unconscious behaviors.

Functions of Nonverbal Communication

© Lesterman/Shutterstock.com

Nonverbal cues perform several functions in communication. There are six basic jobs they do, along with one that would be best undone.

They emphasize verbal information (Knapp and Hall, 1997).

When you are angry and stomp your foot as you say, "I am so mad!" the foot stomping doesn't give more information, but it stresses how strongly you feel. It's the same thing with raising your voice. It is a nonverbal exclamation point.

They illustrate a verbal message (Jaffe, 2013; Knapp and Hall, 1997).

This visual can be done one of two ways. The first is by *giving additional information*. If you say, "I have a bruise right here," the sentence has no meaning unless the listener can see where you are pointing. Nonverbal messages can also *repeat a message* that has been given. If you say, "He called me four times," and hold up four fingers, you are giving the same message both verbally and nonverbally. Either way, a gesture that shows the meaning of the words either through supplementing or reiterating a verbal message is called an illustrator.

They contradict a verbal message (Knapp and Hall, 1997).

Have you ever been introduced to someone who never looked up from checking their text messages as they said, "It's nice to meet you"? If you have, you know that their failure to make eye contact didn't agree with the words you heard. The nonverbal message was clearly that they were not interested in you. Hopefully, our mothers have taught us to think before we speak, but we still give ourselves away by our facial expression, voice tone, and gestures. When things slip out nonverbally that we didn't intend to share, it's called leakage (Ekman and Friesen, 1975). Actually, sarcasm is intentionally saying one message with the words while sending a contradictory message with the nonverbal communication. If you drop your tray in the cafeteria and the entire room applauds, that's sarcasm. You know that though the applause complimented your gracefulness, the meaning was clearly that you were clumsy.

They regulate the flow of conversation (Knapp and Hall, 1997).

When you walk into your home to find your mom on the phone, she may hold up her index finger with the rest of the fingers curled in. You know to wait a minute until she is off the phone. Then again, if you've ever started talking and gotten a dirty look from someone, you also know to shut up. All these are regulators in action. A regulator is a gesture that stops or changes the flow of conversation (Ekman & Frisen, 1975).

They can take the place of words (Knapp and Hall, 1997).

You know the gestures that stand in for words: a wave, thumbs up, clapping, bowing, and shrugging your shoulders are all examples. Each of these gestures has a specific definition. A wave says either "hello" or

Illustrator
a gesture that shows the meaning of the words either through supplementing or reiterating a verbal message

Leakage
when things slip out nonverbally that we didn't intend to share

Sarcasm
intentionally saying one message with the words while sending a contradictory message with nonverbal communication

Regulator
a gesture that stops or changes the flow of conversation

© schankz/Shutterstock.com

"goodbye." Clapping says, "Good job"; bowing says "thank you." Shrugging says "I don't know." These have a one-to-one substitution of gesture for words. In fact there is a name for these types of gestures. They are called emblems. **Emblems** are culturally recognized gestures that have a direct interpretation into a few words (Ekman & Frisen, 1975).

They help us adapt to uncomfortable situations.

Gestures that help us feel better are called **adaptors** (Ekman & Frisen, 1975). They include fanning ourselves when we are hot and shivering when we are cold. Rubbing an aching body part is another example. They also include the things we do when we are nervous or bored, like jingling the change in our pocket, twisting our jewelry, or rocking back and forth to comfort ourselves when we are giving a speech.

They can be used to bully or harass others.

Bullying is using nonverbal and/or verbal communication to control, threaten, or intimidate others. There are many ways to use nonverbal communication to bully others (Swearer & Doll, 2001; Underwood, 2004). Not all bullies are children. You know that sometimes people can walk up to you way too close, and you can tell by the way they look into your eyes and the tone of their voice that they are trying to intimidate you. That is a form of bullying. Edesu and Burgoon (1996) identified several things that people do to use nonverbal communication to overpower another, such as:

- Touching you more than you can touch them
- Using your things without asking you
- Using more negative (frowning, scowling) and fewer positive (smiling) facial expressions than you
- Interrupting and talking over you
- Using eye contact less often, but more intently
- Having to start and end all conversations and periods of silence
- Doing most of the talking in a conversation
- Using their voice in an aggressive way (talking louder, using more angry inflections and tones of voice)

"HR has told me I 'loom'."

© Cartoon Resource/Shutterstock.com

All of these things can be used to make you feel afraid, off balance, or insecure. That can put the bully at an advantage and the victim at a disadvantage. You may look at some of those things and think, "I've seen that in my own relationships!" Not all controlling nonverbal gestures come from enemies; sometimes friends and family can use power plays on us. Deborah Tannen (2001) says that most close relationships have some degree of power inequality, and it is not really unusual for the higher power person to use one or more of these techniques to maintain their position. Very often, the degree of difference is so slight that we don't notice the use of a few of the power techniques; we just chalk it up to that person's individual communication style.

Workplace harassment is a form of bullying that happens at a workplace in which the bully usually is in a position of official power over the victim, like a boss or supervisor, or a commanding officer in the military. This is not always the case, but it's pretty typical. Often, when we think of harassment we think of sexual harassment (unwanted sexual advances on the victim, such as standing too close, inappropriate touching, lewd comments, etc.), but sometimes a supervisor can simply "pick on" an individual in such a way as to make them miserable. That's called "creating a hostile workplace." Examples of this behavior would be a manager "correcting" an employee using bullying nonverbal communication like yelling, sneering, or standing too close and using an aggressive tone of voice.

Workplace harrassment
a form of bullying that happens at a workplace in which the bully is usually in a position of official power over the victim

Types of Nonverbal Communication

If asked to give examples of nonverbal communication, most of us would quickly come up with gestures and eye contact, and some of us would include the way we use objects or our personal space. But the list is much, much longer. Here we go . . .

Gestures

This is the easy one. We all understand that gestures are the way a person uses their hands and body to add meaning to a message. We've already discussed emblems (gestures that substitute for words), illustrators (gestures that add to or illustrate the meaning of a message), regulators (which affect the flow of conversation) and adaptors (which help us deal with uncomfortable situations or help us think). If you've been watching the references, you saw that Ekman and Friesen (1975), identified all these terms and how they function. We tend to think of gestures as being done only with our hands, but we can also include posture and big muscle movements as well. Tension in the shoulders signals an individual who is stressed. The way a person stands says a lot about their confidence in a given situation. It also reveals their emotions. You know when someone you love is down simply by the way they carry themselves, or when they are happy because they may literally "jump for joy." These outbursts of feeling are called *displays of emotion* (Ekman & Friesen, 1975).

Gestures
the way a person uses their hands and body to add meaning to a message

© Champion studio/Shutterstock.com

Eye Messages

Has anyone ever "made eyes" at you? That old fashioned phrase for flirting sums it up pretty well. We send a lot of messages with our eyes. Those are called eye messages. Sure, we all recognize that winking, raised eyebrows, and rolling our eyes send messages, but if you think about it, you recognize that direct eye contact can also ask a question, make a statement, or issue a challenge. Our eyes are very expressive. We use all the flesh surrounding our eyes to communicate, including our eyebrows (Ekman, 2013). Even length of gaze tells us something. Most of the time, in American culture, we look someone in the eye for three or four seconds

Eye messages
messages sent with our eyes

(Argyle & Ingman, 1972). Beyond that time, someone has to look away. Why? Because it is perceived as an intimate gaze. Prolonged gaze is one of the markers of flirtation. It is somewhat invasive, and we break eye contact to "repel" the advance or hold the gaze to signal our receptivity. It can also be perceived as a challenge or an invasion of privacy. Remember what I said earlier about not looking people in the eye if the elevator is crowded? Have you ever seen someone try to provoke a fight by saying, "You lookin' at me?" It's the same thing.

Facial Expression

Facial expression is the use of the face to send messages. It is closely connected to eye messages. Examples of facial expressions include smiling, the furrowed brow of concentration, the lopsided grin of the smirk, and the "surprised face" (eyebrows way up, mouth in the "oh" position). The face can be divided into three basic sections that work together to communicate (see Sidebar 4A): the brow, the nose, and the area around the mouth (Ekman & Friesen, 1975). We can use them independently or combine them to bring subtleties of meaning. For example, you can furrow your brow to show concentration, but if you purse your lips it can mean you are confused. You can smile with your mouth and not your eyes (but everyone knows that is not a friendly smile), or you can smile with your eyes, and we all know that is genuine. The eyes seem to be essential in communicating warmth.

There are a few universal facial expressions that do not vary in meaning from culture to culture (Ekman & Friesen, 1975). They denote fear, anger, happiness, sadness, disgust, and surprise. I don't need to describe what any of these look like because you

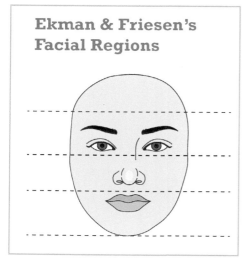

Ekman & Friesen's Facial Regions

Sidebar 4A
© Kendall Hunt Publishing Company

There are six universal facial expressions: happiness, sadness, fear, anger, surprise, and disgust.

already know; that knowledge is programmed into you. Apparently, they are hardwired into humans (Ekman & Friesen, 1975).

Proxemics

Proxemics is the use of space as understood in a particular culture (Hall, 1966). It includes our use of the bubble of space we need around ourselves, as well as how much space we feel we "own." The way we use space is especially culture specific, but since all the authors live and teach in the United States, we decided to approach proxemics from the American perspective. First, let's talk about the proxemic zones Edward Hall (1966) identified for the United States (see Sidebar 4B). The *intimate zone* includes the area directly around the body outward. This zone is strictly limited access for those with whom you have an intimate relationship, hence the name. This includes close family, someone you're dating or married to, and only the closest of friends. You have to really trust someone to let them in here. In most areas of the U.S., we need from 15-18" for the intimate zone. The *personal zone* extends out from our intimate space to three and a half or four feet, depending on the region. It is used for friends, social acquaintances, and strangers in public situations, like standing in line at a bank, or sitting near someone in church or at a concert. We use this to interact with people in a friendly, personable way in social set-tings. It's a "friendly" space. The *social zone* extends from the edge of your personal zone to about twelve feet in the United States. It is used to be friendly but not in a personal way. If you see someone walking toward you, you will wait until they are in that zone before you speak to them. Beyond that a normal speaking voice just doesn't work. You may greet strangers in this zone, but usually only to smile or say "Good morning." We expect to be acknowledged in that zone, but we don't usually invite conversation unless we know the other person. The *public zone* goes from 12 to 25 feet and is used for public speaking or performance events. It requires you to raise your voice, so the boundaries are pretty much set by the reach of the human voice. Beyond that, you must have some form of amplification (a micro-phone or megaphone). You can speak to anyone in the audience, but because it is used for public communication, very little of the message will be directed to one particular person. It's for the group.

Another way we use space to communicate has to do with the space we claim, like our office, home, car, or dorm room. This space is called our **territory**, and the business of staking ownership to one's space is called territoriality (Hickson et al., 2004). The way we decorate it and keep it (clean and in good repair—or not!) tells something about us. What sort of games do you play? What do you read? What sorts of art are on the walls? All these things send messages about you.

Proxemics
the way that we use space to send a message

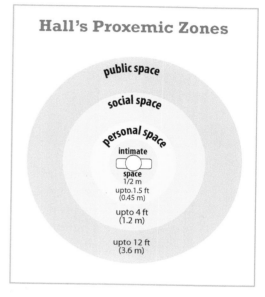

Sidebar 4B
(c) Kendall Hunt Publishing Company

Territory
the space we claim

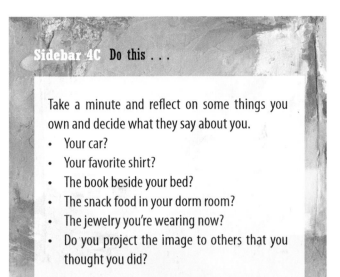

Artifacts
objects that reveal something about someone

Chronemics
messages sent by the way time is structured and used

© ANAID studio/Shutterstock.com

The quantity and location of space a person is entitled to also communicates something. We know that the chairman of the board gets a big office on the top floor with a great view. That person holds power. The custodian gets only a cramped, often dreary closet, and the closet isn't for the custodian; it's for cleaning supplies. Putting up a picture of family members is about as aggressively as the custodian can claim the space.

Artifacts

Artifacts are objects that reveal something about someone. The kind of clothes or jewelry you choose to wear tells something about you, just like your car, the sound system in your dorm room, or the kind of books you read (Dobkin & Pace, 2003). Based on the setting, your shoes can tell a lot about you. If you come to class all dressed up, I can infer that you like being dressed up, or you have just come from some location where you are expected to dress up, or you are out of other clean clothes. The contents of your backpack will tell me what classes you are taking, whether you prefer taking notes on paper or electronically, or not at all. If you carry an expensive pen, it tells me something about you that carrying the bottom-of-the-line Bic will not say. All these are artifacts that you could use to mine information about the owner of the object. It is closely connected to territoriality. Territoriality tells us how you chose to use space, but analyzing the contents of that space is artifactics.

Chronemics

How we spend our time says a lot about us. The term chronemics refers to how we use and structure time (Hickson, et al., 2004). If you spend a lot of time studying, people will probably think you make a priority of your schoolwork and assume you are a good student. If you spend it on socializing, people are likely to think you like people and that the social experience is of primary importance to you. We communicate a lot about our self-image by the way we use time, but we also communicate a lot about what we think of others.

How long a person can keep another waiting or be kept waiting themselves is an indicator of a person's status and power. How long would you wait for your professor? How long would you wait for the president of the United States? See the difference? When we are habitually on time, it sends the message that we are respectful of others' time. If we are always late, we are unintentionally sending the message that our time is more important than that of others. It is a message of selfishness within the United States, but *not* in some other parts of the world. Why? Culture plays a big role in that. The interpretations we make of time use and management is strongly affected by culture (Hall, 1984). Different cultures have different understandings of time. In some parts of the world, you are even *expected* to be late for social engagements by anywhere from a few minutes to a few hours. Just a quick aside: another culture's understanding of time usage is every bit as legitimate as that of your own culture. Just because the American way of doing things seems right to Americans, does not mean that it is the only right way.

Scent

As a form of communication, **scent** refers to the nonverbal messages sent by smell. Most of the research in this area has been on the links between smell and memory, or the effects of hormonal messages released and perceived unconsciously (Hickson, et al., 2004), but we do consciously attempt to manipulate our smell. What is the purpose of wearing perfume or cologne? To smell good so people will think about you in the way you want to be perceived. You pick your fragrance because you like how it smells but also for the message it sends about you. You wear deodorant because you don't want to smell of perspiration. You spray air freshener to make the room smell nice when you have guests so they won't think you are a slob. We hang those cardboard pine trees from the rearview mirrors of our cars so they smell clean. We even identify the "new car smell" with status (Hickson, et al., 2004). Of course, like so many things in communication, your culture plays a major role in what smells "good" to you (Hickson, et al., 2004).

© Asier Romero/Shutterstock.com

Scent
the nonverbal messages sent by smell

Vocalics

Vocalics is the meaning that comes from the way the words are said rather than the meaning of the words. We've all had the experience of someone saying to us "Don't speak to me in that tone of voice!" That is vocalics in action. You have surely had times you got into an argument, not because the things that were said but because of the way they were said. Even the way we breathe can communicate how we're feeling (Rodenburg, 2000), like when we gasp or snort or hold our breath. **Vocal fillers** (sounds like "uh" and "um") also affect our messages in that they indicate that we are searching for the right thing to say; this may indicate that we are unprepared or have been caught with information we don't want to share. Our nonverbal communication is unconscious and is connected to our feelings and attitudes, but it can get us into trouble anyway! Remember leakage?

Four things go into our understanding of vocalics: rate, pitch, volume, and inflection. *Rate* is how fast or slowly we speak. A person who is upset or excited is likely to speak more quickly than someone who is calm; depressed people will often send that message by how slowly they speak. *Pitch* is how high or low our voice is placed

Vocalics
the meaning that comes from the way the words are said rather than the meaning of the words

Vocal fillers
sounds like "uh" and "um"

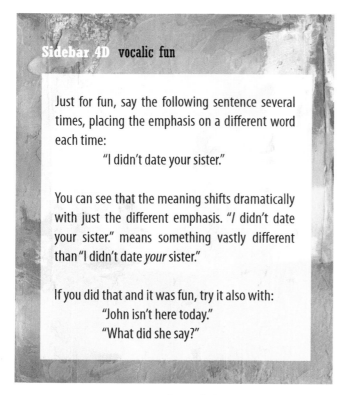
on the musical scale. Pitch often sends the same message as rate. When you are upset or excited, your voice is likely to go up; when you are calmer, your pitch is likely to be lower. It is no accident that we tell people who are upset to calm *down*. *Volume* refers to how loudly or softly we speak. We speak more loudly when we feel something strongly or when we want to assert ourselves in a situation. Speaking softly often shows endearment. We try to achieve a "normal" volume when we are trying to convince someone that we are not upset. All these are uses of volume. The last element is inflection. *Inflection* is the emphasis we put on one particular word rather than another. The emphasis can greatly influence the meaning, not to mention being more interesting to listen to (see Sidebar 4D).

Haptics

Haptics is the use of physical touch to send or receive a message. We hug and shake hands to greet others; we hug, kiss, and gently touch the face of those we love. We may playfully swat at friends. All these are ways we use touch to communicate. We may even push, slap, or hit those with whom we are angry, though this is clearly an unhealthy use of touch.

Haptics
the use of physical touch to send or receive a message

© Andrey Yurlov/Shutterstock.com

There are four types of touch (Knapp, 1978). The first is *intimate touch*, which is touching between people who have intimate roles in each other's lives. The nature of the relationship entitles the right parties not only to be able to be in your intimate space, but also to touch intimately, depending on the nature of the relationship. For example, face touching is pretty much allowed for only those with whom you have that intimate relationship like parents, children, lovers, and best friends. But your boss doesn't have the right to do that. You can see why we want to have careful control of who gets to use intimate touch with us. We know who can and cannot touch us in that way. Individuals who disregard those expectations are perceived as dangerous, and we hold them at arm's length, both literally and figuratively.

Friendship touch is the touch between friends and social acquaintances that are not in your intimate circle. Just like they have reduced spatial access, they have reduced touch access. Touch with these folks is pretty much limited to arms, hands, and back or shoulders, but not face, chest, or legs. That makes sense, right? They are close enough to touch, but not intimately. Examples could include when you fist bump or slap a friend on the back or give what a friend of mine called the "side hug." If the relationship were not good, the touch would be considered an attack, but because it is friendly, it falls into the category of friendship touch.

Politeness touch is the touch allowed to people with whom you must have interaction but who are not considered friends. It includes shaking hands with someone you have just met or must meet in a professional capacity as well as kissing on both cheeks in some Latin cultures. It might include patting someone on the shoulder or hand as a consoling gesture or taking someone by the arm to steer him in a particular direction. It is pretty much limited to shoulders, arms, and hands.

Professional touch is the touch allowed to those whose job requires them to have physical contact with us for a professional reason. Your doctor, your hair stylist, and the person who fits you with shoes at the shoe store are all using professional touch. The places they may touch us are limited by what is needed to do their job.

Intimate touch

Friendship touch

Professional touch

Politeness touch

Ethical Implications

The things we have discussed relate to our behavior in real life in many ways. The first, most overarching item to recognize is that there are rules about how we use nonverbal messages, like touch, personal space, eye contact, or touching other people's things. Respect those rules. They serve a purpose, which is to smooth the difficulties of human interaction. Don't push other people's personal boundaries. That's intimidating, and you know it, so respect their space. Don't touch people inappropriately. Even little children know whether or not they want to be touched by a stranger. Don't force eye contact by staring; that's violating. It may also send messages you don't intend to send. Don't bully people. Follow the rules. Play nice.

Because we unconsciously recognize that the nonverbal message surrounding a communication gives a truer representation of reality than the words, most of us recognize sarcasm and are hurt by it when others use it against us. Sarcasm is a very popular way to make jokes in our society, but that does not excuse us from the damage we do in the name of humor. Sticks and stones may break my bones, but words hurt me the most. There are other ways to be funny. Use sarcasm with care.

Don't use nonverbal communication to lie. Even if you don't say it aloud, it's still a lie. Don't fake feelings you don't have. Tell the truth; just be tactful. This is not easy to do. It takes real courage.

When you are in an intercultural communication setting, take that into account. If you go to another culture, you must learn the rules of that culture and adopt them while you are functioning in that community. It's their country; you have to learn the communication rules for that culture. Don't expect the rest of the world to adapt to your comfort zone. For example, if personal space is smaller than you like, you might explain it to individuals of that culture with whom you are conversing, but keep trying to adjust and learn to work with the smaller space. And when someone from another culture accidentally does something that is unacceptable in your society, it is appropriate to kindly tell them so at a time and place that won't expose them to ridicule. To kindly let someone know they are inadvertently making a social mistake within a culture is doing them a favor and may save them grief in the long run, but be tactful and don't embarrass them by talking about it in front of others.

On the same cross-cultural note, as much as possible, learn the emblems that cannot be used in a particular culture before you enter it. Find someone who has been there or is from that culture to give you a brief tutorial. Search online for "cultural gestures" for the country to which you will go. It will not give you the entire encyclopedic knowledge for communicating nonverbally in that culture, but it will give you a heads-up on the things that could offend people and some of the most common cultural differences.

Nonverbal messages vary not just from culture to culture, but also from age group to age group and in different situations, whether formal, educational, professional, or casual. Your grandparents or employer or minister may not accept your nonverbal cues as having the same meanings as you intended. Don't forget that the way you use time sends nonverbal messages, too. Younger people often are not aware how tardiness is perceived among older people and in workplace or educational settings. Older people and those in authority tend to think that lateness is a subtle form of disrespect, so be aware of that. And put down the phone! Many older folks find your texting during a conversation with them or taking phone calls without excusing yourself very rude. Furthermore, the way you keep your workspace, your posture, and your gestures may seem just fine to you and those of your own age group or social situation but may not be received as you meant them. Remember that in the workplace and educational settings, you are moving into someone else's subculture, so you need to learn the rules that show respect for all parties who function there. You get the idea. Play nice in other people's playgrounds.

Summary

Understanding nonverbal communication greatly affects our effectiveness in message reception. Reading nonverbal signals is something we do not think about much. We learn it in childhood through social interaction. Nonverbal communication is not language, and it reveals our inner thoughts emotions, and attitudes. Your body is resistant to lying and will give indicators when doing so unless you've been coached on how to lie. Nonverbal communication is highly affected by context; culture and gender also affect it substantially. It has several jobs in relation to verbal communication. It can emphasize, illustrate, and contradict words, as well as take the place of words or regulate the speed of conversation. Gestures can help us adapt to uncomfortable situations. Nonverbal messages can also be used to intimidate or bully another.

There are nine types of nonverbal communication: gestures, facial expressions, eye contact, proxemics, haptics, scent, vocalics, chronemics, and artifacts. Gestures perform several functions. Culture and length of gaze affect the meaning of eye contact. Proxemics is the use of space, and how close someone can get to us is determined by relationship and purpose. Space that we claim ownership of is territory. There are several types of touch (intimate, friendship, social, and professional), and who can engage in what touch is also determined by relationship and purpose. Scents carry messages, too, and may be the most unconscious of the nonverbal types of communication. Vocalics is how we use the voice, especially tone, volume, speed, and inflection. How we use time sends a message, and status affects how much time we expect to be allowed or to allow others to have. Objects that we possess and surround ourselves with also send messages about who we are and what we think of ourselves.

Vocabulary Words

Adaptors	Gestures	Regulator
Artifacts	Haptics	Sarcasm
Bullying	Illustrators	Scent
Chronemics	Leakage	Territory
Emblems	Micro expression	Vocal fillers
Eye messages	Nonverbal communication	Vocalics
Facial expression	Proxemics	Workplace harassment

Discussion Questions

1. Have you ever interacted with someone who didn't respect your intimate personal space? How did it make you feel?

2. How long would you wait for your teacher? Your doctor? Your university president?
3. Which form of touch do you think is most damaging when it is violent?
4. Think of an object you own that tells a lot about you. What does it say? Are you comfortable with what it says?
5. Name some kinds of eye messages (winking, squinting, etc.).
6. Which function of nonverbal communication does sarcasm do?
7. How many kinds of products did you use today to repress your odor?
8. Have you ever used your nonverbal messages to make someone else do something they didn't want to? How could you have achieved your goal without coercing them into compliance?

References

Anderson, P. A. (1999). *Nonverbal communication: Forms and function.* Mountain View, CA: Mayfield Publishing.

Argyle, M., & Ingman, R. (1972). Gaze, mutual gaze, and proximity. *Semiotica, 6,* 32–49.

Birdwhistell, R. L. (1970). *Kinesics and context: Essays on body motion communication.* Philadelphia: University of Pennsylvania Press.

Birdwhistell, R. L. (1974). The language of the body: The natural environment of words. In A. Silverstein (Ed.), *Human communication: Theoretical explorations* (pp. 203–220). New York: John Wiley & Sons.

Bowers, D., Bauer, R. M., & Heilman, K. M. (1993). The nonverbal affect lexicon: Theoretical perspectives from neuropsychological studies of affects perception. *Neuropsychology, 7,* 433–444.

Brody, J. (1992, August 19). Personal health: Helping children overcome rejection. *New York Times,* p. C12.

Burgoon, J. K., & Saine, T. (1978). *The unspoken dialogue: An introduction to nonverbal communication.* Boston: Houghton Mifflin.

DeVito, J. A. (1989). *The non-verbal communication handbook.* Prospect Heights, IL: Waveland Press.

Dobkin, B. A., & Pace, R. C. (2003). *Communication in a changing world.* New York, NY: McGraw-Hill.

Edesu, A. S., & Burgoon, J. K. (1996). Nonverbal communication. In M. B. Salwan & D. W. Stacks (Eds.), *An integrated approach to communication theory and research* (pp. 345–358). Mahwah, NJ: Lawrence Erlbaum.

Ekman, P., & Friesen, W. V. (1968). Nonverbal behavior in psychotherapy research. *Psychotherapy, 3,* 88–106.

Ekman, P., & Friesen, W. V. (1975). *Unmasking the face.* Englewood Cliff, NJ: Prentice Hall.

Ekman, P. & Friesen, W. V. (1982). Felt, false, and miserable smiles. *Journal of Nonverbal Behavior, 6,* 238–252.

Ekman, P. (2003). *Emotions revealed: Recognizing faces and feelings to improve communication and emotional life.* New York, NY: Holt.

Floyd, K. (2014). *Communication matters* (2nd ed.). New York, NY: McGraw-Hill.

Hall, E. T. (1984). *The dance of life: The other dimension of time.* New York: Anchor.

Hall, E. T. (1996). *The hidden dimension.* Garden City, NY: Doubleday.

Harrison, R. P. (1974). *Beyond words: An introduction to nonverbal communication.* Engle Wood Cliffs, NJ: Prentice Hall.

Hickson, M., III, Stacks, D. W., & Moore, N. (2004). *Nonverbal communication: Studies and applications* (4th ed.). Los Angeles, CA: Roxbury Publishing.

Hybels, S., & Weaver, R. L., II. (2001). *Communicating effectively* (6th ed.). New York, NY: McGraw-Hill.

Jaffe, C. (2013). *Public speaking: Concepts and skills for a diverse society* (7th ed.). Boston, MA: Wadsworth.

Knapp, M. L. (1978). *Nonverbal communication in human interaction* (2nd ed.). New York: Holt, Rinehart, and Winston.

Knapp, M. L., & Hall, J. A. (1997). *Nonverbal communication in human interaction* (3rd ed.). Fort Worth, TX: Harcourt Brace.

Mayo, C., & La France, M. (1978). On the acquisition of nonverbal communication: A review. *Merrill-Palmer Quarterly of Behavior and Development, 24*(4), 213–228.

Mehrabian, *A. Silent messages: Implicit communication of emotions and attitudes* (2nd ed.). Belmont, CA: Wadsworth.

Philpott, J. S. (1983). The relative contribution to meaning of verbal and nonverbal channels of communication. (Unpublished master's thesis). University of Institution, Lincoln, Nebraska.

Richmond, Y., & Gestrin, P. (1998). *Into Africa: Intercultural insights.* Yarmouth, ME: Intercultural Press.

Rodenburg, P. (2000). *The actor speaks: Voice and performer.* New York: St. Martin's Press.

Swearer, S. M., & Doll, B. (2001). Bullying in schools: An ecological framework. *Journal of Emotional Abuse, 2*, 7–23. doi:10.1300/J135v02n02_02

Tannen, D. (1990). *You just don't understand: Women and men in conversation.* New York: Morrow.

Tannen, D. (2001). *I only say this because I love you.* New York: Ballantine.

Underwood, M. K. (2004). Glares of contempt, eye rolls of disgust and turning away to exclude: Non-verbal forms of social aggression among girls. *Feminism & Psychology, 14*(3), 371–375. doi: 10.1177/0959-353504044637

Wood, J. T. (2002). *Interpersonal communication: Everyday encounters* (3rd ed.). Belmont, CA: Wadsworth.

Yan, W., Wu, Q., Liang, J., Chen, Y., & Fu, X. (2013). How fast are the leaked facial expressions: The duration of micro-expressions. *Journal of Nonverbal Behavior, 37*, 217–230.

Additional Readings

The Definitive Book of Body Language

by Barbara Pease

Emotions Revealed

by Paul Eckmann

What Every Body Is Saying

by Joe Navarro

Children's Unspoken Language

by Gwyneth Doherty-Sneddon

The Silent Language

by Edward T. Hall

Better Communicators Are Good Listeners

By Rhonda Gallagher, M.S.

© Monkey Business Images/Shutterstock.com

5

Listening is so important in our lives. It is critical in our function as communicators. It helps us to learn, to interact, to do our jobs, and make and maintain relationships to name just a few of the things we need it for. In fact, it is irreplaceable for properly functioning in our communities and facilitating happy lives, and we also need to learn to listen critically because things are not always as they seem. But before we begin looking into critical listening, let's begin by just learning about the basics of listening, starting with attention.

Attention is absolutely essential for communication to happen. Otherwise, all that information swirling around in your head will never actually hold any meaning for you. Understanding how we get information is very helpful to improving our communication, and listening plays a powerful role. What is listening? How is it different from hearing? As a child, you are told over and over to listen, but no one told you how, or even what it was. **Hearing** is the purely physical process of sound being relayed to the brain along the auditory nerve (Wood, 2002). **Listening** is an active (Emmert, 1996) mental process that involves perceiving sound (usually by hearing), interpreting it, and responding to it. When we think of listening, we tend to think of something that just deals with the sense of hearing; actually, that is not strictly true (Robinshaw, 2007). Not all

Hearing
the physical process of sound being relayed to the brain along the auditory nerve

Listening
an active mental process that involves perceiving sound interpreting it, and responding to it

Passive listeners
people who do not take responsibility for listening

Active listeners
people who participate in listening by keeping attention focused, creating memory aids, and structuring the information received

listening is done with our ears; we often listen with our other senses, especially our eyes (Egan, 1973). Listening is differentiated from purely sensory stimuli by its *purposefulness*. Listening implies a focused energy toward perception, *trying* to perceive. We often perceive information without thinking about it, but listening is done on purpose.

Now, some people don't realize they can do that. They think that listening just sort of happens, like wild flowers in the spring. These are passive listeners. **Passive listeners** are people who do not take responsibility for listening. If a distraction comes along, they just follow it and say, "I couldn't help it!" **Active listeners** are people who participate in listening by keeping attention focused, creating memory aids, and structuring the information received. They work at it. They recognize when they are getting distracted and take steps to bring their minds back to the subject at hand. They resist daydreaming. They take notes or create images in their minds to help them retain what they have heard. There are things you can do to help yourself attend, and we'll talk about those later.

So, let's look at listening more closely, beginning with the steps: attention, interpretation, response, and remembering.

© 9nong/Shutterstock.com

Attention
intentional effort to capture specific sensory information

Interpretation
understanding what you have heard

Steps in Listening

Step 1—Attention

We begin listening with focus, otherwise known as attention. **Attention** is intentional effort to capture specific sensory information (Wood, 2002). We bring our mental faculties to bear on one particular thing. When you go to class, you know you will need to listen to the lecture, so you put conscious work into attending. Even if the teacher is boring, you can still pay attention if you exercise your will, though it's much easier with a riveting public speaker! You have taken control of your mental process and focused it on something in particular.

Step 2—Interpretation

Interpretation is understanding what you have heard. It is figuring out what the information means. Just because you can parrot back what you have heard doesn't mean you understood it. Your understanding doesn't have to be perfect, but if you didn't get some of the meaning, you haven't moved into interpretation yet. I sometimes ask students to explain a concept I just taught them. They try to give an answer but give up, saying, "I understand it; I just can't put it into words." Listen: if you can't put it into your own words, you don't understand. Either I did a poor job teaching the information or they were not fully, actively engaged in listening, or they tried, but just didn't understand.

Step 3—Evaluation

Evaluation is deciding what you think about what you've heard. Essentially, you have to take the idea or information you've been given, turn it over, look at it from different angles, and figure out if it's true or worth anything. For instance, listening to political campaign speeches requires us to consider if the person is telling us the whole story. Are they telling the truth or spinning their descriptions to support their position? We may think they are lying or that they are telling the truth; or maybe we think they are telling us what they think is the truth, but that they are wrong. Evaluating also comes into play when people tell you things you aren't sure are actually true. If Jordan tells you that Anna said her parents kicked her out of the house, you may doubt if she actually said it, or said it in the way that Jordan is presenting it. You'll ask yourself if this story makes sense, based on what you know about Anna and her parents and, to some extent, what you know about Jordan.

Evaluation
deciding what you think about what you've heard

© TAGSTOCK1/Shutterstock.com

Step 4—Response

Response is the reaction you have to what you have heard. Much of the time, we respond nonverbally to show that we understand. That's response. If your biology teacher is sharing a fascinating bit of information about how the human body works, you don't think about making good eye contact and nodding. You just do because you're actively involved in listening. If your professor tells you that the exam has been postponed, you don't plan to smile and say "Thank you!" You just do. But sometimes we know we can't show our response externally. We may work very hard at having a deadpan expression on our faces when we are told bad information. You may not express the reaction, but you most assuredly had one. Not all information gets an external response, but you still had a response if you understood. These middle steps take place in rapid succession. If you understand what you have heard, response is almost immediate and very difficult to hide. Remember nonverbal leakage?

Response
your reaction you have to what you have heard

Step 5—Remembering

The last stage of listening is remembering. **Remembering** is being able to retrieve information from your memory bank. For some kinds of listening, remembering is absolutely essential, but for others not so much. Funny, huh? If the first four stages are connected by solid arrows, the link between response and remembering should be a dotted line arrow (See Sidebar 5A). You may listen effectively and have safely stored a bit of information in your brain that is never, ever retrieved for any reason. Does that mean you did not listen? No. It means the information was catalogued and stored, but never needed. In time, information that is neither needed, nor deeply rooted in an emotional reaction, may simply no longer be intellectually available. I know that at some point in your life, someone has asked you if you remembered something they told you and you said no. You were promptly told, "Then you weren't listening!" But, here's the problem: you probably *were* listening.

Remembering
being able to retrieve information from your memory bank

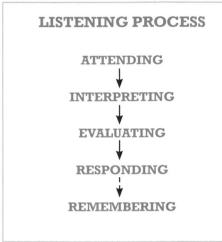

LISTENING PROCESS

ATTENDING
↓
INTERPRETING
↓
EVALUATING
↓
RESPONDING
↓
REMEMBERING

Sidebar 5A

Remembering is a pretty imperfect business. You don't remember everything you hear. You just can't. If you go hear a lecture or speech, just hear it, you will remember roughly 50% immediately. In just eight hours, that can fall to as little as 20% (Nichols, 1995), and even if we recall more, we only remember about 20% accurately (Benoit & Lee, 1986). That doesn't mean you were not listening; you just can't hang on to all of it. Your listening efforts were not wasted; retention is tough. But here is an interesting idea: if you add another form of sensory input, the retention goes up. If the speaker adds visual aids to the speech, your retention the next day goes way up. This is why it helps you remember if you take notes in class. If you can get up and *do* an activity associated with new information, it helps, doesn't it? Those are all ways of increasing sensory input.

Listening Purposes: Why Am I Doing This Again?

We listen for a variety of reasons: to get directions on how to do an assignment, to learn how to change the oil in the car, to get somewhere, to engage in conversation, to enjoy a piece of music, to console a friend in grief or to determine if that roommate is telling us the truth about borrowing our stuff. All of our purposes for listening can be broken down into four categories of things we are listening for: information, empathy, judgment, or fun.

Listening for Information: Tell Me More!

When you go to class or ask directions or watch a how-to video on YouTube, you are listening for information that you want or need to know. Listening for information is applying attentive listening for the purpose of learning something. You are often called upon to do this in real life and few things are more irritating

Listening for information
applying attentive listening for the purpose of learning something

© pathdoc/Shutterstock.com

than being asked for information and having the questioner then fail to listen to what you are saying. There can be serious ramifications that result from poor listening skills in certain situations. You may miss a court date and be fined or take your medications in the wrong way and end up in the hospital! One of the most important places to have good listening skills is at work. Whenever employers are asked to identify the skills they need from their employees, the vast majority of businesses cite communication skills as their most desired skill, and when a thousand human resource professionals were surveyed, they identified listening skills as the most important skill for effective managers (Windsor, Curtis, &

Stephens, 1997). Before moving into higher education, I worked as a corporate trainer, teaching class after class of new hires how to do their jobs. Time and again, new employees who were poor listeners didn't make it. Technical skills can be taught, but an employee who will not listen is a problem from the beginning. Why would anyone *not* listen to their boss? You might be surprised. Occasionally, people will be so nervous that their brains seem unable to form a memory and nothing is retained. Did you know that fear or nervousness can cause you to be unable to listen? (More on this later.) Sometimes, we just have an expectation of what will be said and what we expected is what we hear. When we anticipate what will be said, that is called prediction, and it can be very helpful in processing communication, but it can also present a hindrance to listening.

© wavebreakmedia/Shutterstock.com

So how can we improve our informational listening?

Getting Better

There are several things you can do to improve your skill at listening to information.

Pay attention.

This may seem obvious, but often this is the root of the problem. We have already discussed that attending is an act of the will and requires concentration and effort. It's difficult. They don't call it *paying* attention for nothing; it costs you something. It requires being aware of things that distract you and taking steps to overcome those distractions. It requires discipline, but it yields good results.

Ask clarifying questions.

If a question occurs to you while you are listening, ask. That is not interrupting; it's understanding. If the situation doesn't allow for asking questions until the end, like a speech event, take notes and ask when you can. Often, understanding a piece of new information is dependent on understanding the last one.

Look for the overarching structure.

Listen for the "big picture" stuff and realize that those are the bones on which all the details hang. Unsure if you got the right themes? See the point directly above.

Create memory aids for yourself.

Never despise note-taking, whether you use a phone, tablet, or pen and paper (DeVito, 2009). Writing information down adds a secondary input that increases retention. Close your eyes and visualize the illustrations given to you. If I have to remember a phone number and have nothing to write with, I'll repeat the numbers and move my fingers in the pattern of dialing the number. Come up with story connections. For instance, I wanted to remember the name of a guitarist I knew my husband would love to hear, but I had no pen or paper. His name is Jason Swanson, so I imagined the Greek hero Jason (of Argonaut fame) in a ship with a Swanson canned chicken label on the sail. Sounds silly, I know, but remember his name. See what I mean? Be creative.

Empathetic Listening: Tell Me Your Feelings!

One of the most important listening skills is empathetic listening. Empathetic listening is listening for the purpose of understanding and lending emotional support to another person (Kuhn, 2001). You do that when a friend tells you about something they are feeling or trying to sort through. They could be experiencing almost any emotion, but if they need to talk it out and you listen to them, that's empathetic listening. If your friend has been dumped by his or her significant other and needs to talk/cry it out, if your sister is uncertain if her job is going to work out, if a co-worker is mad at his supervisor and needs to just vent; all of these are opportunities for you to engage in empathetic listening. The goal of empathetic listening is to let the other person sort out their own thoughts. Some of us get called upon to do this more than other folks. Why? Because we are "good listeners". But what does that mean? Is there some cluster of behaviors that we can do to make us better at this? Hybels and Weaver (2003) said there is, and I've been teaching their suggestions to my students for years.

© baranq/Shutterstock.com

Getting Better

Empathize, but keep your objectivity.

Empathy is putting yourself into someone else's shoes and thinking about what they feel. But if you want to really help, you have to keep enough emotional distance to think objectively about what they are saying and doing. That is your best hope of helping them. If your friend has lost his mother, you don't want to be as upset as he is. You can't help him grieve if you are devastated. You can feel compassion for him, but if you lose yourself in his grief, you give up your objectivity and can offer no help. In fact, if you do that, you wind up taking over his situation and making it about you, not him. Think of it this way: you can dip your toe in his ocean of emotion, but you can't get in there and swim.

Avoid giving advice.

One of the real temptations of empathetic listening is to just tell the person what to do to fix the situation, but when you do that, you take away their opportunity to *own the solution*. If you've ever made a birdhouse or knitted a scarf, you know that it is valuable to you because you made it yourself. The same thing is true of solutions we come up with ourselves. We are more invested in them, and we are much more likely to carry them out. Sometimes, what the person needs is not to come up with a solution, but to realize something about themselves or the situation. That *really* can't happen if you tell them how to fix it. Self-knowledge has to be self-constructed. Show caring restraint and let them discover their own answers. Telling people what to do may make you feel like a guru, but it doesn't help them in the long run. Besides, fixing people is God's business, not ours.

Don't overreact to their emotions.

Sometimes when a person is upset, they can be very threatening. They may be so angry you feel frightened, but they aren't angry at you. It isn't personal. Even if they say things like, "I hate that person!" resist the impulse to censor their emotional reaction or deny it. They may later say that they didn't mean it (or they might say that they did!), but you can't tell other people what they feel; you don't know. Emotions are not actions or even moral choices, so don't let them throw you for a loop. They are symptoms of psychological processes, not the actual process. They may be indicators of unresolved issues, but the issues themselves are the issues, not the emotions.

Don't judge the speaker.

They need to talk, and if you get shocked or condemn them, they may stop talking altogether. This person may have just poured out to you a deep confession, and if you judge them, they may never feel safe to open up to anyone again. Besides, Christians should be the hardest people in the world to shock. None of us is really so righteous that we've never said or done anything wrong. However, you *can* judge content. If you think they may actually be a danger to others or themselves based on what they've said, you may need to enlist some outside help for the situation, like a resident advisor, counselor, or pastor, but respect the sensitivity of the situation and their expectation of confidentiality if there was one.

Ask questions.

Asking the right questions can help people identify their feelings, decisions, potential actions, and possible outcomes. If they want to tell the boss to put the job somewhere unsavory, don't tell them, "You can't do that. You'll get fired." Instead, ask them questions that will help them figure that out for themselves, questions like, "What do you think might happen if you did that?" or "How do you think that might help you?" When they figure out that they could get fired, it's time to ask if that is actually what they want or if they have a backup plan.

Don't compete with their pain.

When someone is talking through a problem, they need to remain the center of attention until they have worked through the issue. If you have had a similar experience, this is not the time to say, "I've been through much worse than that!" It might even be true, but it won't help the speaker. It only places you at the center of attention, and while it might be nice for you, it really is not what your friend needs or wants. By taking the focus off of them, you short-circuit their discovery process. Resist the urge. It's not about you this time; it's about them.

Be authentic.

Be genuinely involved in listening. Don't engage in automatic, thoughtless comments. The speaker needs you to be in the moment with them. Sometimes we succumb to the temptation to respond with trite old sayings, like "Every cloud has a silver lining" or "If at first you don't succeed, try, try again" or (as is often said in the church) "Give it to the Lord." Sometimes we even use scripture thoughtlessly in the same way. Your friend says they are afraid they may fail their Spanish class, and you say, "'I can do all things through Christ who strengthens me!'" without ever thinking what they are experiencing. You can see how unhelpful that would be. That is what Langer, Blank, and Chanowitz (1978) called mindlessness. **Mindlessness** is doing and saying things without really thinking about them because we've done it that way so often. Mindless responses don't really help, and they send the message to the speaker that you really don't care about them. Ouch!

Mindlessness
doing and saying things without really thinking about them

© sirtravelalot/Shutterstock.com

Listening for judgment
listening to make a decision about the truth or value of something

Listening for Judgment: All Rise!

The third type of listening is listening for judgment, which is listening to make a decision about the truth or value of something. Sitting on a jury, comparison shopping for the best new computer, or listening to a political speech are all examples of listening for judgment. It's trying to figure out if what you are being told is true, good, or appropriate. Listening for judgment is a part of critical thinking. It requires a healthy dose of careful analysis. If you are by nature a very trusting person, this may be difficult for you, but it is very important to learn to do this. The fact is that not everyone is interested in telling you the truth, so you must be "as wise as serpents and harmless as doves," as the Bible says (Matthew 10:16). Lots of us have it backwards. We are as harmless as serpents and wise as doves. There is no virtue in being bird-brained here. We don't want to be led into foolish or wrong behavior, so it is important to think about the persuasive messages we get. We will be held accountable for our actions, and the decisions we make about veracity can have far-reaching consequences, so we need to think them through. So, how do we get better at this?

Getting Better

Pay close attention.

You can't let your mind wander when you are involved in listening for judgment. If your mind should wander (which happens to all of us at times) don't try to hide it or cover it up or fake it. Ask for the information to be repeated so you are sure you heard right.

Take notes.

You can't remember everything you heard, as we discussed earlier, so backing up information with a paper copy will help you later to remember what you've heard. As an older gentleman once told me, a short pencil beats a long memory any day!

Ask yourself if what you are hearing makes sense.

Do all the parts of the story make sense together? Do they make sense within your understanding of the world? Does the evidence support what you are hearing? (We'll look at this more closely in a couple of pages.)

Consider the source.

Some sources are just more credible than others (Goodall & Goodall, 2006). *Consumer Reports* provides more credible information in my search for a new laptop than my grandmother. If a political candidate tells me his new economic plan will save the taxpayer money, I would be more likely to believe him if he quoted an economics professor than if he quoted his neighbor.

Look for underlying interests.

Does the person giving you information benefit in some way if you believe them (DeVito, 2009; Goodall & Goodall, 2006)? I am less likely to believe the salesperson trying to sell me the more expensive mattress than the friend who recently bought a mattress. Why? Because the sales person may earn a commission or achieve a sales quota if they sell me that mattress. They have an interest in influencing my decision. The student who wants me to excuse an absence in order to avoid a point penalty on a late paper may be tempted to spin the story in order to convince me they were sick, not just cutting class. A note from the doctor is more credible because the doctor has no reason to lie to me.

Keep an open mind.

Listening to someone's arguments for why a thing should be done a particular way doesn't guarantee you will agree with them. Hear them out. They may have good evidence and good logic, or they might not. But if they don't, you'll figure it out. Don't be afraid to hear the idea, and don't be afraid to examine it closely. In my opinion, the most dangerous idea is the one that is unexamined.

Take your time.

Good judgment can't be rushed. Weigh all the evidence and listen to your gut instincts. They are often your subconscious understanding of nonverbal signals that your conscious mind didn't catch, and they are frequently right. However, you must be aware of your own prejudices as well, which may call for some real soul-searching.

Listening for Fun: "Lemme Get My Earbuds!"

Listening for fun
engaging in listening for enjoyment' sake

This kind of listening probably takes less explanation than any of the previous types. Listening for fun is engaging in listening purely for enjoyment's sake. When you listen to music, or watch a movie or TV, or watch your favorite videos online, you are listening for fun. We tend to think of this as "doing nothing," but by definition, if you are listening, it can't be inactive. You must pay attention for it

© Lunda Vandoorne/Shutterstock.com

to be fun, but just like money spent on something you really want, the "pay" in "paying attention" is much easier to do, and we are not often aware of the cost.

Getting Better

Engage in the listening.

Bring your full attention to it (Wood, 2002). Just letting the noise run in the background is not listening. That's not to say you can't do it, but just be aware that isn't truly listening.

Be aware of what you are hearing.

Reserve a small part of your brain to listen for judgment. Otherwise, you'll have no filters on what you hear and may take in ideas that you may not agree with morally and/or ethically. Don't get me wrong. I'm not trying to make you a prude, but often people listen to music or other forms of entertainment without inspecting what they are hearing and wind up singing or repeating things they would find shocking if someone *said* the words to them. Furthermore, you can waste your time if you don't examine the entertaining material for quality. It may be innocent enough but still be just plain junk. Your mind becomes what you put into it. Have some standards for quality and content. Ask yourself if that is what you want to use up your precious grey matter on, or if that is the content you want floating back into your brain when you are home with a fever.

Enjoy some silence occasionally.

Variety makes our lives richer. If you are constantly surrounded by sound and visual input, some silence can take the edge off. According to Johnson et al. (2003), self-imposed silence increases our awareness of the efficacy of our listening and appreciation for the value of listening skills. Overstimulation can dull your life experience. Let your mind rest and reset from time to time. Allow the silence to speak to you. It may enable you to more easily hear God. How can you hear a "still, small voice" when you are surrounded by noise?

Just one last, quick word about the types of listening: We engage in multiple types of listening at the same time. You can (and should) be engaged in listening for judgment when you listen for pleasure. When you are visiting and a friend or family member tells a story, you are gathering information but are also listening for fun and may switch over to empathetic listening with no notice and probably without awareness. Actually, being aware of this sort of stuff makes me aware of how fascinating and amazing the human mind really is!

Listening Obstructions: I Want to Hear You, But Something's in the Way!

No discussion of listening would be complete if we did not examine the obstacles that get in the way of our receiving the message. There are many, and usually, we don't know that they exist, but they keep us from hearing what others are "saying" to us, whether verbally or nonverbally. They include both internal and external factors.

© Sergey Nivens/Shutterstock.com

Let's start with the external barriers. It's an easier list. Basically, anything outside your body that gets in the way of your receiving a message is a listening barrier. It's just external interference. Remember that from Chapter 1? If it's too loud to hear over, or too big to see around, or if the technology breaks down and the phone call breaks up, all those are forms of external interference and they all create barriers to communication. How do you overcome these? Be aware of them and take action. Ask the lady to take off the big hat, ask the guy talking in the theater to whisper, and ask the person on the other end of the phone call to repeat the words. It's external to your body and external to your psyche, so it's the easy one.

Let's go on to the internal barriers. They are tougher, because they are harder to identify and harder to overcome. The first may be the hardest of all: self-centeredness. We all know someone who takes turns talking and lets you have your turn, but you can tell they really aren't listening to you. They are just waiting for you to shut up so they can talk about themselves. Most of us subconsciously think that we are the main character in the great American novel. Oh, we don't think it consciously, but deep within, we are sort of self-absorbed. That can really get in the way of listening to someone else (Wood, 2009). It takes years for a child to develop empathy for others' feelings, and we are all in process.

A second type of interference that we have already discussed in Chapter 1 is semantic interference. Semantic interference is the psychological distraction that comes from your emotional reaction to a symbol that has been used in your presence. If your friend surprises you by using a racial slur in your presence, you might be completely unable to remember anything else they said because you were so

They had a tendency to talk past one another.

© Cartoon Resource/Shutterstock.com

shocked to hear that come out of their mouth. That is a case of semantic interference. Any verbal or nonverbal symbol that causes that sort of reaction can keep you from receiving the rest of the message being sent.

Other things that get in the way of our receptiveness include our preconceived ideas (Wood, 2009). If you believe something and are told something else, you will have trouble listening or paying attention to the new information. Prejudices and stereotypes play into this as well. Assuming we know who a person is because they are "liberal" or "conservative" is an example of those stereotypes preventing us seeing a different perspective. Those labels can serve as mental shortcuts in the thought process that keep us from fully understanding another's position or experience. They stop the conversation and you don't hear anything that's being said.

Fear also affects our ability to perceive messages sent by others. If you are afraid, you just can't pay attention to anything but the thing that frightens you. If you have test anxiety and your teacher announces a pop-test, you may be so freaked out that you may not even hear her say that no grade will be taken.

Another thing that gets in the way of messages we should be receiving is personal investment. If you have committed yourself to a particular action or belief, you will not want to hear anything contradictory to the decision that you have made. It makes you have regret and self-doubt. For example, in a past election, I voted for a candidate that many of my peers did not support. After he won, there was plenty of criticism of him in the media, as is true of any elected official. But I didn't want to hear any of the negative coverage because I felt I had invested myself in that candidate and I didn't want to consider the possibility that I might have made a bad choice.

Cognitive dissonance
the internal turmoil we feel when our actions don't conform to our beliefs

Cognitive dissonance is the internal turmoil we feel when our actions don't conform to our beliefs. One of my psychologist friends says cognitive dissonance is another word for guilt! It can really get in the way of our willingness to listen (Festinger, 1957). For example, let's say you are very concerned about taking care of the planet. You recycle, you ride a skateboard instead of driving short distances, and you work to reduce your carbon footprint. Then, for graduation, your grandparents buy you a new car, and they deliver you a big, shiny, black Hummer! It's beautiful, it has a great sound system, and you feel great driving it. If your best friend makes a comment about it burning a lot of gas, you may feel guilty and make excuses about driving a vehicle that is not in keeping with your "green" position. See what I mean?

Sometimes we don't really listen at all; we just act like we are listening. There is a name for that. **Pseudolistening** is pretending to listen. You know when you are doing it. We all do it, and we do it a lot. If you go to class and the teacher is blathering on about how she spent the weekend and you don't really care, you may act like you are listening when you really are not. You tune out, but you keep nodding and acting like you really are listening, though you are not.

Pseudolistening
pretending to listen

Another listening barrier I should not need to define for you is boredom. If you are bored, it is really hard to pay attention. Your professor may be giving you information that could revitalize your academic or personal life, but if you are struggling with boredom it will probably just wash over you like water over a rock. You won't absorb anything.

Discerning Truth: Tell Me a Story

We expect people to be honest with us. We don't expect them to lie (Grice, 1975). But that is not always the case. People can be evasive, exaggerate, and outright lie to get what they want, so when people tell us stories, we judge whether or not what we're hearing is true. (Fisher, 1989) There are a few things we listen for to determine if the story is true or not. The first is coherence. **Coherence** means that all the parts of the story hold together and make sense together (Fisher, 1989). The people involved act consistently with their own behavior patterns. A friend of mine knew a young couple who got in trouble with the law while a third party (let's call her Gertrude) was living with them. Gertrude had a police record, and my friend felt she was bad for the young couple. The couple had a tendency to allow drug addicts to stay with them and lie when it suited their purposes. My friend was approached by the couple for help. They swore that Gertrude had moved out. However, when she went to visit the young couple, she found an air mattress leaned up against the wall in the couple's bedroom where it had obviously been moved before my friend went to the apartment. She also found Gertrude's toiletries in the bathroom. The story she had been told lacked coherence, and so my friend was pretty sure she was not being told the truth.

Coherence
all parts of the story hold together and make sense together

Another way we test a story is to check it for fidelity. A story has **fidelity** when it is consistent with the way the world as we know it works (Fisher, 1989). Imagine a friend applying for a job at a fast-food restaurant. They tell you that they applied, were called back for an interview and were interviewed by the manager. That aligns with our sense of how the world works. But if they told you that they were interviewed by the CEO on a private plane, you would probably not believe them. Parts of the story had coherence, but you would still doubt it because it's unlikely for someone to be interviewed on a private plane by the CEO for a fast-food job. That's just not how the world works. The story lacks fidelity.

fidelity
something is consistent with the way the world as we know it works

While coherence and fidelity play major roles in our assessment of stories, they are not by any means the whole story. (Pardon the pun.) We are quicker to believe some people than others. That doesn't mean that we always assume they are lying to us; we may conclude that they have been deceived. Some folks are just gullible, and so we don't immediately believe them. We feel we need to examine the accounts of events they tell to catch the deception they may not have caught and gently tell them the truth. On the other hand, some people are less trustworthy than others, so we weigh whatever they tell us with great care, even if the story has coherence and fidelity. What we're doing there is engaging in attribution based on what we know of the person and the circumstances. What if we call that personal consistency? A person has consistently proven to be honest in the past, so we assume they are telling us the truth. We know them to be honest, so we believe them.

© Matej Kastelic/Shutterstock.com

Sidebar 5B Listening Styles

By Marinell Scott-Hall, M.A.

They are four syles of listening, but we tend to default to a primary style. The styles are: people-based, action-based, content-based, and time-based. (Briscoe, 2015; Imhof, 2004; Watson, Barker, & Weaver, 1995). Your personal primary style of listening is revealed by what you focus on in a conversation.

People-based listeners respond to feelings and emotions and are looking to connect with the speaker. They are more likely to be empathic listeners and collaborative communicators. If the speaker is too emotional it can distract people-based listeners from the message. They will also see verbal and nonverbal cues as they listen. However, this style of listener can also pry and get too involved with other people's issues if they are not careful. Be sensitive to how much involvement is healthy.

Action-based listeners are focused on what needs to be done. In other words, this is a problem-solving person. If the speaker is long-winded or beats around the bush explaining, this listener will lose interest. In an effort to get to the main point, this type of listener could finish your sentences or make assumptions about what you are trying to say. Someone who doesn't want to know the story concerning the task, but just want to know what needs to be done, might be an action-based listener.

A content-based listeners are interested in the message itself. In this style, the listeners are usually in a critical listening mode. They will weigh the information heard, gather other information, look for pros and cons, and judge if the message is credible. Also, they will take their time making a final decision, and not rush to any judgements.

Finally, time-based listeners are clock watchers. In other words, they want to know how much time this conversation is going to take. These listeners want short, concise answers with detail. They may get impatient and look away, or at the clock or phone. They also need a "to do list" and to have structure, so they can get lots done in a short time. They are busy people and have a limited time to listen.

Which sort of listener are you?

Listening to Other Speakers

Another area in which it is important to be aware of our listening is when . . .

(Wait! You may not like this much. It's an area where we as a culture really are rude to others, and your instinct may be to shut me off on this one, but resist the temptation! One day, you too will be in a position to need this, so listen carefully! Are you ready?)

. . . you're listening to someone give a speech. We can and should be considerate listeners when someone is giving a speech (O'Hair et al., 2013). That speaker has probably done a lot of work and preparation, and they may be there to improve the quality of your life, so you owe it to them to act respectfully and really listen to what they have to say. Unless you fully engage in the listening experience, you cannot know if the speaker has anything valid to say or not. This can take place in a lot of settings, like class, church, public meetings, and lectures. The advantage to listening respectfully and critically evaluating the speaker's content is that you can learn something, and build the skills of being a leader who can communicate with people who disagree with them. During the last couple of weeks of the semester, when speeches are being given in my classes, a lot of students are behind on their work, so they want to pull out a textbook or open their computer and study during speeches. Ouch! The speaker needs the audience members to be supportive, smiling and making eye contact. Tuning out on a speech is hurtful to the speaker, and if you don't care about that, remember this: you, too, will deliver a speech before this class is over. Is that how you want your audience to respond to you? But this happens in lots of other situations, too, like required meetings and at church. At some Christian colleges, they have mandatory chapel services, and some people feel that because they are required to attend, they have the right to mentally "check out." They may talk with someone nearby and show them pictures on their phone, or update their Facebook page, or tweet about what's happening. The problem with this is that not only are you missing out on what that speaker has worked to bring you, but you are distracting another person, and you're being rude to the speaker right to their face! You may think that the speaker cannot see you out in the crowd on your phone or talking to someone, but I promise you, they can! If you don't believe me, just go up onto the stage sometime in a public venue and look around. The room looks a lot smaller from up there than it does from the back, and the stage is raised so the speaker can see and be seen all over the room. They can *see* you ignoring them and being disrespectful of all their hard work. Jesus said to treat other people like you want them to treat you (Matthew 7:12). The Bible also says that whatever you do will come back to you (Galatians. 6:7). Is that what you want coming back to you? I'm just sayin' here . . . .

Ethical Implications

What are our moral responsibilities to another when we are the recipients of their messages? First and foremost, we must pay attention. We may think we are the center of the universe and that others must wait on our good pleasure to share whatever they have to say, but "it just ain't so." We need to have our antennae out all the time. Things are going on with or without our attention, and if we aren't paying attention, we're going to miss things.

Listening is not something people do well naturally. Don't assume just because you said it that the other person heard it, or more accurately, listened to it. Remember that not everything that is heard is retained. It's not possible, so for Heaven's sake, don't get mad when someone forgets some detail you told them. Be generous and allow others to have the occasional lapse.

Now if you are one of the passive listeners in life, you may think that your failure to "hear" or retain will excuse you. Not so. If the boss gives you a job to do and you miss that order, he will not be pleased. Do it multiple times and you may find yourself looking for a new job. The fact is that you just have to work at this listening thing whether you like it or not.

If you are going to do empathetic listening, do it correctly. Don't try to "fix" the person. That's God's job, not yours. Just help them talk their way through to the best answer for them. Resist the urge to tell them what is wrong or what to do. Sometimes our growth is dependent on our struggle. Let the person talking to you own and learn from their own experience.

When you engage in listening for judgment, it is very hard, because so often you have to really engage in attribution as well as discern the facts. Don't be discouraged that it is hard. It will get better with practice. By the way, you have to do this same sort of thing with sermons. Just because the speech comes from a pulpit doesn't mean it is infallible.

Be skeptical, but keep an open mind. You can entertain an idea without accepting it, just like you can entertain someone for dinner. Just because you invited them in to eat doesn't mean you're going to let them move in. It's the same with the idea. Hear it out, and if you don't like it, you can kick it out just like a bad guest.

When you're listening to another person, hear out the whole story before you hand down judgment, especially your children. When they are explaining something to you, listen fully, and take your time. If you judge your child or friend guilty when they are not, they will feel betrayed and hurt. It may take years to overcome that. Remember do not be rushed in your decision making, especially if you're angry. You may have to calm down before you can decide.

Summary

Listening is the process of hearing sound (physical transmission of that sound from the eardrum to the brain) and interpreting it, evaluating it, reacting to it, and remembering it later. We don't remember everything we hear or see. There are four purposes for listening: information, empathy, judgment, and fun. We often shift from one to another or do them simultaneously, and there are ways to get better at all of them. Empathetic listening is serving others by listening to their problems and helping them develop their own answers by asking questions. There are techniques for doing it correctly. Listening for information is just that—listening to gather information, and that can also be improved. Listening for judgment is used to tell if what you're hearing is good, true, correct, or valuable, and of course, there are steps for improving it. Lastly, listening for fun is recreational listening, and there are steps that will help you get better at that. Barriers to reception of messages affect our listening and perception. They include external barriers, which are easier to control, and internal barriers, which reflect our feelings, beliefs, and prejudices. These are harder to control. Self-centeredness causes us to discount the importance of others and their messages, so we pay little attention. Cognitive dissonance is the distraction that results from being confronted by our contradictory ideas and behavior, and this makes us unable to receive additional information. Personal investment causes us to want to reject messages that imply that a decision we have made was a bad one because we have invested ourselves in the decision. Finally, we can fail to be receptive just because we are afraid, have preconceived ideas, or are bored and our attention wanders. Pseudolistening is faking your listening. We test stories we hear for truthfulness by looking for coherence (all the parts of the story make sense together) and fidelity (the story as a whole seems to be realistic). Listening respectfully is a unique opportunity to be kind, especially when listening to public speakers.

Vocabulary Words

Active listeners
Attention
Cognitive dissonance
Coherence
Empathetic listening
Empathy
Evaluation

Fidelity
Hearing
Interpretation
Listening
Listening for fun
Listening for information
Listening for judgment

Mindlessness
Passive listeners
Pseudolistening
Remembering
Response

Discussion Questions

1. What is the difference between hearing and listening?
2. What makes a good listener?
3. When you are called upon to do empathetic listening, what do you do right? What do you do wrong?
4. What are some of the listening barriers? Which ones get you into trouble, especially when you are listening for information?
5. What is your listening style?
6. What could you do that would make you a better listener?
7. Is there someone who lies to you frequently? How can you tell?
8. Who are you not good at listening to? Why?

References

Benoit, S. S., & Lee, J. W. (1986). Listening: It can be taught. *Journal of Education for Business, 63,* 229–232.

Briscoe, W. (2015). *You hear me, but are you listening?* Denver: Colorado Press.

DeVito, J. (2009). *The interpersonal communication book* (12th ed.). Boston, MA: Pearson.

Emmert, P. (1996). President's perspective. *ILA Listening Post, 56,* 2–3.

Egan, G. (1973). Listening as empathetic support. In J. Stewart (Ed.), *Bridges, not walls.* Reading, MA: Addison-Wesley.

Festinger, L. (1957). *A theory of cognitive dissonance.* Stanford, CA: Stanford University.

Fisher, W. R. (1989). *Human communication as narration: Toward a philosophy of reason, value and action.* Columbia, SC: University of South Carolina Press.

Goodall, Jr., H. L., & Goodall, S. (2006). *Communicating in professional contexts.* Belmont, CA: Thomson Wadsworth.

Grice, H. P. (1975). Logic and converation. In P. Cole and J. L. Morgan (Eds), *Syntax and semantics: Speech acts.* (Vol 3, pp. 41-58). New York: Seminar Press.

Hybels, S., & Weaver, R. L., II. (2001). *Communicating effectively* (6th ed.). New York: McGraw-Hill.

Imhof, M. (2004). Who are we as we listen? Individual listening profiles in varying contexts. *International Journal of Listening, 18,* 36–45.

Johnson, I. W., Pearce, C. G., Tuten, T. L., & Sinclair, L. (2003). Self-imposed silence and perceived listening effectiveness. *Business Communication Quarterly, 66*(2), 23–45.

Kuhn, J. L. (2001). Toward an ecological humanistic psychology. *Journal of Humanistic Psychology, 41,* 9–24.

Langer, E., Blank, A., & Chanowitz, B. (1978). The mindlessness of ostensibly thoughtful action: The role of "placebic" information in interpersonal interaction. *Journal of Personality and Social Psychology, 36,* 635–642.

Nichols, M. P. (1995). *The lost art of listening.* New York: Guilford.

O'Hair, D., Rubenstein, H., & Stewart, R. (2013). *A pocket guide to public Speaking* (4th ed.). Boston, MA: Bedford/St. Martin's.

Robinshaw, H. (2007). Acquisition of hearing, listening and speech skills by and during key stage 1. *Early Child Development and Care, 177*(6–7), 661–678. doi: 10.1080/03004430701379090

Watson, K. W., Barker, L. L., & Weaver, J. B. (1995). The listening styles profile (LSP-16): Development and validation of an instrument to assess four listening styles. *International Journal of Listening, 9,* 1–13.

Windsor, J. L., Curtis, D. B., & Stephens, R. D. National preferences in business and communication education: An update. *Journal of the Association for Communication Administration, 3,* 170–179.

Wood, J. T. (2002). *Interpersonal communication: Everyday encounters* (3rd ed.). Belmont, CA: Wadsworth.

Additional Readings

People Skills: How to Assert Yourself, Listen to Others, and Resolve Conflicts

by Robert Bolton, Ph.D.

Listening: The Forgotten Skill

by Madelyn Burley-Allen

The Listening Life: Embracing Attentiveness in a World of Distraction

by Adam S. McHugh

The Lost Art of Listening: How Learning to Listen Can Improve Relationships

By Michael P. Nichols, Ph.D.

Better Communicators Are Connected

By Rhonda Gallagher, M.S.

6

© Syda Productions/Shutterstock.com

What does it mean to be connected? Knowing some people? Having a tight group of friends? Having a steady boyfriend/girlfriend? Marriage? Actually, it can mean all these things. You need a few close friends to share your life with. One of the first things the Bible tells us about people is that God said, "It is not good for man to be alone" (Genesis 2:18). God's answer to that was to make a woman, and history has been "interesting" ever since! But seriously, humans are designed for community. Seldom do you find healthy individuals choosing to live their lives entirely alone. We need other people. In fact, one of the most severe punishments our society uses in prison is solitary confinement. John Townsend (Cloud & Townsend, 2005) says that "Human relationships are a spiritual and supernatural activity." So, we need more than a few people in our lives and we need to know a few of them pretty well. On the flip side, we don't want to be "joined at the hip," either. So, think for a minute: with whom are you closely connected and why?

Interpersonal communication is the interaction among a limited number of people that is customized for the individuals and the relationship. You can't take a close, intimate relationship between two people and substitute another person to replace one of them without changing the dynamic completely.

That is another way of saying that we are connected to them. It is easy to think that any time two individuals interact it is interpersonal communication, but that is not true. There are some basic characteristics of interpersonal communication that pretty much all experts agree about and that's as good a place as any to begin our discussion.

Characteristics of Interpersonal Communication: Beginning at the Beginning

© Nejron Photo/Shutterstock.com

Interpersonal communication happens in a relationship.

You *know* the person with whom you have interpersonal communication, at least a little. So, having the server at your favorite fast-food place ask if you want fries with your meal is not interpersonal. That is business communication because she is not treating you like an individual, but a customer (Stewart & Logan, 1998). You aren't interacting with her as if she were a person, either. She is a company representative; that is all. But if you tell her that you like her earrings, that moment is interpersonal because you are treating her like a person, not just a server, and you have initiated a relationship with her, though it is brand new and tiny.

Interpersonal communication is tailored to fit the people involved.

That tailoring process occurs over time. As you get to know a person, you build a special shared frame of reference that is unique to that relationship. You may even share a unique "language." My husband's family owns property on the Frio River in Texas and has gone there together for decades. All extended family members are aware of that connection, so if one family member asks if another has been to "the river" this summer, no one has to ask to which river they are referring. Think of your best friend: you may tease each other playfully based on something that has happened in the past, and it may become part of the landscape of the friendship. Nobody else will get the joke because they are not part of the relationship. Or you might learn things your friend is sensitive about and avoid a topic or situation out of respect for that.

© Photographee.eu/Shutterstock.com

Interpersonal communication is affected by culture and gender.

In the United States, women often express connection and friendship by doing grooming activities together, like getting pedicures. Men might compete with each other about competence instead, like who grills a better steak, or who has the nicer lawn, house, car, etc. We know those cultural expectations because they are learned as we grow up (Wood, 1994). In many places in the Middle East, it is not at all unusual to see men holding hands on the street. No big deal. The meaning of that mark of friendship changes drastically from culture to culture. In the U.S. it carries a very different meaning. In China, older married couples do not express affection in public. That might seem very cold to Americans, but that expression of affection is not considered appropriate in public.

Risks and Rewards Self-Disclosure: Is It Worth It?

In order to form real connections, we must open ourselves to others a little bit. Self-revelation has many rewards, but it carries with it some risks. As we learned in chapter 2, the process of telling someone information about ourselves that is not public knowledge is called self-disclosure, and that is what moves a relationship along.

First, let's examine the risks. You may share a piece of information that you wouldn't tell to just anyone with someone you think is safe, and they may tell someone else. They violate your trust, and now your secret is out there for everyone to know and discuss. Or they may reject you because they are shocked or disgusted by what you have told them. They might judge you, and feeling you need a lesson in morality, give you a lecture on how you should behave. They might use that knowledge against you in the future. They could hold that information in their own little treasure vault, and when you make a mistake or make them angry, they may bring it out and beat you with it.

© leolintag/Shutterstock.com

So, if all these things can happen, why would you ever put yourself in that vulnerable position? Because there can also be rewards to self-disclosure! As I mentioned before, when we make ourselves vulnerable to others it can pave the way for deepening the relationship. When you put trust in another, they often then feel safe and will share in kind. Also, if you have been carrying a secret inside for some time, there can be tremendous relief in telling someone else (Kelly, Klusas, von-Weis, & Kenny, 2001); you are no longer alone. Furthermore, if you tell your secret, and the other party accepts the secret without judgment, there can be a lot of healing in that validation. They may even give you a perspective you had not seen before, and if the issue is creating difficulty for you, you could get some new ideas for handling the problem.

How do we determine when it is safe to share or not? The unspoken rule for self-disclosure is that when someone shares, you share back, and the sharing should be of about equal amount and of an equal degree of vulnerability (Gouldner, 1960; Miller & Kenny, 1986). You also don't share everything right away. You have to see if the person you're self-disclosing to will be responsible with the information and not tell anyone else. It is a dance. You share a small piece and see how the recipient responds. If they respond by sharing a reasonably equal piece, then you can wait a few days and share a little more and see how they respond. In that way a relationship can be developed over time and in a safe way.

Social Penetration Theory: Getting to Know You

Social Penetration Theory
a theory that says that we reveal information about ourselves in layers

There is actually a theory that explains how we share in relationships called Social Penetration Theory (Altman & Taylor, 1973). It says that we reveal information about ourselves in layers, like peeling the layers off an onion. In the early stages of a relationship, we share very superficial stuff, like where we're from, and if we like Greek food. But as time passes, and we relax with the other person and sort out what knowledge they can be trusted with. Then, we can open up about more personal things, like how we feel about a political or cultural situation. If we continue to enjoy the interaction and they are also participating in the self-disclosure, we may tell them even more sensitive things, like what we hope to do with our lives, or some of our deepest hurts. If all goes well, the relationship can move to deeper and deeper levels of disclosure all the way down to the core of our self-concept. But, just because someone is around us a lot and we have fun with them doesn't mean we want to share deeply with them. That is where two new terms come in: depth and breadth. **Depth** refers to the level of relationship that allows a person to talk about more personal and sensitive information. If you have a closer relationship with someone, you know them well enough to share deep things about yourself, things that you protect and are close to your heart. That's a relationship marked by depth. On the other hand, breadth deals with how many different topics you can discuss with them. Altman and Taylor (1973) describe the self-disclosure as a wedge that opens up the deeper layers of the person, but also enables the people involved to talk about more related issues around the self-disclosure so that the breadth is also broadened. Surely, if you can tell them about the friend who betrayed you in junior high school, you can talk about which bands you like best, right? You'd think so, but not always. It's not guaranteed that depth and breadth will go together, but they often do. All relationships are different, and each relationship is fitted to the people involved, right?

© EM Arts/Shutterstock.com

Depth
to the level of relationship that allows a person to talk about more personal and sensitive information

Breadth
how many different topics you can discuss with someone

The Nature of Friendship

There are certain characteristics friendships share that separate them from other kinds of close relationships (Floyd, 2014). That is not meant to imply that friendships are worth more than other types of connections; they are simply different.

FRIENDSHIP RULES

Jeff Hall (2001) compiled a list of important friendship rules. Here are some:
- Be loyal.
- Provide support when they need it.
- Be truthful and trustworthy.
- Self-disclose to your friends.
- Include your friends in what you're doing.
- Make time to spend with them.
- Offer money or resources when the friend needs them.

Sidebar 6A

First, *friendship is voluntary*. You cannot command friendship. We have some control over whether or not we will be connected to a person; nobody can force us to befriend another person if we don't want to. We might go through the motions, but it wouldn't be a true friendship. This is not true with family relationships. Families can place certain demands on us, and to some degree we can refuse, but we usually try to do as is expected. If your family plans a Thanksgiving dinner, you will probably go and interact, and you will probably have a good time, but there is some degree of pressure to attend. If a friend asks you to do something, you can do it or decline; it is pretty much up to you (Wright, 1984). It depends on how hard you want to work to maintain the friendship.

Friendship is usually between peers. Both people have fairly equal status in the relationship, so you can speak your mind and no official consequences will result because your place in the relationship is just as powerful as that of the partner (Floyd, 2014). That is not to say that we cannot make friends with people who have more or less influential positions in our lives, but it is rarer. There will always be a power differential between you. Your boss may be friendly and informal with you, but that doesn't make you friends. Don't confuse informality with friendship. You're just not going to become great friends with your academic dean, or even one of your professors, until they are no longer in that position over you.

*There are behavioral rules for friendship*s (Shimanoff, 1980). We all know them subconsciously. If you told a friend's secret, you'd probably feel guilty about it because you know that you don't do that to a friend. You don't try to steal their boyfriend or girlfriend. Don't gripe all the time. Be respectful of their feelings. You get the idea. (See Sidebar 6A for more.)

Finally, *friendships with members of the opposite sex are different than friend-ships with members of the same sex* (Floyd, 2014; Hall, 2011). You can be friends with members of the opposite sex, but you have different expectations of them than you do of same-sex friends. That's because we have role expectations of men and women that have to do with being masculine or feminine even in a non-romantic relationship. If you're a female, most of your male friends will open the door for you, even though you are not their significant other. You don't expect that of your girl-friends, nor would the man do it for his friends. He might, however, expect you to help him help him pick out a gift for his mom or sister. He probably wouldn't expect that of his male friends.

Romantic Relationships: Ah, Romance . . .

In individualist cultures like the U.S., Canada, Australia, and the U.K., we expect the romantic ideal of love (Dion & Dion, 1996). It is pretty well entrenched in our cultural subconscious, and it impacts our relationships deeply. There are certain things we expect from a romantic relationship that we don't expect from any other. Kory Floyd (2014) identified some basic characteristics of romantic relationships.

First, *we expect affection, love, and sexual expression where appropriate*. If you just wanted something to cuddle with, you'd get a cat! No, we need that love and belonging met in a way that is uniquely deep and committed. A cat just can't do that. We are looking for an extraordinary level of acceptance, loyalty, and affirmation that can only be found in a romantic/sexual bond. We need interaction that recognizes us as sexual beings, even if expression of those feelings are limited by personal or religious conviction or other constraints.

Exclusivity
the belief that your romantic partner will not be involved with another person while your relationship lasts

Second, *we expect exclusivity*. Exclusivity is the belief that your romantic partner will not be involved with another person while your relationship lasts. We want to be the "only one," and we realize that our partner expects the same of us. If there is anyone else involved in the relationship, the deep bond feels compromised; so, we tacitly agree not to see anyone else. We know the rules. We don't call seeing someone else on the side "cheating" for nothing.

Next, *we expect the commitment to be voluntary*. If someone has to force you to stay in a relationship, it sort of negates the feeling of being treasured. Of course, like anything else in communication, culture plays a big role. There are plenty of cultures in which parents arrange marriages without considering the wishes of the bride and groom, while in others a spouse may be discontent, but legally incapable of divorce.

Marriage is a sexual and financial contract, so those things figure largely into our romantic relationships, though most communication experts don't seem to worry too much about the money part. However, culture can strongly affect these basic expectations of marriage. For cultures in which romance doesn't play a big role in marriage, the financial aspect may be more pronounced, so families may choose spouses for their children. Ironically, in Western culture (because we value romantic love) we think that we should pick our own mates, but in those cultures where marriage is arranged, that careful choice by the parents, and acceptance by the child is usually viewed as an act of love between parent and child. The presence of love and affection between partners at the time of marriage is less important. The expectation is that love will grow between the bride and groom over time. In the same way, as I said before, the expectation of voluntariness also diminishes when marriages are arranged. Similarly, some cultures have different beliefs about exclusivity. Where polygamy (simultaneous marriage to multiple spouses) is practiced, one might be prepared to share the husband or wife with another spouse, but even so, the belief is that there will be no *other* partners who are not part of the marriage contract. There may be other wives, but there will be no mistresses! That would be "cheating"!

Knapp's Stages of Relationship Development: How We Come Together . . . and Apart

As you know, when you meet someone, you have to grow the relationship. It doesn't spring to life fully formed. Knapp and Vangelisti discussed the stages of relationship development and disintegration (1996). I've seen this theory applied to all friendships, but Knapp and Vangelisti's focus was more on romantic relationships, so we'll follow their lead and keep our attention on the same spot. Try to think of relationship stages like a hill: it starts low but builds to higher levels of connection, and if the relationship dissolves, it slowly comes down the hill to the bottom on the other side (see Sidebar 6B).

© Maridav/Shutterstock.com

Let's start with getting people together. The first stage of this theory is the **initiating** phase. That is when people meet for the first time and make small talk. They look each other over and evaluate how appealing the other person is, and if the prospects look good, they begin to cultivate the attraction. They are just starting the

Initiating
first stage in a relationship when people meet for the first time and make small talk

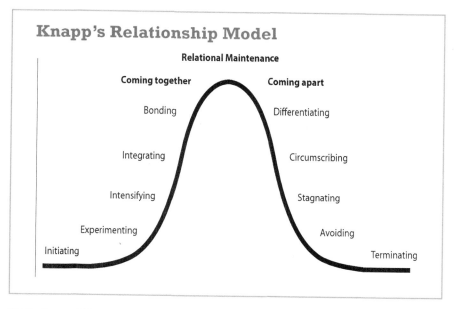

Knapp's Relationship Model

Relational Maintenance

Coming together — Coming apart

Bonding — Differentiating

Integrating — Circumscribing

Intensifying — Stagnating

Experimenting — Avoiding

Initiating — Terminating

Sidebar 6B

connection that may follow, so they play it safe. They may be a little nervous with each other. They introduce themselves and ask basic questions like, "What's your major?" or "Where are you from?" Remember Social Penetration Theory? This is the outer layer of the onion.

Experimentation
stage when one of the parties may move the conversation onto more risky information

If that goes well, one of the parties may move the conversation onto more risky information. This stage is called experimentation. It's where we offer some tidbit about ourselves to the other person to see how they will react. You might mention how you voted in the last election or that you actually hate the newest hot band. The idea is to toss out something that might be objectionable to see if that person will be scared away by that knowledge. We feel some degree of connection to each other at this stage. It is a relaxed, uncritical time in the relationship, though we are unsure if anything will come of it. You're moving deeper into the onion. If the person with whom you have shared that more dangerous bit of information hasn't lost interest, you may feel it is safe to pursue the relationship further.

Intensifying
relationship stage when you really start to get to know the other party

The next stage is called intensifying. In this stage, you really start to get to know the other party. You share hopes, dreams, and fears. The couple spends significantly more time together. They go to movies, go for walks, meet for coffee, etc. They are becoming better and better friends. The physical closeness is very pleasant, so there is usually hand-holding, hugging, nuzzling, etc. They might have nicknames for each other and begin to have enough history together to be able to use verbal shortcuts to reference past events or experiences. The couple begins sharing deeper secrets and increases vulnerability, thus demonstrating a greater degree of trust in each other. They begin making plans together, like deciding to spend fall break at the home of one of them.

Integration
stage when the relationship has become special, and the couple may be unhappy when they are separated

At a certain point, the friends become so connected that people expect to see them together and will ask about the missing partner if one of them is seen alone. The relationship has become special, and the couple may be unhappy when they are separated. This stage is called integration. One partner will know whether or not the other would like a particular book or movie. They can exchange an eye message across the room and probably know what the other is thinking. In integrating, the self-disclosure becomes increasingly revelatory, even sharing their self-concept concerns.

Bonding
relationship stage marked by a formal commitment that makes it more difficult to dissolve the relationship

The last stage of coming together is bonding. Bonding is marked by a formal commitment that makes it more difficult to dissolve the relationship. Couples get engaged: that's a formal commitment. So is marriage. It assumes voluntary, exclusive, love and acceptance. They make plans together for the future (what sort of home to buy, where to live, how many children they want to have, etc.), and the degree of acceptance they feel produces a sense of deep happiness and contentment.

Differentiating
stage in a relationship where the couple discovers significant differences between themselves

Coming apart can be much less pleasant. Differentiating is the stage in a relationship where the couple discovers significant differences between themselves. They are not so enchanted by the close interdependence they had in the bonding stage.

They begin to see the partner's flaws, and conflict arises. When this conflict is not settled in a satisfactory way, the partners focuses on the differences they have, not the things they have in common. However, differentiation is not necessarily the beginning of the end for a relationship. It depends on how the couple handles the differences; if there is conflict, and the couple handles the conflict in a way that satisfies both parties, they learn new things about each other, re-enter the integration phase, and re-bond at a deeper level. Healthy couples routinely cycle through the stages of integration, bonding, and differentiation.

Love Languages

Dr. Gary Chapman (1995) identified five ways we can show our love to others. They are:
1. Words of affirmation—That's telling someone that you love them, giving compliments, or asking questions to show that you care about them.
2. Touch—This includes hugging, kissing, patting, caressing, or anything that expresses love with touching.
3. Acts of service—When you do something for another because you love them, that is an act of service, like cooking a meal, or helping them wash the car, or babysitting.
4. Quality time—It serves as a love language when you spend time with someone. You don't have to be doing anything special; it's just the act of making time for that person and giving your attention to them that makes it loving.
5. Gifts—For some people, receiving a gift from another makes them feel loved. The gift doesn't have to be expensive if it shows thoughtfulness. A coupon you clipped for a friend can be a gift if it is for an item you know they want or are going to need.

We all like to experience love in different ways. Something that says love to one person will not to another. The biggest challenge is learning to love others as they want to be loved, not as we prefer. Looking at how a person shows their love is a good indicator of how they want to be loved.

Sidebar 6C

But if the conflict is not resolved constructively, or is put aside while still unsettled, the couple moves into the next phase, called circumscribing. The conflict has started a rift between the partners. They may revisit the issue repeatedly, trying to resolve it, and if they do, (surprise!) they reintegrate and re-bond. If they continue to argue about it, though, they may come to a place of simply avoiding the topic. It can be a sad, lonely time when they discover that the easy connection of the past is inexplicably strained. The problem isn't resolved, but they just don't want to fight about it anymore. They aren't completely happy about it, but they are just living with the irritant. The sad thing about unresolved conflicts is that they tend to erode connection between people, and as that takes place, the couple becomes more and more unhappy. They spend less and less time together. They pursue separate activities. In public, they continue to project the image of the happy couple, but in private they become distant and show less caring toward one another. They may be depressed or frustrated. Less and less communication takes place: there are fewer interactions, shorter interactions, and more superficial information. Communication becomes limited to safe topics. The relationship isn't dead, but neither is it growing. After a while, the pain of the dying relationship becomes severe and morphs into hostility.

> **Circumscribing**
> relationship stage in which an unresolved conflict has started a rift between the partners

Stagnating
relationship stage where the couple doesn't want to go on like they have been, but they don't want to break up, either

The next stage is called stagnating. The couple doesn't want to go on like they have been, but they don't want to break up, either. So, they're stuck. That is why it is called stagnating. They communicate like strangers and don't talk about the relationship at all. The partners may experience great pain and feel fearful, bored, unloved and hopeless. They may obsess about the misunderstandings and fantasize about what they would like to say to the other party, but they don't actually say it. Eventually, they become so fed up with the situation that they stop trying to protect their public image. They complain about the spouse and begin to move their emotional investments into other people like friends or family.

Avoiding
relationship stage where the couple begins to actively avoid each other

In the next phase, avoiding, the couple begins to actively avoid each other; they may refuse to acknowledge each other's presence in a room, or they may just make a point to always be elsewhere. There is a lot of hostility and conflict; they may feel nervous around each other, annoyed, and helpless. They avoid any real interaction. Any communication that occurs is very superficial; there will be no more than is necessary, and the relationship is not discussed at all.

Terminating
relationship stage where one of the partners wants to terminate the relationship

Finally, one of the partners simply cannot take any more and says aloud that they want out. They want to terminate the relationship. Appropriately, this stage is called terminating. In this phase, there is frequently a great deal of sadness, although there is also relief at having finally ended the relationship. Communication is awkward, as the partners attempt to redefine their roles. There is often negotiation about how resources will be divided or how custody of children or pets will be handled. There is discussion about the future as each partner processes the loss in their own way. They may make predictions about how the relationship will change or make statements about why things went wrong. In essence, they are trying to analyze and make sense of what has happened. According to Dianne Vaughn (1990) there is usually a third person, a transitional person, involved in the breakup. It may be a friend, a counselor, or could even be a lover, but the partner who is most looking to exit the relationship will find someone to temporarily support them and give them the strength to terminate. That transitional person is needed as a launching platform from which to leave the relationship, and when the relationship is ended, the need for the transitional person may end as well, though maybe not as quickly.

Variations on the stages may occur. Quite often one person in the couple will be in one stage while the other person is somewhere else. One member may be ready to bond while the other person is still intensifying. One person may be ready to terminate while the other is still circumscribing (Vaughn, 1990). Furthermore, sometimes a couple may skip stages. A whirlwind romance may get to experimenting and then leap ahead to bonding, but sooner or later, the couple will have to go back and do the work to intensify and integrate if they hope to have a healthy relationship.

Getting Better—Maintaining Romantic Relationships

"Keeping the romance alive" is something that is highly valued in western culture. We really love those hormonal rushes that make romance so much fun, but the fact is that after true bonding happens, those rushes, though still wonderful, are less frequent. So how do we keep the relationship strong and fulfilling?

First, *have realistic expectations*. You are dealing with another real person who has commitments and responsibilities outside the relationship. When a couple is coming together, society and biology both work to help get the couple established. Your body pumps out the hormones, and your friends probably reduce their demands on you for a while until the new relationship has a foundation. People encourage the romance and honk at cars with "Just Married" signs on them by way of encouraging the occupants. But after a while, the honeymoon will be over, and it's *supposed* to be. I don't mean you have to get grumpy with each other, but sooner or later you're supposed to resume your other duties! After a while, the little traits that were endearing when you were dating become less cute. That's normal. Give it time and remember that you're not perfect either. Your morning breath isn't wonderful and you may have put on a couple of pounds since the wedding. Give a little grace; you're going to need it someday. Your turn is coming.

Second, *don't set out to change your partner* (Peterson, 1994). Sometimes, a person will find somebody they think is nearly perfect and subconsciously set out to fix the little things and make that person perfect. Boy, is that a mistake! That is a sincere form of rejection, and it will undermine your relationship in a big way! You need to accept each other honestly and appreciate the differences between you. The differences often bring stability to the relationship; who that other person is complements who you are. Besides, you don't really *know* enough to change the other person for the better; that's God's job. As my friend Mary Alice Baldwin says, "You don't get to be someone else's Holy Spirit."

Third, *tell your partner the truth about yourself, and share your feelings, good and bad*. That has many benefits. It enables you to show your truest face to someone, and when they accept you as you are, that is very healing. It will also invite honest disclosure, and the relationship can grow. In the same way, you need to be honest about your feelings. If something hurts you or makes you angry, or even if your spouse's new idea just seems dumb, those feelings need to be shared. Be tactful, by all means, but trying to hide your feelings doesn't work very well, and the secret will get out eventually. Just be kind as you're sharing. By the way, trying to hide your flaws from your spouse is also a bad idea: they'll figure it out sooner or later. Besides, that's supposed to happen in your integrating phase, not after you're married.

© Olena Yakobchuk/Shutterstock.com

Fourth, *fight fair*. Even in the heat of the argument, don't go for the kill shot. Look back to the first chapter and remember that communication is irrevocable. In a real relationship, information that has been shared makes the partners vulnerable to each other. Don't use that information to hurt each other. Remember that when you calm down, the wounds will remain. Don't say it if you don't want to live with the consequences of having said it. Keep to the issue at hand, and don't resort to character assassination. Dr. Randy Feller (2014) says, "Don't waste a good fight." Based on his counseling experience and his readings in psychology and marital counseling, he told me that a conflict has two stages: tearing down and building up. Anger fuels the conflict, and it can be very destructive. When the anger is gone, often people quit fighting and as a consequence never resolve the issue and rebuild the relationship. It is necessary to follow through to resolution and move on to the rebuilding phase.

Finally, *make the commitment*. Marriage is not like buying a new coat you can return if you decide you don't like it. If you always think in the back of your mind that you can split up if it doesn't work out, your marriage won't make it. Sometimes being married is wonderful, and sometimes it's a pain in the neck. That's why the vows say "for better or for worse." Sometimes it's better being married and sometimes not, but you don't quit just because it gets tough. If you hang in there, eventually it gets better again! Gary L. Thomas (2002) says that marriage is not about making you happy: it's about making you holy. Being married is hard work, but it will make you grow and mature if you embrace it as a learning experience. It will pay dividends over the long haul. Our culture tells us that falling in love is like stumbling upon a fairy castle in the woods, but marriage is like a stone cottage that you build or tear down with your own hands. It's slow going, but it becomes a home for your soul. And you get the benefit of living your life with your best friend!

Family Relationships: All in the Family

© Monkey Business Images/Shutterstock.com

Systems Theory of Family
theory that says that a family is a complex entity unto itself with its own kind of dynamics

No treatment of connection would be complete without looking at families. Family makes up our first primary group. They meet our basic needs and teach us how to function in society. How a family works is very important. Systems Theory of Family (Noller & Fitzpatrick, 1993) says that a family is a complex entity unto itself with its own kind of dynamics. Some of the characteristics of family dynamics that Noller and Fitzpatick identified are:

All families are constantly changing. Children get old enough to take on new responsibilities, new members are added to the family, or someone dies. Someone becomes ill, a job ends, money must be managed more frugally, or a new career brings new luxury. Change is a constant in life, and every family must contend with it.

A change in one member will affect everyone in the family. If your parents are divorced, and your mom finds a new boyfriend, even though all the kids may be happy for her, things change. Mom may not be home to make dinner, or she might be out late and an older sibling may have to put the younger ones to bed. Maybe a child goes off to college, and one parent has been especially close to them. The parent must shift their attention to another child, friend, or the spouse to replace that missing interaction. All these changes require change by other family members.

Each family member plays roles. You know which members of your family play certain roles. There is probably an instigator who tries to move the family in new, more adventurous ways, or you may have a peacemaker who tries to calm conflicts, or there may be a moral monitor who reminds everyone not to cross certain boundaries. In my family, I frequently play the straight man for the family comedians. It's not that I can't be funny; it's just my role to give the other folks someone to play off. If you undergo a serious change in your life (maybe you decide to alter how you respond to another family member's manipulation), your family may refuse to treat you any differently or may ridicule and be angry at you. You are forcing a change in the family roles, and the family will probably resist the change, try to "correct" your behavior, and keep stability.

Family Communication Styles: My Family Has Style!

According to Kantor & Lehr (1975), there are basically three ways family members communicate: open, closed, and random.

The first family communication style is the open family communication style. In these families, the communication style is, well, more open. Flexibility is important, and authentic interaction and responsiveness are valued. They focus on being practical in decision making. This means family members are free to express their thoughts and feelings.

The closed family communication style places value on predictability, structure, consistency, and tradition. Connection between family members is based on loyalty and sincerity. They believe in respect for authority and discipline, and they value certainty and clarity in rules that govern life. Change is not met with approval or acceptance.

Families with a random family communication style value spontaneity, happiness, and individuality. They value free choice, originality, and pursuing individual goals. This sounds like a great way to live; however, these families are more likely to be chaotic than not. Expressed conflict is a given.

People in relationships who come from families with different communication styles have their work cut out for them as they try to work out their differences and establish norms for their homes.

Getting Better—Maintaining Family Relationships

A lot of the things we do to maintain our family relationships are pretty similar to what we do to maintain friendships or romantic relationships.

Open family communication style
a communication style that is more open, where flexibility is important, and authentic interaction and responsiveness are valued

Closed family communication style
a communication style where predictability, structure, consistency and tradition are valued

Random family communication style
a communication style where spontaneity, happiness, and individuality are valued

© Rawpixel.com/Shutterstock.com

Be realistic. You're dealing with people again. Your family members are flawed, and you're not going to fix them. Cut them a little slack. And when they disappoint you, give them some grace with the consequences if there are any. You need grace, too, occasionally. Furthermore, they will be quicker to grant grace to you and others if they've seen you model it.

Parenting Messages

While genetics plays a strong role in setting our personality types, how parents talk to children may be a big factor in how they view the world and the way they learn to control themselves. This is currently being widely debated, but the authors felt this information might be helpful to you as you move into parenting. Noller and Fitzpatrick (1993) identified two types of messages parents give children: control messages and support messages.

- **Control messages** are designed for the purpose of (surprise!) exerting control over the child. Examples would be "Sit down" or "Leave that alone" and they often deal with discipline, like "If you do _____, I'll punish you." These messages essentially come from the view that the child is simply waiting to be given directions. Control messages require parenting to be an ongoing stream of commands, and that often frustrates both parent and child. Constant control messages make the child more aggressive, less secure and creative, and can affect academic performance later (Noller & Fitzpatrick, 1993). Children can feel manipulated and resentful, so an adversarial relationship between parent and child results.
- **Support messages** are designed to help the child feel more comfortable and secure. They sound more like, "If you sit down here, the waiter will bring us a menu, and we can pick what you want to eat" or "If you let me hold the pretty vase, we can look at it and touch it without breaking it." Practically, it looks like enabling your children to be good by directing them in what they want to do. If you're going to a restaurant to eat, take a few small toys that can be played with at the table. That provides the child something to do that will be acceptable. Proactive parenting is more difficult and time-consuming, but the long-term effects on the child are better, and the child's behavior is better in the short run (Noller & Fitzpatrick, 1993). It requires advance preparation for every contingency. This helps provide the safe, nurturing environment the child needs. This helps the child learn decision making and self-direction. It probably will also reduce your stress!

Sidebar 6D

Control messages
messages designed for the purpose of exerting control over the child

---

Support messages
messages designed to help the child feel more comfortable and secure

---

Apologize to your family members when you have wronged them. Even if it was an accident, it's better to apologize twenty times when no offense was taken than fail to apologize the one time it was. This is important with friends and coworkers, but it is *critical* with family members. Be honest. Don't lie to your children and make excuses for your mistakes. If you were wrong, admit it, and apologize with humility.

Treat your family members like people. All people need respect in order to have good self-esteem and function fully. Saying "please" and "thank you" and asking permission before using someone's things are courtesies you'd give to other people who matter less to you than your family, so it only makes sense to have that consideration for your family members. By the way, children are people, too. From birth, they have their own personalities, thoughts, and feelings. They should be treated with the same respect and affection other family members deserve—maybe even more.

Ethical Implications

You are not a lone wolf; you need people, and they need you. When you're struggling, find someone who loves you and connect. God works in our interactions with others. Here's an analogy. You put rocks of all shapes together in a rock tumbler and roll them around. Over time they become smooth from their banging against each other. God uses people in the same way. We rub the rough edges off each other. That often gives rise to disagreements, so it's important that we apply godly principles and seek to see with His eyes when we engage in conflict.

© Cartoon Resource/Shutterstock.com

You can't make someone be your friend, but if they choose to, it makes that friendship more of a gift. You can't rush forming a relationship, either, so don't overshare or push others to share their deep stuff until they are ready. And for heaven's sake, respect their confidences.

Remember that culture and gender alter expectations of relationships. You may think you know what's going on, but if something makes you uncomfortable, it's okay to ask your friend of the opposite sex or from another country about the thing they're doing that seems strange to you. Just be tactful and ask your question in a kind way.

Even though the phrase "my friend" includes the word "my," people are not possessions. You don't get to use guilt or manipulation with the people in your life. Their friendship is a gift, not something you own. Just because one of the benefits of friendship is material help, like helping you move or loaning you money when times are tough, you don't get to take advantage of people. If you do, they won't be your friends for long. Remember that those same friends will expect help from you, so keep your commitment to them. Follow the unspoken rules of friendship.

Just a quick aside here on the marital/sexual bonding thing; in Western culture, we think that we attach to someone because we have a strong attraction to them and we "fall in love." We think we are really connected to the recipient of our affections because of the emotions we feel. But a lot of falling in love is biological, and the part of the brain that truly forms bonds with another person cannot come into play until the hormones die down a little. I once had a pastor who said that you don't really begin to love someone until you don't *feel* in love at all, but you begin to do the *acts* of love, anyway. He said that it is in times of commitment when you actually begin to form the bonds of love. That's *really* falling in love.

Before you make your vows, I would advise you to get premarital counseling from a professional counselor, pastor, or mentor, and for more than just an hour or two. You need to be talking about 1.) how your family communicates with each other, 2.) what topics are never discussed, 3.) how they fight, and 4.) who is responsible for what jobs to name just a few. In all our relationships, we have expectations, and you may not even be aware that you think "good husbands" and "good wives" behave in a particular way until after you're married. Try to know as much about what you and your prospective partner expect before you say "I do." You might not want to "do" what they expect.

© Monkey Business Images/Shutterstock.com

When you do finally get married, don't freak out when you and your spouse begin to differentiate. It's your chance to get to know them better, and when you find an area of disagreement, try to think of it as an opportunity to re-integrate and re-bond. Keep at it until you come to an acceptable resolution, and be sure to fight fair: no name-calling, personal attacks, or physical or psychological threats. The object of the game is to resolve the conflict, not to "win." When winning becomes the goal, you've already lost. If finding the resolution seems to be out of your league, get professional help. Calling a marriage counselor is a way better move than calling a divorce attorney, and it's probably cheaper! Who knows? You might even find an area in which you need to grow as well.

Treat your family kindly, like you want to be treated. The Golden Rule applies to family, *especially* to family. We can be real jerks at home. If there are any people to whom you owe respect and courtesy, it's the people who put up with you every day when you are least likely to be putting your best foot forward. They may not be perfect, but you aren't, either.

Treat your children like people, and they'll return the favor. They learn more by observing their caregivers than they will ever learn in pre-school or Sunday school. They are born as smart as the rest of us. They don't know everything we know yet, but that's lack of experience, not lack of intelligence. They will learn. They have love and belonging needs from the start just like you do, and they need to feel secure. Everyone should be treated well, especially those little people God

© iofoto/Shutterstock.com

put into your care. They belonged to Him before He gave them to you, and you'll give an account to Him for what you did with them. Use those support messages, and it will pay benefits. And when you make a mistake, own it. Admitting to your children that you were wrong will teach them how to do that, fostering humility in them and in you. This does not mean that you need to be friends with your children. The time for that comes later. Pastor Willie George says that friendship with your adult children is the reward for parenting them when they were young.

By the way, as you try to discipline your children, you need to know that parents don't really discipline a child. They create a set of circumstances in which it is so advantageous for the child to do as the parent has instructed that the child learns to *discipline him/herself* and obey. Discipline is a character trait that is grown within a person; no one else produces it but the person who disciplines themselves. The hardest part of disciplining your children is disciplining yourself to be patient and consistent.

Summary

Humans need other people. Interpersonal communication is two people interacting with each other and treating each other in a way that is tailored to the relationship and the people involved. The characteristics of interpersonal communication are that it occurs in relationships, is tailored to fit the people involved, and culture and gender affect how we interact. Self-disclosure is sharing deep things with another person. It carries with it some risks, like rejection or betrayal of trust, but it also has positives, like freedom from rejection and fear, and emotional healing. Knowing when to self-disclose is a complex social dance that should be followed to minimize the dangers. Social Penetration Theory explains the stages of sharing we go through. Breadth and depth both play a role in our close relationships. The characteristics of friendship are that it is voluntary, takes place between peers, and relationships with same sex friends are different than friendships between people of the opposite sex. Romantic relationships in the West have attached expectations: love/affection, exclusivity, and voluntariness. Culture plays a huge role in which of these expectations are valued in a particular relationship. Knapp and Vangelisti postulated five stages to a relationship coming together (initiation, experimentation, intensifying, integrating, and bonding) and five for coming apart (differentiating, circumscribing, stagnating, avoiding, and terminating). There are things we can do to nurture our romantic relationships, like being realistic, not trying to change our partners, being honest, fighting fair, and remaining committed to the relationship. Systems Theory of Family says that change is constant in families, change in one family member will affect all other members, and family members play roles within the group. There are three types of family communication styles: open, closed, and random. We can maintain our family relationships by being realistic, giving grace to others, apologizing when we are wrong, and treating all family members with love and respect.

Vocabulary Words

Avoiding

Bonding

Breadth

Circumscribing

Closed family
   communication
   style

Control messages

Depth

Differentiating

Exclusivity

Experimentation

Initiating

Integrating

Intensifying

Interpersonal communication

Open family communication
   style

Random family
   communication style

Social Penetration
   Theory

Stagnating

Support messages

Systems Theory of Family

Terminating

Discussion Questions

1. What is more important in a relationship: common interests or shared values?
2. Which rules of friendship are most important? Would you add any to Hall's list?
3. How do you make the decision to move a relationship from friendship to romance?
4. What is the best part of family? What's the worst?
5. How could you be a better friend?
6. What do you think causes romantic relationships to come apart?
7. What kind of family communication does your family have? Is it the same style you want to have in your family when you marry and have children?
8. If you could change one thing about how you do human relationships, what would it be?

References

Altman, I., & Taylor, D. (1973). *Social penetration: The development of interpersonal relationships*. New York: Holt.

Baumeister, R. F. (2012). Need-to-belong theory. In P. Van Lange, A. Kruglanski, & E. T. Higgins (Eds.), *Handbook of social psychology theories* (Vol. 2, pp. 121–140). London: Sage.

Chapman, G. D. (1995). *The five love languages: How to express heartfelt commitment to your mate*. Chicago: Northfield Publishing.

Cloud, H., & Townsend, J. (2005). *Safe people DVD*.

Dion, K. K., & Dion, K. L. (1996). Cultural perspectives on romantic love. *Personal Relationships, 3*, 5–17.

Floyd, K. (2014). *Communicator matters* (2nd ed.). New York: McGraw-Hill.

Gouldner, A. W. (1960). The norm of reciprocity: A preliminary statement. *American Sociological Review, 25*, 161–178.

Hall, J. A. (2011). Sex differences in friendship expectations: A meta-analysis. *Journal of Social and Personal Relationships, 28*, 723–747.

Kantor, D., & Lehr, W. (1975). *Inside the family: Toward a theory of family process*. San Francisco: Jossey-Bass.

Kelly, A. E., Klusas, J. A., von Weiss, R. T., & Kenny, C. (2001). What is it about revealing secrets that is beneficial? *Personality and Social Psychology Bulletin, 27*, 651–665.

Knapp, M. L., & Vangelisti, A. L. (1996). *Interpersonal communication* (3rd ed.). Boston: Allyn and Bacon.

Miller, L. C., & Kenny, D. A. (1986). Reciprocity of self-disclosure at the individual and dyadic levels: A social relations analysis. *Journal of Personality and Social Psychology, 50*, 713–719.

Peterson, K. S. (1994, November 15). Sharing is the key ingredient to a long-lasting marriage. *USA Today*, p. 5D.

Shimanoff, S. B. (1980). *Communication rules: Theory and research.* Beverly Hills, CA: Sage.

Stewart, J., & Logan, C. E. (1998). *Together: Communicating interpersonally.* New York: McGraw-Hill.

Thomas, G. I. (2002). *Sacred marriage: What if God designed marriage to make us more holy than to make us happy?* Grand Rapids: Zondervan.

Vaughn, D. (1990). *Uncoupling: How relationships come apart.* New York: Random House.

Wood, J. T. (1994). *Gendered lives: Communication, gender, and culture.* Belmont, CA: Wadsworth.

Wright, P. H. (1984). Self-referent motivation and the intrinsic quality of friendship. *Journal of Social and Personal Relationships, 1,* 115–130.

Additional Readings

The Relationship Cure: A 5 Step Guide to Strengthening Your Marriage, Family, and Friendships

By John Gotman, Ph.D.

I Only Say This Because I Love You

by Deborah Tannen

The Five Love Languages: How to Express Heartfelt Commitment to Your Mate

by Gary Chapman

I Hear You: The Surprisingly Simple Skill Behind Extraordinary Relationships

By Michael S. Sorensen

The Big Disconnect: Protecting Childhood and Family Relationships in the Digital Age

By Catherine Steiner-Adair, EdD.

Sacred Marriage: What if God Designed Marriage to Make Us Holy More Than to Make Us Happy?

by Gary Thomas

Better Communicators Are Sensitive to Diversity

By Rhonda Gallagher, M.S.

7

© Joseph Sohm/Shutterstock.com

Think back to when you were a little child. Remember that first lost tooth? What did you do with it? If you grew up in the United States, you probably tucked it under your pillow in hopes that the Tooth Fairy would leave you a nice payoff. But, if you grew up in Japan or the Dominican Republic, you might have thrown it on the roof. In the United States, if we get a hamburger, we eat it with our hands, but in some parts of Europe, it's eaten with a knife and fork. You might wonder why, but the answer is simple: cultural differences. By the same token, I feel relatively confident that many of the gentlemen reading this would say that the working of the female mind is sometimes a mystery to you, and some of the ladies probably feel the same about the gentlemen. Why? It may be because of gender distinctives, though what constitutes masculine or feminine behavior is also defined by culture. So, any of these variations between genders that I'll reference in this chapter are a little bit artificial. In fact, in the same way, interacting with a person from another culture might be challenging for you. Still, please bear with me since both culture and gender differences affect how we see the world, and they spring from perspectives that are so deep in our minds that we are quite often completely unaware of them. That's the problem: we take things for granted that may or may not be true. But those distinctives affect our worldview in huge ways! In Galatians 3:28, Paul tells us "There is neither Jew nor Gentile, neither slave nor free, nor is there male or female, for you are all one in Christ

Jesus." In the Kingdom of God, our distinctives are valuable and enable us to serve each other and God. They let us see things through other eyes, and so, while it is not possible to cover all the ways we can be unique, we need to examine a couple of big ones: culture and gender. Let's start with culture.

Culture: Our Lenses

© goodluz/Shutterstock.com

Code
Culture specific rules about communication

Culture, as we learned in chapter 1, is a shared and learned way of life that includes common values, experiences, symbols, and knowledge. It affects every area of our lives. Culture is like a pair of contact lenses. Most of the time, you are totally unaware that you're even wearing lenses, but everything you see passes through them and is altered by them. They change how you see everything. They are the context that shapes every communication: what we talk about, what we can't talk about, what a gesture or voice pitch might mean, how our messages will be interpreted, what will cause conflict or offense, what we can do in what setting . . . the whole enchilada. These communication rules that are specific to a culture are called its cultural or language code.

Another analogy used in reference to culture is an iceberg. So little of the iceberg is seen above the waterline, and it looks like it would be so easy to navigate around it. But so much is below the surface where you can't see it, and just like the iceberg, the places in cultural variation you can't see are the ones with the potential to really do some damage. Some parts of culture are easy to see like particular food, dress, different gestures, use of space, or other nonverbals. We call those things

Cultural artifacts
tangible expressions of a culture

cultural artifacts, which are the tangible expressions of a culture. But simply knowing and recognizing the artifacts of a culture does not mean you understand that culture. There is much, *much* more that you can't see right away. Just like the part of the iceberg under the water, those differences are much more subtle and reflect the worldview of a people group. They often take us by surprise. Those are the cultural attributes we don't even notice until they cause some sort of conflict. Let me give you some examples. In Italian, there is no word for privacy; every evening the people come out into the public squares and take a stroll to see and be seen. This is evidence of a culture that emphasizes shared, communal life. Or here's an even better one: a friend of mine who has lived and taught in China for a number of years related to me her experience with learning to use chopsticks. She said she thought she had achieved "a cultural victory" when she learned to use chopsticks, but soon learned that she was sometimes laughed at by native Chinese. She used the right implements, but she

© Anteromite/Shutterstock.com

still ate like an American—quickly! You see, chopsticks force you to take smaller bites and eat more slowly than using a fork. It is indicative of the way members of cultures who employ them view life. The Chinese feel you should go slowly, savor the moment, and enjoy the food as well as the people with whom you are eating, reflect, and be in the moment. But Americans value efficiency and speed, so much so that we even apply that to the way we eat. We eat quickly so we can get on to something else, always moving toward the next task, seldom savoring the moment. My friend said it took her longer to master the mindset than the utensil.

Many of us belong to multiple cultures. You remember that a culture that exists within a larger culture is called a co-culture, or sometimes, a subculture. A person who belongs to two different cultures usually learns how to interact successfully in either culture, and when they move from one culture to another, they must adjust how they speak and act. That's called **code-switching**—adapting our communication style to the culture of the people with whom we are interacting (Weinreich, 1953). It enables us to function equally well in either setting, allowing us to be equally respectful of either culture and to see the value in each. When I go home to visit my family in rural Missouri, I use different language and inflection than when I'm working at the university where I teach. But when I come back to work, I adjust my language to my colleagues.

© 1000 Words/Shutterstock.com

Code-switching
adapting our communication style to the culture of the people with whom we are interacting

Linguistic Relativity Hypothesis: What's in a Word?

What's in a word? According to Sapir (1958) & Whorf (1940), everything! In "Romeo and Juliet," Juliet laments "What's in a name? That which we call a rose by any other name would smell as sweet," but Shakespeare notwithstanding, the words we know are pretty important. Sapir and Whorf both postulated that the words we learn in childhood transmit the mindset of the culture in which we grow up and that affects how we see the world. This theory is often referred to as the **Linguistic Relativity Hypothesis.** Let me give you an example. You have probably heard that Inuits in Alaska have many words for "snow This implies that in the Inuit culture, the process of learning all those words for snow not only enables a child to understand how important recognizing a type of snow is for survival but provides handles the child needs to hold and manipulate those ideas and apply them. Let's try another one: The Vietnamese word for paternal grandmother is *ba noi*, but the name for the maternal grandmother is *ba ngoai*. What does that tell you about culture of Vietnam? It says that family relationships are very important and knowing the subtle differences of how you're related to someone else is critical. Get the picture? The significance of the Linguistic Relativity Hypothesis is that the process of learning the language of the culture alters how those who use that language to think. The words you know shape how you see the world. Does that blow your mind just a little? It does mine.

Linguistic Relativity Hypothesis
theory that the words we learn from those who rear us transmit the mindset of our culture and that affects how we see the world

© Dragon Images/Shutterstock.com

Cultural Distinctives: What's the Difference?

Cultures can vary from each other in several ways, and there are some very important ways of viewing the world that we need to look at. They resemble continuums, or sliding scales with extremes at either end. Each continuum deals with a particular issue, but the ends are very different from each other. Based in the work of Hall (1984) and Hofstede (1997), they reflect variations of worldview that can greatly affect how one experiences life. Let's look at these in some detail, beginning with context.

High Versus Low Context

High context culture
culture in which a great deal of the meaning is found in the context

Low context cultures
cultures that require direct communication and communicators expect to have information stated aloud

As you recall from the first chapter, context is the setting in which communication takes place, so a high context culture is one in which a great deal of the meaning is found in the context. In other words, so much information is understood within the culture that a lot can simply go unsaid. It is understood by the participants within the cultural group. On the other hand, low context cultures require direct communication and communicators expect to have information stated aloud because that group doesn't take a lot of shared meaning for granted. High context cultures tend to be very old cultures. For example, China has existed as a country for nearly 5,000 years. The people have a lot of shared history, values, and experiences so a great deal of meaning is simply understood. Tradition and community are held in high regard. Courtesy is very important, and communication is rather indirect. There is a strong reliance on unspoken, nonverbal communication. The responsibility for creating understanding is on the listener, who is expected to know the frame of reference for the culture and be able to apply it. Japan is another high context culture. In Japan, you can tell what month of the year it is based on the colors of kimonos the geishas are wearing. There is no way something like that could be understood in the United States, which is a very low context culture. It is a nation of immigrants who come from everywhere and have a limited shared frame of reference; so, in the United States, communication tends to be very direct. The responsibility for understanding rests on the speaker, not the listener. Because meaning must be articulated in words, the speaker (or author) must pick the right words so that those receiving the message will understand. Everything has to be spelled out in great detail because we can't take for granted that

© imtmphoto/Shutterstock.com

anyone else knows what we mean. It's one reason we rely so heavily on contracts and have so many lawyers. To individuals from high context cultures, Americans can often seem unrefined, too direct.

Monochronic Versus Polychronic Time Orientation

People don't all view time the same way (Hall & Hall, 1990). That can seem really weird the first time you think about it, but every difference seems strange to us until we discover that there are multiple ways of doing things. (The world is a big place! We need to embrace that.) The United States has a monochronic time orientation, meaning time is seen like a really long ruler. Every segment of time (minute, hour, week, etc.) is a piece of that ruler, and once it is gone, well folks, it's gone! Because of that, Americans view time as very valuable, as if it were a resource to be managed, like money. They save it, spend it, or waste it. Americans tend to focus on one thing at a time and prioritize the tasks to be done. Traits such as persistence, perseverance, saving, and order are valued. A high premium is placed on being efficient and "on time" (though that phrase can mean a lot of things!). If you are heading to an appointment and something comes up, like a call from your grandfather, you can't stop because you have an appointment and are already committed for that time period. On the other hand, there are cultures that see time very differently. Cultures with a polychronic time orientation see time more like overlapping experiences to be coordinated. The emphasis in these cultures is on social connection and fully experiencing each moment, and individuals in such cultures juggle multiple tasks with multiple people in multiple interactions simultaneously. An employer in a polychronic culture may have a meeting going on in his office, with the door open, and phone calls coming in at the same time, and a new person arriving on the scene slips right into the interaction with the people already there.

Monochronic time orientation
cultural view of time as linear

Polychronic time orientation
cultural view of time as overlapping experiences to be coordinated

Moving back and forth between the tasks is not viewed as interruption as much as engaging multiple sources in the work being done at the same time. Schedules are less important than letting interactions progress organically. Characteristics that are valued in polychronic cultures are respect for tradition, saving face, and reciprocity. Connecting with people and savoring the moment are far more important than accomplishing some arbitrary job. Remember my friend with her chopsticks? She was a monochronic

© Minerva Studio/Shutterstock.com

American in polychronic China. I once had a student from Africa who told me that "Americans have watches; Africans have time." Yes, people in polychronic cultures do understand the passage of time marching toward the future, but they aren't nearly as concerned with it as with the past and the present. Being anchored in the past also means that these cultures tend to be very stable.

Collectivist Versus Individualist

In this continuum, the focus is on who is important: the individual or the group. **Collectivist cultures** value the good of the group over the good of the individual. Humility, loyalty, and cooperation are highly valued. Success is measured by the success of the group, not the individual. Remember the American lady in the chopsticks story? She actually taught in China for a few years. Of course, China is collectivist. When she gave the first exam in her class, the students began to confer with each other about answers and made no effort to hide it. As an individualistic American, she was appalled! She felt they were "cheating", but she eventually realized that in a collectivist culture, helping each other succeed is expected. But there are also individualistic cultures.

Individualistic cultures place the emphasis on the individual. The primary loyalty is to oneself, becoming all that one can be, and developing one's full potential. These cultures are much more competitive, and success is viewed as the result of one's own choices. It should be obvious by now that the United States is individualistic. In fact, it is the most individualistic culture in the world, followed closely by Australia.

Collectivist cultures
cultures that value the good of the group over the good of the individual

Individualistic cultures
cultures that place the emphasis on the individual

© Dirk Ercken/Shutterstock.com

Power Distance

Power distance is the perceived gap in respect and power between the people who govern and those who are governed. All cultures have people who hold more power than others, whether it is political, religious, economic, or social. The degree to which people in those cultures accept that those with power should be obeyed is what makes for power distance. People in high power distance cultures tend to accept their place in the hierarchy. In low power distance cultures, relationships are less hierarchical, even when one person has power over another. For instance, in China, students stand when the professor enters the room. Obviously, the United States is a low power distance culture, and that would not happen here.

Power distance
the perceived gap in respect and power between the people who govern and those who are governed

Now, power distance affects many areas. Our view of power distance can affect how we act in political, religious, and educational settings, too. Some denominations of Christianity are higher power distance, and the pastor can operate pretty much unchallenged in his control of the church. To question him would be seen by some congregants as questioning God's chosen representative. In educational settings in the United States, teachers expect students to interact with them, participate in class discussions and ask questions. This phenomenon can be very difficult for students from high power distance cultures to experience; they may not feel free to question or contradict the professor because they view such behavior as disrespectful. I once had a student who was nearly rejected from a highly competitive major on campus because her professors felt she was dishonest and showed no initiative. Why, you might ask? She was from Egypt, which is high power distance culture. She was raised to believe that it was a challenge to the teacher's authority to look them in the eye, but in the United States, looking someone in the eye is a signal of honesty. She felt she was being respectful, but her professors thought she was hiding something. Why was she regarded as showing no initiative? Because she did not volunteer answers or participate in class. She was waiting to be called on by her instructors; she felt she was honoring them by not speaking up, but they felt she was not taking responsibility.

© DisobeyArt/Shutterstock.com

Masculine Versus Feminine

Now this is a fun one! When we think of masculine and feminine, we tend to think male and female, so imagining cultures with masculine or feminine characteristics can leave us scratching our heads in confusion. But the terms "masculine" and "feminine" also refer to a set of cultural values. Let me explain. **Masculine cultures** tend to be competitive, focused on accomplishment, and materialistic (Hofstede, 1997). The scorecard for success is material possessions. Gender roles are very clearly defined. Men are expected to do "man jobs" like doctor, lawyer, or construction worker. Around the house, they take out the trash, do household maintenance, and keep up the lawn. Women are expected to do "woman jobs" like teaching, nursing, or homemaking. At home, they do most of the housework, shopping, childcare, and so on. Compare that to more feminine cultures like Sweden or France (Hofstede, 2018). **Feminine cultures** value collaboration and nurturance. It's not as important to have lots of stuff as it is for everyone's needs to be met. Furthermore, feminine cultures value quality of life and fulfillment, so gender roles are much more flexible. If a woman wants to be CEO of a major corporation instead of staying home with the children, that's just fine; the worldview is that she should be doing the work that fulfills her. By the same token, if a man wants to be a stay-at-home dad, that's fine, too. If he's a nurturing soul, he should do what he's good at and what brings him joy.

© India Picture/Shutterstock.com

Masculine cultures
cultures that tend to be competitive, focused on accomplishment, materialistic, and where gender roles are clearly defined

Feminine cultures
cultures that value collaboration and nurturance

By now, you may be wondering where the United States falls in the rankings. Actually, the United States is about 10th on the list of most masculine countries in the world. The most masculine cultures tend to be in the Middle East, like Saudi Arabia (Hofstede, 1997). Think about how gender roles are assumed in Arab cultures and how that plays out in the workplace. In contrast, the United States may look pretty feminine, but that is only by comparison. The United States still has pretty clearly defined gender roles. Culture, like language, is not fixed or set in stone; cultures are constantly changing. You should remember that; it's important.

Uncertainty Avoidance

Uncertainty avoidance
the degree to which a culture can tolerate uncertainty

Some cultures can stand a lot of risk-taking and uncertainty while others cannot. That's the heart of uncertainty avoidance, which is the degree to which a culture can tolerate uncertainty. A culture that is high in uncertainty avoidance really doesn't like risk or change and, well, avoids it, hence the name. Those cultures resist change and tend to place a lot of emphasis on rules and regulations. These regulations provide structure and security, allowing members of that culture to interact comfortably and securely. Those guidelines include things like what kind of toast to make at a wedding, what to wear to the wedding, whether or not to bring something if you're invited to dinner, and if you are bringing something, what to bring. That's just the beginning. Many rules can make a person from a high-risk avoidance culture feel safe, and the absence of those guidelines can feel very uncomfortable for them. Imag-

© Dirk Ercken/Shutterstock.com

ine the discomfort a student from Singapore (which is a high uncertainty avoidance culture) has in the United States when invited to a party. They will want to know when to arrive, how long the party is expected to last, what to bring, what to wear, what activities are likely to happen, and so on. And what is the American response? "Don't worry about it. We'll probably start around 7:00 and go until whenever, but you can leave early if you want. Bring food if you want to, or not, either way is OK." You can imagine what that would feel like. On the flip side, an American would probably be very frustrated by all the rules for party attendance in Singapore. It would seem formal, stiff, and stifling. Americans are pretty casual and laid back, with fewer rules governing conduct than in many other countries. We sort of try things out to see what works. In fact, we are gamblers; we seem to *love* risk. Maybe it is because we are the descendants of people who took huge risks to come here and settle this continent. People who don't like taking chances don't *willingly* get onto leaky ships and sail across the ocean. They don't get into covered wagons and head out to God-knows-where. They stay safely at home in the old country. So, you can see how Americans came to be low risk avoidance, right? (I also hope this hints at the idea that shared group history can shape cultural preferences, too.)

Problems of Cultural Differences: When Cultures Collide

There are a couple of things that can go wrong when people interact across cultural differences. They are stereotyping and ethnocentrism.

Stereotyping

Stereotypes are predictions about how someone will behave based on the assumed characteristics of the group to which they belong. We discussed stereotypes in Chapter 2 in relation to self-concept, and in Chapter 3 in relation to perception, but it also relates to how we see people of other cultural groups. (Remember, I told you that all this stuff is connected and will resurface from time to time.) If a family moves in down the street from you of a nationality or ethnicity you don't know anything about, you watch their behavior, and then assume that all people who belong to that group will

© Philip Date/Shutterstock.com

behave in the same way because that is all you know about the supposed characteristics of that group. Humans subconsciously make these sorts of generalizations, but they really get in the way of communicating with individuals. We don't interact with stereotypes; we interact with *people,* and people need to be treated as individuals.

Ethnocentrism

Have you ever noticed that sometimes you automatically assume that the way you were brought up is just naturally better than the way someone else was, and the way you do things is better? That's because most of us tend to be a little ethnocentric. We judge all other groups by the values and standards of our own group. That is ethnocentrism. Ethnocentrism is the belief that one's own culture is superior to all others. In *My Big, Fat, Greek Wedding*, Gus Portokalos tells his daughter that there were two kinds of people in the world: Greeks and people who wish they were

© Giulio_Fornasar/Shutterstock.com

Ethnocentrism
the belief that one's own culture is superior to all others

Racism
believing one's race to be superior to all others

Greek. That's a pretty strong statement about how much better he felt his culture was than any other. Some people confuse it with racism, which is the belief that one's race to be superior to all others, but it's not the same thing. Race is physical; ethnicity is cultural. A lot of what we think of as racism in the world is actually ethnocentrism. If you think about it, many times the things you find off-putting in other people groups have little to do with their physical characteristics. You are much more likely to be offended by their behavior, beliefs, values, and attitudes. Think about that for a minute. Maybe, if we can learn to understand cultures better, we might be less confused, afraid, or frustrated.

We need to be respectful of differences precisely because we are different, so understanding cross-cultural communication (communication between two different cultural groups) becomes even more important.

Gender Communication: Another Gender or Another Culture?

I'm sure that most of you find yourselves scratching your head in confusion at some of the things you see members of the opposite sex doing or saying. That's not too surprising. Some theorists say that differences across the gender divide are so great that they should be treated as cross-cultural communication. At times, it can certainly feel that way! However, that thesis has never been satisfactorily demonstrated; the similarities between the genders are actually far greater than the differences (Andersen, 1999). As vehemently as some experts, such as Tannen (1990) and Gray (1992), claim gender differences are huge and real, others like Canary and Hause (1993) and Wilkins and Andersen (1991) shout "Absurd!" Somewhere in the middle lie more moderate positions that gendered communication patterns are learned (Wood, 2002) and simply knowing about those differences and making appropriate accommodations is helpful (Tingley, 1994). The differences between the sexes are much fewer than the similarities between them, but the variations can be confusing. It would be naive to say that there are no distinctives. There certainly appear to be some significant ones, but neither style of communication, masculine or feminine, is superior to the other; they are just different.

Now, if you were paying close attention a couple of pages back when I talked about stereotypes, you may be thinking that this discussion of gendered communication lends itself to stereotyping. (Congratulations! You get a gold star for attention!) That is probably true, at least according to Canary and Hause (1993). They even put forth a list of preconceived ideas that could affect how a communication researcher conducts research, which could skew results to show gender differences. Besides, those stereotypes aren't much help in predicting an individual's behavior. However, the same might be said of any of the topics previously discussed in relation to culture, and—now pay attention here, this is critical—our intention here is not to make predictions about how a particular person in your life is going to act. It is to give you some tools to help you understand what might have motivated that person to act as they did in that situation.

Patterns for Gendered Communication: "Why Did You Do That?"

Before we consider some of the areas of difference, we need to look at learned patterns of gendered behaviors. For this to make sense, you need to understand some things about how the Western world enculturates its children; most of the research that has been done on gender distinctives has been done in the United States. Men are usually taught from earliest youth to be competitive and demonstrate their strength and competence. According to Tannen (1990), competition and defense of the public image greatly affects masculine communication. Emotional expression is also affected. Males tend to be encouraged to feel and express emotions that demonstrate power, such as anger, rather than fear, sadness, or helplessness (Wood, 2002). Competition trumps collaboration, and men may be inclined to use communication to establish dominance (or power, or leadership, however you'd like to describe being "top dog"). This is not because they are arrogant or egotistical: it's the way they were taught to act to succeed.

Conversely, feminine communication isn't about competition; it's about connection and cooperation. Women are much more likely to extend empathy and respond to it in an effort to establish solidarity and are enculturated early to maintain relationships. Expressions of "strong" or "assertive" emotions like anger are discouraged (Tarvis, 1989), and females are trained to be caring and supportive. That focus on relationship demonstrates prioritization of connection rather than competition (Tingley, 1993).

So, if we have different behavior patterns that we have been taught to have from childhood, how did we ever learn them in the first place?

Gendered Speech Communities: "Where Did You Learn to Do That?"

Remember when we talked about the Linguistic Relativity Hypothesis? It said that the language you know and the patterns of speech that prevail in your culture influence what you can think about and the terms in which you can think about it. Well, gendered communication is nested in culture. Each cultural group has its own ideas about which attributes are more masculine and which more feminine, and those views are reinforced by the language structures of the community. So, to a large degree these contrasting communication styles are *learned* (Wood, 2002). Think back to when you were growing up. You were taught by your parents and those around you to do and say certain things and avoid others. For instance, you were probably taught to say "Excuse me" when you burped (or *to* burp as a compliment to the cook—it depends on the culture, remember!), not to interrupt others when they are speaking, and never speak with your mouth full. All these "do's and don'ts" that you're taught were part of your socialization. Socialization is the process of teaching children how to behave in their social group. You probably do some of those things better than others. (Maybe you talk with your mouth full when you get excited, for example.) In that respect, you are better socialized in some areas than others. That makes sense, right? Well, we are socialized in regards to gender behaviors by gendered speech communities, and the primary setting in which that takes place is going to surprise you. Are you ready? It happens during play (Maltz & Borker, 1982). Crazy, right? I know! You see, the kind of games children play tend to be segregated based on gender, and the games girls have traditionally played exhibit different communication patterns than those played by boys. For instance, girls are more likely to play house, or school, and those games require more talking about how they will be played (who gets to be mommy this time, what part of family life is being reenacted, etc.) than standard boys'

Socialization
the process of teaching children how to behave in their social group

© Andrey_Popov/Shutterstock.com

games. Boys usually play games with more players and fewer, clearer rules, like sports. Even when boys are playing imagination games, like war (Should I say "Star Wars"?) or police, or firefighters, they have goals that are easily distinguished, and each little boy pretty much knows what to do. There is less *need* for talk. Girls' games are often more cooperative and require sensitivity to the other players, while boys' games are usually more competitive, both between competing groups and among members in each group (Wood, 2002). According to Olsen et al. (2015), among members of these competing groups men demonstrate intense loyalty to other group members that might not be seen among females in the same situation. These childhood games shape how boys and girls learn to communicate, which carries over into adulthood.

Adult Gendered Communication: "All Grown Up"

Wood tells us that these communication patterns learned in childhood set the stage for adult communication. It's not surprising that we keep communicating in the ways we've used since childhood.

Just a quick disclaimer here—these generalizations are just that: generalizations. They don't predict how a particular person will behave. They are just useful for understanding a little bit about where an unexpected action comes from when someone acts differently than you would. Just as each person is socialized differently about covering their mouth when they sneeze, they are also gender socialized in myriad ways, and with greater or less efficacy.

So, what do these adult gendered communication patterns look like? First, feminine talk is regarded as more expressive and dealing with more emotional and personal matters, while masculine talk is often more competitive and task oriented. Secondly, the focus of feminine communication is more about forming and maintaining interpersonal connections (Riessman, 1990), while males usually tend to be more concerned with achieving goals and feel that relationships grow by doing things together, like watching a game or working on a project together (Swain, 1989; Wood & Inman, 1993). Next, the genders approach talking about problems differently. Males' tendency toward competitiveness may cause a man to protect his vulnerabilities, and thus, keep problems to himself until he has exhausted other resources for problem solving. Then he may go to another man to discuss how to solve the problem. If so, he's probably looking for suggestions to address the issue, and when approached by another man, he's likely to assume that the sharing comes from a sincere desire for a new perspective or solution. A male friend is likely to offer suggestions by way of helping another man. But because women tend to see talk as the primary means of relationship-building, they don't necessarily feel the need to "fix it." The friendly help offered is usually to listen, be supportive, and validate emotions. Can you see how these different styles can produce misunderstanding? Gentlemen, your lady friend may not be asking you to give her advice; she may just want you to be a witness in her life. Ladies, the man in your life is probably not trying to boss you around; he's probably trying to offer you the advice he would like. Lastly, let's talk about "relationship talk." Because women often see talk as the way to build and keep intimacy, they will probably want to talk about the relationship. But most males have been socialized in their games not to talk about interpersonal things unless there are decisions to be made or problems to be dealt with, so the idea of discussing the relationship can be unsettling (Acitelli, 1988). The request for talk can send the message that there is something wrong in paradise.

So, now that you know why we do things differently, let's see some of the areas of difference and learn to understand each other better.

Verbal Differences

Deborah Tannen (1990) identified gender differences in speech based on her observations of American males and females, mostly at work. Her research has come under fire for generalizing these characteristics that may well be driven by the highly competitive workplace to other cross-gender interactions. (Go back and re-read the section on masculine culture above if you have doubts about the competitive nature of the American workplace.) She used the terms report talk and rapport talk. According to Tannen, **report talk**, the masculine speaking style in Western culture, is focused on sharing information, while **rapport talk**, the feminine speaking style, is intended to create connection between the parties engaging in the communication. (By the way, most of our students mispronounce this word, so let me give you a clue. The "port" part is pronounced "pour," so all together now, it's "ruh-pour." It's French.)

Report talk
the masculine speaking style in western culture that is focused on sharing information

Rapport talk
the feminine speaking style that is intended to create connection between the parties engaging in the communication

Report Talk

Generally speaking, Tannen says men usually use report talk, and the goals of report talk are as follows:

Showing expertise: This means dealing with conversation in a way that masks areas of uncertainty and magnifies areas of competence.

Keeping center stage: It's a form of competition to dominate others, keep the attention on themselves, and keep themselves in a good light. This leads to talking more, interrupting more, and talking over each other.

Earning respect: This usually plays out as a man tells things about himself that make him look good to earn the respect of men and women alike.

Focusing on problem solving: This allows a man to hold center stage, demonstrate his competence, and earn respect. It's unemotional but shows power and ability.

Using more interruptions: In a disagreement, men will often talk over each other until one stops talking. It's a way to assume leadership.

Avoiding posing questions: Asking questions may be seen as undermining an image of strength. (If you ever wondered why your dad might be lost driving around but won't pull over to ask for directions, this is why.)

Attempting to find topics that others don't know about: It provides another chance to hold center stage. It may look like showing off, but it can be a deeply engrained communication expectation.

Rapport Talk

Conversely, women may use rapport talk for particular purposes, and the areas of focus are:

Being expressive: Women are culturally allowed in United States to be emotional and share those emotions with others, thereby allowing other women to be supportive, show solidarity, and form connection.

Being polite: Females are taught in our culture to be polite in interactions and yield the floor if someone else is talking, especially a man. This is generally seen as "being nice."

Using more personal, plural pronouns, more requests for agreement, and more indirect language: Indirect language often allows women to give orders and secure acceptance in ways that are less likely to offend or cause conflict. They may use more words like "us" and "we" as opposed to "I" and "you." This can unconsciously reinforce unity and provide an opportunity for showing cooperation. Requests for agreement are perceived as much less confrontational than direct commands. (So, men, when your female boss says, "We can have that report ready by Friday at 5:00, right?" she's probably not really asking if she can help you with it or if next Tuesday would be better. It's probably a command, just like if your male boss said, "Have that report done by 5:00 Friday afternoon." The difference is that women usually soften language to "make the medicine go down" more easily. The problem is that men, being more direct, sometimes don't recognize a request as an order because the language is indirect. (Women, if you have an order to give, be direct; it's only fair to let people know what they're actually agreeing to and when.)

© antoniodiaz/Shutterstock.com

Using more intensifiers: Females usually get to be as expressive as they like in the United States and overstate things, so they can say "very," "really," and "soooo" a lot more, A LOT MORE! (Notice how I got away with using that all capped intensifier? It's because I'm a woman in a culture that more comfortable with that sort of behavior from women!)

Using more compliments and praise: Listen, anybody can make more friends and achieve their goals better with compliments and praise. It helps build relationship and cooperation. But across the board, women are more likely to use them than men.

Matching and sharing experiences: Women often share common experiences as a way of showing connection and unity.

© thodonal88/Shutterstock.com

Complaining as means of building solidarity: Women frequently share their troubles to connect with each other. It's a way of finding common experiences and bonding.

Nonverbal Differences

Andersen (1999) did show that men and women are more similar than different in the ways that they use nonverbal communication, but there are still differences that are worth noting.

Attentiveness: According to Andersen, women do a better job of reading nonverbal cues and showing attention, essentially demonstrating care and support through their gestures and other nonverbal expressions.

Voice: Just as women use words to express more emotion and intensifiers, they tend to use their vocalics to express a greater range of pitch and inflection. Men in the United States generally talk more loudly than women and employ more verbal fillers, like "um" or "ah."

Gestures and facial expression: Women often reveal their emotions through facial expression and gestures more accurately than men, while most men are more likely to fidget with their hands and feet. Men may make bigger gestures, but ladies usually gesture more often. When happy, women appear to be more likely to smile than men, but much less likely to show anger.

Interpersonal distance: Whether alone or with others, men tend to assume more territory and take up more personal space when interacting. Conversely, women tend to stand closer to others when conversing and take up less space in general. It is interesting that when men interact with women, they usually reduce the amount of space they would normally take when interacting with a man, though they do not usually reduce to the same level another woman would.

Eye contact: Since we use eye contact to connect with another, it is not surprising that most women make and maintain more eye contact than men. Tannen (1990) demonstrated that males and female use eye contact in different ways from early childhood, finding that in conversation females tend to square off face to face and look directly into each other's eyes, while males usually stand or sit side by side and exchange glances. (I call that "eye tag.")

Touch: As a rule of thumb, women generally just touch more than men. Touching behaviors in intimate relationships differ relative to the stage of the relationship. During the courting or dating phase of a romance, males will probably initiate touch more often, but in established intimate relationships, females usually initiate touch more often. However, in long-term, heterosexual relationships, touch is initiated about equally by each sex.

Listening

Listening cues
behaviors that let the speaker know that the listener is actually listening and engaged

© Pressmaster/Shutterstock.com

Men and women listen differently to achieve their own ends (Tannen, 1999). Women often give more listening cues, which are behaviors that let the speaker know that the listener is actually listening and engaged, such as nodding, showing an attentive facial expression, making direct eye contact, possibly touching the speaker, or using encouraging noises (like "go on," "I see," etc.). Men tend to listen very quietly without a lot of listening cues, may look around instead of making direct eye contact (Brownell, 2006), and may interrupt more. This style of listening reflects concentrated attention and that the man may be gathering information in order to help by formulating a solution. Women appear to be more interested in helping by emotional showing support (Tannen, 1990) while men usually lend support through possible solutions (Wood, 2002).

Ethical Implications

We need to *really value* diversity, not just say that we do. Seeing the infinite variety of people can enable us to see multiple views of God. We are made in His image, and we show that image to others just as they show His image to us. Of course, we are all fallen and make mistakes, but the light of God can show up in so many wonderful ways when we keep our eyes open. That's why it's so important to be respectful even when we don't fully understand.

Give people the benefit of the doubt about what they are doing and why. A behavior that seems strange or even offensive to you may come from a really good motive. Remember that those misunderstandings are the icebergs that sink our relationships if we jump to conclusions. Very often we are totally unaware of cultural differences until they produce conflict, but conflict is just a tool to increase understanding if we use it correctly, so seek to understand. How do we do that?

Ask questions! If you don't understand why a person acted in a particular way or used a particular word or phrase, as respectfully as you know how, ask! And if the answer you get seems wrong to you, realize you don't have to agree with everything you hear; just be respectful of differences.

Try to see people as individuals. Regardless of why they do what they do, you have more in common with others than you might think. Even the person you most dislike is like you in some very fundamental ways. Try to imagine what their lives might have been like to bring them to the actions they have committed. Recognize the loyalties people have as just that: loyalties. Loyalty is a good impulse, even if the object of the loyalty may be undeserving in your opinion. But don't minimize the differences; just acknowledge them.

Remember the things you've learned about cultural differences in your daily interaction, especially when you have to work with people from other cultures. People from high risk avoidance cultures are not cowards; they've been socialized to be cautious. People from polychronic cultures aren't disrespectful when they're "late" for a meeting. Different cultures show their value of time in different ways. It doesn't show lack of respect for anyone, or even for time itself. This doesn't mean you can't express your position if there's some confusion, or even conflict; just be mature and respectful when you do it.

Don't be ethnocentric. I don't care how much you love your own culture. It's not the only one with virtues. Try to see the virtues in other cultures.

When you go abroad, adjust to the other culture. The responsibility for adjustment lies with you, not the other culture. If you travel from the United States to a European country, make yourself speak softly in public because that's what the natives do, and it's their home, not yours. If you move to the United States from South America, learn what "on time" means in the United States and adjust yourself to that expectation. If you go to another culture with different table manners, adopt the manners of the culture while you're there. You're a guest; be a good one.

Be aware of gender differences. Try to see members of the opposite sex as people, because they are. If someone goofs, calmly explain what they did to offend you. Yelling and screaming won't help.

It's a funny thing about diversity. The root word for "diversity" is the same as for "division," and we all know that there are areas in which we are different from other people. Sometimes, awareness of our dissimilarity can make us uncomfortable, so we ignore or deny it. Instead of celebrating and enjoying our distinctives, we can end up devaluing them. That's sort of sad. Each of us is a combination of characteristics that set us apart from each other as wonderful, unique creations of God.

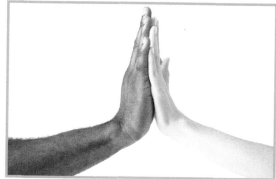
© WAYHOMEstudio/Shutterstock.com

Summary

Culture is a learned way of life that includes shared values, experiences, symbols, and knowledge. It affects our perspective and how we function in every area of our lives. Codes tell us what we can or cannot do in a given cultural setting. We often don't notice cultural differences until they cause conflict. Cultural artifacts are tangible expressions of culture, like what we eat, how we greet each other, and so on. A co-culture is a culture within a culture, and adjusting our communication to the group of people we are with is called code-switching. The Linguistic Relativity Hypothesis says that the words we grow up with in our culture affect the way we think about things. Hall identified two ways cultures differ (high vs. low context and monochromic vs. polychronic time orientation), while Hofstede identified others (collectivism vs. individualism, power distance, masculine vs. feminine, and uncertainty avoidance). Problems that occur between cultures include stereotyping and ethnocentrism.

Cross-gendered communication (communication between males and females) has been called cross-cultural communication by some, but that has been largely rejected by most researchers. We learn gendered communication as children from gendered speech communities, and that affects how we communicate in adulthood in areas of speech, nonverbal communication, and listening. Generally speaking, masculine communication tends to be competitive, and seeks to demonstrate strengths and competence to hold center stage. Feminine communication is more concerned with promoting cooperation and collaboration, being polite, and building connection. Verbal communication styles are different as well, and men tend to use report talk while women use rapport talk more. Nonverbal communication can also be different, with different use of attentiveness, space, touch, gestures, facial expressions, and voice tone. Listening styles are also affected. Men may interrupt more and usually listen more quietly, while women usually show more supportive nonverbal cues.

Vocabulary Words

Code	Individualistic culture	Power distance
Code-switching	Linguistic Relativity Hypothesis	Racism
Collectivist culture	Listening cues	Rapport talk
Cultural artifacts	Low context culture	Report talk
Ethnocentrism	Masculine culture	Socialization
Feminine culture	Monochronic time orientation	Uncertainty avoidance
High context culture	Polychronic time orientation	

Discussion Questions

1. How many reasons can you think of for studying cultural differences?
2. To which different cultures or co-cultures do you belong?
3. Have you ever had a misunderstanding with a person from another culture? What do you think was the real source of the conflict?
4. Which of the cultural differences have you seen in real life? Which confused you the most?
5. When have you had to code-switch? Why?
6. Which gender difference was most surprising to you?
7. How did your own childhood games teach you to behave in gendered ways?
8. Have you seen examples of report talk or rapport talk that closely match Tannen's observations?
9. Do you believe that gendered communication is cross-cultural? Why? Why not?

References

Acitelli, L. (1988). When spouses talk to each other about their relationship. *Journal of Social and Personal Relationships, 5*, 185–199.

Anderson, P. A. (1999). *Nonverbal communication: Forms and function.* Mountain View, CA: Mayfield Publishing.

Brownell, J. (2006). *Listening: Attitudes, principles and skills* (3rd ed.). Boston, MA: Allyn & Bacon.

Canary, D. J., & Hause, I. S. (1993). Is there any reason to research sex differences in communication? *Communication Quarterly, 41*, 129–141.

Gray, J. (1992). *Men are from Mars, women are from Venus.* New York: Harper Collins.

Hall, E. T. (1984). *The dance of life: The other dimensions of time.* New York: Anchor Press/Doubleday.

Hall, E. T., & Hall, M. R. (1990). *Understanding cultural differences: Germans, French, and Americans.* Yarmouth, ME: Intercultural Press.

Hofstede, G. (1997). *Cultures and organizations: Software of the mind.* New York: McGraw-Hill.

Hofstede, G. (2018). *Compare countries.* Retrieved from http://www.hofstede-insights.com/product/compare/countries

Maltz, D. N., & Borker, R. (1982). A cultural approach to male-female miscommunication. In J. J. Gumpertz (Ed.), *Language and social identity* (pp. 196–216). Cambridge, England: Cambridge University Press.

Piaget, J. (1923). *Language et pensée chez l'enfant.* (3rd ed.). *1948 revue it avec un nouvel avant-propos it un nouveau chapitre ll insere utgave bind). Neuchatel: Delachaux et Niestle.*

Olsen, M. R. (2015). *Maturity and the Hispanic male: A grounded theory from the characteristics and experiences that lead to the maturation of the Hispanic male student.* Retrieved from ProQuest Dissertations Publishing.

Riessman, C. K. (1990). *Divorce talk: Women and men make sense of personal relationships*. New Brunswick, NJ: Rutgers University Press.

Sapir, E. (1958). *Culture, language and personality*. Berkeley, CA: University of California Press.

Swain, S. (1989). Covert intimacy: Closeness in men's friendships. In B. Risman & P. Schwartz (Eds.), *Gender and intimate relationships* (pp. 71–86), Belmont, CA: Wadsworth.

Tannen, Deborah (1990). *You just don't understand*. New York: Morrow.

Tavris, C. (1989). *Anger: The misunderstood emotion*. New York: Simon & Schuster.

Tingley, J. (1993). *Genderflex: Men and women speaking each other's language at work*. New York: Amacom.

Weinreich, U. (1953). *Languages in contact*. New York: Linguistic Circle of New York.

Whorf, B. L. (1940). Science and linguistics. *Technology Review, 35,* 229–231, 247–248.

Wilkins, B. M., & Andersen, P. A. (1991). Gender differences and similarities in management communication: A meta-analysis. *Management Communication Quarterly, 5,* 6–35.

Wood, J. T. (2002). Gendered standpoints on personal relationships. In J. Steward (Ed.), *Bridges, not walls* (9th ed., pp. 377–384). New York, NY: McGraw-Hill.

Wood, J. T., & Inman, C. C. (1993). In a different mode: Masculine styles of communicating closeness. *Journal of Applied Communication Research, 21,* 279–295.

Additional Readings

Love and Respect

by Emerson Eggerichs

The Visible Self: Global Perspectives on Dress, Culture, and Society

by JoAnn Eicher & Sandra Lee Evenson

Perception & Deception

by Joe Lurie

You Just Don't Understand: Men and Women in Conversation

by Deborah Tannen

Better Communicators Are Attentive to Words

By Denise Miller, M.A.

8

"It is not the critic who counts; not the man who points out how the strong man stumbles, or where the doer of deeds could have done them better. The credit belongs to the man who is actually in the arena, whose face is marred by dust and sweat and blood . . . . if he fails, at least fails while daring greatly, so that his place shall never be with those cold and timid souls who neither know victory nor defeat."

This excerpt of U.S. President Theodore Roosevelt's "Citizenship in a Republic" exemplifies the power of words to inspire generations. According to the Huffington Post, entertainers Miley Cyrus and Liam Hemsworth have matching tattoos of the quote. Inspiration is only one of the super powers of words. When we haven't decided what we think about a particular issue, verbal processing, talking to a friend, or journaling can help us find clarity. The chapter on perceiving also has tips for discovering our own opinions. This chapter's emphasis on finding useful words can help us as we talk to ourselves, to others and when we speak to large groups in public. We start with the theoretical properties of words, then cover the two types of word power. We finish with the ethical implications of words.

Theodore Roosevelt became the 26th president of the United States.

Words Have Four Properties

Thinking about the basic properties of words may seem tedious and unnecessary. Little children communicate well enough and they are not burdened with such details. But as children become adults, they become responsible for caring for themselves, their environment, and for others (Bandura 1997) and learn that words matter. Words and their arrangements influence how we think and act and how others respond. As we understand the properties of words we can gain social dexterity and better fulfill our destinies, pursue happiness, and affect culture (Comello, 2009).

> "There are two ways to slice easily through life; to believe everything or to doubt everything. Both ways save us from thinking"
>
> -Alfred Korzybski, the father of general semantics

Sidebar 8A

Words Are Symbolic.

Alfred Korzybski (1933) coined the phrase, "The map is not the territory." He used "map" as a metaphor for words and "territory" as a metaphor for reality. A map is only a symbol of a territory and not the territory itself; like a map words represent persons, experiences, places, ideas, and feelings. We can use symbols/words to think about things we've never experienced such as Moses, Tibet, and the 2032 Olympics. With words we can explore intangibles such as creativity, pride, and freedom. Words open to us a world of fantastical things like Santa Claus, Tolkien's Middle Earth, and Roosevelt's sweat-stained man from the opening paragraph of this chapter. Law depends on words. Leaders use words to cast a vision, to help us form a picture of a preferred future. We speak words to describe the person whom we hope to become someday and the products we hope to produce. Symbols/words stand in the place of things, real or imagined. Words work best when the speaker and the listener have the same meanings for the same words. One property of words is that they are symbolic.

Triangle of Meaning

Ogden and Richards (1923) used a triangle to demonstrate that the meanings of words are much more varied than any dictionary definition. See Sidebar 8B.

The line between the word and the concept demonstrates that each individual will attach a unique meaning to a word. The line connecting the referent to the concept demonstrates that a person who has some experience with the referent will have a unique meaning for that person, place, thing, action, or description. For instance, a lamp may remind one person of studying while the same lamp may evoke a fondness for

The symbolic nature of words enables us to create meaning, and cast a vision.

© Susan Schmitz/Shutterstock.com

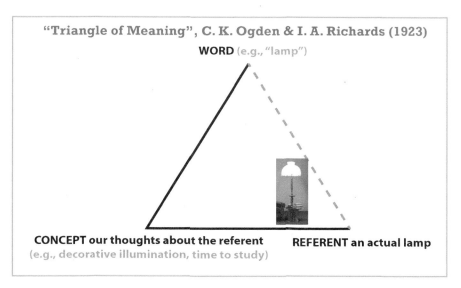

"Triangle of Meaning", C. K. Ogden & I. A. Richards (1923)

WORD (e.g., "lamp")

CONCEPT our thoughts about the referent
(e.g., decorative illumination, time to study)

REFERENT an actual lamp

Sidebar 8B

art deco architectural style for another person. The word "lamp" at the top encompasses the relationship of the three points of the triangle of meaning (Nesterov, 2009).

One reason that we may feel comfortable with our friends and families is that we've learned the special meanings that words have for them and they've learned the meanings that words have for us. We understand one another; we get the same jokes. We are less likely to unintentionally offend them or to sound silly to them. Our concepts of words are more predictable.

Here's an example of the unfortunate effect of different interpretations of words. Trying to help a refugee mother arrange for her child's day care, the social worker offered to fill out some paperwork, but the mom quickly slipped away without any assistance. Later the social worker learned that to some people, using the words, "paperwork" and "childcare" in the same sentence, symbolizes, "The government is taking your child away from you." The longer the social worker interacted with the co-culture, the more he learned what his symbols meant in "their language." We understand language more accurately with people we know or who are similar to us because words are not static realities, words are only symbols (Edwards et al., 2013).

"When I said I could help her with some paperwork for free child care, she thought the government would take her child away!"

© vlada93/Shutterstock.com

Words Are Ambiguous

Not only are words symbolic, standing in for ideas and feelings, but words also have levels of **ambiguity**, or uncertainty of meaning. The first time you hear a significant

Ambiguity
uncertainty of meaning

Concrete
the characteristic of words that refer to an actual instance or a specific thing

other introduce you as "boyfriend" or "girlfriend," you may want to clarify what that word means in your relationship. Does it mean that you have a standing lunch date every weekday? Does it mean that you will stop spending time with certain others? What does "boyfriend" or "girlfriend" status mean to this person? What does it mean to you? What questions will your parents have about a "boyfriend" or "girlfriend"? The same word can mean something different to different people, at different times, and in different contexts. S.I. Hayakawa (1964) used a ladder to demonstrate the ambiguous nature of words. He called it the Ladder of Abstraction. See Sidebar 8D.

The ladder demonstrates that some words are inherently more or less abstract than other words. We call the least abstract words "concrete" because they have an actual instance, person or thing as a referent.

Ladder of Abstraction, Hayakaya (1964)

Abstract

person

citizen

adult

wage-earner

professional

teacher

Mrs. Worth

Concrete

Sidebar 8D

Cultural Politeness Can Be Ambiguous

Polite people use an assortment of ambiguities to express sensitive matters such as failures, bodily functions, or death. We may say, "You're almost right," "She's looking for the restroom," or "He has gone on" instead of "You're wrong," "She needs to urinate," "He's dead." These polite ambiguities vary depending on the context. Some cultures use ambiguity for politeness differently than other cultures. U.S. humorist Dave Barry related his frustration trying to arrange transportation while he was in Asia. He was repeatedly told that the flights he wanted would be "very difficult." Dave repeatedly asserted his willingness to endure whatever "difficulty" necessary to get the flights. Instead of booking him on the flights, the attendant kept repeating that it would be "very difficult." Eventually, Dave discovered that the flights he wanted did not exist. Dave learned that to avoid the harshness of bluntly pointing out "you are talking nonsense, there is no such flight," this group of people says "very difficult." They expect the listener to appreciate the courteous subtlety. Similarly in the U.S. a professor might reply to a student that her grade is "fine" even though she is in danger of failing the course. The professor might use the ambiguous term "fine" to protect the student from the probable judgments of those nearby who might overhear. Different communities use the ambiguous property of words differently to be polite.

© szefei/Shutterstock.com

Public Speaking Can Be Ambiguous

Public speakers have a greater responsibility to consider the ambiguity of words because of the reduced opportunity for the listeners to seek clarification and because of the greater number of listeners who are receiving the public message. Individual audience members assign very different meanings to words. Adjectives and adverbs such as *large, awesome, interesting, or appropriately, dangerously, lavishly* are especially indistinct. In a small group, listeners may inquire, "how large?" or ask why it seemed so appropriate, dangerous, or lavish. In a public setting, those questions often remain unasked. The audience's assumptions may be very near or very far from the speaker's intention. Ambiguity can support or sabotage the goal of a speaker and can mislead a listener.

A wise communicator considers every word as he writes his outline. He may use ambiguity to his advantage, employing more abstract words to avoid being held accountable for details beyond his control, to protect a person or organization, or when he wants the audience to access their imaginations. One example of avoiding ambiguity to serve the listeners and the speaker involves a controversy in Massachusetts.

Barbara Bush, previous first lady of the United States, bravely delivered the 1990 commencement address at Wellesley College amid protests that because she had dropped out of college to be a wife and mother, she was a poor role model for the graduates. Mrs. Bush unquestionably needed to build rapport with this audience. To build rapport, she began by concretely relating her admiration for her audience.

"More than ten years ago, when I was invited here to talk about our experiences in the People's Republic of China, I was struck by both the natural beauty of your campus and the spirit of this place . . . Wellesley, you see, is not just a place but an idea—an experiment in excellence in which diversity is not just tolerated, but

© Cynthia Johnson/Contributor/Getty

is embraced. The essence of this spirit was captured in a moving speech about tolerance given last year by a student body president of one of your sister colleges. She related the story by Robert Fulghum about a young pastor . . ." Had Mrs. Bush omitted the student body president's speech and Fulghum's story, the audience would have been left to assume Mrs. Bush's meaning when she said that she was "struck" by the Wellesley spirit (Bush 1990). Mrs. Bush built rapport at Wellesley by avoiding ambiguity.

We've reviewed the first two properties. Words are symbolic and words are ambiguous. The third property is that words are changeable.

Words Are Changeable

Definitions of words are as fluid as the experiences of the people who use the words. The meanings of words morph over time, and among different cultures, as well as among social, religious, and political contexts. Each new dictionary edition includes not only new words but also new meanings for the old words. Sidebar 8E, adapted from the Huffington Post, includes some examples of the changing property of words.

Words Are Changeable

1) **"Hook up"** used to mean getting some kind of service or appliance, e.g., "hook up cable television." Today, it also means something completely different like a meeting or an intimate encounter.

2) **"Sick"** used to mean ill. Today, it also means something is really amazing.

3) **"Backlog"** during colonial times meant the biggest log in the fire. Today, it means a reserve or a pile of work you still need to plow through.

© Minerva Studio/Shutterstock.com

4) **"Tool"** used to mean something you dug up the garden with. Today, it also means someone who's not intelligent enough to realize they are being used or taken advantage of.

5) **"Message me!"** wouldn't have made sense in 1995 . . . like "Letter me"?

6) **"Bimbo"** used to mean a well-dressed man. Today in Mexico, "Bimbo" is a popular brand of snack foods. Today's Urban dictionary defines "bimbo": A girl who is stupid, wears lots of make-up and is obsessed with boys and clothes.

Sidebar 8E

The listeners' generation, co-cultures, and experiences offer clues to predict how those listeners will define certain words. As people move and change, the definitions of their words move and change. One example is "mango." For many U.S. Americans, "mango" is a tropical fruit, but in central Pennsylvania, they use "mango" for the food that most of the country calls green peppers or bell peppers. Often younger generations innocently use slang that their parents and grandparents consider to be vulgar, rude, and disrespectful. Understanding and complying with generational, cultural, and local linguistic characteristics demonstrates appreciation for the listeners' age, culture, religion, and experience. The same words that open doors into the hearts of one generation in a certain location may slam doors shut with another generation in another place. Meanings of words are not static; meanings of words change.

Insensitivity to the changing definitions of words can seem like disrespect to those we love.
© Iakov Filimonov/Shutterstock.com

Words Are Arbitrary

Words are not only symbolic, ambiguous, and changeable, they are also arbitrary. "Arbitrary" is the fourth property of words. The sounds that comprise a word are random (except in the case of onomatopoeia). There is nothing about the sound of "sh" and "oo" that inherently indicates foot protection or "kuh" and "ee" that naturally indicates the thing that opens locks. As long as the sender and receiver agree that those sets of sounds equal those ideas or feelings then they do.

Arbitrary
the characteristic of words that states the sounds of the words are random and do not affect meaning.

Problems arise when two different communities use the same word/set of sounds for different things. For example, many British English speakers understand that "bin" means a container for rubbish. Many American English speakers understand that "bin" means a container for things they want to keep. It's not hard to imagine the problems that arise. Can you hear the English woman exclaim, "You put my passport in the bin?!" We can remedy such situations by recognizing that the sounds we've been using to communicate are not sacred or fixed. They are arbitrary. We are free to adapt the arbitrary sounds of our words to make them more useful.

Activist librarian Sanford Berman (1982) wrote: "Too often we wrongly assume that other people use words as we do. We therefore wrongly assume that other people mean what we mean. And this is when we have misunderstandings . . . . If you want to lessen misunderstandings, try to find out what people mean, not what words mean."

"If you want to lessen misunderstandings, try to find out what people mean, not what words mean" - Sanford Berman
© Dmytro Gilitukha/Shutterstock.com

Many relational and logistical problems can be prevented or solved by finding the "right" way to say something, the way that transfers your meaning as faithfully as possible to your listener, regardless of dictionary definitions. Ignore these

Sidebar 8F

four properties of words and you risk contention and confusion. Employ the four properties to bring understanding; the choice is yours. Words have four properties; they are symbolic, ambiguous, changeable, and arbitrary.

Words Have Power

In addition to having four properties, words also have two kinds of power: name power and frame power.

Words Have Name Power

Name power means that once something has a name or a label, it becomes malleable and useful. Three stories follow. The first shows the naming power of words to transform a totally dependent, special-needs young woman into an international and political activist. The second story shows the naming power of words to transform an embarrassed scholar and public speaker into a confident professional. The third story demonstrates the naming power of words to oppress or to empower groups of people.

Helen Keller

In the 1880's as an infant, Helen Keller barely survived a terrible fever that left her blind and deaf. By early adolescence, Helen's most common emotions seemed to be rage, self-pity, panic, and angry frustration. She was often hysterical and violent until Anne Sullivan taught her words through sign language (Merrick 2000; Wilkie 1969). As an adolescent, Helen learned to sign words for her ideas, and her environment. With words, she could interact with her family. Although Helen Keller never recovered her sight or hearing, through the use of sign language, she traveled the world as a popular educator, journalist, and public speaker. She co-founded the American Civil Liberties Union (Sullivan 2003). The gift of language transformed Helen's temper tantrums into thoughtful optimism that captured the hearts of audiences around the world. Helen Keller is credited with axioms such as, "The highest result of education is tolerance" and "Walking with a friend in the dark is better than walking alone in the light." The transformation in Helen Keller demonstrates the transformative power of words.

© catwalker/Shutterstock.com

Like Helen, we benefit from each new word we learn. Helen was able to relieve her restless, anxious feelings by labeling and describing the feelings with specific words. We can do the same. Generalities such as, "I have issues" or "I just want it to be over" inhibit thoughtful problem solving. Concrete descriptions of what you mean by "issues," and what being "over" looks like, initiate a foundation for workable solutions and, eventually, increased happiness.

"Brené Brown".

Brené Brown researches, writes books and presents very popular lectures on a very unusual topic. Brown, Ph.D., L.M.S.W. (2010), has focused her career on "shame". She also dabbles in fear and vulnerability. Brown confirms and extends Helen Keller's story about the power of naming things. Brown contends

> "Shame . . . . hates having words wrapped around it - it can't survive being shared. Shame loves secrecy."
> -Brené Brown

that naming troublesome, counter-productive emotions, beliefs and thought processes can strip those feelings of their power. Brown describes her own humiliating, very public failure and how it affected her. She felt terrible (hot face, racing heart, time slowing down, dry mouth and tunnel vision) until she told the story to an accepting friend. The, "I'm such an idiot" shame-loop playing in her head succumbed to the virtues of courage and connection when she voiced the names of the tormenting feelings. Brown asserts that ". . . shame hates it when we reach out and tell our story. It hates having words wrapped around it-it can't survive being shared. Shame loves secrecy. The most dangerous thing to do after a shaming experience is hide or bury our story. When we bury our story, the shame metastasizes" (2010, p. 10–11). Brown's research and Keller's experiences both point to the power of assigning words to ideas, objects, and emotions, but there is also a more clandestine power of vocabulary. Certain subtleties of words can make us more interested or less interested in particular topics.

"Sanford Berman"

Sanford Berman, a self-proclaimed librarian activist (1982) purported, "The kind of language we use in library catalog labels is interconnected to the kind of thinking we do." Berman called some of the labels used in his city's library, such as *Women as accountants* (Would you expect to see *Men as accountants?*) *crippled people,* and *Jewish question* "humanity-degrading, intellect-constricting rubbish" (1982, p. 16). Berman fought long and hard for additional subject headings and for a change of the biased subject headings reflecting what he saw as racism, sexism, and Christo-centrism used by the Library of Congress.

Words have name power. Hellen Keller assigned a name for objects and ideas, empowering her to manipulate the things and use them. Brené Brown used words to weaken the power of shame and fear to live a whole-hearted life. Sanford Berman thoughtfully chose specific labels, to resist oppression. A limited pool of words stagnates thinking and doing. An expanding vocabulary is an expanding mind and influence.

Words Have Frame Power

Framing
the manipulation of perceptions by highlighting certain aspects

Frame power varies from name power. Name power is the influence of a label. Framing is the influence of a set of words used in conjunction with a name. Specifically, framing is the manipulation of perceptions by highlighting certain aspects. Robert Entman (1993) explored the enormous power of framing to influence how receivers interpret a message. As we speak, we frame events, objects, and groups as problems or solutions, as causes or effects, and as good or bad.

© Air Images/Shutterstock.com

I remember my dad's first snow skiing experience. My husband, dad, and I had approached the mountain just after noon. My husband convinced Dad to skip the lessons and ride the lift with us to an advanced intermediate slope where Dad and I were left to traverse the narrow switchbacks overlooking rocky, 50-foot drop-offs. A slip-up would mean a trip to the hospital and possibly the morgue. Dad had almost no experience turning, so his survival strategy was to ski the straight portions, approximately 50 feet, then sit/fall down at the curve so he could turn the skis while he was in a sitting position. He would then push himself up with the poles and repeat this process over and over and over. Hours later the lengthening shadows brought the ski patrol to help us down to the base. Dad was so sore that evening, he could hardly lift his arms to feed himself. We told the waitress that he had skied the "Plunge" and made up magnificent stories of his athletic hero-ism. The telling of this tale always engendered lots of laughs and admiration for Dad, the legendary mountain-survivor, until the day I heard a particular person tell the story as if it were a shameful thing that Dad had trouble getting down the mountain and that he was so sore later. The skiing story, told by one person, framed my dad as a marvel, but told by another person made him appear weak, maybe even shameful. Framing, it's not what you say, but how you say it.

Euphemisms
ambiguities used to protect or benefit the listener, another person, or an organization

Doublespeak
ambiguity used to protect or benefit the speaker, another person, or an organization to purposely deceive the listener

Euphemisms and Doublespeak Are Part of Framing

Euphemisms and doublespeak are two ways to use ambiguities to influence how the receivers interpret a message. Euphemisms use ambiguities to protect or benefit the listener or another person or organization. For example, a fellow might euphemistically

say that his brother's watch "fell off the back of a truck" rather than "is stolen property" in order to protect his brother. **Doublespeak** is like euphemism, but it uses ambiguity to protect the speaker. The intension of a doublespeaker is to deceive or obscure for his or her personal benefit. A divorcing couple who wants to appear happily married in a particular situation may describe their interactions as "discussions" instead of "fights." The frames that we use and that we hear from others including euphemisms and doublespeak, influence how we feel about a topic. Since feelings influence thoughts and actions, euphemisms and doublespeak can significantly change an environment and a relationship.

Vividness Is Part of Framing

Vividness is forming discrete and remarkable mental images. Vividness frames a message as important because it includes action verbs, metaphors, colorful nouns, and descriptors. Look at Roosevelt's "The Man in the Arena" speech from the beginning of the chapter. Roosevelt arrests our attention with the staccato of his diction, "It's not the critic who counts"; and with his word pictures: dust, sweat, blood. In that same speech, Roosevelt used action words and descriptors: "strives," "comes short again and again," "spends himself," "great enthusiasms," and "great devotions." Roosevelt's vividness has invigorated generations.

As they advised families and co-workers, Smalley and Trent (1988) combined the concept of vividness with I-statements as a technique to restore relationships (I-statements are discussed in Chapter 9). Imagine a young wife telling her husband, "When you use my ideas during group discussions without acknowledging me,

Vividness
discrete and remarkable mental images

Sidebar 8H   **MLK Used Vividness**

© Forty3Zero/Shutterstock.com

Look for Reverend Dr. Martin Luther King, Jr. metaphors in this excerpt from his 1963 "I Have a Dream" oration. "But one hundred years later, the Negro is not free. One hundred years later, the life of the Negro is still sadly crippled by the manacles of segregation and the chains of discrimination . . . languished in the corners of American society and finds himself an exile in his own land . . . . I have a dream that my four little children will one day live in a nation where they will not be judged by the color of their skin but by the content of their character."

The vividness of a celebrity association promoted public awareness of the importance of checking pets for ticks.

© Noppadon stocker/Shutterstock.com

I feel like a little slave girl." Her phrase: "I feel like" makes this an I-statement. She accepts the responsibility for her own feelings instead of saying that her husband makes her feel a certain way. "Little slave girl" is a word picture. The concrete nature of word pictures conveys ideas and feelings more efficiently than other more abstract words. Practice painting word pictures and combining those mental images with I-statements. The clarity of this combination may save a relationship or help you know when to end a relationship. See the information about I-statements in chapter 9.

Vividness is enhanced with word pictures, I-statements, and also by involving a colorful celebrity. For example, health professionals and the general public paid much more attention to Lyme disease after rocker Avril Lavigne told her story, energizing her fans to check themselves and their pets for tick bites and the resulting bulls-eye rash. Since the vivid Avril celebrity story, networks have broadcast warnings and anecdotes for their recently interested listeners.

Concision Is Part of Framing

Concision
brevity

The quality of brevity is called concision. Sometimes less is more. When we use more words than necessary, our intended message is diluted. Listeners may get bored, quit listening, and start pseudolistening, occasionally adding a nod or an "oh" just to be polite. Foster the skill of concision. When you want your meaning to be clearly understood, cut clutter words.

Power Talk Is Part of Framing

Powertalkers load their voices with energy eliminating fillers like "um" and "so, yeah." They avoid tag questions that invite affirmation at the end of a statement like, "don't you think?" Powertalkers champion concision to eradicate

---

Cut the Clutter

Here is a list of transitional and filler words that may be better left unsaid:

"that being said"
"in order to"
"I am here to talk about"
"Today, I want to"
"In the world, today"
"basically"
"you know"
"like"

© Tyler Olson/Shutterstock.com

Sidebar 8I

Sidebar 8J

disclaimers and hedges. Hedges are added qualifications or contingencies to lessen the impact, like "kind of." Veteran industry leader, Craig Johnson (1987) found powertalkers to be more attractive, credible, and persuasive than other communicators. Professionals such as medical doctors and professors, even authoritative politicians and parents often use power talk with their patients, students, opponents, and children. Columnist for *The Wall Street Journal,* Sue Shellenbarger (2018) noted that some individuals, especially women, use weak talk. They reduce the importance of their contributions by over justifying their research methods rather than describing their findings. It can be refreshing, motivating, and empowering to hear someone get right to the point. Powertalkers attract followers.

On the negative side, occasionally powertalk inhibits relationship-building and mutual understanding. Potential friends may feel that they must prepare and rehearse before they try engaging with a powertalker. Listeners often feel too rushed, exhilarated, or intimidated to ask the powertalkers to clarify an idea or provide an example. Concision and energy make the speaker seem more intentional and powerful, not necessarily more approachable or friendly.

Refusal Styles are Part of Framing

Which newly health-conscious guy is more likely to resist the temptation of stopping for a double bacon cheese burger and fries on the way home: Paul who says, "I don't eat fast food" or Daniel who says, "I can't eat fast food"? The answer is Paul. Individuals who say, "I don't" instead of "I can't" are more likely to persist in their goals, except under certain conditions (Patrick and Hagtvedt, 2011). "I don't" suggests stability and a personal conviction which empowers us psychologically. Conversely, "I can't" makes us feel deprived and weak. The power of dropping "I can't" in favor of "I don't" supports goal-motivated behavior in other ways as well. When a friend suggests that you should buy a cool, new gadget with your credit card, try, "I don't spend more than I have" instead of "I can't spend more than I have". You may find it easier to stick to your schedule with "I don't watch movies before I finish my work" instead of "I can't watch movies before I finish my work". "Can't" vs. "don't": the subtle nuance of the refusal is powerful.

Words have Ethical Implications

Because of the power of words including euphemisms, doublespeak, and power-talk to influence minds, emotions, and actions, a discussion of ethics is in order.

Responsible Words Promote Civility

As we said in Chapter 1, civility involves valuing others instead of judging them or passing over them. Krista Tippett in *The Art of Conversation* (2015) said that civil communicators suspend their suspicion as they listen to expand their thinking. Tippett sees civility as an attitude of open mindedness, expecting the best of others demonstrated through listening. She described civil speech as more generous, curious, and hospitable and less convincing or advocating. But you might ask, "Aren't civil people called upon at times to convince, advocate, and persuade for good causes?" Of course, they are; but all persuasion does not have to take the same form. Paul Brandeis Raushenbush (2015) of the Huffington Post offered his insight about persuading through listening in contrast to persuading through

Krista Tippett received the 2013 National Humanities Medal from U.S. President Obama.

Alex Wong/Staff/Getty

rhetoric: "Sometimes we have the fortune of talking with someone who is such a good listener that, during the course of the conversation, we learn new things about ourselves and expand our understanding of the world." Raushenbush was describing a way that he has been persuaded not by a well-constructed argument, but by being asked questions that lead him into new ways of thinking and behaving. The Apostle Paul in his letter to the Romans described the divine use of civility for persuasion in Romans 2:4: "God's kindness is intended to lead you to repentance." In some cases, simply expressing curiosity and courtesy may be more persuasive than arguing. Some first steps toward linguistic civility include inclusive language, questioning, I-statements, and proper apologies (see Chapter 9).

Inclusive language
language that avoids expressions that highlight how a person or group is different

Inclusion Promotes Civility

Inclusive language avoids expressions that might separate some of the listeners from the speaker or from the group (Drmmond & Orbe, 2009). One type of language that may exclude others is **jargon**, the vocabulary of a particular group, profession, or trade (Dobkin and Pace, 2006). Heavy use of jargon in the presence of those uninitiated into the colloquialisms may intentionally or unintentionally communicate, "You're not one of us; you don't belong here." A person with no knowledge of basketball or baseball has limited access to a conversation that sounds like *Sports Illustrated* articles describing players "dribbling against the Spurs" and "whiffing against Chicago." The sports jargon may limit opportunities for engaging with potential friends or business contacts. Consider as well the opportunities we have as listeners to set speakers free to communicate in a way that is natural to them when we have knowledge of a broad array of topics and vocabulary. The responsibility of inclusion can be shouldered by both the speaker and the listener.

Jargon
the vocabulary of a particular group, profession, or trade

Talking about events to which only some of the listeners are invited is another example of exclusive conversation that inhibits community building (Cowen & Bochantin 2011). For example, if you are invited to a party for only those with a certain level of income or popularity, etc., your friends who were not invited or not eligible may be interested in hearing you talk about the exclusive event for a while, but continual emphasis on the event that has excluded your friends often results in interpersonal distance. You would be more civil to your uninvited friend if you found topics of general interest with vocabulary understood by all.

Another example of exclusive language is unnecessarily gender-specific words, such as "man," "mankind," and masculine pronouns, he, his, him, because they may be interpreted as excluding women. Inclusive speech trades traditional masculine labels for neutral labels for careers that may be engaged in by either females or males. Because the word includes both sexes we call the word "inclusive." Inclusive language expresses value for the work and the worker.

Inclusive Language

© Joseph Sohm/Shutterstock.com

Exclusion says	Inclusion says
mailman	letter carrier
policeman	police officer
chairman	department chair
congressman	legislator

© John Roman Images/Shutterstock.com

1. How many other words can you think of that may intentionally or unintentionally exclude others?
2. When have you felt excluded by the language of others?
3. When have you excluded others through jargon or unnecessarily gender specific language?

Sidebar 8K

Questions Can Promote Civility

Another step in developing civility, in addition to inclusion is taking the time to find out about others. Individualistic cultures such as the U.S. tend to be egocentric. I am the main character in the movie of me! To appreciate the value of others, the others must have opportunities to express themselves. Asking open-ended, unbiased questions courteously invites the others to share their worth and contributions (Dobkin and Pace 2006). Find more about these types of questions in the interview portion of this textbook. You might record some of your interactions and then compare the number of directives versus the number of questions you speak.

The Creative Power of Words Can Promote Civility

We use words to create our identities on social media as well as in face-to-face encounters (Stritze, Nguyen & Durkin, 2004). Words set systems in motion for families, social groups, economies and governments (Herrmann 2007). Words create relationships (Wood, 1982). Ancient Israel's King Solomon summed it up in Proverbs 18:21. Life and death are in the power of the tongue and those who love it will eat its fruit. Civility is not passivity. Passivity is inaction and can be very dangerous. Civility channels the energies of individuals and groups through inclusion, questions, and creative communication to build a better future. Civility provides the framework that can engage others into the most important conversations.

Sidebar 8L

Record your conversations to count the number of questions you ask.

(c) Bplanet/Shutterstock.com

Summary

This chapter is dedicated to making our words work for us and others. We've reviewed the four properties of words. They are symbolic, ambiguous, changeable, and arbitrary. We have reviewed the power of the words that we say and hear to name and frame the things that we think and the way we think about them. Civility creates and empowers personal, professional, and political relationships. With language comes amplified opportunity and responsibility. Consider choosing an aspect of language to practice for a week. You might adopt the vocabulary of a co-culture, use ambiguity more purposefully, concentrate on understanding people instead of words, expand your vocabulary, limit tag questions and hedges, use inclusive labels, or practice refusals by saying "I don't" instead of "I can't." Unexamined language is like oil on a runaway pig, it keeps you from tackling the situation. Purposeful language is like a handle that helps you get a grip.

© Jenoche/Shutterstock.com

Vocabulary Words

Ambiguity	Doublespeak	Inclusive language
Arbitrary	Euphemism	Vividness
Concision	Framing	
Concrete	Jargon	

Discussion Questions

1. What are some new words that have been made up in your lifetime? New words for old meanings? New meanings for old words?
2. What are some words that have been appropriated from other languages?
3. Besides needing new words for new ideas, why do we change the meanings of words? Who benefits? Who loses?
4. When we are talking about current issues, we sometimes use derogatory terms to refer to people who disagree with us. How does this framing of those people in those terms affect how we approach them? How does it change how we approach the disagreement?
5. When have you used ambiguous language to spare someone's feelings?
6. Can you think of a time a public speaker might have been wise to use more ambiguous language in his speech?
7. What is the connection between civility and inclusive language?
8. Are there words that have particular connotations for you that most other people don't seem to react to in the same way?

References

Bandura, A. (1997). *Self-efficacy: The exercise of control*. New York: Freeman.

Berman, S., & Danky, J. P. (Eds.). (1982). *Alternative library literature: A biennial anthology*. Jefferson, NC: McFarland & Company Inc.

Bush, B. (1990). *Choices and change* (speech). Wellesley, MA. Retrieved from Rhetoric Top 100 Speeches, www.americanrhetoric.com/speeches/ barbarabush-welleslycommencement.html

Brown, B. (2010). *The gifts of imperfection*. Center City, Minnesota: Hazelden Publishing.

Comello, M. L. G. (2009). William James on "Possible Selves": Implications for studying identity in communication contexts. *Communication Theory, 19*, 337–350.

Cowen, R. L, & Bochantin, J.E. (2011). Blue-collar employees' work/life metaphors: Tough similarities, imbalance separation, and opposition. *Qualitative Research Reports in Communication, 12*, 19–26.

Dobkin, B. A., & Pace, R. C. (2006). Communication in a changing world. New York: The McGraw-Hill Companies.

Drummond, D.K., & Orbe, M. P. (2009). "Who are you trying to be?": Identity gaps within interracial encounters. *Qualitative Research Reports in Communication, 10*, 81–87.

Edwards, A., Edwards, C., Wahl, S., & Myers, S. A. (2013). The communication age connecting and engaging. Thousand Oaks, CA: SAGE Publications, Inc.

Entman, R. (1993). Framing: Toward clarification of a fractured paradigm. *Journal of Communication, 43*, 51–58.

Gordon, T. (1977). *Leadership effectiveness training*. New York: The Berkley Publishing Group.

Herrmann, A. F. (2007). "People get emotional about their money": Performing masculinity in a financial discussion board. *Journal of Computer-Mediated Communication, 12*, 165–188.

Johnson, J. A. (2012, November 30). Are "I" statements better than "You" statements? (Blog post). Retrieved from https:/www.psychologytoday.com/blog/ cui-bono/201211/are-i-statements-better-you-statements

Keller, H. (2003). *The story of my life: The restored classic*. New York: Norton, W.W. & Company Inc.

Korzybski, A. (1933). *Science and sanity: An Introduction to non-Aristotelian systems and general semantics*. (5th ed.). Brooklyn, NY: Institute of General Semantics.

Luft, J. (1984). *Group processes: An Introduction to group dynamics* (3rd ed.). Palo Alto, CA; Mayfield.

Merrick, M. (Writer), & Tass, N. (Director). (2000). The miracle worker. In S. Beugen (Producer). United States: Walt Disney Television.

Miley Cyrus, Liam Hemsworth have matching tattoos: Actor gets Teddy Roosevelt quote inked on arm. (2012, October 13). Retrieved from https://www. huffingtonpost.com/2012/10/13/liam-hemsworth-miley-cyrus-matching-tattoo-theodore-roosevelt-quote_n_1963807.html"

Nesterov, A.V. (2009). On semantic, pragmatic, and dialectic triangles. *Automatic-Documentation and Mathematical Linguistics, 43*, 132–137.

Ogden, C. K., & Richards I. A. (1923). *The meaning of meaning.* London: Kegan, Paul, Trench, Trubner.

Patrick, V. and Hagtvedt, H. (2012). "I don't" versus "I can't": when empowered refusal motivates goal-directed behavior. *Journal of Consumer Research, 39*(2), 371–382.

Raushenbush, P. B. (Host). (2015). *Krista Tippett's art of conversation.* Huff-Post Religion (Audiopodcast). Retrieved from https://soundcloud.com/huffpost-religion/krista-tippetts-art-of-conversation

Roosevelt, T. (1910, April 23). *Citizenship in a republic* (speech). Paris, France. Retrieved from design.caltech.edu/erik/Misc/Citizenship_in_a_Republic.pdf

Smalley, G., & Trent, J. (1988). *The language of love.* New York: Simon & Schuster.

Stritzke, W.K., Nguyen, A. & Durkin, L. (2004) Shyness and computer-mediated communication: A self-presentational theory perspective. *Media Psychology, 6*, 1–22.

These 12 everyday words used to have completely different meanings. (2014, February 26). *Huffington Post.* Retrieved from http://www.huffingtonpost.com/2014/02/26/words-that-have-changed-meaning_n_4847343.html

Vaux, B. (2007). *Linguistic field methods.* Eugene, OR: Wipf and Stock Publishers.

Wood, J. T. (1982). Communication and relational culture: Bases for the study of human relationships. *Communication Quarterly, 30*, 75–84.

Additional Readings

Alternative Library Literature: A Biennial Anthology
edited by S. Berman & J. P. Danky

Quiet: The Power of Introverts in a World That Can't Stop Talking
by S. Cain

Nonviolent Communication: A Language of Life
By Marshall Rosenberg, Ph.D., & Deepak Chopra

Better Communicators Are Problem Solvers

By Matthew R. Olsen, Ed.D.

© Sergey Nivens/Shutterstock.com

9

It happens all day, every day, and the better we are at dealing with it, the more enjoyable life can become. What am I talking about? *CONFLICT*. It occurs at school, at work, during the commute, on the bus, in line at the checkout lane, and even while we are getting lunch. It happens all the time. It can be as simple as having to wait at a stoplight when you are a little late for class. It can be deciding whether or not to stop for coffee and be late for class. It can be sitting though the dry and boring lecture about something you don't care about without caffeine. Conflict happens every day. I am not necessarily talking about the screaming in your face, spit flying, red-faced rants, but simple everyday conflict.

Conflict is a state of disagreement, hostility, discord, or argument that can exist between people when they believe their needs, beliefs, goals (Cahn & Abigail, 2007; Folger, Poole, & Stutman, 2009), or characteristics are irreconcilable. Conflict can exist between two individuals, a group of individuals, countries, people groups, family members, or within ourselves.

So we see expressions of external conflict all around us: wars and military exercises on almost every continent, road-raging drivers who are so mad that they will cause an accident, sports fans biting their fingernails to the nubs and weeping when their favorite team misses the final kick/shot/goal. And those are just the external conflicts that are visible to us. We haven't

© Oleg Mikhaylov/Shutterstock.com

Conflict
a state of disagreement, hostility, discord, or argument that can exist between people when they believe their needs, beliefs, or characteristics are irreconcilable

even discussed the internal conflicts that we each deal with on a daily basis. Internal conflict is created by the difficulty of two opposing choices that you must decide by yourself. You may ask yourself: how do you deal with the internal conflict of how to respond to someone who is upset with you? It may be the person in your small group project who has different ideas from yours as to the direction of your group project. Do you voice your concern, anticipating that it will not be well-received, or do you just go along with everyone else? What about the internal pressure of opposing something that you strongly believe in but which is not accepted by your group of close friends? Needless to say, we are plagued by both internal and external conflict throughout our lives and throughout each day. How we deal with it is part of the measure of our maturity.

With all this discussion about conflict, you might think that conflict is only negative and therefore should be avoided like the plague. We tend to want to run from conflict. But, didn't Jesus get upset? Didn't God have strong emotion? Is conflict always bad? I believe that there are times when not expressing frustration and refusing to have conflict is a far worse option than having a good, strong argument. Conflict can be the spark for the change necessary in your life, or it can be the soul-sucking, life-crippling crusher of hope. When are conflict and anger good? When are they destructive? There is good conflict and bad conflict, but both push us to change. Without conflict, there is no motivation for change. Conflict spurs us to change. While change is not always welcomed, change can be good. It's what we do with the conflict that can be part of the problem or part of the solution.

© Iakov Filimonov/Shutterstock.com

Goal incompatibility
one of the most common causes of conflict, in which both people want something different

What causes problems in your life? Really stop and think about it for half a second. Has a relationship not gone the way you wanted it to go? Has something ever taken longer to accomplish than you would have liked it to? Have you wanted a friendship to move to something more than friendship and found the other person is happy with your friendship just like it is? Back into the friend zone you go! We have all had a time when we didn't have enough money to buy something that we really wanted or had a close friend says something critical about us. We can have conflict over disagreements with people; disappointments over unmet expectations of someone; incompatible goals; differences in values, beliefs, and needs; or simply misunderstanding someone or being misunderstood ourselves.

Before we start talking about how to handle problems with respect and dignity, let's look at some of the reasons that cause us to fight with other people. **Goal incompatibility** is one of the most common causes of conflict. You want Italian food, and your friend wants a sandwich for dinner. Neither is good, bad, or for that matter better or worse; it is just different. What you do with this simple incompatibility conflict can either enrich your relationship or not. Tannen (1992), in her book, *That's Not What I Meant! How Conversational Style Makes or Breaks Relationships* explains how when we have conflict, we begin the process of negotiations to see which option gets picked. Negotiations can look like: "We ate where I wanted last time, let's go where you want and get a sandwich." "My ex-boyfriend works at the sandwich shop; I would rather not run into him." This conflict occurs before we even begin to look at the context of the situation and relationship.

Understanding Context: Wait . . . What?

As we learned in earlier chapters, context refers to the circumstances that form the setting of communication. We pick up on nonverbal **context clues** or clearly state the relationship so that we really understand what is being said and what is not being said. **High context communication** refers to a communication situation or relationship in which there are numerous nonverbal cues to which you must adhere. **Low context** refers to situations in which the interaction is governed by clearly expressed expectations. In certain cultures, the status, age, relationship, and education of a person will more greatly influence how you should interact. For instance, you are outside of school, and you see a fellow student and your professor. You have known them for the same amount of time. You will more than likely say hello to your fellow student followed by their first name. "Hey, Mark." "What's up, Matt?" But can you do that to your professor? What if they are an older professor? What if they have an earned doctorate? "Hey, Mark." "Hello, Dr. Olsen." (Don't make the mistake of calling a professor "Mr." or "Mrs." when they have a PhD. Some professors *really* don't like it. Trust me, I know.) Does it matter that the interaction is not taking place in the classroom? Have they asked you to call them by their first name? These questions must be answered in the split second when you see them, and this is just one high context situation in a low context environment.

context clues
hints at the true meaning of the conversation that can be found in the setting of the communication

High context communication
a communication situation or relationship in which there are numerous unstated expectations to which you must adhere

Low context communication
communication situations in which the interaction is governed by clearly expressed expectations

High context situations have a lot of understood requirements that are not verbalized but that influence the interaction. Low context situations have few or no unstated requirements to be acted upon. Historically, men have said what they mean and have been considered low context and women have been considered high context. High context communication and low context communication can also apply to men and women. Men tend to have direct, content-focused listening without reading into the situation and women tend to focus on the overall communication experience (Johnson, 2000; Sargent & Weaver, 2003). Sometimes, men may not pick up on the subtle clues that women can give them. So how do you understand what someone is really meaning in a situation? Pick up on the context clues, which are hints at the true meaning of the conversation. These clues can be part of her

© Monkey Business Images/Shutterstock.com

© Billion Photos/Shutterstock.com

nonverbal communication as well as your communication history. Good communicators are able to evaluate the situation as it is happening and determine how to positively impact that situation. They are also able to build upon past interactions and be part of the solutions to problems rather than the cause of problems.

Dialectical Tensions: or Teeter/Totter Dynamics

Dialectical tensions
the tension that arises between opposing relational needs

So what else brings conflict every day? We also have conflict about different relationship needs whether they are expressed or hidden. We call the tension that arises between opposing relational needs **dialectical tensions** (Baxter, 1988; Baxter & Montgomery, 1997). They are autonomy vs. connection, stability vs. change, and expression vs. privacy. You feel these when someone wants something in your relationship, and you want something different, and they are common in intimate relationships (Baxter & Braithwaite, 2009). As we take a closer look, we need to understand the complexity of these tensions. It is not just one person in the relationship wanting one thing and the other person wanting the other; both parties want both. They just want them to different degrees. Many times dialectical tensions arise within ourselves; these come day-to-day and moment-to-moment and compound the tensions we have with others.

Autonomy vs. connection
tension between wanting to be independent and staying connected to others

The first type we need to look at is **autonomy vs. connection**. It is the need to feel our own independence, paired with the need to feel connection with someone else. It is at the heart of a classic struggle between adolescents and their parents (Peterson & Bush, 1999). This may have occurred when you left home for the first time. You want the autonomy from your parents that comes from being in college, but your parents want the connection that they have had for the past 18 years. I was the last one to leave the house when I left for college, thus making my parents "empty nesters." I was happy to be in college and wanted to start the new chapter in my life; however, my mother didn't have the same ideas. I wanted autonomy, but my mother wanted connection. It took a semester or two until my father and I talked about it. He told me that, due to my strong desire for autonomy, I had left my parents with little in the way of connection. The only time I called was when I needed something. I felt the only time they called me was when they needed nothing. I was communicating for information, and my mom was communicating for relationship. My father asked that I call more often and give my mother what I considered "useless" information so that she felt connected. Then he promised that they would only call me when they had something that needed to be said. We helped solve each other's needs first by communicating and then by seeing through each other's eyes. That way we better understood each other and helped meet each

© Lisa F. Young/Shutterstock.com

other's needs as well as our own. Interestingly enough, as I got older, I wanted more connection with my parents. When I got married, my mother wanted more connection with my wife than with me. It seems that when the mother of two boys had a son (me) who got married, that meant that she got the daughter she wanted. Because of this experience, when my son went away to college, I had the same conversation with him that my father had with me.

© Jakub Zak/Shutterstock.com

The next one to look at is **stability vs. change**. This tension addresses our desire for things to remain relatively constant, expected, and with no surprises against the need to have new experiences, variety, and change. One of the things that I like about higher education is that every semester there is a new set of classes, students, experiences, and people. It feeds my desire for change. My wife, however, likes things to be planned for, consistent, and without surprises. I know it is hard for her when I come in and out of the blue say, "I want to go scuba diving in the Galapagos Islands" or "I want to get a motorcycle" or "Let's fly to New York City for the weekend" or "I want to take a week to go on a 40-mile hiking trek in Colorado and I want to do it by myself." (All of which I have said to her. Actually, one time I just put her in the car and drove her to the airport, bags packed, and we flew to NYC.) For some of you reading this, you think, "Oh, my goodness! I can't imagine being married to this guy." Others may think, "I want to go to there." That may be your own personal preference for stability vs. change.

Stability vs. change
tension that addresses our desire for things to remain relatively constant, expected, and with no surprises against the need to have new experiences, variety, and change

Engage your own personal preference with someone else's preference, mix it together, and you get conflict. When you go out to eat with someone, do you like to eat at a familiar place because you know what you like and what you will get, or do you want to try something new and different? Does the thought of doing the same thing over and over again in a relationship sound suffocating or peaceful to you? Does doing something different every weekend sound adventurous or anxiety producing? The thought of living in a different country for three months during the summer break sounds incredible to me, but it makes my wife want to throw up on my shirt. She realizes that I need the right amount of variety and adventure, or I can be quite a jerk. I realize that without stability and peace, she starts throwing things. By seeing how the other person thinks about dialectical tension not as being wrong but as different, we can be part of the solution instead of the problem. When I told her that there was no way that I could go to the Galapagos Islands because we couldn't afford it, and I would be gone too long, I was valuing her and addressing her valid concerns for stability. I decided not to go. Then she valued my need for change and said that this was a trip of a lifetime, and there is no way that I could not go scuba diving. I almost cried when she told me that, and it WAS the trip of a lifetime. She saw through my eyes and I saw through hers. We were able to resolve the conflict by addressing the dialectical tension between us.

Finally, let's look at the tension of **expression vs. privacy**. Sometimes we want to share information with others, and at other times, we'd just as soon keep it to

Expression vs. privacy
tension regarding sharing personal information

© Dragon Images/Shutterstock.com

ourselves (Vanlear, 1991). This was the classic argument with my mother and father. My mother was from New York and always wanted to be doing something, talking about something, or planning something. My father grew up a farmer's son from Minnesota and didn't like talking about stuff outside of the family. My dad didn't want to let people know we had a new dog. My mom wanted to tell everyone about how I was doing in school, my shoe size, my girlfriend, my sports, my room, my posters, my clothes, and, well, you get the idea. My mother liked to know about things and talk to her friends about them. My father did not. They had to find a balance. Communicators who are problem solvers don't try to rush someone to share more personal information before they are comfortable. They help the other person feel comfortable with them and provide a safe place to share personal information. With the free expression that many young people have, it isn't always a bad thing to keep some things private. Some things don't need to be shared with the world. My friends and I will send out a text to each other instead of a tweet when we only want certain people to know. We use the hashtag #untweetable; this has saved me many times from saying things publicly that I may have regretted later. Just because it *can* be said publicly on social media doesn't mean that it *should* be said publicly.

What are some things that you fight about? Are they different with different people? What are your pet peeves? What really bothers you about your friends? What really bothers you about yourself? When you start to ask these deeper questions instead of just getting mad, you start working toward the solutions to your conflicts. Usually we just get mad; but in order for us to get past the situations to be problem solvers, we need to look at what causes the initial conflict and then address that root.

Conflict Done Poorly: How Not to Do It

© Cartoon Resource/Shutterstock.com

So what do we do about it? How do we handle conflict? How do we become part of the solution to conflict? Before we begin to see how to do it well, let's talk about how we have done it poorly. When we understand the problem of the way we communicate, then we can address the actual problem. In the book of Revelation, the end times of the earth are described as the 4 Horsemen of the Apocalypse. When it come to relationship dynamics, John Gottman (2001) identifies the Four Horsemen of the Apocalypse: criticism, contempt, defensiveness, and stonewalling.

Gottman uses the term "Apocalypse" because the word describes the end times, and these behaviors often bring the end of times of that relationship.

Criticism attacking someone's personality, character, or style in an attempt to make the person wrong rather than their argument wrong. You know that you are using criticism when you don't have anything else to say in regards to your argument, and instead of closing your mouth, you pick on the individual personally, or you point out the most insignificant piece of disagreement, and blow it out of proportion. "Your argument couldn't be right because you haven't finished your degree." "I had to wait out here for five minutes before you came to pick me up and take me out to dinner." "These homemade chocolate chip cookies don't have enough chocolate chips." "When you bring me a cup of coffee, it needs less sugar and more cream." If you ever respond to someone who does any of these things for you, you are stupid—ok, maybe just foolish. Don't focus on the little things that they did wrong and miss what they really did well. The key is to be analytical without being critical. Evaluate and analyze based on the arguments rather than what you think about the person.

In my first job teaching after I finished my master's degree, I was assigned a veteran teacher to mentor me and assist me in not screwing up, or rather teaching better. She was a phenomenal teacher who had many unique (read: INCREDIBLE!) ways of teaching the class. I still use some of the things that she taught me that first semester. She was smart, funny, opinionated, and a great teacher. Our principal, however, did not share my admiration for her. Instead, the principal seemed to be threatened by her ideas, not because she was coming up with new and different ways of teaching something that had been taught the same way for many years, but because she felt threatened by the popularity of this teacher. In many of the staff meetings, this incredible teacher would come up with a great idea to do things better and get shut down by a critical principal who dismissed the person rather than the concept before the idea was even heard. It came to a head one day when the two of us were talking about teaching, and as usual, this teacher came up with another great idea. I told her that she needed to bring it up in staff meeting, and she said that she wouldn't because she would get shut down again. She liked the idea so much that she convinced me to bring the suggestion up in staff meeting and submit it like it was my own. After much convincing, I agreed to bring it up and act like it was my own idea. You know what happened: the principal loved my idea and praised me for thinking so creatively. Just think of how many great ideas were missed because the principal chose to criticize the individual rather than analyze the idea. I wonder how many great ideas were never thought up because of the critical tone that was in place around this teacher.

Contempt includes insulting a person through name-calling, sarcasm, hostility, mockery, sneering, eye-rolling, etc. Complete dismissiveness for the person and their argument. If you thought that criticism was bad, contempt is criticism's nasty older brother. People who use contempt as a tool when arguing, many times, have an

Criticism
attacking someone's personality, character, or style in an attempt to make the person wrong rather than their argument wrong

Contempt
insulting a person through name-calling, sarcasm, hostility, mockery, sneering, eye-rolling, etc.; complete dismissal the person and their argument

© Antonio Gravante/Shutterstock.com

argument with very little substance, so they resort to attacking you personally in order to win. They say, "You are an idiot." "How can you possibly think that way?" "That's stupid." "That's the dumbest thing I have ever heard." "My 10-year-old sister is smarter than you." It is an extremely aggressive approach people use in order to get you thinking less about your argument and more about yourself and your own insecurities. In that way, you are defending personal attacks rather than attempting to find a resolution in the conflict. Contempt can completely sabotage any type of success that you have had during the conflict. It sidetracks the argument from the issues at hand to personally attack the individual. Contempt communicates that you are so stupid that you aren't worth my time. It communicates that the blamed person is less than the accuser, and the criticizer is the better person. Contempt is dismissive and devaluing of a person. Malcolm Gladwell (2005) suggests that contempt is the greatest predictor of divorce. When couples show contempt for each other, their relationship is in real trouble. Contempt is so aggressive an emotion that it can also affect your immune system.

Gottman says that you might think that criticism is harmful because of its global condemnation of a person's character, but contempt is more harmful because it attempts to put someone on a lower plane than you. The accuser feels superior.

Defensiveness is playing the victim in an attempt to divert an attack or perceived attack. Making excuses, blaming the other person for your behavior, taking the smallest correction as a personal attack. While contempt is an over-the-top aggressive and offensive behavior, defensiveness is the opposite; it is a defensive move, thus the name. Defensive people are difficult to deal with since they can take the simplest suggestion and make it out to be something that it is not. Something that is not personal and not a reflection of character is blown way out of proportion. Defensive behavior loses objectivity. This is something I see a lot of my students dealing with on a regular basis.

Leaders who are defensive don't allow their subordinates to question them and take the slightest suggestion as a personal confrontation and attack. Subordinates who are defensive take the simplest correction as a major disappointment to their boss. Don't allow yourself to miss out on some great individuals from whom you can learn because you can't take correction. If you aren't open for correction, people won't want to teach and correct you. When people can't correct you, you will make the same mistakes over and over again. When people can't teach you, you will be dumb. Don't be dumb. Learn to take constructive criticism from people who have more experience and know more about the subject.

Stonewalling is ignoring the other person's argument completely, the silent treatment, muttering to yourself, changing the subject, leaving the situation, ignoring texts, sending calls straight to voicemail. Dealing with people who stonewall can be difficult; you don't know how to address the situation because the other person refuses

Defensiveness
playing the victim in an attempt to divert an attack or perceived attack; making excuses, blaming the other person for your behavior, taking the smallest correction as a personal attack

Stonewalling
ignoring the other person's argument completely, refusing to acknowledge the opponent's attempts at communication, muttering to yourself, changing the subject, leaving the situation as a conflict strategy

BECOMING A BETTER COMMUNICATOR

to engage. For a number of reasons, a stonewaller doesn't know how to interact in an argument and would rather ignore the situation and hope it goes away instead of trying to find the solution. Problem solvers need to pay good attention to "when" a stonewaller may be ready to discuss the situation and not just the "what" of the conversation. Create a safe and private place so that the stonewaller will be comfortable enough to engage in the conversation. Start the conversation with something like, "I would really like to talk about what happened between us last week. Is now a good time?" If they refuse, which is likely to happen, ask them when they would like to discuss it. More

© Spectral-Design/Shutterstock.com

than likely they will say, "I don't know"; you can suggest a couple of times that it would be beneficial to engage the situation. Keep at it. If you are a stonewaller, learn to communicate *before* you feel comfortable communicating. It doesn't have to be perfect, but good friends will be the ones who stick around. Trust them, and be trustworthy with them. You have the opportunity to make friends these next few years that can become lifelong friends. Make the most of these opportunities.

So we have learned what causes conflict and how we poorly address conflict, but before we talk about how to manage it, you might be thinking: What is conflict good for? Can we just live our lives without conflict? Can't we just give peace a chance? Well, there are some great benefits to conflict.

Conflict Can Be Beneficial: It's Not As Bad As You Think

Conflict and stress are bad for you, right? Actually, a 2012 report (Keller, et.al., 2012) suggests that it is not stress and conflict that are harmful for your health, but that your view of stress and conflict has a greater impact positively or negatively. It is your mindset that produces benefits or liabilities from conflict and stress. An additional study in 2012 suggest that when people view their stress and conflict responses as helpful to their situation, they had increased benefits physiologically. So, if you can view conflict as beneficial, you will have personal benefits for your body (Jamieson, et.al., 2012).

© Sandra Matic/Shutterstock.com

Conflict is beneficial (DeVito, 2009) for *establishing boundaries*. You may like to talk to close friends from at least an arm's length away. Your closest friend may think you don't speak loud enough and is a close talker, or an acquaintance always says hello and goodbye by giving long hugs. You, on the other hand, prefer a fist pound or a handshake, or perhaps your roommate uses your things without asking. They might think that's what they did with their siblings; therefore since you are roommates, you get to borrow each other's things. These are very basic boundaries that without conflict would continue to be crossed. The stronger the boundary breach, the greater the need for conflict. Conflict is the catalyst that forces parties to engage in discussions about what appropriate boundaries are for each individual.

Conflict is beneficial for *expressing feelings*. We all have those people and situations that we just have to, I mean get to, put up with. It could be the obnoxious guy down the hall, or the neighbor who doesn't clean his yard, or the co-worker who doesn't have a clue. What happens is that through the conflict of interpersonal relationships, you are forced to not just co-exist but rather engage. We express our feelings to deepen relationships or end those same relationships. Without good or bad conflict, relationships stagnate.

Conflict is beneficial for *identifying individual and group needs*. In group interactions, there are a few different roles that you might play: a task role, a maintenance role, or a disruptive role. Throughout the interactions with groups, you may switch roles as the situation changes. A person in a task role makes sure that the group goal is achieved. If the task is presenting something to the class for an assignment, a task role person takes notes, assigns parts, sets the next meeting, gets opinions, and challenges groupthink, which occurs when all members of a group think the same way and miss glaring holes in their system. A good task role individual will challenge groupthink respectfully by giving an alternate opinion against what everyone thinks. This is called playing the devil's advocate.

Task role
characteristics that individuals use to make sure that the group goal is achieved

Groupthink
when all members of a group think the same way and miss glaring problems in their system

Maintenance role
characteristics that individuals use to focus on people and maintaining good relationships

Disruptive roles
characteristics that individuals use to disrupt the agenda of the group by prioritizing their own needs and agendas in a group

Without a person in a task role, nothing gets done, but without people in maintenance roles, conflict within the group becomes overwhelming, and decisions are made without regard to people's feelings. A person in a maintenance role focuses on people and maintaining good relationships. His or her role is that of encourager, supporter, and someone who seeks to make sure everyone's opinion is heard. We need those people too.

The roles we could do without are those in disruptive roles. People in disruptive roles are prioritizing their own needs and agendas in a group. They could be the cynic who disagrees with every idea without providing any solutions. They could be the spotlight seeker who wants all the attention for themselves. They could be the clown who uses the cheap laugh in an attempt to get people to pay attention to them. Finally, they could be the arguer who just wants a battle. Conflict can shed light on individuals who may be putting their needs above the group's needs.

© Iakov Filimonov/Shutterstock.com

Conflict is beneficial for *balancing power*. We work, live, and interact in places that are governed by people dealing with authority. In error, we often rank ourselves against others with whom we interact. At times, we may think that someone is exerting too much control or has too much power in a relationship, and without even realizing it, we may create conflict in an attempt to balance the power more in our favor.

Conflict is beneficial for **building a history of survival.** A healthy couple that has been married for decades will tell you that it is not the absence of conflict that makes a marriage stronger. It is dealing with conflict that a couple builds on. When relationships are able to weather the storms of conflict and come out stronger on the other side, a deeply rich friendship is experienced. I wonder how many relationships never get deep because we cut and run at the first sign of conflict. Don't run. Work through the conflict and become better because of it. Ships and friendships are tested in the chaos of the open oceans.

How Do We Handle Conflict?

Ok. So there is conflict with your roommate, your professor, your parents, your friends, and yourself. You disagree and want them to do it your way. What do you do about it? There are ways that we attempt to get the other person to come into agreement with us. Some of the ways are healthy and productive, while others are destructive and manipulative. In 1974, Kenneth W. Thomas and Ralph H. Kilmann introduced their Thomas-Kilmann conflict mode instrument which can be used to determine the conflict management style of an individual. They suggested that there are five different behavioral styles for handling conflict.

THOMAS-KILMANN CONFLICT MODE INSTRUMENT

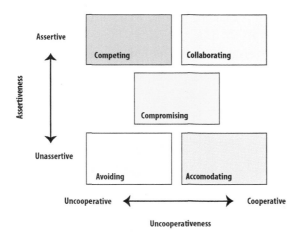

Sidebar 9A

One way that you try to manage conflict is by using a competing style. This suggests that you are more concerned with being right than getting the right answer for the situation. You may inappropriately engage someone by using persuasion or coercion, which is the use of threats, force, violence, or ridicule to get your way. This is not good. Let the strength of your idea and your explanations direct your decisions. If you have to resort to coercion, you may win, but at what cost? Sometimes, your way is not the best way. This is definitely a win-lose situation.

Competing
individuals in a conflict are more concerned with getting what they want than getting the right answer for the situation

© xtock/Shutterstock.com

© Ivelin Radkov/Shutterstock.com

Collaborating
both individuals in a conflict attempt to reach consensus

Another way of managing conflict is through the use of a **collaborating** style. Using this style, individuals attempt to have both parties reach consensus. Both parties try to achieve a win-win scenario (or as Michael Scott would say a "win-win-win" scenario) in which they work together to get what they want. This style is preferred by cultures that set a high importance on relationships. It's always enjoyable to watch people who place a high value on collaborating with others, people who are concerned with more than getting their own way. They care about the individuals they work with in addition to the tasks that they need to get done.

Compromise
each person gives up something in order to come to an acceptable solution

Sometimes complete collaboration is not possible and people could attempt to use **compromise** as the conflict resolution style. Compromise is achieved when each person gives up something in order to come to an acceptable solution. The key word is acceptable. Too many times when I hear someone say, "Let's compromise," what they are really saying is, "You compromise to what I want." In a true compromise, people don't get 100% of what they want, but they also don't give up 100%. They meet somewhere in the middle and don't kid yourself into thinking you are using compromise when you start by asking for much more than what you want so that you have some things to give up in the negotiations. In that situation, you are using a competing style dressed up like compromise. Don't kid yourself. Work together.

Accommodation
give in or sacrifice partially or completely to the other party

As we continue to move away from self-interest into a less assertive stance, we begin to be more **accommodating** in our conflict resolution. People who use accommodation give in or sacrifice partially or completely to the other group. Some Christians may be accommodating to people because they think that it is more godly to not express their wishes or desires in conflict. This is not the case. Don't accommodate just because you think you should or that you are more spiritual. Downplaying the importance of your own issues is not the best policy.

Avoidance
to evade conflict through silence or removing oneself from the situation

Finally, many times people wish to completely eliminate conflict from their lives and will utilize **avoidance** to evade conflict through silence or removing themselves from the situation. At times, people adept at conflict will use avoidance when they are not knowledgeable about the situation or when they believe that the point is so minor that it doesn't need to be addressed. Good problem solvers are able to address issues constructively while dismissing those that could sabotage productive conflict.

Learn How to Apologize: Not "I'm Sorry/Not Sorry"

We've all selfishly offended someone and we've all needed to apologize. Done poorly, apologies can make a problem worse instead of better. "I'm sorry if you're offended" is an example of a poor apology. It indicates that you accept no responsibility beyond underestimating the listener's weakness! Steer clear from making excuses for yourself. Include four parts in your proper apology. Popular single-named blogger JoEllen (Poon, 2014) suggests:

© igorstevanovic/Shutterstock.com

1. I'm sorry for . . . (Be specific.) For example: breaking my promise.
2. I was wrong because . . . (Often the reason it's wrong is because you have betrayed the other's trust)
3. In the future, I will . . . (Relate what you will, not what you won't, do. This should be a definitive, concrete action.)
4. Will you forgive me?

I-statements
statements that begin with I and enable the speakers to be assertive without making accusations

"you" statements
statements that shift the blame to the listener

The Power of I-Statements

In the 1960s, Thomas Gordon developed the concept of **I-statements** in contrast to **"you" statements**. You-statements shift blame to the listener. "Why don't you . . .?" "You don't . . ." "How could you . . .?" "You didn't . . ." You-statements produce defensiveness. Conversely, I-statements, which begin with "I" or have as the subject "I," enable speakers to be assertive without making accusations. I-statements force the speaker to take responsibility for his or her own thoughts and feelings. "I feel bad when you do that" is really different from "You make me feel bad" (Johnson, 2012).

Our passions and emotions are the constructs of our world. If we learn how to master them and utilize them appropriately, our lives consistently get better. An ancient proverb offers this challenge: Conquer your passions and you conquer your world. We can learn how to live and deal with conflict and be the problem solvers of this world.

Sidebar 9B

Practice the four-step formula above in these different scenarios.
You turned your work in late.
You returned a borrowed item damaged.
You betrayed a secret.
You took something that didn't belong to you.
You used language that was too harsh.

Will you forgive me?

© AlexKaplun/Shutterstock.com

Conflict in Unequal Relationships: Good Cop/Bad Cop

Sidebar 9C

Practicing I-Statements

Create an I-statement (to reduce defensiveness in the listener) to substitute for these.

- Why don't you take out the trash?
- Why do you act like that?
- You make me so mad.

Create an I-statement (to make yourself more powerful) to substitute for these.

- He is inconsiderate.
- She talks too much.
- They waste my time.

You have read a lot about conflict in seemingly equal relationships, but what if the relationships are not equal? It could be a parent correcting their misbehaving child, a student addressing a professor about a project that was incorrectly graded, an employee trying to work around a difficult boss, or a driver getting pulled over by a police officer. Each of these interactions represents an unequal relationship so it would be unwise to work through one of the above styles of conflict resolution. "But officer, *both* of us need to compromise what we want in order to find a solution!" As you move into the workforce, there will be more than enough opportunities for you to interact with relational inequality.

When you are in a subordinate role, there are a few things that you can do to help you deal with those in authority. ***First, have respect and communicate respect for the position, regardless of what you think about the individual.*** You may not like the person, but your attitude may be the difference between

© Pepsco Studio/Shutterstock.com

one ticket and three tickets. I find it amazing when someone comes to me with a bad attitude and expects me to do a favor for them. That's not going to happen.

Second, recognize that that person has people in authority over them and is bound by certain requirements. You may think that it would be really easy for a professor to let you take your test at another time, but in reality, there are certain requirements that they must meet in order to allow you to do that.

Third, don't suffer in silence. When there is a problem, a person in authority can't help you if they don't know about it. Your frustrations may increase when nothing changes and you think that the leader isn't doing anything about the problems. Every day you get more frustrated. When it is glaringly obvious to you that things are bad, how could they possibly miss it? Chances are good that they just don't realize it.

Fourth, when you struggle with a leader above you, don't talk behind their back. This only stirs up resentment and paints you as someone with a negative attitude. Don't listen to people who talk about the boss behind their back. If they talk to you and other people about the boss, they will talk about you with other people.

Fifth, admit when you are wrong. This may not always be the right thing when you are getting pulled over by a police officer, but I would rather hear it from my staff that they messed up than get blind-sided by the news in a meeting. Telling the truth even when it is hard is a sign of maturity. Closely related to this is the fake apology. Don't do it. "I'm sorry I didn't do what you said, but this is just something I really feel strongly about." "I'm sorry that you were offended by what I said." "I'm sorry that you didn't understand the heart behind what I said. If you understood, you would have been fine with it." "I'm sorry, but you really made me mad, and I didn't know what else to do." Knowing how to apologize is a skill that you can learn and is just as important is being able to admit when you are wrong.

Choose your mindset. When you let someone frustrate you, they win. You get to choose the way that you respond to an individual no matter how unreasonable they are acting. I have a friend who, when frustrated, will often say, "I will not give them control over my emotions." When you already decide to have a good attitude regardless of how big of an idiot someone is, you are the one who will get better.

Finally, stay professional. When someone acts like a fool, don't follow suit. It's hard to defend yourself when a bystander says that both of you were yelling at each other. It may feel nice temporarily to unload on someone, but it will end up hurting you in the end.

Conflict When You Are In Charge: How to Act When You Are the Big Cheese, the Head Honcho, the One in Charge, or Just Someone Who Has a Teensy-weensy Little Bit of Authority

First, godly leaders are servant leaders. If you would like to lead, get good at serving those above and below you. Serving those who are above you is oftentimes self-serving, but you can tell a lot about an individual when they serve someone who can do nothing for them. Those are the people whom I want leading and following me. As a problem solver, you have a responsibility to serve others and not just to make your own life easier.

© lassedesignen/Shutterstock.com

Second, know that there will always be someone who has authority over you. Think of the Roman centurion who responded to Jesus in Matthew 8:9, "I too am a man under authority." Here is a man who had authority over 100 men but responded that he was under authority. When I look to promote people, I look for those who are not just good leaders but also good followers. While those who are good followers may not be the best leaders, they are a good bet.

***Third, be a good listener and* perceiver.** Leading is more than having minions running around listening to you and doing whatever you want. Godly leaders know how to read a situation and understand what is really going on. Sometimes what is said is important for understanding this, but you also need to listen to what is not said.

Fourth, have stronger ethics than those who follow you. The people you lead will watch the way you do things. If you cut corners and forget your ethics to make things easier for yourself, your followers will take it to the next level. Your lowest standards can become your followers' highest standards. Don't give them permission to live unethically because you are lazy.

Fifth, godly leaders really care about the people who are following them. Chances are good that in the future, you will have a different job from most of the other people in this class. We will all have a different path, however, we all work with people. You know when your leader doesn't really care about you. In the same way, your followers will know if you don't care about them. Genuinely care about them, and empathize with their difficulties. Look for ways that you can help them, and give grace when they need it. If one of your people is having a tough day and you let them leave 30 minutes early, the hard work and loyalty that you get back from them will be worth more than 30 minutes.

Finally, when you get the opportunity to lead, know that you still have a lot to learn. One of the problems I see is that some people get too much authority too early, and they stop growing in their leadership. They think that they need to be perfect and can't admit mistakes. They want to show themselves as strong leaders. Young leaders are just that: young leaders. Know that you have blind spots, and be open to feedback from those who can see your blind spots. Be comfortable enough that you can ask people to critique you and give you suggestions for improvement. Hire people who are better than you are. Don't be intimidated by them. If you only hire people who make it easy for you, you will only be as good as you are. Surround yourself with people who will push you to grow as well.

Ethical Implication

The following are tips that you can try to assist you in working through the problems you are having with people.

- Value listening and attempt to understand what someone is trying to say. Seek to clarify information that you might not understand.
- Don't lose control of your emotions. When you are out of control, very little constructive progress can be made.

- Be honest but kind. You can say uncomfortable things without being a jerk. A good problem solver can disagree without being disagreeable.
- Don't make it personal. If you lose objectivity, you view the other individual incorrectly. You can be wrong and still be a great person. Winning doesn't necessarily mean that you are good.
- Avoid negative persuasion or coercion in your arguments. "Win-Lose" usually means I win now but lose the relationship later.
- Take a break if necessary, and agree to discuss it later. Cooler heads can prevail if you give it a break.
- Communicate respect. When you feel respected and give respect in return, you will be more apt to find a mutually beneficial solution. Don't wait to feel respected before you offer respect to the other party.
- Recognize the dialectical tension both in the relationship and within yourself.
- Use I/you statements.
- Keep perspective. People are more important than things. Change takes place in the context of relationships. Sometimes being right isn't the best thing. Are you going to lose a lot more than what you might gain for being right?
- Practice apologizing.

Summary

Conflict is all around us. It happens when two people have disagreement, hostility, discord, or argument because they feel their needs, beliefs, and characteristics are not compatible. Conflict can be negative, but also positive depending on how it is used. Even God gets angry. We engage in conflict for reasons like incompatible goals, differing communication contexts, and dialectical tensions (autonomy vs. connection, stability vs change, expression vs. privacy). How we handle conflict makes a huge difference in whether it is good or bad. Gottman identified four conflict behaviors that are especially harmful: criticism, contempt, defensiveness, and stonewalling. But conflict also has some benefits, such as establishing boundaries, expressing emotions, identifying needs (individual or group), balancing power, and building a history of survival. In group settings, we can play task roles, maintenance roles, and disruptive roles. Thomas and Kilmann (1977) said different strategies for handling conflict can be defined based on one's level of assertiveness and cooperativeness. They identified five methods: competing, collaborating, compromising, avoiding, and accommodating. When you apologize, be specific about the offense, tell what you'll do differently next time, and ask forgiveness. You-statements accuse the listener, but I-statements shift attention to the feelings of the speaker and can help deescalate conflict. There are tips for handling being in a subordinate position when things don't go well. They include having respect for the person in authority, recognizing they are under someone else's authority, speaking up for yourself, not talking behind the leader's back, admitting if you're wrong, choosing your attitude, and staying professional. When you get to be in charge, you need to remember some things. Be a servant leader. Remember that someone is in authority over you. Be a good listener. Have higher ethical standards than your subordinates. Care about the people who report to you. Finally, be humble and remember you still have things to learn.

Vocabulary Words

Accommodation
Autonomy vs. connection
Avoidance
Collaborating
Competing
Compromise
Conflict
Contempt
Context clues

Criticism
Groupthink
Defensiveness
Dialectical tensions
Disruptive roles
Expression vs. privacy
Goal incompatibility
High context
    communication

I-statements
Low context
    communication
Maintenance roles
Stability vs. change
Stonewalling
Task roles
You-statements

Discussion Questions

1. What are the most common examples of external conflict that you experience?
2. What are some ways that people handle conflict poorly?
3. How have you seen people on social media deal with someone who disagrees with them?
4. Have you seen someone who handles conflict well? How do they do it?
5. What do you need to do to improve your skills in handling conflict?
6. Are there times that refusing to engage in conflict is actually worse than engaging?
7. What are some destructive behaviors you have observed in groups you've been involved in?
8. What are the positive behaviors that should have been utilized in those groups?

References

Baxter, L. A. (1988). A dialectical perspective of communication strategies in relationship development. In S. Duck (Ed.), *Handbook of personal relationships: Theory, research, and interventions* (pp. 257–273). New York, NY: Wiley.

Baxter, L. A. (1990). Dialectical contradictions in relational development. *Journal of Social and Personal Relationships, 7*, 69–88.

Baxter, L. A., & Braithwaite, D. O. (2009). Relational dialectics theory applied. In S. W. Smith and S. R. Wilson (Eds.), *New directions in interpersonal communication research*, pp. 48–68. Thousand Oaks, CA: Sage.

Baxter, L. A., & Montgomery, B. M. (1996). *Relating: Dialogues and dialectics.* New York: Guilford.

Baxter, L. A., & Montgomery, B. M. (1997). Rethinking communication in personal relationships from a dialectical perspective. In S. Duck (Ed.), *Handbook of personal relationships: Theory, research, and interventions* (2nd ed., pp. 325–349). New York, NY: John Wiley, & Sons.

Cahn, D. D., & Abigail, R. A. (2007). *Managing conflict through communication* (3rd ed.). Boston: Allyn & Bacon.

DeVito, J. (2009). *The interpersonal communication book* (12th ed.). Boston, MA: Pearson/Allyn & Bacon.

Folger, J. P., Poole, M. S., & Stutman, R. K. (2009*). Working through conflict: A communication perspective* (6th ed.). Boston: Allyn & Bacon.

Gladwell, M. (2005). *Blink: The power of thinking without thinking.* New York, NY: Little, Brown & Co.

Gottman, J., & DeClaire, J. (2001). *The relationship cure: A five-step guide for building better connections with family, friends, and lovers.* New York, NY: Crown.

Greenleaf, R. K. (2002). *Servant leadership: A journey into the nature of legitimate power and greatness* (25th anniversary ed.). New York: Paulist Press.

Jamieson, J. P., Nock, M. K., & Mendes, W. B. (2012). Mind over matter: Reappraising arousal improves cardiovascular and cognitive responses to stress. *Journal of Experimental Psychology, 141*(3), 417–422.

Johnson, J. A. (2012, November 30). Are "I" statements better than "you" statements? (Blog post). Retrieved from https://wwwpsychologytoday.com/blog/cui-bono/201211/are-i-statements-better-you-statements

Keller, A., Litzelman, K., Wisk, L. E., Maddox, T., Cheng, E. R., Creswell, P. D., & Witt, W. P. (2012). Does the perception that stress affects health matter? *The Association with Health and Mortality. Health Psychology: Official Journal of the Division of Health Psychology, American Psychological Association, 31*(5), 677–684.

Kilmann, R., & Thomas, K. W. (1977). Developing a forced-choice measure of conflict-handling behavior: the "MODE" instrument. *Educational and Psychological Measurement, 37,* 309–325.

Peterson, G. W., & Bush, K. R. (1999). Predicting adolescent autonomy from parents: Relationship connectedness and restrictiveness. *Sociological Inquiry, 69,* 431–457.

Poon, J. (2014, March 30). A better way to say sorry. (Blog post). Retrieved from www.cuppacocoa.com/a-better-way-to-say-sorry

Sargent, S. L., & Weaver, J. B. (2003). Listening styles: Sex differences in perceptions of self and others. *International Journal of Listening, 17,* 5–18.

Tannen, D. (1987). *That's not what I meant!: How conversational style makes or breaks relationships.* New York: Ballantine.

Vanlear, C. A. (1991). Testing a cyclical model of communicative openness in relationship development: Two longitudinal studies. *Communication Monographs, 58,* 337–361.

Additional Readings

David and Goliath: Underdogs, Misfits, and the Art of Battling Giants
by Malcolm Gladwell

Crucial Conversations: Tools for Talking When the Stakes Are High
by Kerry Patterson, Joseph Grenny, Ron McMillan, & Al Switzler

Getting to Yes: Negotiating Agreement Without Giving In
by Roger Fisher & William Ury

Better Communicators Are Group Leaders/Followers

By Agena Farmer, Ed.D. and Matthew Olsen, Ed.D.

© tomertu/Shutterstock.com

10

Anyone can screw up a group. We have examples of bad leaders everywhere. While this may sound like a bad way to start a chapter on good leaders/followers, we started this way to prove a point. Most people avoid group projects because they forfeit their control and feel they turn out a sloppy product. Very few people make friends-for-life in a group project experience. In fact, they tend to avoid even the friends that they had after bad group experiences (Snyder, Lassegard, & Ford, 1986).

One of the famous sayings about groups is "A camel is a horse built by a group." Obviously, a camel is a poor substitute for a beautiful horse. They have humps where horses are sleek and smooth and camels seem to be very irritable. Camels are know for spitting on people. There is a reason why "Prince Charming" seldom rides up to rescue a damsel-in-distress on a camel. So why are we taking the challenge to change your perceptions? Well, the potential for successful group work is multiplied exponentially by getting thoughts and ideas from others. We have watched groups avoid huge mistakes because someone reminded the group of a fact that the rest of the group forgot. Groups usually do better with input from multiple sources.

The purpose of this chapter is to teach you how to communicate effectively in groups regardless of whether it is a good or bad situation. You do this

© Rawpixel.com/Shutterstock.com

by being a good leader (if leading is your calling), or being a good follower (if following is where you find yourself). We want to empower you so you realize that if you know how to communicate you are not at the mercy of a leader's inability or stuck with a bad group if you are a leader. Your ability to communicate well will help you be more successful in a group.

This chapter is being written by two of the authors so if you see an "I" statement, it could be either one of us. If it's good, then it's mine. (Ha ha!) See if you notice the changes in style and voice.

The book of Ecclesiastes reminds us that there is a season for everything; therefore, it's safe to say that regardless of your authority and power, you will function as both a leader and a follower. It's your job to find the balance in the seasons, namely when to talk and when to keep silent, when to lead and when to follow. Our culture has put so much emphasis on leadership that they have inadvertently given total responsibility for the group's success to the person at the top. If the leader is awesome, then you are fortunate. If the leader is bad, you are stuck with a lousy experience. With God's leadership you can help focus a group to do the "God" thing whether you are the leader or not.

Good followers are just as important as good leaders. As the old saying goes, "Someone who has no followers is just taking a walk." As a leader, you should not

© Rawpixel.com/Shutterstock.com

only look behind you, but beside you, and in front of you. Here's another proverb for you from Africa: "If you want to go fast then go by yourself. If you want to go far, go together." The speed with which you reach the destination is immaterial if the destination is wrong.

We propose to give you some background on groups, the characteristics of groups, the characteristics of good leaders, and some problems that can happen with groups.

Beginning of Groups

Since the beginning of time man has looked for order. Genesis 1:2 says, "The earth was without form and void and darkness covered the face of the deep." Realize that as God saw the chaos, He created order by leading. By His speaking, things were ordered and arranged. Light was separated from darkness; the waters were separated from the dry land, etc. Everything was good and in fact, in some places God noted that it was very good. Adam walked with God in the cool of the day and they communicated. God showed him how to organize and structure the beginning by naming the animals. I don't know if you have thought about it this way, but when

Adam named the animals, he was establishing order. When Adam and Eve sinned and they were separated from God, chaos returned.

Humans are no better at establishing or maintaining order in relationships than building roofs - maybe not as good!

© Ken Schulze/Shutterstock.com

Humans were not as successful as God in restoring that order. We still seek order. Small groups (3 or more people who work together interdependently to get something done; Floyd, 2014; Hybels & Weaver, 2001; Myers & Anderson, 2008) can be very helpful for setting things right. However, just as soon as another person comes along, there is a disagreement about how the order can be established and maintained. Communication allows input from all involved (Hybels & Weaver, 2001).

Small groups
3 or more people who work together independently to get something done

Think about leaders you have had in the past. The range of leaders probably included people who seemed mean and bossy and acted like you were not important. You probably also had people who seemed wishy-washy and were so concerned with what everybody thought that they couldn't decide anything. Which frustrated you the most? There is a lot to learn when you are in a group, especially if you are not the leader. Look at the successes of the group. Look at the areas in which things fell apart. When did it function well? When did it seem to stop functioning? Who in the group did not participate? Who participated too much?

How Groups Function

As we examine leadership we need to have a clearer understanding of how groups function. We are going to analyze how groups form, the importance of focusing on the problem instead of people, some considerations for leading a group, and some ways that the group members can be identified.

Stages of Group Formation

Conflict in interpersonal relationships are difficult enough; ironically, conflict plays a very important role in forming a strong, functioning group. Throwing multiple players into the mix of conflict can bring about enormous depth to the difficulty, but if you can understand that conflict is a necessary part of group growth, then you are able to deal with that conflict, and use it. Tuckman (1965) identified four stages of group growth. Let's begin with those.

© sirtravelalot/Shutterstock.com

The forming stage of group growth is characterized by shallow, formal interactions. You are gauging people and getting to know each other. Deep conversations do not take place. Your hopes and dreams do not get discussed. You try to make sure that you are liked and comfortable. Take for example this class. On the first day, you sat by yourself, watched each student come in, and silently sized them up. Could I

forming stage
stage of early group growth that is characterized by shallow, formal interactions

be friends with this person? I wonder if they will be nice. What do they value? Everything is easy and comfortable until someone or something happens that kicks you right into the next stage of group dynamics.

storming stage
stage of group growth that occurs when conflict is introduced

The **storming stage** of group growth occurs when conflict is introduced. There isn't a specific time or day that this happens, but it usually occurs when the group feels bored enough or comfortable enough with each other that their true colors come out. Insecurities, pet peeves, quirks, and idiosyncrasies that we all have tend to come out when we are stressed, tired, hungry, hurt, angry, or lonely. That is usually when the fireworks go off. The group has one of two directions to go in the storming stage: retreat to the forming stage or push through the conflict to the next stage. If you retreat, you will find yourself back in this stage again. Don't get stuck being shallow and formal. Push through conflict and normalize into a stronger group.

norming stage
stage of group growth when conflict has been resolved and some progress is made

When you push through the storming stage, you find yourself in the **norming stage** of group growth. People apologize. Bruised feelings are healed. You see some progress. You find your rhythm. You find your task roles. You find out what the group needs for each member to do and then they do it. This is where the work takes place and where most groups stay. However, there are certain times that group members find their places within the group, and those places complement each other. That is when you can move into the really fun stage.

performing stage
stage of group growth that strong, cohesive groups move to where synergy develops and more work is accomplished together than individually

Strong, cohesive groups can move into the **performing stage** of group growth. When this occurs, group work becomes less of a chore and just fun. You get to do the things that you are good at and really enjoy. Other people get to do the things that they are good at and you HATE to do. You love it. They love it. You start to see a synergy develop, and you accomplish more together than you could individually. This is rare. If you get to experience it, take note and appreciate it.

Focus on the Problem

One of the main things you need to do as a leader is to focus the group. Some situations are fraught with people battling others in the group. Perhaps some are not performing well in their tasks. Maybe someone erred and it cost the company a lot of money; the focus needs to be on the problem (Dobkin & Pace, 2003; Hybels & Weaver, 2001), not the person. For example, if the person setting up the schedules is doing a poor job the problem is that we need to adjust our scheduling process. If we can correct the method, the person doing the job should be able to do a better job. Your problem is not the person as much as the process that the person uses. If the anger is focused on the person making the mistakes, the meeting will be a complaint-fest that will cause a bigger division in the group instead of mending the problem. Your meetings should be problem-focused instead of people-blaming. Your goal is to let everyone feel like they have contributed to the solution without making someone take the blame for the problem. Maybe the system worked well in the past but has become dysfunctional. You can find out by having pre-meetings with some staff individually to help clarify the problem in your mind. With a clear picture of what is going on you can find a way to institute a better system to help take care of the problem. Adjustments to the staff can be made if needed after the new plan has been implemented. Your goal is to solve the problem, not to fight amongst yourselves. Focusing on the problem can make an enormous difference in how your group works together.

On Leading a Group: Putting the Pieces Together

Let's compare a group to a jigsaw puzzle. My family loves to work together to do big jigsaw puzzles. When you look at the picture that you are going to create with the pieces, it looks beautiful. Then you take it out of the box and it is a mess. Most of the pieces look like they couldn't possibly be in the picture at this point. This is like the awkward beginning time in a group. Please don't get frustrated as a follower when the group seems so disconnected. Just like in the puzzle, there are some real nuggets of wisdom (important pieces) that will probably come from members who don't seem to be even paying attention at first. There is a reason they were chosen for this gathering. Watch and learn.

As a leader, choose your group with care (Bennis, 1999; Eisenberg, 1990) by making sure the areas involved in implementing the solution are represented. Be clear in the instructions you give (Devereaux Ferguson, 2008). This lets the group know you are not wasting their time. Let the members get acquainted with each other and then get started on the problem. If there is not clarity in the perception of the problem from the perspective of all of the group members, then the chance of finding a good answer is decreased exponentially. Don't be dismayed by the haphazard way the group is picking at each other at the first. Just continue to refocus them toward the problem at hand.

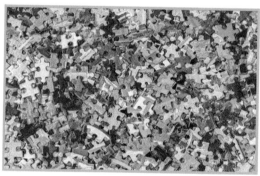
© sirtravelalot/Shutterstock.com

There is sure to be conflict on the way to resolution (Goodall & Goodall, 2006). It is important in groups to allow people freedom to work. Probably group members will be rallying behind different ideas. As long as those ideas are concepts that will further the solution, this time will help the group come up with the most efficient way of solving the problem.

Leaders need to adjust their attitudes toward conflict and realize that by controlling and guiding conflict, the group can use it to become more cohesive. You also have a better chance of coming up with a better answer. Remember that leaders who push for resolution before the facts and options have all been presented end up with flawed answers that are not likely to work. While conflict itself is not bad, uncontrolled fighting is. Watch for emotions. When people start reacting without listening, refocus the discussion back to the problem.

After you have exhausted discussion about options the group makes a decision about which option it will take. Plan a time to check up on the progress of the plan and see if any adjustments should be made. Many answers chosen by groups to solve problems are excellent. It is in the execution that the ideas fall apart.

Now that we have a clearer picture of what will happen with the group, I want to give you some ideas about how to work with the individual people in the group. They are all different and your understanding of their unique qualities will help you interact better and accomplish more.

Who's in the Group?

© Ollyy/Shutterstock.com

A leader can work to identify the kinds of people in the group. This will help in the formation of subgroups and the assigning of tasks. Do you remember the Johari window (Luft, 1969) in Chapter 2 and how you used it to gauge your relationships with others? You measured your ability to listen (receive feedback from others) and your capacity to share with them (how much you talk).

Keeping that in mind, estimate a window for the people in your group. Next, examine the windows you created for each member and identify four possible kinds of windows. Regardless of your title, (leader/follower), each member's window offers different obstacles that must be overcome for the group to gain understanding and finding the best was to work together. Here are the kinds of windows and ideas for ways to respond to that type of person.

Interviewers ask lots of questions but don't share their information. They have a larger hidden window. (See Sidebar 10A) Your job as a leader/follower is to ask them questions so they will share.

Bulls in a China Shop are people who share information indiscriminately and seem to not understand that the feelings of others might be hurt by what they say. (See Sidebar 10B) Your job as leader is to encourage them to listen. You could ask them closed questions and control the conversation by asking other people to share.

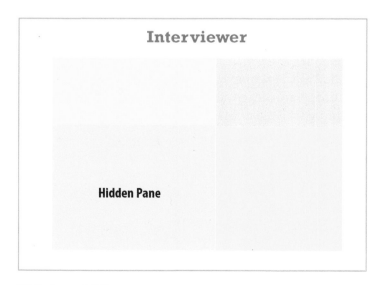

Interviewer

Hidden Pane

Sidebar 10A

Turtles don't share or listen well. They stay to themselves. The information that they have could help the group turn the corner in resolving the problem. (See Sidebar 10C) Your job as leader is to encourage them out of their safe place to participate in the group. Sometimes recognizing their importance to the group can help them come out of their shells. You might praise them for a past accomplishment and then ask them to share about the topic and how it pertains to the problem at hand.

Ideal are both good listeners and sharers. They will encourage others to talk and share. They don't take offense at the harshness of the "bull-in-the-china-shop" and they encourage both the interviewers and turtles to share (See Sidebar 10D). Your job is to work at being an ideal person and to find your ideal types to help you work with the other kinds of windows. Assign them to a turtle. Have them ask the interviewers questions and help the bulls listen.

Now that we have talked about groups, let's move on to the people who lead them.

Lots of Leadership Styles

Our purpose in this section is to offer you a taste of lots of different leadership styles so that you can call on the type that you need at the time a need arises. This information can also help you understand why leaders are going in the direction that they are as they lead. Whether they are focused on the job or the people doing the job, knowing the different kinds of leadership can the group has give you a "heads up" on how to respond to the leader needs in the most effective way. If the group has inventive and creative people the leader needs to give them space. If the job that they are doing is not that exciting but needs to be done, then less freedom and more structure will help them do their job more efficiently.

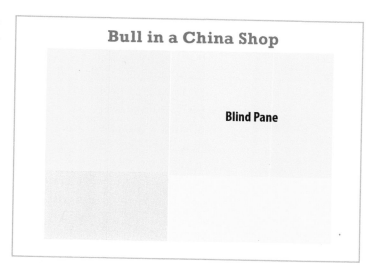

Bull in a China Shop

Blind Pane

Sidebar 10B

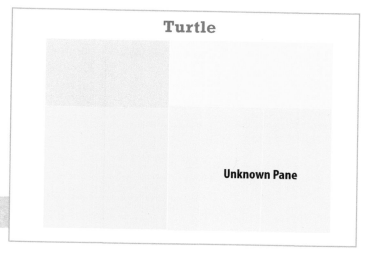

Turtle

Unknown Pane

Sidebar 10C

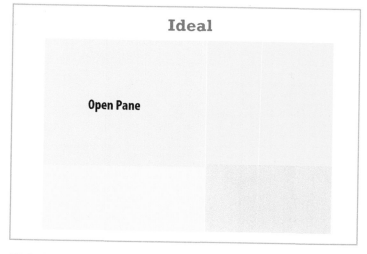

Ideal

Open Pane

Sidebar 10D

Kinds of Leaders

We are surrounded by leaders, those who want to be leaders, or those who just want to boss us around. So, the question that needs to be answered is this: What actually is leadership? **Leadership** is the ability to direct an individual or group of individuals toward a common goal. Some people influence their teams incredibly well and are much better than others while some leaders with a title actually hinder the work of the team. Think about someone who was a great leader for you. What are some characteristics of their good leadership? Was it a coach or a teacher or a pastor who motivated you to do your best work?

© Jirsak/Shutterstock.com

Before we begin discussing the different types of leadership skills, we need to address self-leadership. It is the foundational level of leadership. **Self-leadership** is the development of your own personal leadership style and following it. There are so many books currently published that teach about how to develop yourself and your leadership skills. Heck, there are entire sections in the bookstore completely on self-development and making yourself a better leader. But you need to understand something that I believe in strongly: People are not born great leaders, they develop into great leaders. They don't start out as great leaders but make mistakes and do things wrong. You, like them, can learn how to develop yourself into a better leader. It starts with your desire. The foundational level of leadership is self-leadership. If you want to be a great leader, you must learn to lead yourself. In order to lead yourself, you must develop those characteristics.

Good leaders are willing to grow in their leadership. They take risks and make mistakes. They see other leaders and learn from their mistakes and successes. If you want to develop your leadership, you should do the same. Talk with good leaders and analyze their leadership strengths and weaknesses. Go on a "wisdom tour" to find out more information about leadership from great leaders. Determine questions that you want to know the answers to and then go and ask these wise leaders. You would be surprised at how much good leaders feel responsible to help young leaders become better leaders.

© Dragon Images/Shutterstock.com

Charles Duhigg (2016) in his book *Smarter Faster Better* writes about a study that Google did on the characteristics of good leadership. He describes eight different skills that are present in some of the best leaders. First, good leaders are good coaches. Second, they empower their teams and don't micromanage. Third, they express interest and concern for the well-being and success of their team members. Fourth, they specifically orient themselves to create results. Fifth, good leaders listen to their team and share information with them. Sixth, they help their team foster their own career development. Seventh, they have a clear mission and vision and a strategy to accomplish it. Finally, a good leader has key skills necessary to complete the tasks at hand.

Good leaders are in the development game. Their leadership gets better when the people who work for them become better leaders. Sydney Finkelstein (2016) in his book, *Superbosses*, suggests that developing the people around them is one of the strategies that make great leaders. **Developmental leaders** motivate people by nurturing the strengths and weaknesses of their followers. This is not always an enjoyable process but they seek to make you better by developing you into the best you possible. Development focused leaders are not just focused on the development of their people, but also on their own personal development. They are always reading books, listening to podcasts, attending seminars, joining webinars, and watching TED talks. They lead with development. Don't be threatened when they give you a suggestion about how to improve what you are doing. Yes, it can be annoying when they always tell you something that you are doing wrong, but they are doing so to make you, the department, themselves, and the company better. Thank them for their input and apply what makes sense to you.

Developmental leaders
leaders who motivate people by nurturing the strengths and weaknesses of their followers

In addition to development focused leaders, a strong institutional mission and vision can help bolster a mediocre leader through the process of development. The stronger the mission, whether it is institutional or departmental, the easier it is for a group to support, but a strong mission can never fully compensate for a poor leader. **Missional leaders** continually bring the vision or mission or goal of the group to mind. In essence, they remind people, "This is why we are doing this!" Leading with mission is necessary when the group loses sight of the "why" of what they are doing. When you do something repetitively for a long period of time, you can easily fall into the mindset of just getting it done; we lose purpose. When we lose purpose, it is easy to get sloppy in our work, relationships, school work, or life. For me, when I know the "why" of it, it is easier for me to do something that is difficult or unpleasant to do.

Missional leaders
leaders who lead through an emphasis on the mission and vision or goal of the group

Positional leaders
leaders who rely on their title or position to utilize any type of authority

Authoritarian leadership
leadership style characterized by directive activity without group input

There are three types of leadership styles that are most common and you will most likely interact with throughout your lifetime. **Positional leadership** is the lowest and most common form of leadership. This occurs when leaders rely on their title or position to utilize any type of authority. Their directives are followed by their followers because of their title or position, not the value of their argument. One form of positional leadership is **authoritarian leadership**, which is necessary when the group is in an emergency or a chaotic situation. Authoritarian leaders have all the power and direct the group without any type of input (Dobkin & Pace, 2003; Wood, 2009). One classic example of authoritarian leadership is the military during times of battle. The military commander does not tolerate disobedience or questioning of their decisions.

© Constantin Stanciu/Shutterstock.com

© file404/Shutterstock.com

Laissez-faire leader
leadership style that does not give direction or leadership structure but provides a hands-off approach to leading the group

Democratic leader
leader who delegates decision-making to the group itself

Situational leadership
leadership style that adapts to match the needs of the group members

Directing
leadership stage in which the leader makes most of the decisions for the staff member

Coaching
leadership stage in which the leader will not direct the staff member, but rather analyze their weaknesses and offer correction

At times, authoritarian leadership requires a strong stance that is directive and not open to any type of suggestions from their followers. While difficult, there are times when authoritarian leadership is necessary. Those times, however, should be short and few.

On the opposite end of the leadership spectrum from authoritarian leadership is laissez-faire leadership. A laissez-faire leader does not give direction or leadership structure but provides a hands-off approach to leading the group (Dobkin & Pace, 2003; Wood, 2009). Each group member decides what is best for them without any real oversight or interference from the leader. This type of leadership works well in mature groups that have an existing order to the way they do things.

A third type of leadership involvement is a democratic leader (Dobkin & Pace, 2003; Wood, 2009). This type of leader delegates decision-making to the group itself. The group members themselves make the choices about the direction of the group. They do so as a group and the leader has a voice just like the other members. Democratic leadership is also better tolerated by the group and gets better buy-in. While group leaders have the ability to utilize one type of style exclusively, most will use a variety of styles depending on the situation that the group finds itself in.

Situational Leadership

There are times when the best leaders have to shift their default leadership style to match the needs of each of their group members. Paul Hershey and Ken Blanchard (1977) described this process of successful leaders who can shift their style to every situation and called it situational leadership. The first stage in the situational leadership model is directing which involves the leader making most of the decisions for the staff member. This is necessary when the person may not know the procedures of the job or is new to the position. The supervision is close and the communication about the goals, tasks, and procedures is from the top down. When the staff member becomes skilled and knowledgeable, then the leader will move to the next stage of the situational leadership model.

When a staff member has a level of understanding for the position and is competent in what they are doing, a situational leader will then shift into a coaching role for the staff member. During this phase, the leader will not direct the staff member, but rather analyze their weaknesses and offer correction. Coaching works well when the follower has a desire for improvement and is open to correction. The communication becomes more two-way where the leader seeks suggestions and solutions from the follower. The follower becomes more confident with his own skill and ability to make decisions.

Another phase that leaders could move into is the **supporting** stage. During this phase, the leader watches as the follower makes decisions. The leader offers support when necessary, but allows the follower to choose what needs to be done and how it needs to be done. The leader's role in this stage is motivation rather than direction. The follower knows what to do, but just needs encouragement to do it. The communication changes again to be more follower-initiated and the leader provides advice if requested, needed, or desired by the follower. The role of the leader is finding what the follower needs to become motivated. When the follower is capable and motivated, then the leader moves into the last phase of situational leadership.

© Phovoir/Shutterstock.com

Supporting
leadership stage in which the leader watches as the follower makes decisions and offers support when necessary, but allows the follower to choose what needs to be done and how it needs to be done

The last phase of situational leadership is **delegating**, during which the leader recognizes that the follower has the ability and the motivation to complete the tasks at hand. This requires a high amount of trust so that the leaders can release all control and provide little or no support. The follower has the control of all aspects of the job and communication again becomes one-way. The follower works independently and therefore must inform the leader of their progress, success, and challenges.

Delegating
leadership stage in which the leader recognizes that the follower has the ability and the motivation to complete the tasks at hand and does not provide any support or direction

Servant Leaders
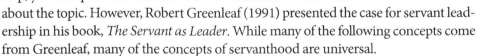

When you hear the term **servant leaders**, you probably think of a lot of different types of leaders that you have seen in the church or in ministry. It is a concept of leadership that many believe was the leadership style of Jesus in which the leader seeks to serve first before leading. While this is true, if you are anything like me, you have probably seen leaders who call themselves servant leaders who are not great at the servant part. However, true servant leaders have certain characteristics that clearly show their leadership style. They don't have to tell people they are servant leaders. If you do a simple Internet search for servant leadership, you are apt to find a number of current authors who write about the topic. However, Robert Greenleaf (1991) presented the case for servant leadership in his book, *The Servant as Leader*. While many of the following concepts come from Greenleaf, many of the concepts of servanthood are universal.

© Monkey Business Images/Shutterstock.com

Servant leaders
leadership style that focuses on serving first before leading

The first concept of servant leaders is *commitment to the growth* of their followers. That doesn't mean that they aren't committed to their own growth, because their own personal development is incredibly important to them also. However, servant leaders realize that when they are focused on developing their followers, their followers are focused on doing the job that they are supposed to be doing. Great businesses focus on their employees and not their customers, because a well-supported employee will focus on the customer. After my initial on-the-job training, I do very little in telling my staff how to do their jobs. I focus on training and developing them into better employees and then push them to tell me how they can do their jobs better. I learn things from them that I would never have realized on my own. That's the power of development.

© WAYHOME studio/Shutterstock.com

Next, servant leaders focus on *listening and understanding* rather than speaking and being understood. Insecure leaders like to hear themselves talk and feel the success of the group depends on their insight. How tragic! Servant leaders can listen to an opposing viewpoint because they realize that the richness of a group can only come when the group feels safe enough to share a dissenting viewpoint. If groups don't feel safe enough to disagree with each other and the leader, my guess is that it is the leader who doesn't listen well or seek to understand. Listening to understand takes time and some leaders don't want to invest the time necessary to really understand. I have found that when I talk with a student who has a complaint, the best thing that I can do is listen and try to really understand their issue rather than just fix it. When a servant leader understands the group, she will help cultivate the solution rather than have to create it.

Next, servant leaders recognize that their followers are broken people just like the rest of us, but have strengths and weaknesses that are the leader's most valuable resource. They treat people with *empathy and acceptance,* loving them in the midst of their brokenness. When mistakes happen, servant leaders address the issue at hand and not the person. This is the difference: address issues and care for people. One of my former leaders had to address an issue that we had messed up pretty badly. He brought about 15 of us into a conference room and explained the situation that had gone wrong. He was not emotional, even though I figured he was mad. He told us that no one was getting fired, and then asked us to evaluate and fix what had gone wrong. It was a difficult and uncomfortable process that I didn't enjoy, but he treated us with empathy and acceptance, even after we messed up. I greatly respect that servant leader.

When a servant leader is focused on development, understanding, and empathy, the next natural expression is that of being a person of *healing*. The leader's view focuses upon their followers, so they can see when things change or are difficult for their staff members. I first realized this when my assistant came back from lunch and it was clear that she had been crying. Her eyes were red, and she had trouble keeping her voice under control. I, brilliantly, deduced that something was wrong. (I know, I'm good like that.) Instead of having her tell me all about it, or telling her to suck it up because we had work to do, I suggested that she could take the rest of the afternoon off and spend time by herself praying and doing what she wanted. She protested, but I knew that there was nothing that she needed to get done before the next day. Ultimately she left the office for the day. I was able to be part of her healing.

Servant leaders who are part of healing move easily into the next component, which is having *foresight and awareness*. They are able to look at their organization, the staff members, the problems, the solutions, and the season and make an appropriate decision for the future. They don't just see the solution to the current problem, but also the solution to future problems and how they interact. Awareness sees the current issues that need to be addressed through both internal intuition and external sensing. This is a leader trusting their gut while at the same time getting all the information that they can get. Foresight sees the future issues that need to be addressed before they become serious issues. Those leaders who do this well have learned how to rely on the Holy Spirit throughout the day doing what they do all the time and not just in their spiritual walk or on Sunday morning.

As servant leaders are externally focused on their staff and followers, their influence is also felt by everyone around them. They have permission to lead, and thus as a result, are *persuasive*. They have influence and they utilize that influence to cultivate the environment that they lead. They are able to be persuasive because they are honest, competent, and knowledgeable. They are able to be persuasive without being manipulative. When my staff members don't agree with the direction that I am leading them, instead of forcing them to follow, I try to explain it a different way so that they are able to better understand what I am saying. Persuasion is never manipulating.

© xtock/Shutterstock.com

Finally, a servant leader *builds community* within their team. They understand the concept, as stated earlier in the chapter, "If you want to travel fast, go alone. If you want to travel far, go as a team." Building a community means focusing not just on those who are comfortable communicating in the team, but also eliciting input from those who aren't as comfortable. Knowing the style of each of your team members can help you appreciate them more. If you want to show appreciation to your team, some might appreciate you spending time with them in a casual setting while another may want to be able to leave early instead of spend time with you. Some want to be appreciated publicly while others want a simple, "good job" where no one else hears it. Knowing them helps you build a strong community. Strong teams who have a sense of community look out for each other (as well as the leader) and make it a joy to work together. Those types of groups don't feel like work; they are a real joy. Good leaders look to build that community.

Focus of Leaders

As we finish this discussion on kinds of leadership, I want to add a word or two about focus. Good leaders/followers can do better work by adjusting their focus to the problem at hand instead of on irritations with members of the group. This means that if the problem appears to be the person

© Syda Productions/Shutterstock.com

scheduling the workers, we need to re-focus the group on evaluating scheduling systems and not on the inadequacies of the scheduler. We need to be focused on problem solving and not people blaming. By focusing the group on the problem and not the people over that area, the group can stay focused on the situation and logically figure out how to make adjustments. If the focus is on the person responsible, the discussion can become petty and emotional. If the system is at fault, even a new-hire will have the same problems. The current person "causing" the problem can give us insight as to the particular things that need adjustment. As the individual ideas of the group members begin to align, the quality of the solution increases. This idea alignment will also help in implementing the plan. Many great answers that make it through development never come to fruition because the care given to creating the answer is not extended to implementation. In other words, great ideas die in the implementation because they are not given the commitment they need so they can be put into place.

The second focus point is to listen to everyone, not only the ones with power. One of the reasons we might not give credibility to possible answers is because the people with the best ideas don't get heard. This can lead to discounting great ideas if they were to come from the less powerful or less popular members. To avoid this we should work to place more value on the people in the group instead of giving value only to their position. This allows us to not be limited to answers from a few members but will help us hear solutions from more of the group. If we are not as intentional and focused on putting the answer in place as we are in finding the answer, we will waste the time we used in finding the better solution. We have the mistaken idea that when we figure out the answer we have reached the end of the process when actually the process is just going to the next level. This is why it is important to include input from the departments that are responsible for putting the plan into place while the plan is being created. Throughout the process, a good leader connects the workers from every level. This allows people with understanding of potential problems to steer the plan toward a viable solution. It will also allow people with power to implement change during implementation so that problems can be found and resolved. Having people with power at every stage, including implementation, enables needed adjustments to be made more easily.

Now that we have looked at focusing on the problem and listening to everyone, let's look at cohesion. **Cohesion** means that all group members are in unity and going in the same direction to reach an expected goal. Cohesive groups seem to have a connection that enables them to work together and support the team so that the focus is on the destination instead of the temporary irritations. It seems that it would be easier to get things done with a group of people who are satisfied with each other, in a group spirit, and committed to the same idea. **Groupthink** is the desire for unanimity that takes precedence over the need to seek out all possible

Cohesion
all group members are in unity and going in the same direction to reach an expected goal

Groupthink
desire for unanimity that takes precedence over the need to seek out all possible answers

"Today's meeting is about Getting Beyond Group Think."

© Cartoon Resource/Shutterstock.com

answers (Janis, 1972). It implies pressure to conform (Janis, 1982). Many times it can happen when the group is under unusual pressure to make a decision and/or working in unchartered territory. The group knows that there is contrary evidence that presents doubt about their plan but they ignore the information in order to stay united against the problem. It's not easy to be considered a dissenter because you spoke against a dynamic leader or a popular point of view. So most people just don't speak up. If this situation arises for you, a good option will be to use information from a recognized source in presenting your argument. It will deflect the criticism away from you and toward the research. As a leader you need to create an atmosphere where questions and opinions are not discouraged. This requires focus because, unless a leader/member is watching for this problem, the likelihood of error is escalated. They say that hindsight is 20/20, so foresight can help you avoid big problems. Remember no one plans to make mistakes; they just seem to happen.

Examples of Groupthink

History is full of stories of very wise people making decisions that became very stupid mistakes. We can learn from the mistakes of others and avoid catastrophe. Here are some groupthink situations:

Pearl Harbor- attack by the Japanese

Watergate - cover-up US government

Penn State University - child abuse cover-up

Space shuttle Challenger explosion - NASA administration

Jonestown Massacre - mass suicide by religious group (This is where the phrase, "Don't drink the Kool-Aid" originated)

Sidebar 10E

Though you may or may not be a government official, you could be in a group situation at work, church, or an organization. It is important to have a clearer picture of groupthink so that your group will not make the same mistake. Many times, when an organization fails it may have many symptoms of groupthink (Janis, 1982). Let's look at what those symptoms are:

1. *Illusion of invulnerability* is the belief that the group is more powerful than they are and, therefore, are not susceptible to attack.
2. *Belief in the inherent morality of the group* is a belief that since the group is good, their goals and decisions must be good also.
3. *Outgroup stereotyping* is when anyone not in the group is perceived as the enemy and is assumed to not understand the situation.
4. *Collective rationalization* causes the group to ignore the warnings about their decisions.
5. *Self-censorship* means the group members minimize their personal doubts and any counter arguments.
6. *Illusion of unanimity* is the belief that silence is consent because no one shares contrary information.
7. *Direct pressure on dissenters* happens when group members coerce those who have objections into supporting the leader and not making waves.
8. *Self-appointed mindguards* are members who decide to shield the group from adverse information.

© g-stockstudio/Shutterstock.com

Keeping these symptoms in mind when your group gets ready to make decisions that will affect your business or ministry or family in a big way, please consider these safeguards as a leader:

1. *As a leader, let the group reach big decisions twice.* See if the group will come up with the same solution the second time.
2. *Don't make the decision by yourself.* As the leader, you need to make sure that it is a decision made by the group and not just your own ideas.
3. *Arrange to have meetings without you, the leader, being present.* You should know that the meeting is happening, but just don't attend. This allows the group to share more freely.
4. *Appoint someone to be the devil's advocate.* If you are not familiar with this term, it means that people in the group are assigned to challenge the proposed solution. They are to stay level-headed and unemotional about the plan. They are allowed to ask the hard questions without being chastised by the group. They can look for problems without retribution.
5. *Divide the larger group into smaller groups and see if they reach the same conclusion.* Members might ask questions in a group of 7 that they wouldn't ask in a group of 25 or more.

In conclusion, when you feel motivated to move or act in a certain way that might be risky, for the sake of the group, proceed carefully. Make wise decisions so that excellent answers can be found and well-functioning groups can implement those plans to resolve the issues.

Ethical Implications

Our desire is that you be ethical in how you handle groups. Now that you can more easily persuade people to go in a particular direction, your task is to make sure you are guiding the group toward the right destination. The saying, "Just because you can, doesn't mean you should" encourages you to be responsible for what you do. Don't lead people in a self-serving manner. Figure out what will be best for the group, choose your leadership style carefully, and lead accordingly.

Proverbs 21:1 says "Good leadership is a channel of water controlled by God; he directs it to whatever ends he chooses" There is a moral responsibility that goes with leadership and the task is daunting. Rest in the fact that He will control the water. Be responsive to the needs of those around you. Don't let the power corrupt you. Serve the needs of those in your group and trust God to help you see what needs to be done.

When you get and have a position of leadership, remember where you came from. Don't be someone who is an overbearing leader just because you have been given a position. In the same way, leaders need followers who are supportive, encouraging, and loyal. Wherever you find yourself, be a good leader and a good follower.

Summary

So you now know about how to be a better group member/leader. We have looked at how groups can function better, and talked about the phases that a group encounters when reaching a decision. We looked at ways to work with people in the group by identifying their characteristics/type. We defined leadership as the ability to direct an individual or group toward a common goal and discussed self-leadership as the foundation level of leadership.

Leaders of all kinds are around us and will be part of our schools, our jobs, our churches, and just about everything we do. Good leaders are a joy to follow. Truly great leaders are rare and are something to behold. Good leadership starts with self-leadership and the development of himself or herself. The focus on development moves into assisting followers in their own development. Developmental leaders focus on development of their staff. Missional leaders focus on adjusting the direction of their departments to align with their mission and vision. Positional and authoritarian leaders are directive and not open to suggestions. They are necessary in a crisis or emergency, but detrimental to creativity. Laissez-faire leaders provide no input and allow their teams to make their own decisions. Democratic leaders seek the input of the team and everyone has equal authority. Situational leaders evaluate each team member to determine which style of leadership that individual needs to be successful at the task at hand. Servant leaders are not only motivating in the direction of their teams, but also transformational in the lives of their individual team members.

© Rawpixel.com/Shutterstock.com

Cohesion and groupthink (both the symptoms and some safeguards) have rounded out the chapter. Our hope is that all of this information will help you be a better leader/follower because you will have more of the tools needed to be successful.

Vocabulary Words

Authoritarian leadership
Coaching
Cohesion
Delegating
Democratic leaders
Developmental leaders
Directing

Forming stage
Groupthink
Laissez-faire leaders
Leadership
Missional leaders
Norming stage
Performing stage

Positional leadership
Self-leadership
Servant leaders
Situational leadership
Small group
Storming stage
Supporting

Discussion Questions

1. Who is your role model for a good leader? (You can't say Jesus!)
2. What is harder: leading or following?
3. Have you ever had a really good leader? What were they like?
4. Have you ever had a bad one? What were they like?
5. What are the characteristics of a good follower?
6. What does a godly leader look like? What about a godly follower?
7. When have you felt the pressure of groupthink?
8. Have you ever been a leader? What sort were you? Were you any good?
9. How could you be a better follower?

References

Bennis, W. (1999). *Managing people is like herding cats: Warren Bennis on leadership.* Provo, UT: Executive Excellence.

Devereaux Ferguson, S. (2008). *Public speaking: Building competency in stages.* New York: Oxford University Press.

Dobkin, B. A., & Pace, R. C. (2003). *Communication in a changing world.* New York: McGraw-Hill.

Duhigg, C. (2016). *Smarter faster better: The secrets of being productive in life and business.* New York, NY: Random House.

Eisenberg, E. (1991). Jamming: Transcendence through organizing. *Communication Research, 17,* 139–164.

Goodall, Jr., H. L., & Goodall, S. (2008). *Communicating in professional contexts: Skills, ethics, and technologies* (2nd ed.). Belmont, CA: Thomson Wadsworth.

Greenleaf, R. K. (1991). *The servant as leader.* Indianapolis, IN: Robert K. Greenleaf Center.

Finkelstein, S. (2016). *Superbosses.* New York, NY: Penguin Random House.

Floyd, K. (2014). *Communication matters.* (2nd ed.). New York: McGraw-Hill.

Hersey, P. and Blanchard, K. H. (1977). *Management of organizational behavior: Utilizing human resources* (3rd ed.). New Jersey: Prentice Hall.

Hybels, S., & Weaver, R. L., II. (2001). *Communicating effectively* (6th ed.). New York: McGraw-Hill.

Janis, I. L. (1972). Victims of groupthink. Boston, MA: Houghton Mifflin.

Janis, I. L. (1982). *Groupthink: Psychological studies of policy decisions and fiascoes.* Boston, MA: Houghton Mifflin.

Luft, J. (1969). *Of human interaction.* Palo Alto, CA: Natural Press.

Mezulis, A. H., Abramson, L. Y., Hyde, J. S., & Hankin, B. L. (2004). Is there a universal positivity bias in attributions?: A meta-analytic review of individual, developmental, and cultural differences in the self-serving attribution bias. *Psychological Bulletin, 130*(5), 711–747. doi:10.1037/0033-2929.130.5.711

Myers, S. A., & Anderson, C. M. (2008). *The fundamentals of small group communication.* Thousand Oaks, CA: Sage.

Snyder, C. R., Lassegard, M., & Ford, C. E. (1986). Distancing after group success and failure: Basking in reflected glory and cutting off reflected failure. *Journal of Personality and Social Psychology, 5*(2), 382–388.

Tuckman, B. W. (1965). Developmental sequence in small groups. *Psychological Bulletin, 63*(6), 384–399.

Wood, J. T. (2009). *Communication in our lives* (5th ed.). Boston, MA: Wadsworth.

Additional Readings

First, Break All the Rules: What the World's Greatest Managers Do Differently
by Marcus Buckman and Curt Coffman

Leaders Eat Last: Why Some Teams Pull Together and Others Don't
by Simon Sinek

100 Worst Bosses: Learning from the Very Worst How to Be Your Very Best
by Jim Stovall

Better Communicators Are Considerate

By Rhonda Gallagher, M.S.

11

What does it mean to be considerate communicators? Have you ever thought about it? In fact, why do we even care? As you know, we (the authors) are doing our best to come at this from a Christian worldview, but even if you are not approaching this from any religious foundation, it is important to become less self-centered if you hope to be a better communicator. You know that we all see the world through our own filters. Our self-concept actually causes us to notice different things when we examine the world. Sometimes selfishness distorts our view of life. We miss out on a lot of information and rewarding relationships by being self-absorbed, and sadly, most of us are. But none of us is the center of the universe. When we approach our communication as if others are as important as we are, we begin to see things differently and often more clearly. In any discussion of being considerate, we must cite the Golden Rule: "Do unto others as you would have them do unto you" (Luke 6:31). Sometimes people look at this and say, "I have to treat everyone else like they are better than I am." That is not what Jesus said. He said to love others as we love ourselves. In this context, "as" is often interpreted to mean "as much as," but it can also mean "at the same time." The idea is that you matter, and I matter, and the person with the worst need takes precedence. Nobody gets to be the "Big It." So, being considerate of how others experience life becomes pretty important, especially in romantic relationships (Wood, 2009), whether you are religious or not. Okay, so with that established, where do we begin?

© Ljupco Smokovski/Shutterstock.com

Being considerate means several things. It means thinking about what other people think, feel, and need, while not taking them for granted. It means expressing gratitude to others who do things for us. Being considerate also means being aware that others may not see things as we do and that we could be wrong. It is making an effort to understand other people's perspectives on things and to be aware of their needs as being as important as your own. It also means considering the needs of others when you make plans, even plans seemingly as small as preparing for a speech. Let's start with . . .

Reasons for Misunderstanding: Me?! Wrong??!! Never!!

Okay, nobody is right all of the time. We simply gather the information from around us through our senses and put it together in the best way we can, but we may perceive situations entirely differently than someone else does. Perception is the process of gathering and transferring information from the world around us and interpreting what it means (Dobkin & Pace, 2003; Floyd, 2014; Wood, 2002), remember? (Go back and re-read chapter 3 if you don't!) The whole process of perception is susceptible to failure. We constantly apply filters to our perception in each step of the process. Let's look at four ways the process can fail us.

First, our self-esteem can influence what stimuli we attend to, causing us to interpret facts inaccurately and overrate our failures (Brown & Minkowski, 1993; Campbell, 1990). Or we might not see the true meaning at all. For example, if you are sensitive about your weight and your friend at lunch says he needs to diet, you may perceive it as being a thinly veiled insult toward yourself. Your weight may never have entered his mind. Your self-concept filtered the conversation for important facts and you interpreted your friend's intent entirely differently. In fact, you might be so wrapped up internally that you could completely miss that your friend is expressing his *own* insecurities at that time. This is a case of your (probably temporary) self-absorption creating a barrier to receiving your friend's message. Do you see how you might fail to be considerate of your friend at that moment?

Your momentary emotional state (what mood you're in) can also affect your mental state (Wood, 2009) and your consideration of another person. Say your significant other just dumped you. You are likely to be too upset to really receive any information from anyone, and lash out at someone who did nothing to deserve it. That's not very considerate.

Our physical state can also affect the way we understand things (Sweet & Wisby, 1998). If you're sick, you may be distracted and have trouble paying attention in class, causing you to misunderstand directions for an assignment or the favor your mother just asked you to do. However, sickness is not the only way your body can get in the way of your mental function; you may also be cold, hot, wet, hungry, itchy, sleepy, or sneezy. The list goes on and on. (It's also starting to sound like the list of Snow White's friends!) Any of those may cause us to be mistaken.

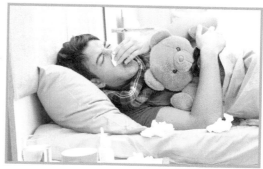

© Elnur/Shutterstock.com

Finally, your surroundings may also distract you and lead to incorrect information, because of sound or visual obstacles. We call that external noise, right? But those are not the only ways we can be wrong and fail to consider others' needs or wants.

Attribution Biases: I'll Take Attribution for $400, Alex.

We can make some dandy mistakes interpreting what is happening, and those mistakes can do disservice to others. **Attribution** is assigning meaning to what someone has done, whether it is we ourselves or someone else (Aronson, 1984; Fehr, 1993; Fehr & Russell, 1991). **Internal attribution** says that a person acts as they do because it reflects who they are. **External attribution** says that a person's actions may be driven by external forces influencing them to behave as they do. If we are not careful, we can judge another person's actions based on an assumed motive and be entirely wrong. Obviously, *that's* not fair.

Attribution
assigning meaning to what someone has done

Internal attribution
assuming a person acts as they do because it reflects who they are

External attribution
assuming a person's actions may be driven by external forces influencing them to behave as they do

There are basically four ways to get attribution wrong. The first mistake is called a **fundamental attribution error**. This is the tendency to assume the cause of any negative behavior by another person is internal rather than external. If you say a person did something bad due to his character rather than factors beyond his control, you made a fundamental attribution error. It's assuming the worst of another person. Once, on the way to work in icy weather, I had to stop at a light beside a hospital. Just as I got the green light and was about to pull into the turn lane, another car cut me off and nearly caused an accident. My passenger was very upset and called the other driver several choice names implying his ignorance and inconsiderate nature. He made a fundamental attribution error. The other driver may have been a wonderful person just trying to get someone to an emergency room, or he could have been the jerk that my passenger thought. I'll never know, but either way, a fundamental attribution error occurred in my car that day.

Fundamental attribution error
the tendency to assume the cause of any negative behavior by another person is internal rather than external

Another attribution error is similarity bias. **Similarity bias** is assuming that a person who is like you in one way will be like you in other ways. For example, if you are from Texas, wear cowboy boots, like country music, and hate opera, you may assume that another Texan who wears cowboy boots also likes country music and

Similarity bias
assuming that a person who is like you in one way will be like you in other ways

"What if, and I know this sounds kooky, we communicated with the employees."

© Cartoon Resource/Shutterstock.com

Attractiveness bias
the tendency to ascribe better motives for actions to attractive people than we would to less attractive people in the same circumstances

Jeff J Mitchell/Staff/Getty

Self-serving bias
the tendency to give ourselves credit for the best of motives, but when others in the same situation act in the same way, we assume bad things about their reasons

hates opera. Because he appears to be like you in a couple of areas, you assume he is like you in others. You may be wrong. He may love opera. Another way this can get us into trouble is that we often assume that people we like have the same values and beliefs we have, and we operate accordingly only to discover later that their values may be entirely different from ours.

The third type of attribution bias is called attractiveness bias (Aronsonn, 1984). **Attractiveness bias** is the tendency to ascribe better motives for actions to attractive people than we would to less attractive people in the same circumstances. That is all good if you are beautiful, but if you are not-so-great looking, it can create real problems for you. Remember when Susan Boyle made it big on *Britain's Got Talent*? That YouTube clip illustrates attractiveness bias very well. The treatment she received was very dismissive in the beginning of her performance. She didn't look very "put together." Both the judges and the audience appeared to have very low expectations of what she would sound like. Everyone was surprised when she actually sounded good. Some theorists think that attractiveness bias is hard wired into us (see Sidebar 11A). We do know that attractive people get more dates (no surprise there) and experience professional (Hosoda & Stone-Romero, 2006) and educational benefits (Talamas, Mavor, & Perrett, 2016). Van Leeuwen & Macrae (2004) found that attractiveness does elicit more positive responses, and Aronson (1984) found that attractive people are held accountable for their actions less than the rest of us. On behalf of the "plain" people, I'd like to assert that this is totally unfair, but there it is.

The last (and I think most prevalent) kind of attribution error is **self-serving bias**. That is when we give ourselves credit for the best of motives, but when others in the same situation act in the same way, we assume bad things about their reasons. Mezulius et al. (2004) confirmed the existence of this bias in the general population. Here's how that works: If a coworker takes my soft drink out of the fridge at work, I could call that theft, pure and simple. But if I take her drink, I think to myself that I was just "borrowing" it and would replace it as soon as possible, which might or might not happen. The action is the same, but I have given myself the benefit of the doubt by making that attribution. I might or might not do the same for others. This is pretty common, and sadly, most of us never even realize we are doing it. It's really tough to avoid, but in order to not be influenced by attribution biases, the first step is to become aware that we have them. Measuring yourself by the same standard that you apply to others is called integrity. Ethical behavior demands that we not expect better behavior from others than we would expect of ourselves.

Perspective Taking: Do You See What I See?

Another thing that gets us into interpersonal trouble is our failure to realize that other people don't necessarily "see things" the same way we do. They may come from a different background or culture, or they may have a different focus or need something different from an interaction than we do. That doesn't negate the validity of our needs or theirs, but we need to realize that they may see things differently. We need to put ourselves in the other person's shoes, especially when we are deeply invested in our own position. That process of seeing an issue from the other person's point of view is called **perspective taking**. It is tempting to only look at things from our own point of view, but the other person's viewpoint may be as valid as our own, and even if it is not, we must be respectful of it. We must just do the work and try to see what the other person sees. I'll give you an example from real life. I was raised to be very frugal. Every purchase was closely inspected for necessity and financial responsibility. I used to do customer service work (a profession that is notorious for not paying especially well) with a young man who was working only part-time and struggling to make ends meet. He came to work one day wearing a really nice, new sweater, and we all commented on it. I asked him if he could really afford something so expensive. His response was that he had been taught that buying the best quality was always the best choice because it would last longer and bring him pleasure every time he wore the garment. This forced me to step back and consider his position. Without engaging in that perception check, I would not have understood him.

So, how do you know if you're wrong? Ask! That's a perception check. What is a perception check you may ask? A **perception check** is asking another person to be certain that one is right in interpreting an even or situation. Simply getting another point of view can be very helpful making certain we don't mess it up. So, how do we get it right if we're confused or uncertain of our understanding of events or actions? We ask. It sounds so simple, you'd think we'd be willing to do it more often.

Perspective taking
process of seeing an issue from the other person's point of view

Perception check
asking another person to be certain that one is right in interpreting an event or situation

© JensHN/Shutterstock.com

Considerate Public Speaking: Tell It So I'll Understand!

On the flipside, what is your job as a speaker, and where does the audience come into that equation? Okay, here it is. Are you ready?

Public speaking is service.

Did you get that? That's your job, pure and simple. If you don't remember anything else I tell you about public speaking, remember this: you are there to *serve* the audience (Schultz, 2006). Being a servant does not make you a slave, but anticipating and responding to the needs of the audience is crucial. The act of speaking is not about you. It's not about showing everyone how smart you are, preventing your own humiliation, or even how great you look in a suit. (BTW, you look great!) It's about serving the audience (Hoff, 1988) and serving the subject. You find out what the audience needs, and you focus on giving them that, whatever it is. In I Cor. 9:20-23, Paul said he made himself like his audience members so that they would be able and willing to receive his message. He was doing exactly what I'm talking about. He was serving the audience and the subject, and God by extension.

Serving the audience comes with a wonderful and unexpected benefit: when you are centered on the audience instead of yourself, you usually relax a little bit! Now, I won't lie to you and tell you that you won't feel nervous at all, but the worst of it often passes when you take your focus off yourself and put it on the audience where it belongs. In fact, when you're focused on getting your ideas across, you might actually discover that you are having a good time and even feeling a little bit fulfilled by the experience. Consideration is a powerful thing.

Look at the diagram below. Notice that the arrow only goes in one direction. Think of this line as having a fixed point on the left and a rubber band that pulls over to the right. The standard informative speech represents what the audience already knows and puts no pressure on the rubber band. As you go further to the right, more tension is introduced to the audience and the harder the speech

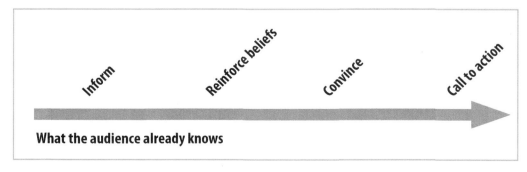

Sidebar 11B

is to do successfully. Tension comes when what the audience members know is challenged. Next to that is the first type of persuasive speech, the **speech to reinforce**, in which the audience's beliefs or behaviors are not challenged. In a speech to reinforce, you're not changing what they believe or do, but you are encouraging them to continue to believe or do what they already believe or do. A little further over is the **speech to convince**, which is getting the audience to believe something different than they already believe. This is obviously a persuasive speech that takes more work and is harder than reinforcement, but it only involves changing the audience's mind, not prompting them to act. The furthest speech to the right is the **call to action speech**. That requires the audience to actually *do* something. I hope it is apparent that this is the hardest type of persuasive speech. Getting people to do something is hard. But don't worry; we're going to save that for the chapter on persuasion.

So, we need to examine how a considerate speaker approaches these tasks, beginning with analyzing the audience.

Picking a Topic

First, we need to select a topic. As we discussed earlier, the task of the speaker is to serve the audience, and it is important to find a topic that fits you, the audience, and the occasion (Hybels & Weaver, 2001). A topic that fits you should be something that you (1) already know something about and (2) care enough about to commit to doing the research. The topic should also (3) be a good fit for the audience. Finally, (4) the topic should fit the speaking occasion. Great speeches have the *right* speaker giving the *right* message to the *right* audience at the *right* time (Jaffe, 2013).

Ask yourself: Are you knowledgeable about the topic (DeVito, 2000; Fraleigh & Tuman, 2017)? Sometimes a teacher will ask you to start with a topic you know nothing about, research it, and speak on it. The intent of this activity is usually to hone your research skills. But in real life you will seldom, if ever, be asked to speak on something about which you know nothing. You'll be asked to speak precisely because you *do* know something. When a speaker is chosen for a group meeting or event, they are chosen specifically because of their expertise.

Are you passionate about the topic? A passionate speaker can make even a boring topic interesting, and the speeches people hear have the potential to change

Speech to reinforce
persuasive speech to reinforce the audience's beliefs or behaviors

Speech to convince
persuasive speech to get the audience to believe something different than they already believe

Call to action speech
persuasive speech that requires the audience to actually do something

Sidebar 11 C Finding a topic . . . .

- Consider topics that interest you.
- Examine your activities and hobbies.
- Think about beliefs or ideas that you think are really important.
- Look at current events.
- Consider ideas related to your major.
- Look at the charities or humanitarian efforts you support.
- Browse the Internet.
- Flip through magazines or other periodicals.
- Ask your friends/classmates what would interest them.

their lives. It's a chance to strike a blow for the cause you hold dear (Wood, 2009). My sister is alive because a young man donated an organ. Someone *persuaded* him to be an organ donor. He wasn't born with a donor form in his hand. How many lives could be saved if you show the audience how easy it is to become an organ donor? How many children's futures could be saved if your audience members considered being foster parents? These are important issues and reasonable, worthwhile ideas to consider. Treat your speech topic like it matters, because it does! One of the benefits of passion is that it keeps you focused. Adequately researching and preparing for a speech takes a lot of time and energy, so you had better love what you are speaking about, or you'll hate every minute of the process and probably not do a very good job. Additionally, you need passion because you'll never sell an audience on an idea that you aren't really sold on yourself!

Will the audience care about this topic? Pick a topic that has significance to the audience (Fraleigh & Tuman, 2017; O'Hair, Rubenstein, & Stewart, 2013; Wood, 2009). That means it is suited to their needs and concerns. You should consider what they already know about the topic. You can get a fair idea about what they will think about a particular topic by doing a demographic analysis of the audience; it should also give you some idea about their beliefs and attitudes about the topic in question. That's one reason we do audience analysis in the first place! If the audience has no connection or interest in the topic, why are you giving the speech anyway? It's supposed to be for them; however, the topic needs to work for you, as well.

Will this topic work for the occasion? *Consider if the topic works* for the purpose of the event, the mood people will be in, the location of the speech, and the time of day, as well as how long you can speak (DeVito, 2000; O'Hair, Rubenstein, & Stewart, 2013). All these things should help you narrow down the options on a topic until you have a good fit for the occasion, the audience, and the speaker.

Audience Analysis: Who is your audience, anyway?

One of the major jobs a speaker has to do is audience analysis. Audience analysis is figuring out what the audience knows, thinks, and feels in order to adapt your topic, content, visuals, and delivery to meet their needs (Schultz, 2006). It's an excellent example of perspective taking, which we discussed earlier. By doing an audience analysis, you are trying to put yourself into the shoes of the audience and figure out what they see. My friend and co-author, Susan McMurray, says that when we look at a picture in which we appear, we look first for ourselves. The same is true of an audience. They are looking for how they can relate to your speech. Start with some questions. What do they already know about your topic? What do they believe about it? What is important to them?

Audience analysis
process of figuring out what the audience knows, thinks and feels in order to adapt your topic, content, visuals, and delivery to meet their needs

© sirtravelalot/Shutterstock.com

What do they need? You need to get an idea of what they already know, value, and believe. That helps you know where to begin giving new information, anticipate what questions may arise, and figure out how to overcome their objections.

What are their attitudes about the topic?

Knowing your audience's attitudes is crucial to building a well-received speech. If you know what they value and what they identify as important, you have gone a long way toward being able to serve them (Devereaux Ferguson, 2008; Hybels & Weaver, 2001). If you are speaking to raise money for a homeless shelter, and you know the audience is made up of people who are committed to one of the major world faiths that value caring for the poor, you can use that to motivate them to give. If, on the other hand, they belong to a group that stresses personal financial responsibility, you may have to find another way to get them to give, like showing them how the shelter benefits the community and actually builds the local economy.

What are the audience's expectations?

Of course, they expect you to respect their time. But they also have other expectations (Dobkin & Pace, 2003). First, they expect you to be informed. If you don't know any more than they do, why would they give you a piece of their precious time? Secondly, they expect you to be prepared. If you don't remember what you intend to talk about next, or your visuals are sloppy, they will figure out pretty quickly that you didn't do your homework and they will probably lose a lot of respect for you. Finally, they expect you to look nice, not just clean; they expect professional appearance.

What are the audience demographics?

You can get a pretty good idea by asking whoever invited you to speak what the audience is like, but you may also be able to get access to some demographics about the audience. Demographics refers to basic, quantifiable information you know about the audience. Several kinds of demographic data can be secured about an audience, including:

Demographics
basic, quantifiable information you know about the audience

Age—Various age groups approach certain topics differently. If you are talking about reforming Social Security, an audience of young people will be interested in how sustainable it will be, while the older folks may be concerned with how reform will affect their benefits.

Gender—Men may receive a topic differently than women. Women are likely to be less interested in a speech about reinstating the draft to military service than men.

Socioeconomic Status (SES)—Often, we can make basic assumptions about social or political views based on SES. For example, if your audience is mostly middle class, you can expect that most will think college is important for young adults; however, this may or may not be the case among people who live in poverty.

The purpose of the gathering has a great effect on how a speech is planned.

© hxdbzxy/Shutterstock.com

© JiriCastka/Shutterstock.com

Nationality/Race/Ethnicity—People of different ethnicities often experience elements of life differently. For example, a group of Latinos will likely feel differently about immigration reform than a group of white Midwesterners.

Educational Level—If your audience members are college students, you can take for granted a basic level of knowledge about vocabulary, cultural history, and critical thinking, especially as it relates to persuasion. Just remember that a lack of education doesn't equate to a lack of intelligence.

Group Affiliation—Finally, look at whether your audience members all belong to a particular group. A group of commuter students will feel probably differently about abolition of on-campus curfews than a group of students who live on campus.

Taking demographics into account is a major part of audience analysis and a way of helping the audience by addressing their particular needs and concerns. Many people think that the speaker paying attention to the audience all takes place during the speech, but a tremendous amount happens in advance. Both are very important.

Occasion Analysis: Does the setting make any difference?

You bet it does! Before and during public speaking, there are different elements of context you need to examine carefully in order to adjust to the setting. Occasion analysis is considering the purpose of the gathering, the timing of the speech, the mood of the audience, and the social rules that govern interaction in public speaking communication.

First, be aware of the mood of the gathering. The mood for a wedding toast is entirely different than that of a funeral eulogy. The audience has expectations. If you go to church, you expect something entirely different than if you go to a public lecture, even if the topic is the same.

Second, be aware of time. The audience expects you to conform to the time limits you were given. They have committed to give you a small segment of their lives. Respect what that means! Time also includes time of day, so be aware that *when*

Occasion analysis
process of considering the purpose of the gathering, the timing of the speech, the mood of the audience, and the social rules that govern interaction in public speaking communication

you speak during the day will affect how receptive the audience is likely to be. Right after lunch, the audience may be drowsy, so deliver your speech with energy.

Finally, remember that public speaking is a conversation between you and the audience. You get to do most of the talking, and the audience's feedback is largely nonverbal, but it is a conversation nonetheless. There are unspoken rules about the ways an audience can interact with a speaker, and you should be prepared to view and interpret their reactions through that lens. They can't come right out and call you a liar if they don't believe you, but they can frown, turn their heads to the side, and look skeptical. Be prepared to be sensitive to their feedback.

© sebra/Shutterstock.com

Ethical Implications

Considerate communicators are careful about how they treat people and make judgments about them. Only God can see another's heart. The scriptures tell us not to judge another (Matt. 7:1), and the more of life I see, the more I realize that I can't really know anyone else's motives for certain. It's nearly impossible to avoid judging someone else once in a while, but we can surely try to give others the benefit of the doubt.

About attribution, just be aware of it. You're probably going to do it, like making judgments about others. This is probably not right but we're likely to do it, so we need to try to get better. Don't assume that everyone thinks the same way you do. Don't hold others to standards you cannot maintain. Not everyone is pretty by society's standards, but they are all still made in the image of God and should be treated that way.

Now, about perception checks and gossip . . . . a good way to tell if you're gossiping is to really examine your motive for asking for confirmation from the other person. Unless you are genuinely confused, it's probably not a perception check. If it gives you that perverse little thrill inside, it's not a perception check. It's gossip. Be honest with yourself and hold yourself accountable to the same standards you would use to evaluate the actions of anyone else.

Remember that we are not all alike. Appreciate those differences. Sometimes I think our culture says we are "valuing diversity" when we pretend we are all the same, instead of genuinely valuing the things that make us unique. God likes diversity! Surely a few types of tropical fish would have been enough, but He wanted lots of them, so that's what He made. He made every person unique, so we need to try to see and appreciate the wonder each person is.

When you are involved in public speaking, whether listening or speaking, remember that speakers and audiences both need to be respected and appreciated. An attitude of humility serves us well both when listening to a speech and when preparing for one.

Finally, being considerate of others often calls for sacrifice, which may not be fun, but it is very rewarding. When we see someone else's needs and perspectives as being as significant as our own, we are practicing empathy, developing the ability to see another point of view, and cultivating humility.

Summary

It is important that we not be self-centered and realize we could be wrong in our interpretations. The perceptual process is susceptible to failure when we are not considerate of others because of our self-concept, emotional state, or incorrect attribution, especially with similarity bias, fundamental attribution error, attractiveness bias, and self-serving bias. Perception checks enable us to verify what we heard, and perspective taking lets us see the world from another point of view. Public speakers must be especially considerate of others. The speaker is a servant both to the topic and to the audience. Consider your audience and their needs, values, and beliefs as you pick your topic and plan your speech. Take the setting of the speech into consideration as well. Your topic should be one about which you already know something and about which you care deeply.

Vocabulary Words

Attractiveness bias
Attribution
Audience analysis
Call to action speech
Demographics
External attribution

Fundamental attribution
   error
Internal attribution
Occasion analysis
Perception check
Perspective taking

Self-serving bias
Similarity bias
Speech to convince
Speech to reinforce

Discussion Questions

1. Which attribution bias are you most likely to commit?
2. Are you as tough on yourself when you examine your actions as you are on others?
3. What role does respect play in being considerate?
4. When have you been surprised to find an area that someone was significantly different from you?
5. Have you ever heard a speech where the speaker clearly put no thought into the audience's perspective?
6. What do you know about your audience? What do they care about?
7. What topic would be interesting to them? What do they know/believe about that topic?
8. Will that topic interest you? Do you already know about it?

References

Aronson, E. (1984). *The social animal* (4th ed.). New York: W. H. Freeman.

Brown, J. D., & Mankowski, T. A. (1993). Self-esteem, mood, and self-evaluation: Changes in mood and the way you see you. *Journal of Personality and Social Psychology, 64,* 421–430.

Campbell, J. D. (1990). Self-esteem and clarity of the self-concept. *Journal of Personality and Social Psychology, 59,* 538–549.

Devereaux Ferguson, S. (2008). *Public speaking: Building competency in stages.* New York: Oxford University Press.

DeVito, J. A. (2000). *The elements of public speaking* (7th ed.). New York: Longman.

Dobkin, B. A., & Pace, R. C. (2003). *Communication in a changing world.* New York: McGraw-Hill.

Fehr, B. (1993). How do I love thee?: Let me consult my prototype. In S. W. Duck (Ed.), *Understanding relationship processes, 1: Individual relationships* (pp. 87–122). Newbury Park, CA: Sage.

Fehr, B., & Russell, J. A. (1991). Concept of love viewed from a prototype perspective. *Journal of Personality and Social Psychology, 60,* 425–438.

Floyd, K. (2014). *Communication matters.* (2nd ed.). New York: McGraw-Hill.

Fraleigh, D. M., & Tuman, J. S. (2017). *Speak up!: An illustrated guide to public speaking* (4th ed.). Boston, MA: Bedford/ St. Martin's.

Hoff, R. (1988). *I can see you naked.* Kansas City, MO: Andrews & McMeel.

Hosoda, M., & Stone-Romero, E. F. (2006). The effects of physical attractiveness on job-related outcomes: A meta-analysis of experimental studies. *Personnel Psychology, 56*(2), 431–462. doi:10.1111/j.1744-6570.2003,tb00157.x

Hybels, S., & Weaver, R. L., II. (2001). *Communicating effectively* (6th ed.). New York, NY: McGraw-Hill.

Jaffe, C. I. (2013). *Public speaking: Concepts and skills for a diverse society* (7th ed.). Boston, MA: Wadsworth.

O'Hair, D., Rubenstein, H., & Stewart, R. (2013). *A pocket guide to public speaking* (4th ed.). Boston, MA: Bedford/St. Martin's.

Schultz, Q. (2006). *An essential guide to public speaking: Serving your audience with faith, skill, and virtue.* Grand Rapids, MI: Baker Academic.

Sweet, L., & Wisby, G. (1998, June 25). From A's to Z's: Later school start, fresher pupils sought. *Chicago Sun-Times,* p. 4.

Talamas, S. N., Mavor, K. I., & Perrett, D. I. (2016) Blinded by Beauty: Attractiveness Bias and Accurate Perceptions of Academic Performance. *PLoS One 11*(2): e0148284. https://doi.org/10.1371/journal.pone.0148284

Van Leeuwen, M. L., & Macrae, C. N. (2004). Is beautiful always good? Implicit benefits of facial attractiveness. *Social Cognition, 22*(6), 637–649. doi: 10.1521/soco.22.6.637.54819

Wood, J. T. (2002) Gendered standpoints on personal relationships. In J. Steward (Ed.), *Bridges, not walls* (9th ed., pp. 377–384). New York, NY: McGraw-Hill.

Wood, J. T. (2009). *Communication in our lives* (5th ed.). Boston, MA: Wadsworth.

Additional Readings

The Power of Context: How to Manage Our Bias and Improve Our Understanding of Others

by Daniel R. Stalder

Give Your Speech, Change the World: How to Move Your Audience to Action

by Nick Morgan

Better Communicators Are Informative

By Rhonda Gallagher, M.S.

12

Well, friends, if you are reading this chapter, then you are a member of a blessed and highly favored group. You see, most universities dictate that the first communication class will focus on either (a) public speaking or (b) interpersonal communication. But there are a few schools that believe that you need all of it to be a competent communicator, and they choose to offer a course that is roughly half interpersonal communication and half public speaking. If you're reading this, then your teacher wants you to have a taste of it all, and you're about to get introduced to informative speaking along with a study of the ethical choices we make in the process! You see, public speaking can be scary for most of us (Davidson & Dwyer, 2012; Richmond & McCroskey, 1998), but it's really important for both our professional lives and to be civically involved (Jaffe, 2013; Parvis, 2001).

So, what is public speaking? **Public speaking** is the act of one speaker addressing a large group of people in person. Usually, the distance is between 12 and 25 feet (Hall, 1969), and the speaker has one clear goal to accomplish. An informative speech focuses on simply sharing information. But, first, let's begin by looking at why we engage in public speaking.

Public speaking
the act of one speaker addressing a
large group of people in person

© michaeljung/Shutterstock.com

Forensics
the study of public speaking

Why Speak?

Public speaking has a long and venerated history. We call the study of public speaking **forensics**, and it first arose in ancient Greece in the 5th century B.C.E. (Jaffe, 2013; O'Hair, Rubenstein, & Stewart, 2013). You've heard of some of the ancient greats: Cicero, Socrates, Plato, Aristotle, and Jesus. Cicero was a politician; Socrates and Plato were teachers; Aristotle was a philosopher; and Jesus sort of did it all. But they all had one thing in common: they used their gift for speaking to serve the community. As I said in the last chapter, public speaking is about service. Let me say that again because it bears repeating. Schultz (2006) stated that the role of the speaker, especially a Christian speaker, is to serve. It's not about looking good, impressing people, or even getting what you want. It's not about you. It's about serving the topic and the audience, and by extension, God. It brings information and ideas to light in a public setting and focuses the attention of everyone there on something important (Hogan, Andrews, Andrews, & Williams, 2017). The speaker brings the audience's attention to bear on the issue in such a way that they can no longer ignore its existence, as if to say to the listener, "Well, now you know; what are you going to do about it?" Public speakers often force us to examine things we might just as happily avoid, but by doing so, they force us to deal with problems and can help us make the world a better place. In essence, they force honesty in the way we examine our world.

Many people fear public speaking . . . a lot! (I'm not sure why; it was never an issue for me, but then again, that may be why I *teach* it. Hmmm . . . .). Some surveys actually show that it is the second strongest fear, right behind death (Davidson & Dwyer, 2012). In fact, some people really, truly would rather die than give a speech. It's a funny thing, though; if you put your focus on the service to the audience, it helps take the attention off of yourself, and your speech anxiety may decrease because it's not about you anymore!

Informative Speech Types

Think about informational speeches you've listened to in the past. They probably didn't all seem alike. That's because they weren't. A speech to show you how to sew on a button is very different than a speech that explains the lifecycle of a mosquito. There are basically four types of informative speeches (Dobkin & Pace, 2003).

1. **Speeches that describe** just tell what something is like. If you describe what the Taj Mahal looks like, where it is situated, what it is made of, its romantic history, etc., you are giving a speech to describe.

2. **Speeches that explain** tell how a process works or why a thing happens as it does, for example, telling how the Electoral College works or how the Vatican became its own country.

3. **Speeches to demonstrate** are "how to" speeches. These are great jumping off points for people who have never given a speech before. You can show an audience how to make cookies, paint their toenails, gift wrap a present, or do any other skill that humans practice. If you choose a speech to demonstrate, it's a good idea to select a skill that is simple to do, and requires little space and needs only a few supplies. While I suppose it's been done before as a demonstration speech, how to shear a sheep would be a pretty impractical topic for most speaking situations. (Especially in my class. I thank you in advance for not choosing that topic!) It is especially important to practice for these speeches using both the objects to repeat the process, and the words you mean to say (Fraleigh & Tuman, 2017).

4. **Speeches to narrate** tell a story. Usually we associate these with "what I did on my summer vacation" speeches. You might share about what happened on a mission trip you took or the life event that caused you to choose a particular major. Of course, you can also tell about historical events in story fashion, like telling about the discovery of Tutankhamun's tomb.

Speeches that describe
speeches that tell what something is like

Speeches that explain
speeches that tell how a process works or why a thing happens as it does

Speeches to demonstrate
"how to" speeches

Speeches to narrate
speeches that tell a story

This demonstration speech is serving the audience and the community.
© SpeedKingz/Shutterstock.com

There are certain things we need to keep in mind as we prepare an informative speech and they provide a nice structure for the rest of the chapter. They are: keep your focus on your topic, know what you're talking about, and be organized.

Speech Purposes: Focus, People, Focus!

There are basically two types of speech purposes: the general speech purpose and the specific speech purpose (Gregory, 2002). Let's start with the big one first. The **general speech purpose** is the big goal of the speech, and there are generally four recognized, though that can vary (Ferguson, 2008; O'Hair et al., 2013): to inform, to persuade, to entertain, and to address a special occasion. (There is also a specific speech purpose for every speech, and we'll get to more about that in the next chapter.)

© Ollyy/Shutterstock.com

General speech purpose
the big goal of the speech

Informative speaking
speaking to give information to the audience

Informative speaking is just that: giving information to the audience. There is no agenda beyond that (Goodall & Goodall, 2006). You may feel strongly about the topic; you may even *want* to persuade the audience to believe or do something, but don't try to do that. In an informative speech, you give the best, balanced information that you can, and you let the information speak for itself. You might give a speech about the life of a college freshman to a group of high school students. You might want them to realize that they ought to study harder so that they can get a scholarship, but you won't tell them that. You are just there to give information. That's all. Save your persuasion for persuasive speaking.

Persuasive speaking
speaking to make the audience believe or do something

In **persuasive speaking,** you set out to make the audience believe or do something. You want a group of businesspeople to roll up their sleeves and give blood on the spot, so you *set out to persuade them* to do so. You may tell them all the things donated blood is used for, which is sharing information, but only as it serves the purpose of persuasion. You can have a perfectly good informative speech without any persuasion in it, but you can't have a good persuasive speech without any information. A persuasive speech without information to support your claims is just a rant. Supplying the audience with good evidence strengthens your argument and your credibility, but everyone should know that you are trying to be persuasive, not just informative. You tell them right up front that persuasion is your plan.

Entertainment speaking
speaking to help the audience relax and have fun

© stock_photo_world/Shutterstock.com

The purpose of **entertainment speaking** is to help the audience relax and have some fun. You may have another point that you would like to get across, but the *most important* thing you're doing is helping the audience enjoy the time. Entertainment speaking often occurs at a banquet during the after dinner speech, which is a funny speech given after a meal to make the evening more enjoyable. You might see a good example of one at a Toastmasters' meeting. (Toastmasters is group of people who meet regularly to give speeches to each other and improve their public speaking skills.) You also see it when a standup comedian gives a monologue. Entertainment speaking is probably the most specialized type of public speaking, and we actually see very few of these given in person.

Special occasion speaking
speaking done at a special occasion

Special occasion speaking is speaking at a special occasion, hence the name. They are addressed in Appendix A. You should read it.

Now you know a little bit about the general speech purpose and how to identify various types of speeches, but you can't begin to build an informative speech until you get informed.

Research: Know What You're Talking About!

This might be the most important part of informative speaking. *You can't be informative without being informed!* Your audience has other things to do with their time, so have something worth hearing, and do a good job saying it. You owe it to them. If you don't know about your topic, why should anyone listen to you, anyway? The audience will figure out pretty quickly if you aren't knowledgeable, and they'll tune you out. Do the research so that you can give the audience something that will help them understand or improve their lives in some way. And when you do your research, keep some things in mind:

Get good quality information.

It should come from a variety of sources, including electronic resources (especially electronic journals, but also the Internet, if the quality is good), print materials (like books and periodicals), interviews you have conducted, and your own personal experiences. Just don't cite yourself in the bibliography. (Don't laugh; I've seen it happen. Right there in the "M"s: "Myself"!)

Reference librarians can be a LOT of help!

© Phovoir/Shutterstock.com

Get lots of information.

To begin with, you already chose a topic you knew a lot about, so you may be tempted not to do additional research. The reason you do more research is to improve the quality of what you give your audience. Don't scrimp on this step. You need to pick the best evidence to give to the audience, so you need a lot to choose from. I always tell my classes to unearth a wheelbarrow full of information so that you, the speaker, can pick through and choose the best bowlful to use in the speech.

Use a variety of types of information.

There are several types of information, including quotes, analogies, examples, and visual aids, among others. Don't worry about getting the whole list now. We'll do that in the next chapter. The key here is to think about getting a variety of types of data (DeVito, 2000; O'Hair et al., 2013; Reynolds & Burgoon, 2002). Some audiences will be attracted to particular types of

© Sergey Nivens/Shutterstock.com

evidence. A group of Christians will be more likely to respond well to quotations from the New Testament. A group of doctors may prefer statistics and case studies. Different people respond to different kinds of evidence, so having a variety helps you engage everyone. Getting several types of information does something else as well that's just for you: it increases your credibility (Floyd, 2014). It shows the audience that you did the study to know what you are talking about, so they trust you more, and that in turn improves the quality of their experience.

So where can you get good information? There are basically four places to look.

Information Sources

Library materials

There's a reason why teachers will go to this source first. You're going to get better quality information from a library source, and if you know how, library databases are just as easy to use as the Internet. Of course, the library has many excellent print materials like books and magazines (just because it's in print doesn't automatically mean it's out of date!), but it also has access to online journals, which are probably the best sources to use for academic research. Let me explain. In order for an article to be published in an academic journal, either online or on paper, it has to be submitted to a group of experts in the field. They review the article and determine if the author knows anything worth repeating. Those articles are then catalogued in online databases for which libraries pay a subscription fee. Then, students and faculty can log onto the library site, access the database, and find really good information just as easily as they can on the Internet. There are several databases for different fields of study, like ERIC for education or PsychLIT for social sciences, but EBSCOhost is usually a good place to start. I recommend that my students actually go to the library, find the reference section, and talk to a real, live reference librarian. Reference librarians can show you how to access the databases and use them to actually *find* stuff, as well as how to access the university library databases online. It takes a special kind of person to be a true reference librarian. They tend to be sort of obsessed with finding things out. They will know where you should look and how to find whatever you need.

Internet

Now, you can also get information from the Internet. Recent studies show that many users find the Internet at least as credible than traditional news sources (Flanagin & Metzger, 2000; Johnson & Kaye, 1998), but while many may trust the Internet, they seldom verify that it is accurate (Flanagin & Metzger, 2000; Metzger, Flanagin, & Zwarun, 2003), and maybe less than they should. The good thing about the Internet is that you can access the Internet from anywhere, and you don't have to go through a library or university server to get to it. The downside is that there is no organization that validates the accuracy of postings. Many online sources have great information, but look for websites that are accurate, balanced and credible (Floyd, 2014). Pay attention to the extensions. Use .edu, .gov, or .org.

Those tend to be better quality information. Use .coms and .nets with care. If it is a news site, like nytimes.com or msnbc.com, you can trust the reputation of the source, but most .coms have an agenda to part you from your money, not spread the truth. If you don't have access to online library databases, try googlescholar.com. It can be accessed through google.com and has only academic sources, similar to a library database.

Informational Interviews

The third source for information is personal interviews that you conduct. An interview is just a conversation with a purpose. An informational interview is a conversation in which one person asks questions of another person in order to gain information. So, you need to know something, and someone else has the answers. How do you get those answers? Some guidelines are helpful if you've never conducted an informational interview before.

Interview
a conversation with a purpose

Informational interview
a conversation in which one person asks questions of another person in order to gain information

1. ***Pick a credible person to interview*** (Ferguson, 2008). Interview someone who knows what they are talking about. There are two ways a person can be a credible source. If they have studied a topic extensively, like a researcher, doctor, or teacher in a given area, then they are knowledgeable. A source who has personal experience with something is also credible. If you need to know about chemotherapy, you can interview a doctor, a cancer patient, or a caregiver of a cancer patient, because all of them have experience and knowledge about the topic, though the *kind* of knowledge they have is different. Realize that the guy across the hall in your dorm is not a credible source, unless he is a doctor, cancer patient, or a caregiver. Get the picture? Be careful picking the person you should interview.

You can only record an interview if the interviewee agrees!

© pan_kung/Shutterstock.com

2. ***Do some preliminary research before the interview*** (Ferguson, 2008). You need to know enough to ask an intelligent question. An interview is a great place to get information that was unavailable to you or that you couldn't find on your own. Use the interview to plug holes in your knowledge. If you don't know anything about the topic before the interview, you are actually insulting the interviewee by implying that their topic was not important enough to learn about before meeting with them, and you send the message that their time is not valuable.

3. ***Prepare your questions in advance*** (Wood, 2009). You should have five or six interview questions written and ready before you ever begin the interview. Word them carefully so that they are clear and easy to understand. Vague or unclear questions waste time and may confuse or frustrate the interviewee. Avoid double-barreled questions. Those are questions that include two or more questions together before the interviewee has an opportunity to answer

Double-barreled questions
questions that include two or more questions asked at the same time.

either. You should carefully choose wording that asks only one question at a time. Furthermore, your questions should be open-ended questions (those that allow the interviewee to determine the amount and depth of information they want to give). These questions invite the interviewee to share. They start with "why," "describe," "please explain," "what," or "how," and let the interviewee cover a lot of ground quickly, sort of like a paint roller covering a wall. The opposite of an open-ended question is a close-ended question. It is a question geared to solicit answers of one or two words. (These questions start with "did," "would," "could," "have.") If an open-ended question is like a paint roller, a closed-ended question is more like a detail brush that fills in the edges.

4. *Ask neutral questions* (Ferguson, 2008). Some interviewers try to steer the interviewee in a particular direction or trap them with their own words. Do I even need to say that is wrong? A neutral question does not reveal any interviewer bias and lets the interviewee respond however they choose. For example, you might ask, "What are your feelings about domestic violence?" A leading question reveals to the interviewee how the interviewer wants them to answer by the way it's worded. For example, "Domestic violence is a terrible thing, wouldn't you say?" A loaded question is one that is worded as a closed-ended question and causes the interviewee to be unable to answer without saying something bad about him/herself. Loaded questions blow up in the interviewee's face, hence the name. Of course, the classic example is "When did you stop beating your wife?" If the interviewee says "never," he's admitting that he has beaten his wife in the past, and if he says he hasn't stopped, he's saying that he is still beating his wife. Don't do that to people. It's just mean.

5. *Ask follow-up questions.* A Follow-up question is a question that comes up in your own mind during the conversation in response to what you hear the interviewee saying. A lot of good information can be obtained by just pursuing a line of thought for a while.

6. *Pay attention to the interviewee's nonverbal feedback* (Hybels & Weaver, 2001). Often, an interviewee will give you extra information by the use of their face, pauses, or eye movements. They may also telegraph by their posture or body language that they are not telling you everything. Pay attention. The clues they are sending indicate that more important information can be gained by asking some follow-up questions. Of course, you can do phone or online interviews, but you'll be losing this valuable source of unspoken information. I prefer face-to-face interviews when I have a choice.

It might be good to insert just a quick note here about listening during an interview. Be sure to *really* listen. Be fully present. Put away your phone and give that person your full attention, not just with your ears, but also with your eyes so that you notice the subtle non-verbal cues they may be giving you. When the interviewee finishes an answer, it's sometimes good to be silent for a couple of seconds longer than you would

© Ollyy/Shutterstock.com

ordinarily. It may give them a sense of your permission to elaborate. If you can record the meeting (only with their permission [Ferguson, 2008; Wood, 2009], of course), you don't need to worry so much about taking notes, and that will free up more of your attention, as well.

Personal Experience

You have had experiences from which you've gained information and insight that you can use to enhance your speech (Dobkin & Pace, 2003). Not only is it additional information, it gives a human face to the content and also helps the audience identify with you. Yes, your own life experiences provide valuable information, but don't list yourself in the bibliography (as I've already mentioned). The bibliography lists the sources you used to get additional information *beyond* what you already knew, so you don't get to be part of the bibliography. Sorry.

Who could you interview?

When gathering information for a speech, the interviewee needs to be knowledgeable about the topic. They can either have expertise because of their own personal experiences, or they might have studied the topic. Who might be a credible source for the following topics?

| Blood donation | Car repair | Flower arranging | Civil War |
| Leonardo DaVinci | Investing | Water shortages | Pet care |

Sidebar 12A Reference librarians can be a LOT of help!

© Phovoir/Shutterstock.com

Plagiarism: That's Cheating!

Just a word to the wise here: when you're doing research, be sure to take good notes. You can plagiarize unintentionally so easily if you don't take extra special care to cite sources in the outline, in the speech, and in the bibliography. Plagiarism is using someone else's words or original ideas without giving them credit. Just because you put a source in the bibliography doesn't indicate where in the outline or speech you used another person's words, and if you reference another person's words or original idea, you must cite that person *immediately* and show quotation marks if you gave their exact words. A journalist

© Jacob Lund/Shutterstock.com

Plagiarism
using someone else's words or
original ideas without giving them
credit

friend of mine, Dana Sterling, says a good standard for avoiding plagiarism is to cite anything of five or more words in a row. That's a pretty strict standard: pay attention!

Another good idea is to actually keep a working bibliography while you are doing research. As soon as you take one piece of information from a source, get that source into your bibliography immediately. Then, when you're done and ready to finalize the bibliography, it will be a simple process to weed out the sources you didn't use instead of a frantic search for information about a source that you can no longer find.

Outlining the Speech

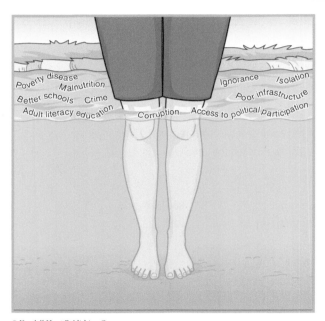

© Kendall Hunt Publishing Company

Order is so important in a speech. Let me say that again. Order is so important in a speech. Why? Because it serves both the audience and the speaker. If the information is organized in the right way, it makes it easier for the audience to understand, and it also makes it easier for the speaker to remember. Order is a blessing from God. So how do you know how things should go together?

Well, if you do as I suggested previously and find a lot of information in the research process, some bits should begin gathering together in your mind into the important ideas you want to say in the speech. It's like going wading in a pond. The more you move the stuff underfoot around, the more stuff floats to the surface. It's the same with data when you're researching. Good stuff should be floating to the top and naturally begin to clump together into idea groups. Those groups become the main ideas you want to cover. They just sort of present themselves. Not everything that comes to the top has to be addressed, but the groupings of ideas should begin to emerge and enable you to decide which ideas to address.

Organizational pattern
the structured order of the
main points, or Roman
numerals of a speech

Once the main ideas have clustered on the surface of the research, look at the organizational patterns available and see which one fits it best (Floyd, 2013). An **organizational pattern** is the structured order of the main points, or Roman numerals. There are five that can be used for informative speeches, but we'll go into those in depth in the next chapter on organization. For now, just realize that some organizational patterns fit some types of topics and speeches, while other organizational patterns fit other topics and speeches. An understandable order is more important than saying everything you want to say, because if the audience can't understand the connections, they won't retain what you said anyway (Chesebro, 2003; Houser, 2006).

Ethical Implications

Remember that the purpose of speaking is to serve the audience and the subject, disclosing anything you have to gain. Don't try to be sneaky and tell an audience your speech is informative if you actually mean to persuade them, and if you will gain any personal benefit by persuading them, tell them so up front. That's just fair play.

Don't waste people's time making noise if you haven't done the research or prepared something good to say (Floyd, 2014). The audience is trusting you to tell them the truth (DeVito, 2000; Floyd, 2014; Fraleigh & Tuman, 2017) and they have agreed to give you a short portion of their lives while you present the speech. Their time is a precious commodity. Don't be flippant about it. Do the research, and tell the truth. It is better to tell them an ugly truth than a pretty lie.

When you do an interview, be respectful of the interviewee's time, and don't try to trick them into saying something they don't want to say. If your information is good, it will stand up to critical thinking, so don't try to twist it around to make it fit your purpose.

Summary

The study of public speaking, also known as forensics, is about service. The four general purposes of speaking are informative, persuasive, entertainment, and commemoration of a special time/event. There are four types of informative speeches: speeches to explain, to describe, to demonstrate, and to narrate. Be sure to do plenty of research before you start building the outline. You can find information in library sources, on the Internet, in your personal experiences, and through informational interviews that you conduct. Pick the organizational pattern that best fits the information and the needs of your audience.

Vocabulary Words

Closed-ended question	Interview	Public speaking
Double-barreled question	Leading question	Special occasion speech
Entertainment speaking	Loaded question	Speeches that demonstrate
Follow-up question	Neutral question	Speeches that describe
Forensics	Open-ended question	Speeches that explain
General speech purpose	Organizational pattern	Speeches that narrate
Informational interview	Persuasive speaking	
Informative speaking	Plagiarism	

Discussion Questions

1. When have you listened to an informative speech in the past?
2. Think of informative speakers you have seen in the past. What did they do well? What did they do badly?
3. When have you ever given an informative speech?
4. What did you struggle with? In what ways were you successful?
5. What topic have you chosen for your upcoming speech?
6. Have you ever done an informational interview?
7. Who could you interview about your topic? What sorts of questions might you need to ask them?

References

Chesebro, J. L. (2003). Effects of teacher clarity and non-verbal immediacy on student learning, receiver apprehension, and affect. *Communication Education, 52*, 135–147.

Davidson, K. K., & Dwyer, M. M. (2012). Is public speaking really more feared than death? *Communication Research Reports, 29*(2), 99–107. doi:10.1080/08824096.2012.667772

Devito, J. (2000). *The elements of public speaking* (7th ed.). New York, NY: Longman.

Dobkin, B. A., & Pace, R. C. (2003). Communication in a changing world. New York, NY: McGraw-Hill.

Ferguson, S. D. (2008). *Public speaking: Building competency in stages.* New York, NY: Oxford University Press.

Flanagin, A. J., & Metzger, M. J. (2000). Perceptions of Internet information credibility. *Journalism & Mass Communication Quarterly, 77*(3), 515–540. doi: 10.1177/107769900007700304

Floyd, K. (2014). *Communication matters* (2nd ed.). New York, NY: McGraw-Hill.

Fraleigh, D. M., & Tuman, J. S. (2017). *Speak up!: An illustrated guide to public speaking* (4th ed.). Boston, MA: Bedford/St. Martin's.

Goodall, H. L., & Goodall, S. G. (2006). *Communication in professional contexts.* Belmont, CA: Thomson Wadsworth.

Gregory, H. (2002). *Public speaking for college and career.* New York: McGraw-Hill.

Hall, E. T. (1969). *The hidden dimension.* Garden City, NY: Anchor Books.

Hogan, J. M., Andrews, P. H., Andrews, J. R., & Williams, G. (2017). *Public speaking and civic engagement* (4th ed.). Boston, MA: Pearson.

Houser, M. L. (2006). Expectancy violation of instructor communication as predictors of motivation and learning: A comparison of traditional and nontraditional students. *Communication Quarterly, 54,* 331–349.

Hybels, S., & Weaver, R. L., II. (2001). *Communicating effectively* (6th ed.). New York, NY: McGraw-Hill.

Jaffe, C. (2013). *Public speaking: Concepts and skills for a diverse society* (7th ed.). Boston, MA: Wadsworth.

Johnson, T. J., & Kaye, B. K. (1998). Cruising is believing?: Comparing Internet and traditional sources on media credibility measures. *Journalism & Mass Communication Quarterly, 75*(2), 325–340. doi:10.1177/107769909807500208

Metzger, M. J., Flanagin, A. J., & Zwarun, L. (2003). College student Web use, perceptions of information credibility, and verification behavior. *Computers and Education, 41*(3), 271–290. doi:10.1016/S0360-1315(03)00049-6

O'Hair, D., Rubenstein, H., & Stewart, R. (2013). *A pocket guide to public speaking* (4th ed.). Boston, MA: Bedford/St. Martin's.

Parvis, L. F. (2001) The importance of communication and public speaking skills. *Journal of Environmental Health, 63*(9), 44–45.

Reynolds, R. & Burgoon, M. (2002). Evidence. In J. P. Dillard and M. Pfau (Eds.), *The persuasion handbook: Developments in theory and practice* (pp. 427–444). Thousand Oaks, CA: Sage.

Richmond, V. P., & McCroskey, J. C. (1998). *Communication apprehension, avoidance, and effectiveness* (5th ed.). Boston, MA: Allyn & Bacon.

Schultz, Q. (2006). *An essential guide to public speaking: Serving your audience with faith, skill, and virtue.* Grand Rapids, MI: Baker Academic.

Wood, J. T. (2009). *Communication in our lives* (5th ed.). Boston, MA: Wadsworth Cengage.

Additional Readings

The Elements of Library Research: What Every Student Needs to Know

by Mary W. George

I Can See You Naked

by Ron Hoff

Speaking With a Purpose (9th ed.)

by Arthur Koch & Jason Schmitt

Better Communicators Are Organized

By Rhonda Gallagher, M.S.

13

When I was in college, I had an education professor who said that "organization is the key to success." He must have repeated that every class period, and as I have lived and learned to navigate the expectations of adult life, I have learned that he was right. That should come as no surprise to you or me. The Bible says that "God is not a God of disorder" (I Corinthians 14:33). In fact, think about the first chapter of Genesis: first we learn that God is eternal, then we learn that He is creative, and then that He is organized. The text says that at the beginning of the world, God created the world but everything was in chaos, and the first thing He did when confronted with chaos was begin to bring order to it. I think God likes order.

Organization is so important when we think about public speaking, and many of the basic ideas about helping others understand a speech also flow nicely over into helping people understand us in everyday conversation (Littlejohn & Foss, 2011). It's just much easier to understand someone who organizes their ideas. This is an American expectation of public speakers (Jaffe, 2013). So, is this chapter supposed to be all about cleaning your room and keeping your car clean? No, though those things do nonverbally communicate information about you to other people (remember Chapter 4?), but our messages to others must be organized if we want our content to be understood and remembered (Fransden & Clement, 1984;

© S.Pytel/Shutterstock.com

Garner, 1992; Miller & McCown, 1986). It also boosts our speaker credibility (Pascella et al., 1996). We're going to focus on how organization applies to public speaking, and you can extrapolate how the basic concepts translate to workplace communication and daily life.

Organizing and Outlining a Speech

Outline
a visual representation of how speech ideas relate to each other

There are several things that need to be done to create an organized speech, and they begin with organizing the outline. An **outline** is a visual representation of how speech ideas relate to each other (Hybels & Weaver, 2001). I'm sure you have encountered outlines before and wondered why ideas have to be indented or particular symbols are used. The reason is that the arrangement on the page shows how the ideas are connected. That is why you never put more than one idea on a line; if there are two or more ideas, it is impossible to see how the ideas relate to each other. Look at the example below:

Specific Speech Purpose: to inform the audience about the major art works of Michelangelo

I. *Michelangelo made sculptures.*
    A. *He carved the Pieta.*
    B. *He carved the David.*
    C. *He carved the Moses.*
II. *Michelangelo made paintings.*
    A. *The Sistine Chapel was his creation.*
    B. *The Madonna and Child was his creation.*
III. *Michelangelo designed architecture.*
    A. *He designed the dome of St. Peter's Basilica.*
    B. *He designed the Medici tombs.*

Sidebar 13A

Clearly, this is not a complete outline: it has no supporting materials at all, but you can see that each main idea points back to the speech goal. Each main idea is indicated by a Roman numeral, and the main ideas are all indented the same number of spaces from the margin. That is how we know they are all of equal importance, because they are all indented equally. By the same token, the sub-points are all indented further; they are listed under the heading to which they relate. Finally, there is only one idea on each line, so we can see the relationship between points. Do you see what I mean? The order and indentation show how the ideas relate to each other.

Building the Outline from the Inside Out: It's Alive!

There is an order we need to follow when creating an outline, and the order is not from the top of the outline to the bottom. Many students want to write the title first because it is the first thing that shows up on the page, but it is actually almost the last thing you do. You'll write the body portion before you even start the introduction (O'Hair et al., 2013). How can you write the introduction before you know what you're going to say? Just like the first thing to form in a baby's body is the heart, the main goal of the speech (we call that the specific speech purpose, but we'll talk more about that in a minute) is the first thing that needs to be written (Devereaux Ferguson, 2008). The steps in creating an outline parallel the forming of a human body so well that we can use that analogy to see how each part functions and in what order to do things. So, let's play Dr. Frankenstein, build an outline, and see if it comes to life! (This assumes you've done your research and know what you're talking about. If not, read the previous chapter and get to the library immediately!)

© Anton_Ivanov/Shutterstock.com

Step 1: Write the Specific Speech Purpose

Similar to a thesis statement, a specific speech purpose is what you hope to accomplish in the speech (Dobkin & Pace, 2003; Hybels & Weaver, 2001; Wood, 2009). Writing a specific speech purpose is vitally important. It is like the heart of the speech. The heart is central to any animal. It provides the driving force of the creature, and it is the first thing to form in an embryo. In the same way, the specific speech purpose is the center and driving force of the speech (Floyd, 2014), and it is the first thing you write. Just like the heart has a very specific design, the specific speech purpose has a set pattern and uses very specific language. Why so specific? Because the specific speech purpose is the target the speaker is shooting for, and you can only aim at one target at a time if you mean to actually hit it. It keeps the speaker focused and on task. So, how is a specific speech purpose written?

© Chinnapong/Shutterstock.com

First, the specific speech purpose is labeled. That puts the goal of the speech before the eyes of the speaker right away. Second, it uses an infinitive clause. Remember what an infinitive clause is? It's "to" plus a verb. In this case, to inform. (If you were to write one of these for a persuasive speech, it would say "to persuade.") Third, it is geared toward the audience (Dobkin & Pace, 2003). You should be focusing on helping the audience understand. They are the audience, after all, and the speech is for them, so you should be fitting what you hope to do to their needs, not your own. Next, it should give the topic in clear, concise terms (Floyd, 2014). Don't

Specific speech purpose
what you hope to accomplish in the speech

use flowery language or try to doll it up. Make what you're trying to do as clear and simple as possible. Finally, it should have only one idea, specifically, the idea you want to get across to the audience. Some teachers feel that the main points of the speech should be listed in the specific speech purpose; others think it should just be the topic. Either works. Ask your teacher what they want. By now, some of you have started saying, "Well, if you start with the label and follow it with the infinitive clause, all that remains is to fill in the blank with the one idea. That's easy!" You're right! It is easy! It's fill-in-the-blank, and it looks like this example:

Specific Speech Purpose: to inform the audience about the effects of alcohol on the body.

See? It has a label ("Specific Speech Purpose"), is an infinitive clause ("to inform . . . "), is audience centered ("the audience"), and presents only one idea ("about the effects of alcohol on the body"). Very tidy and predictable, right? The beauty of tidy and predictable is that it is hard to mess up if you know what you want to accomplish, and if you refer back to it periodically, it will keep you right on track.

(When you prepare your persuasive speech, you actually write a position statement as a starting point for your speech instead of a specific speech purpose. We'll discuss that more in Chapter 15.)

Step 2: Select the Main Points

Main points
the most important ideas that the audience needs to know

Sub-points
the ideas that support the main ideas

The next step in the outlining process is selecting the main points of the speech. If the specific speech purpose is the heart, the main points are the bones. Just like the skeleton in your body, the main points provide the framework upon which the speech rests. The **main points** are the most important ideas that you feel the audience needs to know, and they relate directly back to the specific speech purpose (Fraleigh & Tuman, 2017; Hybels & Weaver, 2001). Any time you see the words "main points," think "Roman numerals." The **sub-points** are the ideas that support the main ideas and when you see "sub-points," think "capital letters." Recall that in the last chapter we discussed how to determine which ideas will be the main ideas of the speech. They are the clusters of ideas that form as we do research and they present themselves as main issues that need to be addressed. Again, be sure that the main points are simple ideas. Many students confuse bits of critical evidence with central ideas. For instance, if the speech is about proper care of cats, one main idea may be that cats need regular veterinary visits, but a student may mistakenly state the main point as "Only twenty percent of pet owners actually take pets for regular veterinary care." The statistic is supporting information, not one of the big ideas of the speech. The correct way to say it would be "Cats need regular

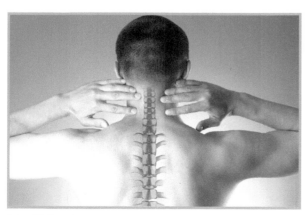

© staras/Shutterstock.com

veterinary care," and then give the statistic under that Roman numeral to support the big idea. Wait to give specifics until you are ready to support the main ideas. (By the way, I made up all those statistics for clarification purposes. Don't quote me!)

© wavebreakmedia/Shutterstock.com

For each group of ideas, whether main ideas (Roman numerals) or sub-points (capital letters), you need two to five ideas. If you have only one idea, that is actually just a restatement of the specific speech purpose. You need at least two (Devereaux Ferguson, 2008), and no more than five points given in a group because the audience will have trouble remembering more ideas than that (Fraleigh & Tuman, 2017). In the same way, each group of sub-points (capital letters) needs at least two points under it and no more than five. Go back and look at the example at the start of this chapter. You'll see two to five ideas per grouping and only one idea on a line. See how clear that makes the ideas?

The main point and sub-points resemble the skeleton in another way as well. They must be parallel (Devereaux Ferguson, 2008). In the same way, the main points and sub-points must "look alike." **Parallel sentence structure** is a sentence arrangement in which each sentence in a grouping follows the order of the first, and the sentences sound as much alike as possible. You have a mirror image of each of your bones on either side of your body; they look alike. In the same way, your Roman numerals and capital letters are arranged in parallel sentence structure. They look alike. (Yes, I know this is a somewhat flawed analogy; all analogies break down eventually, but it should help you remember, and that's what I care about!) Look at the beginning outline again. See how the ideas are written in parallel sentence structure? The purpose of using parallel sentence structure is that it forces the speaker to be sure the ideas are of equal importance and relate to each other in the same way. Another benefit is that it makes it easier for the audience to remember, and finally, it makes the outline easier for the speaker to remember as well. That's good!

Parallel sentence structure
sentence arrangement in which each sentence follows the order of the first, and the sentences sound as much alike as possible

Step 3: Select the Organizational Pattern

Once the main points are selected, we must decide how to arrange them. If the specific speech purpose is the heart, and the main points and sub-points are the bones, then the organizational pattern is the DNA. Your DNA determines how your body is put together, and the organizational pattern determines the order of the main points. The organizational pattern is the way the main points of an outline are put together. Organizational patterns for informative speeches differ from those for persuasive speeches. This is because some ways of organizing information facilitate the dissemination of information for learning (informative speech) while others progress logically from point to point in such a way as to lead the listener's mind to come to a particular conclusion or conviction (persuasive speech).

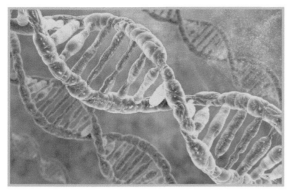
© vitstudio/Shutterstock.com

The key to choosing the right organizational pattern is picking the pattern that makes the most sense for the information you want to share. And it should be obvious to the audience (Kushner, 2004) because if they can't identify it, it's no help to them at all. The right pattern makes understanding and remembering the main points easier and helps the speaker remember the ideas just as much as it helps the audience.

Informative organizational patterns

There are basically five organizational patterns for informative speaking (Devereaux Ferguson, 2008). They are:

1. *Spatial*—The spatial organizational pattern delivers the material in a pattern that can be followed in a physical way from one location to another (top to bottom, left to right, front to back, east to west, etc.). If you explain the settlement of the United States, you will naturally go from east to west. You might discuss trade goods made in Peru from north to south. Here's an example:

Spatial Organizational Pattern

Specific Speech Purpose: to inform the audience about three ancient sites in England from east to west
I.   London is an ancient site in eastern England.
II.   Stonehenge is an ancient site in central England.
III. Bath is an ancient site in western England.

Sidebar 13B

2. *Chronological*—The chronological organizational pattern gives the information in the order that the events took place. You tell what happens first, second, etc. An example would be explaining the history of ancient cultures of Italy beginning with the Etruscans, then the Greeks, then the Romans, as shown below:

Chronological Organizational Pattern

Specific Speech Purpose: to inform the audience about three ancient cultures of Italy.
I.   The Etruscans conquered Italy from Tuscany.
II.   The Greeks conquered Italy from Greece.
III. The Romans conquered Italy from Rome.

Sidebar 13C

3. *Comparison*—The comparison organizational pattern shows the ways in which two things (occasionally three) are alike and/or how they are different. If you want to compare high school to college, use a comparison organizational pattern. Pick out a few areas (like academics, social life, and financial considerations) and focus on those things. You can either make two Roman numerals (high school and college) with academics, social life, and finances as the capital letters, or you can make three Roman numerals of academics, social life, and finances, with high school and college as the two capital letters under each. It's really up to you.

Comparison Organizational Pattern

Specific Speech Purpose: to inform the audience about the similarities between high school and college.

I. High school has characteristics.
II. College has characteristics.

Sidebar 13D

4. *Topical*—The topical organizational pattern uses main ideas that have nothing in common with each other except that they all relate to the main topic. For instance, if you are talking about the Caribbean, you might talk about the culture, the food, and the music. Those things have nothing in common except that they relate to the Caribbean. I think of this one as the mental equivalent of the "catch-all drawer" in the kitchen. The stuff in there is not related, but it all goes in that drawer. This organizational pattern can have anywhere from two to five main ideas.

Topical Organizational Pattern

Specific Speech Purpose: to inform the audience about the culture, food, and music of the Caribbean

I. The Caribbean has interesting culture.
II. The Caribbean has tasty food.
III. The Caribbean has great music.

Sidebar 13E

5. *Narrative*—The narrative organizational pattern does just what it says. It tells a story. The structure goes from start to finish, similar to a chronological pattern, but it is a specific type of chronological order because the list of events make up a story. Relating the story of the life of Frederick Douglass is narrative. One challenge of using this organizational pattern is finding a variety of supporting material, not just explaining and showing speaking aids, so think carefully at that step in the process.

Narrative Organizational Pattern

Specific Speech Purpose: to inform the audience about the life of Frederick Douglass.

I.   Frederick Douglass was born in slavery.
II. Frederick Douglass escaped slavery.
III. Frederick Douglass opposed slavery.

Sidebar 13F

The Magic Line

Nowhere in my studies have I found a concept comparable to this, but it is so helpful I teach it to my students. As you know, the main ideas and main sub-points (think Roman numerals and capital letters) must be ideas; they must be written in simple, declarative sentences; and must be in parallel sentence structure. Once the outline has moved into further detail, it becomes artificial and cumbersome to try to maintain the simple, parallel, declarative sentence structure, and the material at that level becomes supporting material, not big ideas. Here is the correct order for representing content in an outline:

```
I
  A
     1
        a
          (1)
             (a)
```

Now, imagine it with a line that divides the big ideas into simple, declarative, parallel sentence structure on the left of the line (Let's call that the "I zone" for the big ideas.), and the evidence, which can be stated in any structure of sentence or fragment that the writer chooses on the right. (We'll call this the "E zone" for supporting evidence.)

```
I  |
  A|
   | 1
   |   a
   |    (1)
   |       (a)
```

Do you see how much easier it is to know where to put information?

Sidebar 13G

Step 4: Develop Your Main Idea with Supporting Material

Next, we need to support the main ideas with information. To keep with the analogy of the body as a parallel to creating a speech, let's move on to supporting material (also called evidence or backing). Supporting material refers to the little bits of information that help the audience understand the ideas the speaker is trying to share. Just as the main ideas are like the skeleton, the supporting material is like

---

Supporting material
bits of information that help the audience understand the ideas the speaker is trying to share

the muscle. It provides the strength of the speech like the muscle provides the strength for the body to move. It adds clarity to the main points.

© Tuzemka/Shutterstock.com

The second job of the supporting material is to fill out the speech. Like the muscle is the meat on the body, the supporting material provides the "meat" of the speech. It "fleshes out" (forgive the pun) the main ideas. Most of what is said in a speech is supporting material.

Supporting material comes in many different types. Many first-time speakers make the mistake of trying to build the entire speech on explanation and statistics. What's even worse is that some speakers only explain. We call them boring speakers (Fraleigh & Tuman, 2017). That's a mistake. It sounds amateurish and leaves a lot of the audience unengaged. Mix it up! Different forms of supporting material speak to different kinds of people because people learn in different ways (Fraleigh & Tuman, 2017). Some people don't care about the numbers; they just want an explanation of how the thing happens. Others don't care about explanation; they want stories of affected people. Some don't care about stories; they want to know what the authorities say. Finally, others don't care what you say; they won't understand what you mean without examples. You need to mix it up a little and try to meet the needs of all the listeners.

Types of Supporting Materials

Explanation—When a speaker explains something, they are telling the audience about a process, how or why something is the way it is, or how something works or doesn't work. That is explanation. For instance, imagine you want to explain how a tree grows. You would tell us how the layer of living tissue of the tree is really only two layers of living cells in the tree; the wood forms from the dead cells inside of the living layers, and the bark forms from dead cells on the outside of the living layers. With each growing season, a new layer of living cells forms between the two old layers that were alive the last season and have since died. The buildup of dead layers creates the wood on the inside and bark on the outside. That is how the tree grows. (Pardon the length of the example and the biology lesson, but I wanted you to see how explanation actually makes something easier to understand. A drawing would help even more, and that's why visual aids are also considered supporting material.)

Explanation
telling the audience about a process, how or why something is the way it is, or how something works or doesn't work

Analogy—Analogy is using an idea we understand to help us with one we don't yet understand (Devereaux Ferguson, 2008; Goodman, 1976; Thayer, 2000). For instance, I have been using the analogy of the body to help you understand the parts of a speech throughout this entire chapter. (I hope it's working!) Analogies come in two forms: literal and figurative. Want to know the difference? Read Sidebar H below.

Analogy
an idea that we understand that helps us with one we don't yet understand

Literal vs. Figurative Analogies

The word "literally" can get you into trouble if you don't understand all the meanings. Recently, it has become an intensifier, like "really." For instance, someone might say to you "I am literally drowning in homework!" meaning they have a lot of homework. The problem with this is that teachers tend to think of more concrete meanings of literally, like "actually." In that application, you can't literally drown in homework; it's impossible. To drown in something, you must be inhaling liquid into your lungs. Your teacher would say you were using a figurative meaning of drown, not literal. So how does that apply to analogies in a speech? A **literal analogy** compares things in concrete ways, like saying the heart is like a pump. A **figurative analogy** tells us how something seems or feels, like saying having your own business is like having twins, or doing a marathon on your hands and knees. It tells us what the experience feels like; it's really hard, but no one really thinks you build a business by crawling on your hands and knees for 26 miles.

Sidebar 13H

Literal analogy
analogy that compares things in concrete ways

Figurative analogy
analogy that tells us how something seems or feels to help us understand

Expert opinion
what an expert thinks about a conditionx, situation, or experience

Expert opinion—Expert opinion is sharing what a knowledgeable person thinks about a condition, situation, or experience. It includes quotes and paraphrases. First, let's talk about quotes. Sometimes another person just said it so well, you simply cannot improve on their wording. In those cases, you want to use their words, but you have to give credit for the construction of the phrases and sentences. You do that by using quotation marks for written quotes. For example, "The Lord is my Shepherd; I shall not want" (Psalm 23:1). You *have* to give the source. To avoid plagiarism (remember that plagiarism is using someone else's words or original ideas without giving them credit), you have to be really aware of it. If you use more than five words in a row of someone else's, put them in quotation marks and provide a citation. That is because the way the words are put together is *their* work, and they deserve credit for what they have done. When you include a quote in something you write, you need to do an in-text citation according to MLA (Modern Language Association) or APA (American Psychological Association) formatting, depending on your professor's instruction. You do that aloud during the speech by saying, "according to _____" or "in the words of _____" and say "quote" and "unquote" at the beginning and end of the quoted material. (You can also hang "finger quotes" in the air when you are speaking to indicate that you have cited someone else, but you always have to give the source. There is some debate about whether finger quotes are really professional. Check with your teacher.)

We paraphrase when we want to use an idea that is originally someone else's, but the wording is nothing special or too long to be practical, so we just want to represent the idea. Once again, someone else came up with the idea, and it is his/her intellectual property, so we have to give credit to them for creating the idea, even though we didn't use their words. In those cases we use paraphrasing to put the idea into our own words, but we must still include the source of the idea. C.S. Lewis said that human cultures have many of the same mythical types of gods because God has built that vocabulary of ideas into all humans to point them to Him. The way I shared that is an example of paraphrasing. C.S. Lewis said it, so I have to give him credit, even though I didn't use his exact words in quotation marks. In a written document, you show a paraphrase by giving the citation in the same way you would a direct quote, but you don't use quotation marks.

Wait! We haven't actually talked about what makes a person an expert, have we? I think of a person as an expert if they know more about a topic than the average person on the street. Those can come from either study or experience. My favorite example to tell my classes is that a marine biologist would be an expert on the subject of shark attacks, but the person who's been bitten by one has an expertise of a whole other kind!

Statistics—**Statistics** are number facts. You can share statistics by giving raw numbers, such as the number of people in the U.S. who are food insecure. Percentages are also considered statistics, for example, "98% of all statistics are made up on the spot." (Actually, no one knows what the stats are on that one!) You can also use fractions, like "Roughly 1/3 of first marriages, 2/3 of all second marriages, and 4/5 of third marriages end in divorce in the United States." The beauty of statistics is that they feel very authoritative, and so they can be a great way of making a point. Remember that the audience is never going to retain raw numbers if they are too specific; you'll do better by rounding numbers, like rounding 422,612 to 423,000. Or try to relate raw numbers to something we can understand, like if you give the square miles in Italy, go on to tell us that is relatively the same size as California. In other words, for those kinds of numbers consider using analogy to supplement statistics. We simply cannot remember too much numeric detail, so keep it simple. Visual aids help us to retain information, especially when you are comparing two or three sets of figures. Pie charts help us *see* how big a percentage is, and bar graphs do a nice job of showing us how different groups compare to each other.

Statistics
number facts

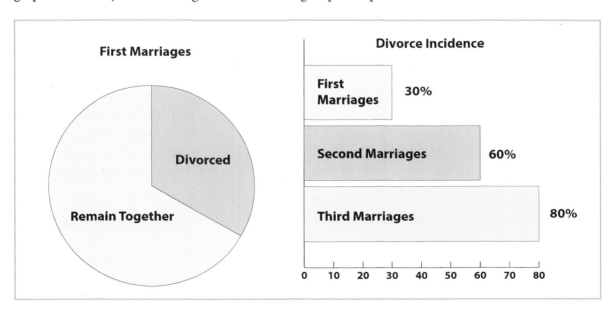

Sidebar 13I Graphs can make statistics more meaningful

Examples—Do I need to define examples? I guess I do, so let me try. An **example** is one item in a large group that enables the audience to better understand the larger group. We usually give two or three examples for clarity's sake. For instance, examples of shoes include sneakers, boots, and sandals. It's hard to imagine that

Example
one item in a large group that enables the audience to better understand the larger group

someone wouldn't already know what a shoe was, but if they didn't, and they knew what a sneaker, sandal, or boot was, they could extrapolate that a shoe is an outer-most garment worn on the foot.

Illustrations
stories that demonstrate an idea by showing how it played out in someone's life

Illustrations—Illustrations are stories that demonstrate an idea by showing how it played out in someone's life. For example, if you were speaking on the importance of applying early for scholarships, you might tell the story of Dameon, who began applying for scholarships in January before he was supposed to start college in the fall. He was offered scholarships at four different colleges and was able to choose the college that provided the most money while still meeting his academic needs. His story shows the audience that it's important to apply for scholarships early. Illustrations can be factual (meaning they happened to a real person) or hypo-thetical (meaning the story is made up to make a your point). You can use either one in a speech, but if you use a hypothetical illustration, you have to tell us that it's hypothetical if you're going to be an ethical speaker. An easy way to do that is to introduce the story by saying "Let's imagine how this might look" or "Imagine a woman named Shontay." See what I mean? You are sending an indicator that the story is made up, so that the audience doesn't go away under the impression that you did all this research and found a real woman named Shontay who had that experience. Obviously, factual illustrations carry more weight with an audience than hypothetical ones.

Facts
Facts are supporting bits of information that are established knowledge.

Facts—How did I ever forget this until now? Speakers use a lot of simple facts to aid the audience in understanding the contents of the speech. Facts are supporting bits of information that are established knowledge. They don't require citations because they are not either original ideas, nor directly using someone else's words. You cite when you use a paraphrase of an original idea, but facts are widely known in the group of people who are knowledgeable about a particular subject. Let me give you an example. A speaker talking about heart disease may explain how the heart func-tions, and say that the heart has two atria and two ventricles. The audience needs to know how the heart is built to understand how it heart functions, so the speaker gives them the parts of the heart. But that piece of knowledge about atria and ven-tricles has been around so long that no speaker tells where it came from; they just say it.

By the way, not everything you find in a source requires citation. If the infor-mation is common knowledge, you don't have to cite a source. If you find the information in multiple sources and there are no citations included with it, you don't need to cite it. In the explanation of how trees grow, I didn't need to include a source, because that information has been found in biological literature for so long it has become common knowledge. In other words, you don't have to give a citation on every line of your outline. You do need sources for quotes, paraphrases, and occasionally, for statistics if they are so shocking the reader or audience may question if they are true. (In that case, citing the source provides data that proves the speaker has done their homework, and that builds their credibility, so it's worth doing.) But plenty of things in the outline will not require the source where you found the information. Work hard where you need to, but don't waste your time on something that is unnecessary.

Speaking aids—**Speaking aids** are items that you show or play for the audience to observe in order to build their understanding or retention. Many times, we think of them as just visual aids, but audio clips are also speaking aids even though they must be heard. If you're talking about the emotional effects of music, you just about *have* to play some sound clips. For the most part, though, if you say visual aids, most people know what you're talking about. A lot of your decisions about which speaking aids you use will be determined by the technological capabilities of your speaking space and what you're trying to accomplish. More technologically demanding forms of speaking aids include video clips, audio clips, and presentation programs like Prezi and PowerPoint. These aids add excitement to the presentation (Devereaux Ferguson, 2008; Fraleigh & Tuman, 2017) and can be used to show images and sound in a format that everyone can see and hear. Less technologically demanding forms of visual aids include real objects and models, among others (DeVito, 2000; Fraleigh &Tuman, 2017). Use models for representing items that cannot be brought into the speaking space because they are too large or too small (like the solar system) or too hard to get possession of (like the Hope Diamond). Objects and models bring a level of reality that stimulates interest in the audience in ways that most visuals simply cannot inspire. However, they can be difficult to make or obtain and awkward to haul around. And depending on their size, they may still be hard for audience members to see. The least exciting forms of speaking aids include posters and handouts. Other forms of visual aids may be more exciting, but these can be very effective and have highly valuable qualities like ease of production, portability, and reliability. Do not despise these low-tech options. Often, they are actually the most efficient and easy to use.

Speaking aids
items you show to or play for the audience in order to build their understanding or retention

A quick word of advice about speaking aids: they should be ready at least 24 hours in advance of the speaking engagement to facilitate peace of mind and enable you to practice with them sufficiently for comfort, and you *should* practice with them (Fraleigh & Tuman, 2017)! They should be things you can control, too. Dogs are cute, but they can steal the show and keep your speech from having the impact you wanted. Also, anytime you use a high-tech option, be sure you know how to operate the equipment in advance of the speech. Have some form of low-tech backup. Technology sometimes fails or doesn't do what was expected. It is important to realize that just because your presentation pulls up just fine on your personal computer does not mean it will work the

© Matej Kastelic/Shutterstock.com

same way when your computer is plugged into an LCD projector by an adaptor. Also be sure to transport the file in a couple of different ways, like emailing it to yourself and also carrying it on a flash drive. Be prepared for *all* contingencies, and always have a low tech backup!

Sidebar 13J

Step 5: Write Your Transitions

Transitions
the sentences that connect main points to each other

The next step is to ease us from one point into the next. Ok, so the specific speaking purpose is the heart, the organizational pattern is the DNA, the main points and sub-points are the skeleton, and the supporting material is the muscle, right? Well, the transitions are the connective tissues. Just like your ligaments and tendons connect your bones together, in the same way, the transitions connect the main points. Transitions are the sentences that connect main points to each other. They make a smooth, easy-to-follow switch from one idea to the next (DeVito, 2000; Dobkin & Pace, 2003; Floyd, 2014; Fraleigh & Tuman, 2017; O'Hair et al., 2013). They should be short and simple, and that will make them sweet. There are basically three ways to do them.

The first method of doing a transition is to begin the sentence with what I call time words, like "first," "next," "now," "thirdly," or "finally." An example would be, "First, let's look at the problems inherent in the Electoral College." These simple, direct sentences announce your next main point and facilitate you moving into your sub-points.

The second method is taking the idea you just came from and putting it together with the next idea. An example would be, "Now that we have considered the problems in the Electoral College, let's examine a proposed solution."

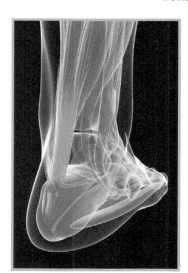

© Sebastian Kaulitzki/Shutterstock.com

The third method is probably the superior method. It's called an internal summary, which provides the audience with a recap of each point that has been covered so far and prepares them for the next point (O'Hair, et al., 2013). For instance: "Now that we have examined the problems with the Electoral College and how an amendment to the Constitution could correct these problems, let's look at some common objections to change." See? Each point was recapped before moving on.

Internal summary
transitions that provide the audience with a recap of each point that has been covered so far and prepares them for the next point

Transitions are placed between the introduction and the first main point, before each subsequent main point, and before the conclusion (DeVito, 2000; Floyd, 2014; Fraleigh & Tuman, 2017; O'Hair et al., 2013). They should be included in the outline. It's sort of like driving a standard transmission. Just like you engage the clutch before shifting, you need a transition before changing directions in the speech. While most transitions looks forward to the next point, the last one is the most difficult to write because it requires that you acknowledge the point you just came from. Resist the temptation to simply say "In conclusion . . . ". You're just getting ready to conclude; you're not there yet. Instead try, "As you can see . . ." or "It is clearly evident . . . " and reference the last point. So to revisit the Electoral College example again, you might say, "As you can see, change to this venerable institution is possible but opposition is inevitable."

Step 6: Writing the Introduction and Conclusion

If you have kept up with all the preceding main ideas, you probably think that I'm going to talk about a body part to compare with your speech's introduction and conclusion. Well, you're right! The introduction and conclusion are like the skin that encloses it all. (However, finding images to put with that might be difficult to do for a "G-Rated" textbook, so we'll pass on that, OK?) Both the introduction and conclusion have functions they must perform, so let's take a look at them.

The Introduction

Your introduction is your first chance to get the audience's attention and bring them on board with your agenda. It's important, so don't mess it up! When you give your speeches, regardless of the delivery method (extemporaneous, manuscript, or memorized), your introduction needs to be memorized. So what does that tell you about your introduction? You need to make it as short as it can be while ensuring it's effective and doing the job for which it was designed. So, the jobs are . . .

1. Get them to listen.

In other words, you need to catch the audience's attention. One thing that makes my heart sink is hearing a speaker open with, "My name is _____ and I'm going to tell you about . . . ." That's a purpose statement and the audience isn't ready for that yet, not to

© Aspen Photo/Shutterstock.com

mention it's just boring. They aren't *ready* to listen. What a waste! The first words of a speech are *so* critical. Don't waste them! You can get the audience's attention by opening with a question, a short story related to the topic, a quote, a shocking statistic or factoid (Fraleigh & Tuman, 2017), or showing a surprising visual/audio aid. For example: "Were you aware that lung cancer for non-smokers is more fatal than for smokers? Second-hand smoke kills!" (See? Got your attention with that, didn't I?) Almost anything that will get the audience to sit up and listen to you will work. I say almost because I once had a student open his speech by clapping his hands for attention. That may get the audience's attention, but not in a way that makes them like you and want to listen to you. That's a problem, because the second job of the introduction is . . .

2. Get them to like you.

Rapport
getting the audience to identify with you

This is called **rapport**, which is getting the audience to identify with you. "Now, why does this matter?" you wonder. Because if the audience likes you, they are more likely to believe you. We should approach listening to speeches with some level of skepticism. (Remember listening for judgment?) Your audience will have some defenses up before you ever begin speaking, and you want to lower those as much as you can, so your message will get through, especially when you are doing persuasive speaking. So how do you get them to like you? Smile, use a friendly tone of voice, and show an open body posture (face forward, with arms loose and not crossed in front of you). Make eye contact so that they know you recognize them as individuals, and require them to do the same. Come out from behind the podium so that nothing separates them from you. These are called immediacy behaviors. Show the audience how you are like them. (Here's an area where your audience analysis helps you.) Mention similarities you share with them and use terms like "we" and "us." Grouping yourself with the audience is a smart move because they know that they are "good people," and so they think you must be, too! All these things make you somewhat socially vulnerable to them, and when they see that, they are more likely to lower their defenses.

3. Tell them why they should listen.

Let's face it: just because an issue is important to you doesn't mean it's important to your audience. Why should they care? You have to show them how the topic relates to them (Petty & Cacioppo, 1986; Maslow, 1966; O'Hair et al., 2013; Reardon, 1991). Your audience analysis is invaluable here as well! If you know who they are, you can get a better idea about what matters to them. For instance, public speaking matters to me very much because I teach it, and I see the importance of it in a civil democracy (Jaffe, 2013; Parvis, 2001). But unless you are a prelaw major, (or education, or business, or political science, or ministry, or theater . . .), you may not see the significance of it yet. So how can I show you that it matters to you? Did you see my references to some of the professions that make extensive use of public speaking? Hopefully, that got a few of you. I might also point out that Christians have a right and responsibility to participate in government and ministry to serve others and future generations. That probably got a few more of you.

I can probably get the rest of you by pointing out that you'll be doing speeches in this class on which you will be graded, and you need to do well on those. It would be great if you had such great personal charm that the audience would just listen to you because they want to bask in your presence, but if you don't have that, showing them why your topic matters to them helps a *lot*.

4. Tell them why they should listen to you.

Even if the audience likes you and the topic relates to them, their skepticism will still be in place to some degree. You need to show them that they can trust what you say to them—that your content is trustworthy. That comes from credibility, which is believability. Credibility comes in four forms. First, there is initial credibility, which is knowledge you get from your personal experience or reputation before the speech begins (Dobkin & Pace, 2003; Wood, 2009). If you're talking about fire prevention and and have written a book on the topic, the audience probably knows that coming into the speech. The audience knows before the enter the room that you know what you're talking about. Another form of credibility is derived credibility. That means you built it during the speech (Dobkin & Pace, 2003; Wood, 2009). Professional dress and presentation along with sharp looking visual aids all contribute to this, but it also includes the credibility you demonstrate by use of good use of evidence. A teacher who is a fire safety engineer may never have fought fires or been in a fire, but he is trustworthy for the content because of the level of study he demonstrates with his resources, organization (Wood, 2009), and delivery. Now an interesting thing about this is while you can *tell* us initial credibility, you have to *show* us derived credibility. You can't just tell us that you studied the material; you must demonstrate by sharing a statistic, quote, or fact that you couldn't have known unless you had really studied it. A marine biologist can have derived credibility because of his good research and delivery, but a shark attack victim has initial credibility. The third type of credibility is charisma, which is really just likability (Dobkin & Pace, 2003). It includes your warm, friendly delivery but also your dynamism and enthusiasm. Remember that we believe non-verbal messages over verbal ones, so even if you say your topic is critical to the lives of everyone in the audience, we aren't going to believe you if your words are spoken without conviction (Weaver, 1996). (I know I just discussed this when I talked about rapport, but it's all connected.) The last type of credibility is enduring credibility (Dobkin & Pace, 2003), sometimes called terminal credibility (Wood, 2009). Enduring credibility is the credibility the audience carries away from the speech. Then, the next time they see you speak, before you even begin to speak, they will automatically think "Oh, I remember this guy! He's a good speaker!" This is the credibility we either carry with us from one speech to the next. Of course, if you didn't do so well, your lack of credibility may be something you *drag* along with you from speech to speech.

Now, before we move on, it's important to recognize one thing relating to credibility, so pay attention here. Ready? *Your credibility must be established in the*

Credibility
believability

Initial credibility
credibility you get from knowledge of personal experience or reputation

Derived credibility
credibility built during the speech based on appearance, presentation skills, and quality of evidence

Charisma
likability

Enduring credibility
credibility a speaker gets from the audience's previous experiences with that speaker

minds of the audience members. Even if you have all the forms of credibility, if your audience isn't convinced of it, you're not authoritative. That's why we take such pains to demonstrate our expertise fully. If they don't believe you, then you're not believable. You must show yourself to be credible.

5. Tell them what to listen for.

Purpose statement
what the speaker is trying to do

Preview
listing the main points to be covered

The last function of the introduction is to give the **purpose statement** (what you're trying to do) and clearly preview the speech. A **preview** is just listing the main points to be covered. This might seem very boring to you, but it is critical for your audience because it lets them see what's coming up and prepare to listen (Fraleigh & Tuman, 2017; Wood, 2009). You see, we unconsciously spend the first few seconds of every conversation deciding what kind of conversation it will be so that we know what to listen for. Behind the scenes, your brain is unconsciously making decisions about how to process the material it's about to receive as if it's deciding which "form" to fill out. When you preview the main ideas of a speech, you are *creating* a form for the audience which facilitates their understanding and retention of the material. Remember I said that public speaking is about service? A preview is a service to the audience, and it may be the most important function of the introduction. It doesn't need to be elaborate; it needs to be clear. An example of a clear preview of three aspects of Midwestern culture would be: "There are three elements of Midwestern culture that bear examination: the speech, the foods, and the sporting traditions." See? Simple, direct, and to the point. The professor will thank you and so will the audience.

The Conclusion

The conclusion is your last chance to drive home your theme and make your point, so you can't mess that up either. Malcolm Kusner (2004) likens failing to have a conclusion for your speech to crash landing a plane. Even a great flight doesn't count if you crash at the end. According to Gregory (2002), a conclusion should summarize the main points and reinforce the central idea of the speech with a powerful closing statement. Let's look at those things in a little more depth.

© Nata-Lia/Shutterstock.com

1. Recap the main ideas.

A conclusion should wrap up the speech in a nice neat package.

Just like the preview prepares the audience to understand and retain, the recap of the main ideas helps them see how the ideas relate to each other and remember them (Devito, 2000; Floyd, 2014; Fraleigh & Tuman, 2017; Wood, 2009). It is their last chance to set their understanding. Your recap can be as simple as "So, the three elements of Midwestern culture we have discussed today are the speech, the foods, and the sporting traditions." One of the major things the conclusion does is help tie up the loose ends, and the recap of the main ideas helps them do that. That's why it is so important not to give the audience any new information in the conclusion (DeVito, 2000). If you have tied up the package of ideas and some new bit of information is presented, the audience has to open the package back up again. You can see how this would not be a good thing, right?

2. Motivate the audience to your desired response.

What was the theme, the one main idea, the specific speech purpose you were trying to get across? After the recap, you are ready to come back and reinforce that main idea (Floyd, 2013; Wood, 2009). So if you're showing the audience that three main characteristics of Midwestern culture are the speech, the food, and the sporting traditions, your main idea is probably that the culture reflects a people who value honesty, simplicity, hard work, and teamwork. That is the conclusion you want them to reach. That's your desired response.

3. Close with power.

The closing statement should be relatively short, and powerful, something that the audience will remember (Devereaux Ferguson, 2008; Devito, 2000; Floyd, 2014; Fraleigh & Tuman, 2017; Wood, 2009). The final statement is so important; it must, must, *must* have impact, and the strongest wording should come last in the statement. Relative to the Midwest culture, a strong closing statement would be "These are people shaped by hardship, but it has not made them hard. It has made them strong, and that strength has, in turn, benefited and shaped this nation. It has made *us* strong." See how the punch comes at the end? Imagine if the speaker had said "It has made them strong. It has made us strong, and that strength has benefited and shaped this nation." It wastes the power of the word "strong" by moving it too far from the end of the sentence. Finally, the impulse most of us feel is to end our speeches with "Thank you" (or worse yet, "That's all I have"). The ending is the most vulnerable you will feel in the speech and many of us simply cannot take that pressure. We feel we must telegraph to the audience that we're done; don't worry, they'll catch on. Don't end with "Thank you"; it dilutes your closing statement. Make your strong statement and let it hang there. If it has strength, it will stand, and the audience will know you're done; you don't have to tell them.

Step 7: Write the Title

The purpose of the title is to pique the curiosity of the potential audience and draw them in to see the speech. The title is bait, a teaser, like a movie trailer. It's a preview of things to come; whatever the title is like, the audience will assume the speech will be too. So, what makes a potential audience bite? First, the title has to be brief (DeVito, 2000). If it's too long, the audience will lose interest or think you'll be as long-winded as the

© Cindy Creighton/Shutterstock.com

title. Secondly, it has to be original. If they've heard the title before, the audience will think they have heard the *speech* before, and again, lose interest. Used titles are boring, so they expect the speech to be boring as well. Next, it should grab the attention of the audience (DeVito, 2000). It should be clever or snappy. If the title is fun and interesting, the audience will assume the speech will be, too. Finally, it should suggest the topic without actually telling what it is. It's a puzzle for the audience to figure out what the speech might be about, a game if you will, so you have to give enough clues for them to figure it out, but there still has to be some mystery. If the title is interesting, maybe the speech will be too. See what I mean? If you intend to talk about the dangers of second-hand smoke, don't call it "The Hazards of Second-Hand Smoke." Yes, it's brief, but it's hardly original or grabs attention, and there is no mystery. Try something like "Up in Smoke" or "Deadly Haze." Make it fun! Of course, use good taste. If the topic is very serious, like human trafficking, don't try to make a joke out of it. Be sensitive and use good sense.

Step 8: Compile the Bibliography

Bibliography
the list of sources you used to gather material for the speech.

© SFIO CRACHO/Shutterstock.com

The **bibliography** is the list of sources you used to gather material for the speech. The research should have been done before you even wrote the outline. As discussed in the informative chapter, you need to have good quality sources. Sources like books, news sources, and professional journals will have better information than the Internet. Remember that just because you accessed information online doesn't make it more or less credible, but if you get it from an academic online database like Ebscohost, ERIC, PsychLit, or even Google Scholar, you're going to get much better information than going to just any search engine like Google. So, while both print and electronic sources can be good, be sure you use good quality sources. (The same principle applies to print copies. *Time* magazine is more reputable than *People* magazine.) You should also conduct interviews to gather information but be sure to pick people who really have credibility about the topic. And, of course, you can use your own experiences in the speech. Another important thing to remember is to mix it up; don't cite all books, or all websites, or all documentaries. Variety increases your chances of getting good information.

Your sources should be listed in the bibliography in alphabetical sequence and cited in either MLA (Modern Language Association) or APA (American Psychological Association) formatting (Hybels & Weaver, 2001), depending on what your teacher wants. The formatting requirements for both of those organizations do change from time to time, so you can visit their websites to find out how to structure bibliographical citations. Or you could actually use a website to format the citations for you. A couple of good ones are citationmachine.org and easybib.com.

Ethical Implications

While so much of this chapter is focused on mechanics, there are still ethical considerations. When you pick your topic, do your research, select the speech purpose, and structure the outline, always keep the needs of the audience in mind. You are there to serve the audience, so prepare everything to make it as easy as possible for the audience to understand and remember, including organizational patterns, use of transitions, and previews and recaps of main points.

Do high quality research and avoid plagiarism by taking good notes and citing your sources for original ideas or exact wording. Use your evidence responsibly, and present an even-handed perspective of the issues. All speeches should treat the opposing viewpoint respectfully. There are two sides to every argument for a reason; there are good arguments on both sides. Arguments by their very nature have opposing viewpoints with components that have validity. Even if you think an idea is stupid, that doesn't make the people who believe it stupid. Furthermore, you don't know what it cost someone to arrive at a particular belief or opinion. Their experiences are different from yours, and you see things differently for that reason. Later you may change your mind about the issue and be on the opposite side, so be kind.

Summary

Organization aids retention and understanding and helps speakers be successful. An outline shows how ideas relate to each other. Indentation indicates whether ideas are main points, sub-points, or evidence. When you do your research, pick good quality information from a variety of sources. Take careful notes to avoid plagiarism. The specific speech purpose tells your goal in clear, singular, audience-centered terms and is labeled. The main points are the big ideas you want to cover in the speech, and the sub-points support the main ideas. All are written in simple, declarative, parallel sentences. The organizational pattern determines what order the main points are covered in, and there are different patterns for informative and persuasive speeches. A beginning list of informative outline patterns includes narrative, spatial, chronological, comparison, and topical. Supporting material develops and supports the sub-points. Expert opinion, examples, statistics, analogies, explanation, illustrations, facts, and speaking aids are all types of supporting material. Transitions carry us from one main idea to the next and should be short—one or two sentences. The introduction has five jobs: to get the audience to pay attention, to make them like you, to show why the topic is important to the audience, to demonstrate your credibility, and to preview the main points. Remember that if your audience doesn't find you credible, then you're not. The conclusion should recap the main points, drive home the main idea of the speech, and have a powerful closing sentence. The bibliography is the list of sources used for the speech and should be written in either MLA or APA format.

Vocabulary Words

Analogy
Bibliography
Charisma
Credibility
Derived credibility
Enduring credibility
Example
Expert opinion
Explanation
Facts

Figurative analogy
Illustration
Initial credibility
Internal summary
Literal analogy
Main point
Organizational pattern
Outline
Parallel sentence
     structure

Preview
Purpose statement
Rapport
Speaking aids
Specific speech purpose
Statistics
Sub-points
Supporting materials
Transition

Discussion Questions

1. Have you ever heard a speech that had no sense of order? What was it like to listen to?
2. What past experiences have you had applying order to something that was disorganized? What was it like to do that?

3. What topic do you have in mind for your informative speech? If you don't have anything in mind, where might you look for ideas?

4. What kind of thing might interest your audience? Which organizational patterns would best fit the topic?

5. What makes you a credible source for your chosen topic?

6. Why might your audience be interested in your topic? If that is not readily apparent, how could you help them see the connection between them and the topic?

7. If you need help formatting your bibliography, where could you find help on how to do it?

8. What sort of visual aids will best help the audience to remember the content? Which will best help you, the speaker, remember and share the content?

References

Devereaux Ferguson, S. (2008). *Public speaking: Building competency in stages*. New York: Oxford University Press.

Dobkin, B. A., & Pace, R. C. (2003). *Communicating in a changing world*. New York, NY: McGraw-Hill.

Floyd, K. (2014). *Communication matters* (2nd ed.). New York, NY: McGraw-Hill.

Frandsen, K. D., & Clement, D. A. (1984). The functions of human communication in information: Communication and processing of information. In C. C. Arnold & J. W. Bowers (Eds.), *Handbook of rhetorical and communication theory* (pp. 338–399). Boston, MA: Allyn & Bacon.

Garner, R. (1992). Learning from school texts. *Educational Psychologist, 27*, 53–63.

Goodman, N. (1976). *Languages of art*. Indianapolis, IN: Hackett Publishing Co.

Gregory, H. (2002). *Public speaking for college and career*. New York: McGraw-Hill.

Hybels, S., & Weaver, R. L., II. (2001). *Communicating effectively* (6th ed.). New York, NY: McGraw-Hill.

Jaffe, C. (2013). *Public speaking: Concepts and skills for a diverse society* (7th ed.). Boston, MA: Wadsworth.

Kushner, M. (2004). *Speaking for dummies* (2nd ed.). Hoboken, NJ: Wiley Publishing.

Littlejohn, S. W., & Foss, K. A. (2011). *Theories of human communication* (10th ed.). Long Grove, IL: Waveland Press.

Maslow, A. (1966). *The psychology of science: A* reconnaissance. New York: Harper & Row.

Maxwell, A., Curtis, G. J., & Vardanega, L. (2008). Does culture influence understanding and perceived seriousness of plagiarism? *International Journal for Educational Integrity, 4*(2). http://dx.doi.org/10.21913/IJEI.v4i2.412

Miller, R. B., & McCown, R. R. (1986). Effects of text coherence and elaboration on recall of sentences within paragraphs. *Contemporary Educational Psychology, 11*, 127–138.

O'Hair, D., Rubenstein, H., & Stewart, R. (2013). *A pocket guide to public speaking* (4th ed.). Boston, MA: Bedford/St. Martin's.

Parvis, L. F. (2001) The importance of communication and public speaking skills. *Journal of Environmental Health, 63*(9), 44–45.

Pascarella, E., Edison, M., Nora, A., Hagedon, L. S., & Braxton, J. (1996). Effects of teacher organization/preparation and teacher skill/clarity on general cognitive skills in college. *Journal of College Student Development, 37*, 7–19.

Petty, R. E., & Cacioppo, J. T. (1986). *Communication and persuasion: Central and peripheral routes to attitude change.* New York: Springer-Verlag.

Reardon, K. (1991). *Persuasion in practice.* Newbury Park, CA: Sage.

Sowden, C. (2005). Plagiarism and the culture of multilingual students in higher education. *ELT Journal, 59*(3), 226–233. doi:10.1093/let/cci042

Thayer-Bacon, B. J. (2000). *Transforming critical thinking: Thinking constructively.* New York: Teachers College Press.

Weaver, R. L. (1996). Motivating the motivators: Eight characteristics for empowering those to empower others. *Executive Speeches, 11*(1), 35–38.

Wood, J. T. (2009). *Communication in our lives* (5th ed.). Boston, MA: Wadsworth/Cengage.

Additional Readings

Beyond Bullet Points: Using PowerPoint to Tell a Persuasive Story that Gets Results
by Cliff Atkinson

Writing Great Speeches: Professional Tips You Can Use
by Alan M. Perlman

Public Speaking Survival Guide: 37 Things You Must Know When You Start Public Speaking
by Ramakrishna Reddy

Better Communicators Are Confident

By Susan McMurray, M.A.

© Tom Wang/Shutterstock.com

14

I don't know about you, but sometimes the thought of getting up and speaking in front of others is just frightful. Why do some of the communication situations that we have to participate in cause us so much anxiety? Speeches, job interviews, meetings, impromptu talks- can I please just hide under the table with my teddy bear and never come out? What's worse than our own fear of speaking in public is that some people just really know how to rub it in. You know the ones. Those charismatic, dynamic, funny, charming individuals who command an audience. The ones who effortlessly float up to the front of the room and deliver an articulate, witty talk with their audience hanging on every word. Those who tell the funniest stories at parties and really know how to work a room. I call them the "naturals." The "naturals" make it look so easy. When they get up to speak their voices don't crack. Their armpits don't produce a bucket of sweat. They don't use hundreds of nonsensical "ums" and "uhs." Their hands don't shake when they hold their notes. Wait, these people don't even need notes because they're so fluent in their speaking and their words just flow out of their mouths like a host of angelic beings!

Would you feel any better if I told you that you too could be a "natural"? Yes, you. All of us! Your current level of like or dislike of public speaking doesn't matter. What if I told you that public speaking is like a muscle? Yes, a muscle that you need to work to make stronger. I once heard Adam

© DeymosHR/Shutterstock.com

Levine, lead singer for Maroon 5, use this very analogy. When he first started performing at 18, he was extremely nervous. If you look back at videos of his early years, you see that he very rarely even looks at his audience when he sings. He said it took years for him to get comfortable being on stage. He likened the experience to a muscle. Being in front of others was a muscle he had to develop. The more he performed, the stronger the "muscle" got and the more "natural" he became in front of others. Speaking is a skill. Just like a musician's skills or an athlete's skills. You don't getter better unless you practice—a lot! You won't get better until you put yourself out there—for others to see. You won't ever really excel at communication unless you take some risks. We can be encouraged by Adam Levine's story. It's time to develop our public speaking muscle! God put an important message in you to share with others. Philippians 2:13 says, "For it is God who works in you, both to will and to do of His good pleasure." The amplified version says it like this, "[Not in your own strength] for it is God Who is all the while effectually at work in you [energizing and creating in you the power and desire], both to will and to work for His good pleasure *and* satisfaction *and* delight." Let's remember that it's God's good purpose that you be an excellent communicator. He will anoint you for such a task. So let's learn how to develop that muscle!

Confident Communication: What's at Stake?

There's a lot at stake with our confident communication, or lack thereof. Have you ever really considered what's truly at stake when we can't deliver a speech with confidence? Well before we really explore how much is at stake let me diverge with a story. Oh, and I promise there is a point . . .

Many years ago my husband and I traveled with our friends John and Andrea to Cozumel, Mexico. Our friend John had the "brilliant" idea of going scuba diving. When I say "brilliant," I mean everyone but I thought it was brilliant. The thought of being down in the ocean depths with nothing but a small oxygen tank supporting my very existence wasn't overly appealing to me. I was terrified! The day before our big dive we got resort certified to go scuba diving the next day. This sounds very official, but all it meant was taking a few dunks in the resort pool with our oxygen tanks. I still didn't feel any better about scuba diving. In fact, I was so scared it was beginning to ruin my entire vacation. I couldn't eat, I didn't sleep, I was a nervous wreck! The next morning, we woke up and got on the boat for the journey to the diving site. I think I was sweating buckets and maybe even beginning to shake uncontrollably. I distinctly remember my husband looking over at me with slight concern and encouraged me saying, "You will scuba dive and you will like it!" Before I knew it, I had plunged into the ocean, with mask and tank. All I remember is breathing. All I could think about was breathing. In fact I was breathing so heavily the scuba master had to bring me up early because I used my oxygen up too quickly. When my husband and friends finished their dive and came back up on the boat, they were in awe of what they had seen in God's beautiful ocean. (Did I mention that Cozumel is the second best place to scuba dive in the *entire* world? Second only to The Great Barrier Reef in Australia!) I heard them saying, "Did you see that octo-

© Billion Photos/Shutterstock.com

pus?," "The coral reef was more breathtaking than I could have ever imagined." "What about the schools of fish—more colorful than anything I've ever seen!" What? How had I missed all this? What octopus? What coral reef? What colorful schools of fish? Why did I not see these things? Oh that's right, all I could think about down there was breathing. I saw nothing but my fear. Fortunately, I had a chance for redemption in my second dive. After a forty-five minute break we got to dive again. This time I gave myself a little pep talk. I decided I wasn't going to let my fear rob me of this experience, a once-in-a-lifetime experience. I took the plunge, trusted my oxygen tank, and opened my eyes to the world below.

I told you my story would have a point, and here it is. Where are you when you are speaking in front of your audience? In your fear? Thinking about your breathing, or your nervousness, or how nauseous you feel? Or are you surveying the beauty of what's out there. Your audience . . . their needs . . . the importance of your God-given message. We can, no we must, get out of our fear when we speak. We have an important message to share. There's too much at stake if we don't get out of our fear. God would never call you to speak without anointing you for such a task. We can do it, so let's take the plunge!

Why Do I Feel Nervous When I Speak?

If you wonder why you are nervous when you speak, it's how we were designed. God has created our bodies with a certain chemical that might make us feel nervous when we are in situations such as public speaking, musical performances, athletic events, or dangerous, life-harrowing catastrophes. This chemical is called adrenaline. Maybe you've heard of it? It's the chemical that prepares us for "flight or fight." You see, God wants us to fight so he's given us adrenaline. Adrenaline is God's provision for having that extra boost of energy our bodies need to perform well in physically demanding situations. Have you ever heard of those people who perform super-human feats in extremely dangerous

Adrenaline

a hormone secreted by the adrenal glands, especially in conditions of stress that increases rates of blood circulation, breathing, and carbohydrate metabolism, causing a noticeable increase in strength and performance, as well as heightened awareness situations? The man who, with his bare hands, picked up and threw a car off his son who was trapped underneath? Or the lady who held a child in each arm while fighting off an intruder with amazing karate-like kicks? Yep, that's adrenaline. According to The Hormone Health Network (2016), "Adrenaline causes a noticeable increase in strength and performance, as well as heightened awareness, in stressful times."

So now that we know what adrenaline is and that God has created it with a specific purpose to actually help us, it's time to realign our thinking. The next time we have to give a speech, rather than saying, "Oh, I'm so nervous." Let's instead say, "Oh, I have so much energy to help me for this task."

Communication Apprehension: Is This Stage Fright or Am I About to Pass Out?

© cunaplus/Shutterstock.com

Communication apprehension
the fear or anxiety associated with either real or anticipated communication with another person or persons

The official word for the fear associated with public speaking is **communication apprehension** and is defined as "the fear or anxiety associated with either real or anticipated communication with another person or persons" (McCroskey, 2001, p. 40). Also known as stage fright, speech fright, and public speaking anxiety, McCroskey (2009), one of the leading researchers on communication apprehension, has been studying this topic for four decades. Although we may understand communication apprehension and how to overcome it better through decades of study, McCroskey still concedes that it can be a very real and serious fear for individuals to overcome. Did you know that nearly 75% of all individuals experience some sort of fear associated with public speaking? This type of anxiety can also trigger a fear response when the presentation is weeks or months away (Croston, 2014). Communication apprehension is a psychological fear of being evaluated when we speak, manifested through physical symptoms (such as shaky knees or a cracking voice). So the bad news is that we all experience some degree of communication apprehension. None of us are immune from it, Darn that adrenaline! However, communication apprehension can affect individuals in varying degrees. The good news is that we can manage and overcome whatever degree of communication apprehension we personally struggle with, and the physical manifestations that might be associated with that apprehension.

In order to learn better how to work through our communication apprehension, it's important to understand where it comes from. The apprehension, or anxiety, we face in various communication contexts can be attributed to two main types:

situational and trait. **Situational anxiety** is the anxiety that we can face in any communication situation we participate in. It's the aspects of the situation that might cause us to feel anxiety about getting up in front of a particular audience (Motley, 1995). Think about when you have to give a speech. What aspects of the situation are new and different that cause you to feel nervous? Are you nervous because you are being graded? Do you have to speak in front of a large audience? Are the members of your audience of high status? Do you have to speak early in the morning and you really don't do your best work until early afternoon? Is the topic new to you and you're not comfortable with your knowledge level? These are all examples of situational anxiety. It doesn't matter what the presentation is, there will always be aspects of the situation that will cause you some amount of anxiety when you speak.

Situational anxiety
anxiety caused by factors present in a specific speaking situation

"Of course you're allowed to have stage fright. As soon as your talk is over."

© Cartoon Resource/Shutterstock.com

Trait anxiety is the internal anxiety a speaker brings to the speaking situation and it usually stems from personal feelings of inadequacy (Beatty, Balfantz, & Kuwabara, 1989). There are several reasons that might cause us to experience trait anxiety. One of the main reasons for experiencing trait anxiety is that we feel subordinate to others, especially those in our audience. A poor self-esteem can be a strong predictor of communication anxiety. Another reason for experiencing trait anxiety is that we've had a negative experience with public speaking in the past and we tend to bring that experience with us to the next speech. We let our negative self-talk predict the outcome of our next speech. It can become a vicious cycle we have a hard time breaking free from (Beatty, 1998). Someone dealing with severe trait anxiety might be so fearful of speaking they find themselves physically paralyzed when giving a speech. Those of us who experience severe trait anxiety will have to work harder to overcome our public speaking anxiety. But we can—and we will!

Trait anxiety
internal anxieties an individual brings to the speaking situation, usually stemming from feelings of inadequacy

Managing Situational Anxiety: Overcoming the Sweating, Peeing, Throwing Up (and Other Unmentionables)

We'll talk about overcoming trait anxiety later. Let's first talk about how to handle situational anxiety. The very first thing I would say to you about handling this pesky situational anxiety is this—don't fight it, embrace it! Remember, none of us are immune from the effects of situational anxiety in our presentations;

© Mike Focus/Shutterstock.com

there will always be something about every speaking situation that causes us some degree of nervousness. Don't forget that those little butterflies you are feeling before a speech are actually a good thing. It's the adrenaline at work, giving your body that extra boost of energy you need to do an excellent job on your speech! I once heard a famous rock star, Bonnie Raitt, say this when asked about the anxiety she faces before a concert, "The day I don't feel nervous before a concert is the day I quit my job as a musician. If I'm not a little bit nervous, it means I don't care about the audience." So embrace your nerves, and just know that they mean you care.

Now unfortunately when we are feeling nervous before a speech, our body tends to do some really strange things and betray us to all the world; well, at least to our audience. Garcia-Lopez (2013) says that "you may feel faint, excitable, or jittery when experiencing stage fright. Your heart might race, your mouth might feel dry and you may feel out of breath or suddenly nauseous. These are all normal sensations and reactions that can be overcome." So what are some of the physical effects of nervousness you experience before a speech? I'll go first. I tend to talk way too fast, my ears and neck turn red, and I tend to get away from my outline and just start rambling. Look over the checklist in Sidebar 14A. Think about what physical symptoms you succumb to when speaking, and check all that apply.

Now that you've identified the physical symptoms of nervousness that you tend to deal with during a speech, don't panic! Let's talk about how to get your body to cooperate when you are feeling nervous. But first let me ask you this, when you are giving a speech, how long do you really feel nervous before you hit your groove? You know, that point in your speech when the nervousness subsides and you hit your sweet spot. Does that nervousness last the entire speech? If you think about it, the nervousness tends to go away fairly early on in your

---

What-my-stupid-body-does-when-I'm-nervous-during-a-speech Checklist:

❏ I sweat.   ❏ I shiver.   ❏ I want to throw up.
❏ I want to pee.   ❏ My hands shake.   ❏ My knees knock.
❏ My voice cracks.   ❏ I use vocal fillers.   ❏ I talk too much.
❏ My mind goes blank.   ❏ I look at the floor.   ❏ I pace or sway.
❏ I stutter.   ❏ I laugh nervously.   ❏ I have busy hands.
❏ I don't use my hands at all.
❏ Insert other unique, quirky nervous symptom you may experience here _____.

Sidebar 14A

BECOMING A BETTER COMMUNICATOR

speech. Maybe within the first few minutes. Wouldn't you agree? So, one secret to dealing with the physical symptoms of nervousness is simply patience. Start your speech, remain calm, and know that your nerves will subside.

Besides patience, let me give you some other techniques that will help your body overcome the physical symptoms of nervousness. Do you struggle with a cracking voice? Or maybe you can't even complete an entire sentence because you run out of air. Do you talk too fast during a speech? Here's what you need to do: breathe. Yes, you heard me, just breathe. A speech takes a tremendous toll on your body, and oxygen is a necessary life support. However, when we are nervous, we tend to take very shallow breaths of air from our chest. What we need to be doing is taking deep breaths from our diaphragms. I would encourage you to practice deep breathing when you are practicing for your speech. What's more critical, however, is that before you get up to speak, make sure you've taken several deep breaths to support you when you start your speech. And don't forget to breathe during

© ArtmannWitte/Shutterstock.com

your speech. It's okay to pause during your speech and take a deep breath. Also plan for pauses in your introduction to breathe to help you during that time when you tend to feel more nervous. By providing your body ample amounts of oxygen, you will likely diminish the effects of a weak, cracking voice. You will also avoid talking too fast by regulating your breathing. You might be surprised how adequate amounts of oxygen will support your body in many other ways to help you give a strong speech (such as clearer thinking and helping you release tension).

What about shaking hands and knees, or nervous pacing? Oh that's an easy fix—just move. If you have an opportunity to do a quick walk right before your speech, do it! Getting your blood circulating will combat the "shakes." Don't forget to move during your speech too. Don't be one of those speakers who stays in one place during their speech, locking their knees. If all you do is stand behind a podium during your speech, you're not doing your body any favors. Get that blood circulating before your speech, and keep it circulating during your speech with purposeful movement. We'll talk more about movement later in this chapter when we talk about confident delivery.

Besides deep breathing and movement, you should also participate in some relaxation exercises before you give your speech. Relaxation exercises incorporate muscle relaxation and deep breathing to help you relax and combat symptoms of anxiety before a speech. When the relaxation response is activated through relaxation exercises your heart rate decreases, breathing becomes slower and deeper, blood pressure drops or stabilizes, and your muscles relax. Relaxation exercises also increase energy and focus (Robinson, Segal, Segal, & Smith, 2016). When we feel stressed, we tend to tense up all over. Do you ever feel cold before a speech? Maybe you start shivering all over? Maybe you feel a

Relaxation exercises
the deliberate use of muscle relaxation and deep breathing that helps one relax and combat symptoms of anxiety before a speech

little nauseous? You likely feel this way because you are so tense. It's your job to remind your body to relax. Some specific things you could do before your speech is to tense up certain parts of your body, breathe deep, and then relax. I suggest a head-to-toe relaxation routine. Tense your neck, breathe, relax. Tense your shoulders, breathe, relax. Tense your hands, breathe, relax. You get the idea. And your body will get the idea too.

Our wardrobe choices can also help us with some of our other wacky signs of nervousness, or at least hide them. Do you sweat a lot during a speech? Wear a blazer. Blazers have a magical ability to hide sweat. Does your neck get splotchy when you are nervous? Wear a high-collared shirt, turtleneck, or a scarf. Viola! Ladies, do

© Mangostar/Shutterstock.com

you mess with your bangs when nervous? Wear your hair back. Do you feel like you look especially thin and attractive in your favorite suit? Wear it. If you feel like you look good, you will likely deliver a more confident speech.

Here are a few other pointers to help combat your nerves. Plan an introduction that puts you (and your audience) at ease. Tell a personal story at the beginning of your speech. It's much easier to tell our own stories versus reciting facts. Audiences like stories too. Tell a joke. When your audience laughs, it will help break the ice between you and them (Detz, 2000). (Word of caution: make sure the joke is appropriate, and that you don't mess up the punch line. I usually mess up punch lines so I avoid telling jokes in my speeches.) How about showing a powerful visual? When your audience is looking at your visual, it helps you relax. Don't forget that it's perfectly acceptable to use your speech notes to support your speaking. Unless you are required to memorize your speech, extemporaneous speaking, or speaking from an outline, is the preferred method for public speaking. You can easily glance down at your outline to keep you on track during your entire speech. Notice how I said "glance down at" and not "read" your speech notes. And please don't forget to sleep and eat. I know I am asking the impossible from a group of college students. Sleeping and eating? Who has time for that? But you really must support your body with the necessary amounts of rest and food. Both are critical factors to your body having the needed energy to perform well during a speech.

One of the best words of advice for combating situational anxiety is this . . . listen closely . . . this is very important . . . ***prepare in private to be proficient in public.*** You must do your part first. You must work hard during all phases of your speech preparation. Work hard when researching your speech, work hard when outlining and writing your speech. Practice until you really know your speech. One of the main contributors to our nervousness is that we just don't feel well prepared to deliver our speeches. If you put in the work beforehand, you will enjoy greater confidence during your speech. You will enjoy delivering your speech. Your audience will enjoy hearing your speech. God will enjoy helping you give an excellent speech. It's a win-win for everyone!

Managing Trait Anxiety: It's All in Your Head

Trait anxiety tends to build up over time and those who experience this type of anxiety may already be people who are naturally shy and self-conscious (Lumen, 2018). Trait anxiety tends to stem from two main areas: low self-esteem, and a history of negative public speaking experiences (Hamilton, 2006). Perhaps we are dealing with low self-esteem regarding our ability to get up and speak in front of others. Trait anxiety also tends to rear its ugly head when we compare ourselves to others. We might see ourselves as subordinate to our audience members. Or maybe we think that our classmates just have it all together. They are so witty and funny, and they appear to exert no effort whatsoever when they deliver their brilliant speeches. We think we just can't speak like them. Secondly, maybe we've really done poorly on a speech in the past. We can take that bad experience with us to future speeches. We then expect to have a really bad speech the next time, usually because we speak negative emotions over the upcoming speech. Have you ever caught yourself saying anything like this, "I'm really going to bomb this speech"? "I'm so nervous, I'll probably just draw a blank when I give this speech"? Remember the self-fulfilling prophecy is a belief that comes true because we are acting as if it is already true.

Not everyone struggles with this more severe form of communication anxiety. But for those who do, trait anxiety is a bit stubborn. This type of speaking anxiety really wants to hang around and cause us troubles, and can be a bit more difficult to overcome. You see trait anxiety tends to be more of a mental game. Yes, it's all in our head. But the good news is that God has given us the tools to overcome this type of anxiety too. And if you don't particularly struggle with trait anxiety, remember that if you know how to manage the "mental game" associated with confident and successful public speaking, you can help others manage their trait anxiety.

The most important thing we must remember when dealing with our trait anxiety is that we've got to learn to realign our thinking when it comes to public speaking. Remember I said God has already given us the tools for this? Well, here they are: pictures and words. Yes, two simple things will make a huge contribution in helping us be the confident speakers God has called us to be. I once heard my pastor say that our words are the elevator to our hearts. You see, we all deal with doubt and discouragement. It's when we speak words of failure and negativity that we tend to accept them. And, act on them—a.k.a "The self-fulfilling prophecy." But this can work both ways. When it's time to deliver our next speech, instead

© Brian A Jackson/Shutterstock.com

of seeing ourselves in our minds doing a poor job, and then speaking that failure over the speech, we can realign our pictures and our words. Instead of seeing failure, we can train our minds to see ourselves delivering a confident, successful speech and backing it up with our words. For example instead of saying, "I'm so nervous, I'm going to do a terrible job on this speech" we can instead say, "I have so much energy for this speech, thank you Lord that you are helping me to give an excellent speech." It really is all in our heads (and our words)!

© charnsitr/Shutterstock.com

Positive imagery
a technique used to evoke positive mental images, feelings, and thoughts

Positive imagery is an excellent tool to help realign our thinking. **Positive imagery** is a technique used to evoke positive mental images, feelings, and thoughts when thinking about an anxiety-producing situation. Positive imagery entails seeing yourself, in your mind, giving a confident, dynamic presentation. It might mean visualizing yourself successfully walking through every aspect of the speech, from research, to practice, to presentation (Ayers, 1998). Athletes, musicians, actors, and speakers have all used positive imagery in helping them overcome their performance anxiety. Have you ever been on a sports team and your coach made you incorporate positive imagery as a regular part of your practice? My daughter plays competitive volleyball. In addition to physically practicing her serve, her coach makes her visually practice her serve. She must visualize every aspect of the serve from her stance, through the throw, to the hit. Coaches know the power of conquering a demanding physical performance in the mind first.

© Monkey Business Images/Shutterstock.com

But why does positive imagery work? I'm glad you asked. Positive imagery works for many reasons. First, positive imagery helps you deal with an anxiety-producing event before the actual event. For example, if you've already dealt with the feelings of fear and anxiety before a big speech, you're likely feeling much more confident about the speech when the big day arrives. Also, our subconscious never wants to push us out of our comfort zones. Practicing positive imagery will help you to feel confident to take risks to do things you never thought you could do . . . to be the speaker you never thought you could be . . . to get past the limitations of your mind (Hamilton, 2006).

But some of you may be thinking, "Eeek, this sounds a little out there!" "I'm not comfortable with meditation." What do you think? Does God's Word support positive imagery? Oh you bet it does. Look over to Sidebar 14B to see what God has to say about aligning our words and pictures. I challenge you to let His words sink deep into your heart. God doesn't want you to fail when you give a speech. He wants you to succeed. He has given you an important message. Your speech just might change the world.

No matter what your level of anxiety when facing your next speech, I encourage you to align your thoughts with the Word of God. Do what you need to do to prepare

Sidebar 14B

yourself for a successful speech. See yourself being the confident speaker God has created you to be. Care about your audience and remember that you have an important message to share. Trust God to do through you, through your words, what you cannot do yourself. Then sit back, relax, have fun, and enjoy the journey.

Confident Delivery: Seeing Is Believing

Now that we know how to manage the anxiety associated with public speaking, let's look at how our confidence is communicated in the delivery of our speeches. Do you remember when we talked about nonverbal communication? Specifically, the part about how if one's verbal communication and nonverbal communication conflict, we tend to believe what the nonverbal cues are communicating over the verbal? The same principle applies to the delivery of our speeches. In regard to our speech delivery, it's important to understand the difference between the verbal and the nonverbal codes we use when we present our speeches. There are three codes (Douglas, 2014) we utilize as a speaker during our presentations: the verbal, vocal, and visual. These codes are the channels that deliver our message. The verbal code is the words we speak when we give a speech. The vocal code is composed of our tone of voice, such as our vocal expression, rate, pitch, and loudness.

Verbal code
the words one speaks when giving a speech

Vocal code
a nonverbal code composed of a speaker's tone of voice, which includes vocal expression, rate, pitch, and volume

Visual code

a nonverbal code comprised of anything an audience member sees of a speaker's delivery, such as their facial expressions, movement, gestures, and visual aids

The **visual code** is anything our audience members see with their eyes. This would be the actual components of a speaker's delivery such as their posture, clothing, facial expressions, movement, and gestures. Visual aids are also something that our audience members see with their eyes during a speech, so they are also part of the visual code. Now two of these codes are nonverbal, and one is verbal. Obviously a speaker's words make up the verbal code. That means the vocal and visual codes are the nonverbal codes. Remember back when we learned about nonverbal communication in Chapter 4, we learned that if one's verbal and nonverbal communication contradict each other, another tends to believe the nonverbal cues over the verbal. Here's where our confidence comes into play. We can spend hours researching, writing, and practicing our speeches. We can use all the right words during our speech, *but*, if our nonverbal communication (our tone of voice and physical delivery), do not confidently align with our words, our audience members will judge us as speakers who lack credibility. As Lynda Katz Wilner, author of *Successfully Speaking,* puts it, "In general, it's not just what we say, but how we say it, and how we look when we say it. When delivering information, the non-verbal aspects of vocal tone and body language influence the actual verbal message." It's imperative then that we learn how to communicate confidence in each component of our vocal and visual delivery so the verbal and nonverbal codes are congruent.

Immediate Delivery: I Don't Get It

© Blend Images/Shutterstock.com

Before we get into the specifics of what delivery looks like, let's take a few minutes to talk about a very important, yet often overlooked, aspect of delivery. Let's call it the "it" factor. "It" varies in its names. "It" is rather intangible (hard to define exactly) and hard to put a finger on what qualities make a speaker someone who has "it." Maybe you've even thought to yourself when listening to a speaker, that they really have "it" going on. So let's put a name to "it." Some might reference a speaker who has this quality as someone with "charisma," or a speaker who's very "dynamic," or a presenter whose "energy" is infectious. It may feel like this quality is unattainable, only reserved for the talented few. I'm here to tell you that that's not true. You too can have the "it" factor when you present your speeches. Do you know what having "it" is really all about? Simply put, "it" is just about how you "connect" with your audience. As speakers, there are tangible things we can do to connect better with our audiences. Connection can be learned, and developed, and refined.

Immediacy behaviors

verbal and nonverbal behaviors that a speaker uses to build closeness and connection with audience members and makes the speaker more likable

So how do we connect well with our audiences? In order to be that energetic speaker who has a good connection with the audience, it's important you learn how to incorporate immediacy behaviors in the delivery of your speeches. **Immediacy behaviors** are defined as those behaviors that help us build closeness and connection with our audience members and make us more likable. Think about a speaker you really enjoy listening to. They might be speaking to an audience of hundreds, but you feel connected to them. You like them. Now think about the aspects of their delivery that make them relatable, likable, open. What did you think of? You probably thought about the immediacy behaviors they used without even realizing it. Immediacy behaviors can be verbal and nonverbal. When speakers demonstrate verbal immediacy they might incorporate the following in their speeches: humor, telling stories and sharing personal examples, calling audience members by name, being available to talk with the audience before and after their presentation, and using inclusive language such as "us" and "we" when they speak. A speaker who incorporates nonverbal immediacy is a speaker who has excellent eye contact with their audience and great energy when they speak (Beebe, Mottet, & Roach, 2013). Energy comprises expressive facial expressions and voice, varied movement, and expressive gestures. So that's the good news! You already have everything you need to be a good speaker who has that charismatic quality, that dynamism, that engaging presence, that "it" factor. I am not asking you to be anybody else when you speak. I'm just asking you to be yourself, at your most energetic.

Movement: Getting Past the Line-of-Terror

Now that we understand the overriding goal of being a speaker who connects well with their audience, let's take some time to learn about these specific components of delivery and look at what our goals should be for each.

© dotshock/Shutterstock.com

Let's start with confident movement. It may be an easy temptation to get comfortable behind the podium and never move. A speaker who doesn't move is afraid to pass the line-of-terror. If you're wondering what the "line-of-terror" is, imagine a speaking environment in your mind. The **line-of-terror** is that imaginary line that a speaker is afraid to move past. It's typically the line that is represented by the front of the podium. Many speakers are afraid to venture past that imaginary line during a speech, keeping a safe distance between themselves and their audience. But here's the thing, if you really want to communicate warmth, connection, and energy, you must walk past that imaginary line and prove to your audience that you really do like them (Reimold & Reimold, 2003).

Line-of-terror
that imaginary line a speaker is afraid to move past, typically level with the front of the podium

Purposeful movement is a necessary part of your confident delivery. In fact movement is a key component of communicating your energy and enthusiasm for your audience and your topic. I might even go as far as to say that standing in one place during a speech is boring. Now, there are certain speaking occasions where it might be more appropriate to incorporate little movement as a speaker, and perhaps even stay behind a podium, such as at a formal event, or when the speaking environment has a very small stage. Otherwise, don't stay behind the podium. You look bored (and maybe a little lifeless too). The closer you get to your audience members, the more they feel connected to you (a nonverbal immediacy behavior). That's why it's important to walk out from the "line-of-terror" during a speech.

So incorporate movement during your speech, but be sure you use purposeful movement, not pointless movement. Pacing is not purposeful movement, it's pointless. Swaying back and forth is also not purposeful movement. Pacing and swaying also communicate nervousness, not confidence. So what does purposeful movement look like during a speech? Instead of pacing, try the walk-stop-talk method. For example, let's say you just delivered your introduction front and center on the topic of college students and stress. As you transition into the body of your speech, you might move to another part of the room while saying, "Let's begin by looking at the causes of stress in college students' lives." Then you would spend some time in that part of the room during your first main point. As you transition to the second main point, you might move again as you say, "Next, let's look at the effects of stress on college students" and stay in that part of the room for a bit before you move again. As you can tell, movement and transitions work really well together. Then after main point two, you might move back to the center of the room and spend time front-and-center as you deliver your third main point. Although planned for, remember to always strive to make your movement as a speaker look natural and varied, not scripted. Use your movement as a speaker with purpose, allowing you to make friends with audience members in all parts of the room. Oh by the way, by incorporating movement during your speech, you also keep your blood flowing, which reduces nervousness while you speak. Bonus points!

Let's also think about our speaking posture here, since posture is so closely connected to our movement. The goal for our posture when we speak is to have an upright, confident, yet relaxed posture. Head up, shoulders back, and arms open is a good goal for confident speaking posture. Gripping the podium tightly and refusing to move as if our feet have been cemented in concrete is not the posture we're striving for. Appropriate posture communicates that a speaker is confident, yet comfortable, when standing in front of his audience.

Gestures: It's All in the Hands

It's a mysterious phenomenon that happens to us when get up to deliver a speech. We suddenly forget what to do with our hands. All of a sudden we are strangely cognizant that we have these huge, heavy appendages hanging at the side of our bodies. We become keenly aware that we're not quite sure how to include our hands in the speech. Perhaps that's why our hands start misbehaving during a speech. They feel left out and are trying desperately to get attention. Let's look at some of the ways our hand gestures do not make a good impression (or no impression at all) on our audience members. First, there's what I call the "tedious" hands. Tedious hands are when a speaker keeps their hands moving during their entire speech with small, repetitive motions. There's also "crazy" hands. Crazy hands are when the speaker keeps moving their hands in large, repetitive motions throughout their entire speech. When our hands are moving all the time, they become distractions and fail to be a helpful component of our delivery. There are numerous other examples of misbehaving hands: the "white-knuckle-death-grip" (hands gripped so tightly to the podium that our knuckles turn white); wringing hands; hands fidgeting with notes (or hair, or our tie, or whatever); as well as hands stuffed in pockets.

© hasan eroglu/Shutterstock.com

So what should our hand gestures look like? First of all, remember that hand gestures should be varied and natural, not scripted. Gestures should also be large and dramatic expressions that highlight key components of our verbal message. Our gestures should also complement our message and look like natural extensions of a speaker's energy during their speech. Knowing how to use gestures to complement your message is the sign of a savvy speaker. Did you know that nearly 65% of the population are visual learners? This means the majority of individuals learn through seeing primarily (as opposed to auditory learners who learn mainly through hearing). This means you should be mindful to incorporate gestures that complement your words, and add meaning. Let's give it a try. Think about a gesture that complements the following words: surround, oppose, and elevate. Did you immediately think of a gesture that would represent that specific word? It wasn't too hard was it (Reimold & Reimold, 2003)? Remember too, it's okay to let your hands rest. Hands do not, and should not, be moving the entire time you are speaking. To sum it up, don't let your hands take over the speech. When you incorporate gestures shoot for large expressive gestures (not small, repetitive gestures) that highlight key ideas, are varied, and are natural.

Eye Contact: Do I Really Have to Look at my Audience?

The answer is yes! Remember what we learned about immediate speakers? They have good eye contact with their audience. Good eye contact creates connection with our audience. Nervous speakers may find themselves looking at their notes, the ceiling, the floor, or a myriad of other places. Confident speakers look at their audience. Nervous speakers don't. Immediate speakers care about their audience

© sirtravelalot/Shutterstock.com

and want to talk with them as friends. When we remember that, it shouldn't be too intimidating to look our audience members squarely in the eyes. Good eye contact during a speech does not look like a tennis match. You know, the predictable shifting of eye movement from one side of the room to the other. Instead try this. Take some time in your presentation to squarely face each member of your audience, look them in the eye, have a time of personal communication with that audience member, and then randomly move on to other members of the audience in the same fashion. Eye contact is a critical element of expressing your connection with your audience, enabling you to connect with each audience member on an individual level. Eye contact also enables you to see what's going on out there with your audience and helps you make adjustments during your speech to meet your audience members' needs.

Vocal Delivery: Variety and Expression

© leungchopan/Shutterstock.com

Vocal expression is a critical part of your speech delivery. Here's the thing—if you haven't got any variety or expression in your voice you run the risk of putting your listeners to sleep. Your speech content may be excellent. It could match your audience's needs very well but unless you deliver it in an interesting way, few people will actively listen. A talented public speaker knows how to use their voice masterfully to communicate their message effectively. During a presentation, your vocal delivery consists of how effectively you use your voice. Specifically, how effectively you use volume, rate, and pitch. As we look at all these components individually, remember that your overall goal for your vocal delivery is to strive for an expressive, yet natural, vocal delivery.

Let's review the basics of vocal delivery as defined by The University of Pittsburg (2007). Be sure to speak loudly enough for your entire audience to be able to hear you when you speak. A speaker who consistently speaks too softly will fatigue their audience members. Audience members will tire of trying to strain to hear the soft-spoken speaker and will likely just quit listening. Speakers who consistently speak too loudly will frankly just annoy their audience. No one likes to be shouted at. (Well, unless you're in a burning building and someone yells "FIRE!"). Strive to use the appropriate volume during your speech, and be mindful of how to use varying volume as a way to emphasize key points. For example, you may consider speaking a bit louder for a short time to emphasize an important point in your content. You might also speak just a bit softer for a time to emphasize important ideas, allowing your audience members to really hear and take in what you are saying. When audience members

BECOMING A BETTER COMMUNICATOR

hear a change in volume, their ears tend to perk up and they listen a bit more attentively. So you see, how we control our vocal volume can be a tremendous asset in our speeches.

Rate also works much like volume when it comes to our vocal variety. Rate is how quickly or how slowly you speak during a speech and is a critical part of your vocal expression. For the most part, you should strive for a rate that your audience members can comfortably keep up with. A speaker who consistently speaks too slowly is boring. A speaker who consistently speaks too fast is tiring. But, speaking at the same rate during our entire speech is not necessarily what we're shooting for either, and is not what we should aim for when trying to solve the problem of speaking too fast or too slow. Instead of a "one-rate-fits-all" mentality, be sure to vary your speaking rate to meet the needs of your content and your audience. Just as we did with volume, use rate to emphasize important ideas in your speech and also to communicate your energy for your topic. Think back to a time you told a friend a story about something you were very excited about. What happened to your rate? You probably sped up as you were telling your story, and your friend sensed your excitement and passion for the topic. Or think about a time you heard another person speak slowly and deliberately to ensure accurate understanding of a message. The same technique of slowing down for a time to stress important points can also be applied in our speeches. When practicing your speech, try slowing down or slightly increasing your speaking rate to emphasize points.

Pitch is another part of our vocal delivery that is important to master. If you look at the dictionary definition of pitch, you will find a wordy explanation that includes words such as "vibrations" and "vocal folds." (Say what?) A simpler definition of pitch is the highness or lowness of your voice. Changes in your pitch are also known as inflections. Pitch is really just the natural range of highs and lows in which your voice operates. We all have a comfortable range of highness and lowness in which we speak. Those with a greater range of pitch tend to have more expressive voices. Those with a shorter range of pitch tend to have monotone voices. So when delivering a speech, remember to vary your vocal inflection to add emphasis and expression in your voice.

Before we finish our discussion about vocal delivery, don't forget about pauses. Pauses are temporary "stops" within our speeches that are useful, necessary, and deliberate. When giving a speech you do not need to talk non-stop for the entire speech, all the time, until you are completely out of breath, and want to gasp for air, and pass out from exhaustion. How did you feel after reading that last sentence? Tired? Well that's how your audience feels when you don't pause. When giving a speech you should plan for strategic pauses. For example, you might pause for a moment when you've shared a shocking statistic, or a new term, or a thoughtful point. This will give your audience members time to think and reflect on what was just said. Avoid using too many pauses. This will make your speech feel incoherent and choppy and it may communicate that you are

Rate
how fast or how slowly one speaks during a speech

Pitch
the highness or lowness of one's voice

Pause
a temporary stop or rest within the speech used deliberately by the speaker to emphasize a point or catch a breath

not well prepared because you have to pause so often to think. Whatever you do, avoid filling your pauses with vocal fillers such as "um," "uh," or "you know." Let me also encourage you by saying that pauses can be a presenter's best pal when speaking. Pauses allow us to catch our breath, and even get back on track when something has gone wrong during a speech (such as finding our place in our speaking notes when we've lost our train of thought). To sum up the critical role that pauses play in our speeches, let me say that speakers need pauses, and audience members need pauses. Everyone wins when pauses are used appropriately in our speeches.

Visual Aids

© Anton Gvozdikov/Shutterstock.com

Before we finish talking about the specifics of confident delivery, I want to say a quick word about what our delivery should look like when using visual aids during a speech. Remember, if they are designed well, visuals should complement your verbal message. Visuals should be the teacher's aide (get it?) and not be the teacher! As the speaker, you are the one your audience members came for. They did not come for your PowerPoint presentation. Your audience also did not show up to read your PowerPoint presentation, or to watch *you* read your PowerPoint presentation. When incorporating visuals into your speech, you must maintain that same confident delivery, all the while connecting and engaging with your audience. Do not push the pause button on good delivery when using a visual aid during your speech. For example, don't turn your back to your audience to read your visuals from the projector screen, or turn the lights out, stand in a corner, and look only at your Prezi while you speak. Instead, keep moving, and gesturing, and competently relaying your content to the audience as you speak. Keep that same good eye contact with your audience when showing them the objects you brought. Practice with your visuals before your speech so you are comfortable using them. Arrive at your speaking environment early to set up your visuals and work through any technology issues that may arise. I would also encourage you to practice your presentation one time without the use of your visuals. Let's say you get to your speech location and the computer isn't working, or you can't pull up the presentation that you emailed to yourself, or you forgot the objects that you were planning to use in your demonstration. Remember that the show must go on. As a presenter, you may need to be prepared to give your speech without your visuals. I would also encourage you to have a plan B. For example, if you can't pull up the PowerPoint presentation what is your back up plan? Perhaps you could have a low-tech back up such as printing out a few of your most important slides and showing them on the document camera. When it comes to delivering with your visual aids, still incorporate good delivery and plan for a perfect presentation, but also plan to be flexible.

Ethical Implications

In previous chapters we discussed the ethical obligation of a speaker to be well researched when presenting information. However, how often have we stopped to think about the role confident delivery plays in the ethics of public speaking? Sometimes we forget that our role as a speaker is that of a servant. Our ultimate purpose when speaking is to give a presentation tailored around the audience's needs. Pure and simple. If we're too focused on the applause we'll garner at the end of our speech, we'll forget about the merits of the work required before we even deliver our speech. Confident speakers plant seeds at the front-end of the speaking process knowing there's a great harvest to reap at the end. A speaker who takes the time to practice their speech and learn how to manage their nervous energy is a speaker who not only invests in themselves as a speaker, but one who ultimately cares about the audience.

If we have the most profound, eloquent message to share, but our delivery lacks confidence and is poorly received, we've failed. Our message will not be received as it should because our audience doubts our credibility based on our nervous delivery. An ethical public speaker is a servant. A servant who believes in their audience . . . their needs . . . and the importance of their God-given message. We can, no we must, get out of our fear when we speak. We have an important message to share. There's too much at stake if we don't get out of our fear. God would never call you to speak without anointing you for such a task. So remember that you are just an instrument. An instrument used by God to share a message that will help others. You have something important to say! Why not say it confidently?

Summary

Good communicators are confident. This doesn't mean good communicators never experience communication anxiety. We've learned that communication anxiety is a natural part of the speaking process. Adrenaline actually helps provide a speaker the extra energy and strength needed to succeed in any given speech performance. Learning how to manage the symptoms of situational and trait anxiety will help a speaker overcome the fear associated with giving a presentation. Providing our bodies adequate support through deep breathing and increased movement will help tame the physical feelings of nervousness one might experience. The use of positive imagery and relaxation techniques will help one overcome the more serious symptoms associated with trait anxiety. Adequate practice and preparation will further strengthen our proficiency as a public speaker.

Confident speakers know how to connect effectively with their audiences. Through the use of verbal and nonverbal immediacy behaviors, speakers promote a sense of closeness with their audiences and are deemed more likable. Immediacy behaviors also help us understand how to deliver a speech in an energetic and dynamic fashion. Good eye contact, expressive facials and gestures, vocal expression, and varied movement help us deliver dynamic and engaging speeches.

Vocabulary Words

Adrenaline
Communication apprehension
Immediacy behaviors
Line-of-Terror
Pause

Pitch
Positive imagery
Rate
Relaxation exercises
Situational anxiety

Trait anxiety
Verbal code
Visual code
Vocal code

Discussion Questions

1. What aspects of situational anxiety tend to cause you the most apprehension?
2. Do you fear public speaking? If so, what specifically would you consider to be the reason for your unease?
3. Look at Sidebar 14A. What physical symptoms do you most struggle with when delivering your speeches? Based on what you have learned, what will you specifically do to better manage these physical symptoms when delivering your speeches?
4. Which components of confident delivery are the hardest for you? Which are easier for you?
5. Begin to create an action plan for improving your delivery. What specifically will you do to get your speaking skills to the next level? (For example, "I will

look confidently at all audience members when I speak." Or, "I will incorporate purposeful movement in my next speech by walking past the line-of-terror and moving to all parts of my speaking environment.")

6. How do visual aids help you be a more dynamic and confident speaker? Cite some examples of ways you have seen speakers use their visuals well or poorly.

7. Do you agree that a public speaker is a servant? Why or why not?

8. Who could you practice with? Who can you get to time your speech to make sure you will be able to complete it in the assigned time frame?

9. If your speech is too long, what can you do? (You can't just talk faster!)

References

Ayers, J. (1998). Coping with speech anxiety: The power of positive thinking. *Communication Education, 37,* 289–285.

Beatty, M. J. (1988). Situational and predispositional correlates of public speaking anxiety. *Communication Education, 37,* 28–39.

Beatty, M. J., Balfantz, G. L., & Kuwabara, A. Y. (1989). Trait-like qualities of selected variables assumed to be transient causes of performance state anxiety. *Communication Education, 38,* 277–289.

Beebe, S., Mottet, T., & Roach, K. (2013). *Training and development: Communicating for success.* Boston: Pearson Education Inc.

Croston, G. (2012). The real story of risk: The thing we fear more than death. *Psychology Today.* (Blog post). Retrieved from https://www.psychologytoday.com/us/blog/the-real-story-risk

Detz, J. (2000). *It's not what you say, it's how you say it.* New York: St. Martin's.

Douglas, A. (2014). Three elements of communication: Vocal, visual, verbal. Retrieved from http://www.asls.com.au/three-elements-of-communication-vocal-visual-verbal/

Garcia-Lopez, L.J. (2013). Treating . . . social anxiety disorder. Madrid: Piramide.

Grice, G. L. (2015). *Mastering public speaking* (9th ed.). New York: Pearson.

Hamilton, C. (2006). *Essentials of public speaking.* Boston, MA: Wadsworth Cengage Learning.

The Hormone Health Network. (2018). *What does adrenaline do?* Retrieved from: http://www.hormone.org/hormones-and-health/what-do-hormones-do/adrenaline

Lumen Learning. (2018). *Understanding anxiety.* Retrieved from: https://courses.lumenlearning.com/boundlesscommunications/chapter/understanding-anxiety

McCroskey, J. C. (2001). *An introduction to rhetorical communication.* Boston, MA: Allyn & Bacon.

McCroskey, J. C. (2009). Communication apprehension: What have we learned in the last four decades. *Human Communication 12*(2), 157–172.

Motley, M. (1995). *Overcoming your fear of public speaking: A proven method.* New York: McGraw-Hill.

Reimold, C., & Reimold, P. (2003). *The short road to great presentations: How to reach any audience through focused preparation, inspired delivery, and smart use of technology.* Hoboken, NJ: John Wiley & Sons.

Robinson, L., Segal, R., Segal, J., & Smith, M. (2016). Relaxation techniques for stress relief. Retrieved from http://www.helpguide.org/articles/stress/relaxation-techniques-or-stress-relief.htm

The University of Pittsburgh. (2007). Verbal delivery tips: Communication across the curriculum. Retrieved from http://www.speaking.pitt.edu/student/public-speaking/suggestions-verbal.html

Wilner, L. (2013, June 29). *Successfully speaking: The three V's of communication.* Retrieved from http://successfully-speaking.com/blog/the-three-vs-of-communication

Additional Readings

Talk Like TED: The 9 Public-Speaking Secrets of the World's Top Minds
by Carmine Gallo

I Can See You Naked

by Ron Hoff

Speak Like Yourself . . . No, Really! Follow Your Strengths and Skills to Great Public Speaking

by Jezra Kayne

On Speaking Well

by Peggy Noonan

Better Communicators Are Persuasive

By Agena Farmer, Ed.D.

15

Congratulations! By this part of the course you have learned how to connect better with people, how to work in groups, how to analyze an audience, how to choose and research a topic, and you have given your first informative speech. Now you are preparing to do your final speech. This chapter adds another tool to your toolbox by giving you insight on persuasion. A **persuasive speech** is one that helps someone change their mind about the way they think or act, and maybe change the world a little (Jaffe, 2013). If you are going to communicate most effectively you are going to have to learn how to be more strategic when you speak. Realize that the strategic part includes not only what you say, but also how you say it, organize it, and support it. This chapter will help you synthesize the material that you have learned about listening and reading nonverbal behavior so you can be more empathetic to the viewpoints of others.

I am going to give you a different perspective on outlining a persuasive speech. The reason I am giving you a different slant on the outline is because we are persuading now, and not informing. Abraham Maslow (1966) said that when you have a hammer, every problem is a nail. My hammer is debate because I am a debate coach so this persuasive speech problem "nail" can be handled with ease by my debate hammer. We are discussing arguments and so as a debate coach I can give you some rules on how to write and deliver a great speech to persuade. I brought up the debate thing with some

© ArtOfPhotos/Shutterstock.com

Persuasive speech
a speech that helps someone change their mind about the way they think or act

trepidation because it is hard to convince people that I am not going to crush them like a grape if they bring up a point that I think is wrong. I am a relatively calm person, but I really enjoy analyzing arguments.

Connecting with the Audience

I'm sure I will talk about the connection with the audience many times in this chapter, but your understanding of *why* the audience believes what they believe is crucial to your choosing your arguments. I call this being empathetic because you understand why they think the way they do about a topic but you don't necessarily feel the same way. For instance, if some classmates had friends who won several beauty pageants and used the scholarships to pay for their schooling, you would understand why they thought the pageants were not portraying women in a sexist light. You might not have believed the same thing, but you would understand why your classmates thought what they did. You also would know that if you were to give a persuasive speech in class about how the media presents sexist stereotypes of women, which create unrealistic expectations of how a woman should look, you should stay away from the beauty/scholarship pageant examples. If you wanted to fight, you could pick on pageants. But if you wanted to discuss sexist images of women, there are plenty of examples you could use without offending the class with a pageant slur.

© yuris/Shutterstock.com

Put yourself in the audience's shoes.

For the sake of argument and since you already have definitions for sympathy and empathy, I am going to offer you a rationale for my definitions. Realize that this does not make the definitions the supreme ruling definition for everyone in the world, I am just defining them so you will know that what *I* mean by "sympathy" and "empathy" during this discussion. According to psychologist Carl Rogers (1962), sympathy is when you feel the same way the other person does. If they are sad, you are sad with them. Empathy means you know the situation well enough to understand why they feel the way that they do without feeling the same way. You can understand why they are upset without becoming emotional about the situation. For example, if Jennifer, a friend of yours, came to you in tears because she had lost her job, and your response was to cry with her and call the people who fired her evil, you would be sympathizing with her. The end result would be two people who were miserable, mad, and upset. Instead, you said, "That is too bad. I know how much that job meant to you and what a financial strain that puts on you and your family. Were you dismissed or did you resign?" While allowing your friend to express anger at the company, you did not also become angry and emotional. You continued to ask questions at appropriate intervals and found that your friend had been asked to resign and she was to turn in a letter of resignation tomorrow. You would then be able to help her construct a letter and ask for a recommendation from her employer. If she had been fired, the task-at-hand would change. In this instance, you would be empathizing with her. You would understand how and why she was feeling the way she was, but you didn't get caught up in the emotions of the moment and were able to help her figure out her next steps. Now let's connect this to the audience. According to my terms, sympathy happens when you agree with the audience about an idea. No persuasion is necessary. On the other hand, empathy is when you understand why they believe what they do without taking on the same belief. We are obligated to understand why the audience believes the way they do whether we agree or not (Dobkin & Pace, 2003; Fraleigh & Tuman, 2017; Oh'Hair et al., 2013). When we can empathize with the audience, we can move our persuasion to a whole new level.

I want to clarify some definitions with you before we continue. Whether informative or persuasive, any good speech is clear about its intent. For example, when I talk about argument I am talking about a logical discussion about an issue. When I talk about a fight, I am talking about people not listening to each other, becoming very emotional and loud, and saying things that are not supported by information. When you recognize the difference between a discussion and an emotional outburst, you are ready to discuss persuasion.

Persuasive Speech Tasks

Keep these three tasks in mind when you are prepping for a good persuasive speech. First, *analyze the audience* to have a basic understanding of what they think. (See chapter 11 for how to conduct an audience analysis.) Second, *have some idea of why the audience thinks what they do (empathizing).*

The third thing is something we haven't really talked about in much detail before this chapter. We have to *be responsible for using our persuasive skills for the good of the audience. We should* not mislead them or encourage them to do something they should not. Interestingly enough, this has to do more and more with our ability to respond. Often, we don't take time to think before we answer. Because of the ease with which we can communicate our ideas online through social media, we respond without thinking through our ideas. We are *quick to talk, slow to listen,* and *quick to condemn* the other person's ideas in the name of truth. We want to win the argument, and so while the other person is presenting their ideas we are planning our next biting remark. This is not very effective and instead of coming to agreement through a discussion of ideas, it results in two angry people and no consensus. Nothing is resolved and further discussion of the topic is almost impossible because I have "un-friend-ed" you and I don't "follow" you on social media any more.

Quick-Slow-Quick Thinking

Our *quick-slow-quick* doesn't work according to the scripture. If you look in your search tool on your Bible app, you will find that in James 1:19, we are encouraged to be "swift to hear, slow to speak, slow to wrath," according to the King James version. I like the way that the God's Word translation says it, "Remember this, my dear brothers and sisters: Everyone should be quick to listen, slow to speak, and should not get angry easily. An angry person doesn't do what God approves of. So get rid of all immoral behavior and all the wicked things you do. Humbly accept the word that God has placed in you. This word can save you." James 1:16-21 GW. I added the extra verses to give you context for the verse. The reason we work harder at communicating is to show honor to what God has created. It is with respect toward God that we also respect the ideas of others to hear what they have to say. Another scripture says, "Everything you say should be kind and well thought out so that you know how to answer everyone" Col 4:6.

Sidebar 15A

Coercion and Persuasion

I am suggesting you change your goal from winning at all costs through the quick-slow-quick focus, to using the blending of ideas so that you and your audience both can win. This means we are not working for the utter defeat of one idea by another. This is what we need to change. It would be more beneficial to get others to go in our direction because they want to, not because we tricked them (Reardon, 1991). If we use the skills we have learned from the listening chapter and add those to skills about using the time between our thoughts and our responses correctly, we can be more successful in our communication, period, not just in our speeches, but in all of our lives (Jaffe, 2013).

Please realize that sometimes it's more important for you to be heard and understood than it is to win the argument. We would like to help you express yourself well while doing it at an appropriate time and in a more constructive way.

Your objective as a speaker then, is to help the audience empathize with your perspective, not to tell them what to think. Let's start by looking at the role persuasion has played in our lives.

You've Done This Before!

We are persuaded from our birth. This explains why as infants we would eat those green beans and peas—we were persuaded. (What have you used to persuade babies to eat food they don't like—the choo-choo train or the airplane, etc.?) After being successfully persuaded by others, we started to use those same methods on others to encourage them to do the things we wanted them to do. We figured out how to get a favorite aunt to bring us some juice. We also learned as a child that proper behavior earned

© Photo by MHIN/Shutterstock.com

a reward. For instance, I didn't want to keep my room clean but the idea of being able to do something fun in return made making my bed worth the effort. I had been persuaded.

We are also persuading from birth. As we grew we learned the "tricks" or subtleties of the trade and we found out how, because of our victories and defeats, to find the best way to persuade those around us. If we wanted our parents to do something for us, our behavior was "very good" in the days leading up to the event. This made them more willing to agree to our requests.

During high school years we learned to persuade on a much grander scale. After all, an afternoon at the playground is not as expensive as a car, or money for a trip, or a down payment on an apartment. As we grew, the numbers of people to be persuaded grew and the importance of what we were persuading them to do increased exponentially. Now that we have a higher level of education, we have entered into a higher level of responsibility for acting in a moral and just way.

Responsibility of Critical Thought

At a university level our pursuit to learn the ins and outs of persuasion intensifies. The university's focus is on teaching you *how* to think logically, not *what* to think. Pause for a moment and think about that. When people stop telling you what to think you become more responsible for the consequences of what you believe. The criticism of your ideas comes back to you. You can't play the "Well, that's what my dad says" card and it get you off the hook. You are now responsible for putting the "stuff" you know together and making sense of it all. You have no one to blame for inaccurate thoughts. Also, it is harder to persuade people who are thinking for themselves. When they think a particular thing because someone told them to, they will dump the idea more easily. If they have arrived at that conclusion on their own, it is harder to change their minds. They will ignore a professor's idea much faster than they will an idea that they have birthed on their own. You have received a sufficient base of information through your elementary, middle school, and high school years to be able to make decisions for yourself, and what you didn't learn in school, you could access by the touch of a finger.

You might ask then, "If I can find the answers then why am I here at the university?" Proverbs 4:5 says that as you are getting knowledge, you also need to get wisdom. The professors in your classes are helping you learn to use the knowledge tool by giving you the new wisdom tool. The goal is to enable you to justify or think through why you should do things a certain way. This wisdom also helps you be more persuasive when you are trying to change someone else's mind and can make you more empathetic.

Say Yes To Change

© Cartoon Resource/Shutterstock.com

Now, let's look at the connection between listening and responding. Notice that I said listening and responding, and not just hearing and talking. The reason we need to tweak this definition to include understanding and adjusting ideas is that if all we do is hear and talk, there is very little hope for meaningful communication. We can make noise. The Bible says in I Corinthians 13:1 "If I speak with human eloquence and angelic ecstasy but don't love, I'm nothing but the creaking of a rusty gate" (MSG). The point is this: speaking and persuading calls for us to do more than just make noise. Serious communication and connection with others requires that we give our best. Listen to hear what the other person is saying. It is hard to respond wisely and correctly when you haven't really heard what was said. If you have listened well and heard the other person's viewpoint, you may have just now understood the viewpoint of someone who may think completely differently than you. Empathetic listening is risky. But by hearing the other person you have a better chance of persuading them because you know what they think and why.

One of the reasons you need to set up the most logical argument is because people who don't know you have no reason to believe what you say. This is especially true when you are trying to convince them that your idea is better than theirs.

There are basically three types of speeches that we use to persuade: *to reinforce (encourages the audience to keep on believing what they believe), to convince (gets the audience to believe something different), and a call to tangible action (motivates the audience to act in a way that is concrete so that compliance is doable).*

Social Judgment Theory

Social Judgment Theory (Doeherty & Kurz, 2010; Sherif, Sherif, & Nebergall, 1965) says that the more invested people are in an idea, the harder it is to persuade them to change their minds.

Social Judgment Theory states that you have three latitudes of attitude:

1. **Latitude of acceptance**—this is what we believe.
2. **Latitude of non-commitment**—this is what we haven't decided yet.
3. **Latitude of rejection**—these are things we know are wrong.

If you had 10 statements about a topic running from one extreme to the other, somewhere in the list of statements there would be the one that resembled your belief about the topic. This is called your **anchor**. There would be a couple of statements on each side that you would still agree with, but the anchor was your favorite. That is your latitude of acceptance. On each side of that latitude of acceptance would be a latitude of non-commitment, meaning that you really haven't thought a lot about it but you might go either way (for or against). On either side of those latitudes would be your latitudes of rejection, meaning that you would not agree with these statements on either end because they are too extreme for you.

To explain how this would work, let's imagine that you were thinking about purchasing a car. There would be a particular amount of money you would be willing to spend. The cars would range on the scale from a junk heap car for very little money to a very expensive car with lots of extras, like seat heaters and coolers, a very expensive stereo system, etc. so the car could range from a few thousand

Social Judgment Theory
the range of attitude that explains why the more invested people are in an idea, the harder it is to persuade them to change their minds

Latitude of acceptance
what we believe

Latitude of non-commitment
what we haven't yet formed a definite opinion

Latitude of rejection
things we are convinced are wrong

Anchor
one's strongest belief about the topic

It would look like this:

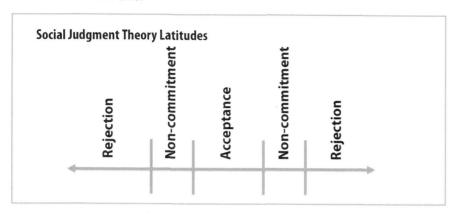

Social Judgment Theory Latitudes

Rejection | Non-commitment | Acceptance | Non-commitment | Rejection

Sidebar 15B

dollars to over $75,000. Good car salespeople would be interested in finding out how much money they could encourage you to spend. They would check to see which cars you are examining in the showroom and then chat with you to see how much you might be willing to spend. This is in your latitude of acceptance. This is strategic. If they show you cars that are too cheap, they would be in your latitude of rejection, and you would be insulted and leave. If they show you a car that is too expensive, you will also become frustrated and leave because it is also in your latitude of rejection. Somewhere between those two is your latitude of acceptance, the amount of money that you would feel comfortable spending. The amount of money you planned to spend is what the theory calls your anchor. The

amounts that you would feel comfortable spending compose your latitude of acceptance. The prices a little higher and lower than this latitude are your latitudes of non-commitment. The prices that are totally unacceptable (on the high end and on the low end) are your latitudes of rejection. The salesperson could probably encourage you to spend more money if they worked within the latitudes of acceptance and non-commitment. Once the buyer gets in their latitude of rejection they will ignore all of the information given by that salesperson. Therefore the best communicators analyze an audience's latitudes of rejection and acceptance before they give the speech.

© ESB Professional/Shutterstock.com

If people really believe that something is right they will have a very narrow latitude of acceptance, an almost nonexistent latitude of non-commitment, and very wide latitudes of rejection on either side. Chances are that your topic is very significant to both you and your audience. Therefore, you are going to have to work harder to understand the other side of your issue, and your audience is going to have to give you the benefit of the doubt that you are not trying to manipulate them.

If someone doesn't know us they won't believe us without evidence. We have to have evidence to encourage someone to be persuaded. So in order to clarify the

Credibility

Credibility is just believability. It is a big part of *ethos*, and comes in four forms.

1. Initial Credibility is based on personal experiences the speaker has had. If you've grown up with person with a mental illness, you know something about it, and if that is your topic, you can build your credibility with your audience by telling them.

2. Derived Credibility comes from outside you. It can come from your study and research, but you can't tell the audience derived credibility. You have to show them by sharing something you learned that they wouldn't know. Another part of derived credibility comes from your grooming and dress, as well as your well-prepared visuals.

3. Charisma is tied to vision and likability and to how your authentic nonverbal communication matches your words, such as eye contact, gestures, and verbal inflection.

4. Enduring credibility is the impression of the speaker that an audience member has formed from past contact with the speaker. If you did well on a previous speech that an audience member saw, they are likely to go into the new speech believing you.

Sidebar 15C

© Giannis Papnikos/Shutterstock.com

evidence part of the speech, let me introduce you to Aristotle. He was the Greek philosopher responsible for drafting the Rhetorical Theory that has been used ever since to help us construct convincing speeches and persuade audiences (Sherif, Sherif, & Nebergall, 1965).

Proof by Aristotle

Aristotle was one of the first people to write about teaching the ethical part of persuasion (DeVito, 2000). During his time, some educated people without any moral compass were using their skills to persuade others. So those who were rich and educated could manipulate the government, the religion, and the uneducated people. Aristotle taught that speakers were responsible for using emotion and logic ethically. They were also responsible for demonstrating their integrity (O'Hair et al., 2013). Can you think of a time when *you* or someone else manipulated someone? How did it feel? Aristotle wanted speakers to be responsible to the audience. I call it the "just because you can, doesn't mean you should" rule. Just because I can evoke people's emotions and make them do something doesn't mean that I should. This is true in speaking situations whether they are in a public forum or with one other person.

Public speaking and everyday communication are connected. The kinds of proof (also known as appeals) that we are discussing are what you use when you talk to a friend, and are even more important when you are public speaking (Wood, 2009). Aristotle's **proofs** are methods used to persuade people using logic, emotion, or ethics (DeVito, 2000; Kennedy, 1991; Schultz, 2006). There are several ways to modify what you are already doing naturally in your everyday conversations. In fact, anytime you are not communicating well you have probably erred in one of the areas that Aristotle covered in his discussion of proofs. For instance, if the audience thinks you are telling them this for your good and not theirs, you need *ethos*; if you haven't piqued their interest enough to care about what you are talking about, you have a *pathos* deficit; if they don't believe you because you have no facts to prove your statement, you need *logos*. These three proofs are interwoven. You can't speak well without all three (Schultz, 2006).

Ethos

The speaker's job of establishing credibility with the audience is what Aristotle called **ethos**. It is the connection that you create to let them know that you won't intentionally hurt them. You have to establish yourself as an expert and convince the audience to believe you. This usually happens in the introduction of the speech. It is your responsibility to find evidence from reputable sources to establish your argument. We learned in our Chapter 12 how to use the introduction to establish credibility and to show goodwill to the audience. They must believe that you are motivated for the greater good of humanity.

Ethos is affected by your presentation style. If you stumble through your information, have sloppy slides, or you look like you just got out of bed, you lose all credibility. There are four kinds of credibility that are explained in the sidebar. (If you are a reader who bleeps over the sidebar because you don't want to take the extra time, I would suggest that you check these out because they seem like ideal questions for an exam over this information.)

Pathos

Aristotle called the emotional appeals. pathos which means appealing to the emotions of the audience, such as anger, love, fear, pity, envy, etc. Emotion can be used to persuade people and motivate them to make a change (Shelton & Rogers, 1981).

Aristotle cautioned engaging the emotions without logic so that the audience would understand their emotional response and would not act irrationally. For instance, imagine you listened to someone speak and were moved to tears, but later you couldn't remember any facts. People cannot make lasting change if they don't remember why they are changing their behavior.

Logos

Next Aristotle advocated organizing logical arguments using facts, statistics, literal comparisons, and quotes from authorities. Logos is the information organized throughout the speech. Its purpose is to document that your ideas are logically structured and believable. Logos shifts the blame from you to the source. That is why you acknowledge them during the speech. "According to the *Washington Post*, '24,000 jobs will be lost in the private sector when the bill becomes law.'" The *Washington Post* is a credible source and the pressure is not on you to prove anything; the credibility comes from the source you use.

We have now looked at three kinds of proof that Aristotle said were important to use in an argument: *logos, ethos,* and *pathos.* Anytime an argument tips too strongly to one of these types of proof, the position being offered is on shaky ground. Aristotle compared it to a three-legged stool, meaning that you need to use each of the kinds of proof. The audience needs to know you care about them (ethos*),* that you have researched multiple viewpoints on this topic and are giving them information (logos*)* in such a way as to appeal to their emotions (pathos*)* so that there will be a change of heart, but there is enough logical structure for enduring change. A good speech includes these kinds of proof because individual audience members are motivated by different things. If you are a logical person you are more receptive to logos. If you are more emotional, pathos will appeal more strongly. Also, if speakers have deceived you in the past, you will be checking out the ethos so you won't be manipulated again (Kennedy, 1991).

Proofs
methods used to persuade people using logic, emotion, or ethics

Ethos
credibility established with the audience

Pathos
emotional appeals

Logos
logical organization of information throughout the speech

Most of Aristotle's ideas are things that you do unconsciously. You are looking for ethos as you examine opinions offered by different media sources, meaning you are judging whether the people are sharing a particular story because it benefits them, or if they are telling it because it benefits you or a greater good. Anytime you are in a discussion with others and they are angry (pathos), you have to decide if there is enough information (logos) to give their position credibility, or if you should ignore their argument because they are too emotional. Some people are ready to discuss and some are ready to fight. Your key to which group you are working with is identifying whether pathos is their motivator and not logos. If they are running on pathos, don't count on changing their minds. They are not listening anyway. (Remember the *quick to talk-slow to listen-quick to condemn* sidebar.)

Fallacies

© TypoArt BS/Shutterstock.com

Fallacy
a mistake in logical reasoning

Before we leave reasoning, let me give you another tool. Have you ever been listening to someone and heard them make a statement that just didn't ring true? Many times this happens because he is emotional, frustrated, or just tired of defending himself. He is guilty of using a fallacy, which is a mistake in logical reasoning (Wood, 2009) to make a point. But by making a fallacious statement, he jeopardizes his ethos and all the "truths" (logos) that he has shared are now in question. This is sad because almost any time a fallacy is used to prove a point, there are better ways to accomplish the same end. Good logic could be used to prove the point, and because the speaker didn't take time to establish a better argument, the speech is jeopardized. Stay alert for these fallacies as you listen and speak.

Begging the question—inserting the question into the answer without answering the question asked

Ad Populum (bandwagon appeal)—justifying an idea because everyone else thinks it or is doing it

False Dilemma—setting up an either-or situation that offers only two choices when there are more choices available

Hasty Generalization—justifying the conclusion without enough data to support it

Slippery Slope—assuming that if one thing happens it will lead to a chain of events that will cause something else to happen without supplying the connection between the two events

Post Hoc—blaming something that really has no connection to the problem

Ad Misericordiam—appealing to the other person's sympathy instead of answering the question

False Analogy—incorrectly comparing unlike things

Dicto Simpliciter—basing an argument on an unqualified generalization

Ad Hominem—attacking the person instead of the argument

Sidebar 15D

The Three Cornerstones of Persuasion

Now let's talk about the way to establish a logical argument to help you outline your speech. Aristotle used the term syllogism to explain that a logical argument. A **syllogism** is a way of logically connecting two related ideas to reach a judgement. It has a major premise, a minor premise, and a conclusion. The **major premise** establishes a generalization, the **minor premise** establishes a specific case, and the **conclusion** is the inescapable judgment resulting from the connecting of the premises. If there is an error with any part of the syllogism or underlying assumptions about their meanings, the conclusion can be wrong (Dickstein, 1975, 1981). Here is an example:

> Major premise: *All men are mortal,*
> Minor premise: *Socrates is a man,*
> Conclusion: *Therefore, Socrates is mortal.*

Syllogism
A syllogism is a way of logically connecting two related ideas to reach a judgement

Major premise
establishes a generalization

Minor premise
establishes a specific case

Conclusion
the inescapable judgment resulting from the connecting of the premises

Finding Solutions

Any good debater will tell you that you go into an argument with a real disadvantage. People don't want to change. They may not be satisfied with the way things are going, but they don't want to change. They want someone else to take care of the problem. There are four things we need to address: harm, blame, cure, and cost. You need to convince people that the problem is significant enough to require action (**harm**). You then need to identify the source of the problem (**blame**). Only

Harm
convince people that a problem is significant enough to require action

Blame
identify the source of the problem

© Kenishirotie/Shutterstock.com

Cure
an acceptable solution

Cost
necessary expenditure of resources to address the problem.

after establishing harm and blame can you show them an acceptable solution (**cure**) that won't **cost** them too much, and then show them what they can do to help make it happen. Any time you set out to change someone's mind, you have to do all four of those things (harm, blame, cure, and cost). Let's look at an example: You have come to college without a car. You need one badly. Your family isn't interested in helping you cover those costs. Before you have the "car fight" one more time, think about the situation from a persuasive perspective. You have had this fight before so you already know they have legitimate arguments. As you plan your position, you need to take those things into consideration (audience analysis). If you come up with a way to show them a different perspective on the situation (harm and blame) and you have a way to answer their objections (cure and cost), you will have a chance to persuade them to change their position and help you get a car.

Persuasive Proposition Statements: Let Me Propose Something

© Phase4Studios/Shutterstock.com

Proposition of fact
gives the justification for the audience to accept that a statement is true

Proposition of value
gives the justification for how a viewpoint is good or bad and centers on what the speaker thinks about an issue

For any persuasive speech, you are trying to persuade the audience to believe or do something. We call that something a proposition. There are three kinds: fact, value, and policy.

If you want the audience to accept that a factual statement is true, you have a **proposition of fact**. If you are arguing a proposition of fact, your goal is to pull together all of the information you can to substantiate what you think. You are not to make moral judgments or try to get them to do anything. Your sole purpose it to convince them that your proposition is true. For example, "Sex trafficking is increasing at an overwhelming rate." Look for good strong evidence: statistics, quotes from experts, perhaps some true stories from people who have lived through it, and comparisons to how much smaller the numbers were in the past (see Chapter 13 for more explanations).

A **proposition of value** shows how something is good or bad and centers on what the speaker thinks about an issue. For instance, the speaker might contend that "Protecting the rights of gun owners is justifiable." information might center around data that shows that the most heinous of gun deaths are caused by people who acquire guns outside of the law. Therefore, taking away the rights of people who are obeying the law will not solve the problem. If arguing a proposition of value, arguments using examples and stories are good kinds of evidence.

The **proposition of policy** covers our procedures for doing something. If you are offering a proposition of policy, you are suggesting a better way to do something. There is usually a "should" in the statement. For example, "The federal government should offer loan forgiveness for federally subsidized student loans." Then you set up a plan that is practical and will solve the problem of student indebtedness. Toulmin (1969) suggests that you support your argument with the following information. You could start with data that shows how much students owe on their education when they graduate, then establish how hard it is for students to get a job that will pay enough to live on *and* pay down on their college loans. After you show that it is a significant problem and it is exacerbated by the method in which students are legally bound to pay back federal loan money, you can offer a new way to receive loan forgiveness and show them how it will help the students and the economy to change the system. The latest statistics are more significant when you are convincing people to change methods because the speech encourages them to change to the *new and improved* method of doing things.

Proposition of policy
gives the justification for a plan to change procedures for doing something

Persuasive Organizational Patterns

Now that we know the difference between the kinds of propositions, let's look at ways to arrange the outlines. Certain patterns are more conducive to different types of the three propositions. Patterns that include an action step are inherently propositions of policy. Similarly, patterns without an action step are fact or value.

Cause/Effect (with or without Action) –We can use this pattern for propositions of fact when the speaker is attempting simply to convince the audience to believe something is true. An example would be tying an economic recession (effect) to particular governmental policies (cause). With the addition of the action step, it can also be used for propositions of policy when the speaker is trying to get the audience to take an action. For example, the speaker might go on to ask the audience to write their legislator (action). Quickly, here's how they would look:

Proposition of Fact:		Proposition of Policy:
I. Cause	OR	I. Cause
II. Effect		II. Effect
		III. Action

Sidebar 15E

Claim—Don't let the name confuse you; this is an organizational pattern, as well. This is similar to the topical organizational pattern for informative speeches, but instead of each main idea being a sub-point of the main topic, each main point is a reason that the proposition is true. For instance, if the proposition says that the death penalty should be made illegal in all states, the first main idea would be that it is ineffective as a deterrent. The second main idea is it risks executing the innocent. The third is that it is costlier than life imprisonment. The fourth is that it is condemned by most countries in the free world. Each of those ideas is an argument for why the main statement is true. A good way to test to be sure you are using claim organizational pattern correctly is to say your proposition, adding "because" and then adding each main point to see if they make sense. For instance, "The death penalty should be made illegal in all states because it is ineffective as a deterrent." If the sentences make sense, then you can use that idea as a reason your claim (proposition) is correct. The claim organizational pattern can be used for any of the propositions.

Proposition of Fact:	Proposition of Value	Proposition of Policy
I. Reason #1	I. Reason #1	I. Reason #1
II. Reason #2	II. Reason # 2	II. Reason # 2
(Can have up to five reasons)	(Can have up to five reasons)	III. Action
		(Can have up to four reasons)

Sidebar 15F

Comparative Advantage—This pattern is similar to the comparison pattern used for informative speaking, but instead of comparing two things in general, the speaker is comparing two solutions to a particular problem and arguing in favor of one of the options. An example would be the problem of a childhood disease like measles. The speaker might compare vaccinating children at an early age to withholding vaccinations and treating disease symptoms as they arise. That speaker would argue for one position or the other, but both responses are ways that the problem of measles could be addressed. Comparative advantage only works with propositions of value. Here's how that would look:

Proposition of Value:
I. Solution A
II. Solution B
III. Why B is better

Sidebar 15G

Problem-Solution (with or without Action)—This pattern is pretty direct. It presents a problem, and it proposes a solution. Depending on whether a call to action is being made in the proposition, the outline may or may not need an action step. For instance, a speaker might say the problem of public school failure can be fixed with better primary education (used for propositions of fact). Or, she may choose to call for more parent involvement in primary school volunteering (proposition of policy). The application of the pattern to the different proposition alters the organizational pattern somewhat, as seen below:

Proposition of Fact		Proposition of Policy
I. Problem		I. Problem
II. Solution	OR	II. Solution
III. Benefits (optional)		III. Action

Sidebar 15H   Sidebar 15I

Monroe's Motivated Sequence
an organizational pattern with five steps that is used for calling an audience to action

Monroe's Motivated Sequence—This pattern is problem-solution-action with an extra step pattern. He called the parts *attention, need, satisfaction, visualization of the future,* and *action.* It has five steps, but only four Roman numerals. Attention is in the introduction and the four Roman numerals are: I. the problem (need), II. the solution (satisfaction), III. the projected future if the solution plan is accepted or if it is rejected (visualization) and IV. the action that the audience must take to bring about the solution (action). For example, you might say that many foster care children are suffering neglect (problem), additional support can help foster care families (solution), that children will be safe and happy (visualization), and that the audience members should volunteer to help foster parents (action). Since this pattern can only be used for calls to action, it will be used only for propositions of policy. Here's what that would look like:

Proposition of Policy
Intro—Action
I.   Need
II.   Satisfaction
III. Visualization
IV.   Action

Sidebar 15J

Ethical Implications

The power to persuade can be both a blessing and a curse. Almost everything that we do, both verbally and nonverbally, persuades those around us of something, whether that is to our benefit or our detriment. There was an idea presented by researchers in Palo Alto, California, that regardless of whether we were talking or not, we were communicating all the time. When someone stopped talking and stomped out of the room during a discussion they communicated that they were angry whether they were speaking or not. So whether or not you believe that a person "cannot not communicate," it is important to remember that every communication leaves a mark. My dad said that communication is like a nail in a board. Even if you decide you don't want the nail there and pull it out, the hole is still in the board. You can't un-communicate. Saying "I'm sorry" may pull the nail out of the board but the hole is still in the heart of the person you hurt. You have a responsibility as a servant to your audience to be wise about what you try to persuade them to do. The Bible says we are responsible for the words that we speak (Psalm 19:14 KJV). As we talk about the skill set necessary for being a persuader, our ability to do it makes us more responsible for the way we use those skills. Evangelism is persuasive. Convincing someone to marry you is persuasive. How successful you are at your job today depends on how well you communicated with others yesterday. We all need to be more responsible in our communication and recognize the power available to us when we persuade.

Summary

The goal of this chapter was to help you hone your interpersonal skills by giving you insight on persuasion. We discussed the basics (Aristotle's syllogism) so that you could see how you should construct an argument and talked about the kinds of proof (logos, ethos, and pathos) necessary to convince your audience to change. The discussions about the audience included Social Judgment theory and being responsible for not misleading them with fallacious arguments. We also looked at how to organize an outline to set up your best argument. We looked at the differences between arguments of fact, value, and policy. All of this was to help you recognize strengths and weaknesses in your arguments and the positions of other people. Only by understanding both sides can you hope to persuade the other people to consider your views.

Vocabulary Words

Anchor
Blame
Conclusion
Cost
Cure
Ethos
Fallacy
Harm
Latitude of
    acceptance

Latitude of
    non-commitment
Latitude of
    rejection
Logos
Major Premise
Minor Premise
Monroe's Motivated Sequence
Pathos

Persuasive speech
Proofs
Proposition of fact
Proposition of policy
Proposition of value
Social Judgment Theory
Syllogism

Discussion Questions

1. All this information can be used in everyday life to persuade someone to do something. What are some examples you can think of?
2. Have you ever been in an argument and known there was something wrong with the other person's position, but couldn't figure out exactly what? Was it because their line of reasoning contained fallacies?
3. What fallacies do we see people use in daily conversations?
4. What are the moral responsibilities of any persuader?
5. What are some moral "fouls" that a person might employ in their attempts to persuade others?
6. What sort of speech topic do you think would be helpful for your audience? How will you ask them to change their beliefs or to take action?

7. When have you heard a speech that showed the harm, the blame, and the cure, but never addressed the cost? How can that hurt an audience?
8. What sort of proposition will you write?
9. Which organizational pattern will you use to accomplish your goals?

References

DeVito, J. A. (2000). *The elements of public speaking* (7th ed.). New York: Longman.

Dickstein, L. S. (1975). Effects of instructions and premise order on errors in syllogistic reasoning. *Journal of Experimental Psychology: Human Learning and Memory, 1*(4), 376–384. doi: 10.1037/0278-7393.1.4.376

Dickstein, L. S. (1981). Conversion and possibility in syllogistic reasoning. *Bulletin of the Psychonomic Society, 18*(5), 229–232. doi:10.3758/BF03333612

Dobkin, B. A., & Pace, R. C. (2003). *Communication in a changing world.* New York: McGraw-Hill.

Doherty, M. E., & Kurz, E. M. (2010). Social judgment theory. *Thinking & Reasoning, 2,* 109–140. doi:10.1080/135467896394474

Fisher, W. (1987). *Human communication as narration: Toward a philosophy of reason, value, and action.* Columbia, SC: University of South Carolina Press.

Fraleigh, D. M., & Tuman, J. S. (2017). *Speak up!: An illustrated guide to public speaking* (4th ed.). Boston, MA: Bedford/St. Martin's.

Jaffe, C. (2013). *Public speaking: Concepts and skills for a diverse society* (7th ed.). Boston, MA: Wadsworth.

Kennedy, G. (Ed. & Trans.). (1991). *Aristotle on rhetoric.* London: Oxford University Press.

O'Hair, D., Rubenstein, H., & Stewart, R. (2013). *A pocket guide to public speaking* (4th ed.). Boston, MA: Bedford/St. Martin's.

Maslow, A. (1966). *The psychology of science: A reconnaissance by Abraham H. Maslow.* New York: Harper & Row.

Reardon, K. (1991). *Persuasion in practice.* Newbury Park, CA: Sage.

Rogers, C. (1962). The interpersonal relationships: The core of guidance. *Harvard Educational Review, 32,* 416–429.

Schultz, Q. (2006). *An essential guide to public speaking: Serving your audience with faith, skill, and virtue.* Grand Rapids, MI: Baker Academic.

Shelton, M. L., & Rogers, R. W. (1981). Fear-arousing and empathy-arousing appeals to help: The pathos of persuasion. *Journal of Applied Psychology, 11*(4), 366–378. doi:10.1111/j.1559-1816.tb00829.x

Sherif, C., Sherif, M., & Nebergall, R. (1965). *Attitude and attitude change: The social judgment-involvement approach.* Philadelphia, PA: W. B. Saunders.

Wood, J. T. (2009). *Communication in our lives.* (5th ed.). Boston, MA: Wadsworth.

Additional Readings

Influence: Science and Practice

by Robert B. Cialdini

One Lousy Friday Before Easter: A Journey From Faith to Despair, and Back Again
by Bob Keith Bonebreak

Return to Reason

by Stephen Toulman

Uses of Argument

by Stephen Toulman

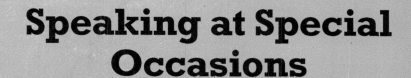

Speaking at Special Occasions

By Rhonda Gallagher & Susan McMurray

© Ekaterina_Molchanova/Shutterstock.com

A

A special occasion speech is one prepared for a specific occasion and for a purpose dictated by that occasion. These speeches can take several forms. You might introduce another speaker at an event. At the risk of sounding obvious, that's called an **introduction**. Just because another person is going to speak as well doesn't negate the fact that you're giving a short speech first. If you win an award, you may have to give an **acceptance speech**. Or you might do an **award presentation**. You might give an **inspirational speech** to encourage a group not to give up in the face of adversity. Speeches that take place to honor a special event or a particular person or group are called **commemorative speeches**. This includes any speech of tribute, a toast, or eulogy. You might give a **toast** at a celebration, or a **eulogy** at a funeral. There are other kinds of special occasion speeches, like roasts, after-dinner speeches, or speeches to gain goodwill (DeVito, 2000), but we need to limit ourselves somewhat, so we'll leave those for your advanced classes in public speaking. One thing all of these have in common is that a special event outside of everyday experience has come about. The speech recognizes that and helps the audience process what is

© Kues/Shutterstock.com

Special occasion speech
Speech prepared for a specific, special kind of occasion

Introduction
speech to introduce another speaker

Acceptance speech
speech given by the honoree at a formal event to thank a group for an award they have given to the speaker

award presentation
A speech given for awarding an honor to someone

Inspirational speech
speech to encourage a group not to give up in adversity

Commemorative speech
speech given at a special event to honor a particular person, group, or event.

Toast
brief speech in preparation for drinking a beverage to honor a person or event

Eulogy
speech to show honor for the deceased at a funeral

happening. A eulogy helps people understand and handle their grief. A toast to the bride and groom recognizes the special nature of the gathering. The Oscars only come once a year. Inspirational speeches don't come up every day, either. That's the key: the occasion is out of the ordinary. It is your job as the speaker to identify the emotional component of the event. These kinds of speeches are sort of a mix of informative and persuasive speeches (O'Hair, Rubenstein, & Stewart, 2013). They do make use of pathos. Remember with this type of speaking to use the sorts of supporting evidence that inspires, like quotes, and stories, and the use of vivid language. Concrete language (as opposed to abstract) will help you paint the mental pictures that embody the emotional impact of the occasion.

So what do you put into each of these kinds of speeches? Well . . .

For an introduction of a speaker:

— Talk about this speaker's qualifications (DeVito, 2000).
— Generate interest (Fraleigh & Tuman, 2017).
— Preview the topic.
— Ask the audience to help you welcome the speaker.
— Be brief!

For presentation of an award:

— Tell the name of the award, why it was established, and criteria for winning.
— Give the name of the winner, qualities that made them a good candidate, and specific examples of their actions that show those qualities.
— Tell why you're proud and happy to deliver the award (Ferguson, 2008).
— Be brief!

For an acceptance speech:

— Express your appreciation for the award, and thank the organization that gave it.
— Be humble (Ferguson, 2008; Fraleigh & Tuman, 2017; O'Hair et al., 2013)!
— Thank the people who helped you succeed (God, family, mentors, the caterer, the dog walker, whoever helped you—you get the idea!).
— Show you're happy to get the award.
— Finish by saying thank you again, and . . .
— Be brief!

For a commemorative speech:

— Recognize the cause or event that perpetrated the event.
— Honor the appropriate parties' hard work and/or sacrifice.
— Reference common values (Ferguson, 2008).
— Inspire the audience to emulate the honorees, and continue to assist in achieving the higher goals of the movement or group (Ferguson, 2008).

For a toast: (Wedding or celebratory)

— Prepare in advance! It may look impromptu, but it's not (O'Hair, et al., 2013). You'll forget important things if you don't prepare. The emotion is too high and the event too important to not give the speech the preparation time it needs.
— Introduce yourself for a wedding toast. Not everyone will know who you are or why you were chosen to give the toast (Ferguson, 2008).
— Tell why the person (or couple) being toasted is special.
— Tell a story about the honoree(s) that is poignant, and humorous if that is appropriate to the occasion (Ferguson, 2008; Fraleigh & Tuman, 2017).
— Be brief!

For a eulogy:

* There is no real-organizational pattern for a eulogy (Ferguson, 2008), so follow these guidelines as they fit the situation.

— Console the audience in their loss, and facilitate their expression of their grief. This is an important part of healing, so by giving the speech, you lead them in reflecting and experiencing their emotions (O'Hair et al., 2013). Be sure to acknowledge the family. The funeral is primarily to help them deal with the loss.
— Remind them that even though the deceased is no longer with them, they still have a relationship with that person through their memories. It is different than it was, but it still exists.
— Follow a general theme of the person's life (e.g., generosity, kindness, public service, love of life, patience, etc.) and give specific examples of that characteristic (Ferguson, 2008). Focus on the deceased's positive characteristics, but don't praise to the point of excess (O'Hair et al., 2013).
— If the deceased was a Christian, remind the family that their loved one is now with God, and is joyfully celebrating the end of life's troubles.

For an inspirational speech:

— Build your credibility on your personal commitment (Dobkin & Pace, 2003; Ferguson, 2008).
— Reference shared group values (Dobkin & Pace, 2003).
— Be passionate!
— Have a powerful closing statement (O'Hair et al., 2013).

I hope as you read through these things you found a couple of themes emerging. First, be passionate, and secondly, be brief, or at least, succinct. So, now you've got a starting place for that speech the future is bringing to you.

Vocabulary Words

Acceptance speech

Award presentation

Commemorative speech

Eulogy

Inspirational speech

Introduction

Special occasion speech

Toast

References

DeVito, J. A. (2000). *The elements of public speaking* (7th ed.). New York, NY: Longman.

Dobkin, B. A., & Pace, R. C. (2003). *Communication in a changing world.* New York, NY: McGraw-Hill.

Ferguson, S. D. (2008). *Public speaking: Building competency in stages.* New York, NY: Oxford University Press.

Fraleigh, D. M., & Tuman, J. S. (2017). *Speak up!: An illustrated guide to public speaking.* Boston, MA: Bedford/St. Martin's.

O'Hair, D., Rubenstein, H., & Stewart, R. (2013). *A pocket guide to public speaking.* Boston, MA: Bedford/St. Martin's.

The Employment Interview

By Susan McMurray, M.A.

B

One very important communication skill, and something that all of us will need to be able to do effectively at some time in our lives and career, is knowing how to effectively and confidently interview. An employment interview is one type of selection interview. The basic purpose of the selection interview is for an organization to be able to choose individuals who they consider the most qualified from a pool of candidates. Essentially, the interviewer is conducting the interview to "select" the person who is the best fit for the position they need to fill (Stewart & Cash, 2014). Sometimes we think we will only need to participate in this type of interview when we are looking to get hired for that dream job. But in reality, you may find yourself participating in a selection interview in a myriad of situations such as being selected for an internship, a summer job, a leadership position at your college, acceptance into graduate school, or even as a babysitter, house sitter, or dog walker. Let's look at some important steps you will want to do before, during, and after to succeed and ace your next employment interview.

© fizkes/Shutterstock.com

selection interview
an interview in which an organization chooses a
candidate to receive a job, internship, or award

© Olivier Le Moal/Shutterstock.com

Before the Employment Interview

Know Yourself

I would be a bit remiss if I didn't mention how important it is to do a thorough self-analysis before you set out in search of your dream job. Remember that an employment interview is a two-way street. Not only is the employer going to try and select a candidate who is the best fit for the position they are trying to fill, but the candidate should also be evaluating the employer to determine if that position, in that organization, is the right fit for them. Bolles (2018), author of the best-selling job-hunting book, *What Color Is Your Parachute*, encourages all job hunters to do a self-analysis before they start looking for a job. A self-analysis is essentially a self-inventory of your talents and skills that help you discover what you love to do and how you work best. Doing a self-analysis serves two major purposes: to help you make wiser career decisions, and to help you answer questions during the employment interview. A self-analysis doesn't have to be complicated and is simply taking an inventory of your "What" and "Where". WHAT are you good at? What are your talents, gifts, and skills? And secondly, WHERE do you want to use your skills? For example, I had a student years ago who was an excellent public speaker, and had strong interpersonal communication skills. He really had a desire to go into a profession that served others. However, he knew he wasn't a "cubicle" kind of guy and wanted a profession that involved working outdoors. Today he's a forest ranger in Colorado. He's using his strong communication skills in the great outdoors. By doing a thorough self-analysis, you will have taken the time to inventory what you're good at and how you would like to use your strengths professionally. This helps you be very strategic in the types of jobs you are searching for, and ultimately helps you get that job where you will likely be more satisfied because you are using your true talents. If you're looking for additional resources to help you take a self-inventory to help you determine the talents and skill-sets that you use to do your best work, I strongly suggest you read books such as *What Color Is Your Parachute* by Richard Bolles, or *StrengthsFinder 2.0* by Tom Rath. Even a visit to your university's career center to take a career inventory will give you insight into careers that line up with your talents.

self-analysis
a self-inventory of one's talents and skills

Research

Once you've applied for a position and have been invited to the interview, it is critical that you do your research beforehand. I highly recommend that you specifically research two areas before you walk into that interview: the organization, and the position. When researching the organization, you should be thoroughly knowledgeable about their product or services, their financial status, their competitors, mission statement, and especially their core values. I've known many employers to "test out" an applicant's research by asking questions during the employment interview such as "What is our mission statement?" or "Who is our main competitor?" and even "What is our stock price at currently?". You should also take time to research the person who is interviewing you. This may not be as necessary for the first interview when perhaps a recruiter or human resource representative is conducting that first interview. It is however critical for the second interview and all those thereafter, when the hiring manager is typically conducting the interview. You should be thoroughly briefed on who the interviewer is, their role in the organization, and even what they have accomplished in their career. You can usually find this information by looking on the organization's website, conducting a general Internet search, asking others, or even looking at the interviewer's LinkedIn page.

Secondly, you should also thoroughly research the position you are applying for. You should be well aware of the job description or typical responsibilities, advancement opportunities, challenges of the position, and even salary. Again you can look at the organization's website, conduct an Internet search or even research occupational handbooks that give lots of information on a variety of careers. Doing the necessary research to prepare for a job interview is important because employers want to know that the people they hire are truly excited and passionate to

© Jacob Lund/Shutterstock.com

work for them, and by doing your research you show a potential employer that you care. It demonstrates that you are someone who pays attention to the details and gives 110%. Doing your research will also help you to more effectively answer the questions you will get during the interview and show yourself to be a good fit to that particular position and organization. I remember going to a selection interview for an internship when I was in college. The interviewer clearly wanted to see that I was knowledgeable about the industry I would be interning in and asked me "What are the professional journals of our industry?" I stared back at her with a blank look in my eye and sheepishly said, "I don't know." Guess who didn't get the internship? Yep, me. So do your research and don't find yourself in the same embarrassing position as I did.

During the Employment Interview

First Impressions

Before I get into specific question–answer strategies, let me talk about the *most* important 30 seconds of the entire job interview: the *first* 30 seconds. I've heard that we formulate first impressions of another person in as quickly as 7 seconds! Wow! That sure puts a lot of pressure on us when we first walk into the interview and meet the interviewer. A **first impression** can be defined as what a person thinks of you when they first meet you. It is the feeling that they get or the initial evaluation that a person forms of you when they first meet you. First impressions are formed in an instant and can even last for several years (Demarais & White, 2004).

© djrandco/Shutterstock.com

Sometimes, first impressions can be hard to overcome, especially if we've made a bad one. So let me give you three simple things to be mindful of when creating the right first impression for the job interview: appearance, manners, and attitude. First, let's look at some practical tips regarding your appearance. Of course, you should dress professionally and appropriately for the job interview. Even though our work places have become more casual, this does not necessarily mean you should show up to your interview dressed business casual. If you are interviewing for an entry-level professional position, then you should dress business professional. This means wearing a professional suit in conservative colors such as black, gray, navy or khaki. It also means you should be well groomed with conservative choices in hair style, make-up, jewelry, and shoes. You should also avoid wearing cologne or perfume, as you don't want to be remembered by how strong your cologne or perfume is.

Secondly, remember your manners. In regards to a job interview, this means arriving about 10–15 minutes early (never, never be late for a job interview!), greeting the interviewer by their name, extending a firm handshake, engaging in direct eye-contact, offering a warm smile, and words of thanks and appreciation to the interviewer for the time they have given you. Don't forget to greet the receptionist nicely and show respect for all organizational employees that you interact with before, during, or after the interview. You never know who's being asked to help assess your behavior when considering your suitability for hire.

Lastly, your attitude during the interview is essential. This is where appropriate nonverbal communication will tell a lot about your confidence and potential competency for the position. Short of saying, "I'm so excited for this interview!", it's more likely your nonverbal communication will be the true indicator of your enthusiasm for the job. So here are some tips to help ensure your nonverbal communication delivers the right message to a potential employer. Have a confident, yet relaxed upright posture when sitting, even leaning slightly forward to show engagement. Have direct eye-contact with the interviewer and use warm and engaging facial expressions. Use a fluid and expressive vocal delivery to demonstrate your confidence and energy. And remember to be a good listener and facilitator of conversation too. Show the interviewer that you are interested in what they have to say and eager to learn more about the position and organization.

Answering Questions

There are so many questions one should be prepared to answer during an employment interview and it's difficult to anticipate every question you might be asked. I always recommend to my students that one of the best ways to prepare for answering questions in a job interview is to do an Internet search for the "most common interviewing questions" and simply practice answering them out loud before the interview. Questions on topics such as professional strengths, professional weaknesses, and future goals will likely be asked and you can come up with a strategy for answering these types of questions before the interview. In addition, be well briefed on your resume and fully competent to talk about your past educational and professional experiences. Most employers will walk through your resume during the interview and ask you about your current and previous jobs. The interviewer may also ask you what was most satisfying and challenging about those jobs, what your supervisor and co-workers would say about you, and why you left each position.

© fizkes/Shutterstock.com

I do want to give you a strategy for answering two types of questions that are asked quite frequently in job interviews. The first type of question that you will likely get at the very beginning of the employment interview is "Before we begin, tell me about yourself." Employers may ask this question for a variety of reasons. Is a candidate self-aware? Can they articulately and succinctly describe who they are and give a recap of their previous experiences? Can the interviewee strategically show themselves to be a good fit for the position in under 2 minutes? This question is also just a great way for interviewers to transition from the opening of the job interview to the body. How you answer this question will do a lot to build your confidence and set the tone for the rest of the interview. The best way to answer this question is to give your **elevator speech**. Collamer (2013) defines the elevator speech as "the 30-second speech that summarizes who you are, what you do, and why you'd be a perfect candidate." So the best way to answer the "Tell me about yourself." question is to give a recent and relevant description of where you are professionally. For example, a student right out of college might say, "I'm a recent graduate from Southwestern University with a degree in Public Relations and Advertising. I recently had the opportunity to work in a 12-month internship with Jones and Meyers Public Relations Firm. Through my bachelor's degree and my internship, I learned how to effectively write press releases, put together branding statements and campaign strategies, plan community events, and use social media for marketing campaigns. I hope to bring my experience and love for public relations to help your organization."

> **elevator speech**
> a 30 second speech that summarizes your character, skills, and suitability for a position

The second common type of question is the behavioral question, or competency-based question. According to Business Dictionary, a **behavioral question** is a job interviewing technique whereby the applicant is asked to describe past behavior in order to determine whether he or she is suitable for a position. This type of question usually starts with "Tell me about a time . . .". For example, an interviewer may ask "Tell me about a time when you were facing multiple deadlines. How did you get everything done?" An interviewee's responses are expected to give an indication of his or her professional conduct in the future based on how he or she handled these type of situations in their previous experiences. These may sound easy to answer, but according to Michael Higgins (2014) from Guardian Careers, "in the heat of the interview, it's easy to give an unstructured answer, miss out key details, or let the story peter to a halt." So, let me share with you a technique and memorable acronym to help you answer the behavioral question effectively every time. The acronym is CAR which stands for

> **behavioral question**
> an interview question that focuses on past behavior for purposes of assessment of suitability for a position

Context, Action, and Results (Spodek, 2014). Before I show you how to walk through this acronym, it is important to prepare for this type of question by identifying several stories from your past experiences that you may draw from to help you answer behavioral questions and demonstrate that you already have the behavioral competencies an employer may be looking for in a candidate (such as leadership skills, decision making, stress management, creativity, and cooperation). I used to do a lot of employment interviewing, and one time I asked an applicant interviewing for a management position the question "Tell me about a time you had a difficult decision to make on the job. How did you do it?" This particular candidate was just a few years out of college but walked through the CAR acronym as follows:

> **Context:** "In my position as Resident Advisor for the university I recently graduated from, I had a friend I caught drinking on our wing. Drinking alcohol is not allowed in the student dormitories."
>
> **Action:** "Even though this was a good friend of mine, I knew that it was my responsibility as a resident advisor to uphold university policy, as well as ensure the safety of all the men I was responsible for on my wing. As difficult as it was, I knew it was necessary to report my friend to the Dean of Men."
>
> **Results:** "Although my friend was angry at me, I knew I made the right decision in my job as Resident Advisor by upholding the rules and regulations of the university and ensuring the safety of all 32 men on the wing."

As a final encouragement, know that you will never be able to anticipate all the questions you might be asked during an interview, so also be prepared to be flexible and think quickly. One time in an interview, the interviewer asked me, "If you were a food, what would you be?" I remember thinking that this was the stupidest question I've ever heard and why would he ask me such a question? But I kept my cool and came up with a pretty good response. I said, "I would be a pizza because it's the entire meal—meat, vegetable, and bread." Later my interviewer confessed that he asked me that question to see how creative my response would be and to see if I would keep my composure or get rattled. Experienced and savvy interviewers always have a very specific strategy behind each question, so do your best to show the interviewer that you have the skill-set they're looking for. (Or at least show yourself to be a good sport and one who is willing to take a stab at every question with a good attitude).

Asking Questions

Toward the end of an employment interview, you will likely have the opportunity to ask the employer questions. You should always ask the employer at least one question. Avoid asking questions that have a "what's in it for me" focus such as:

- "What's the salary?"
- "How many vacation days will I get?"
- "Does this position offer tuition-reimbursement benefits?"

Yes, those questions are important to know, but don't let them be the first questions out of your mouth. If the interviewer doesn't answer this information for you, then ask these types of questions much later in the interview process (such as the second or third interview).

The types of questions you could ask instead are:

- "How do you incorporate teams in your organization?"
- "What skills and experiences would make an ideal candidate?"
- "What duties are most important for this job?"
- "How is this job important to the company?"
- "What have you most enjoyed about working here?"
- "Why did the person you're replacing leave this position?"
- "Now that we've talked about my qualifications and the job, do you have any concerns about my being successful in this position?"

© SK Design/Shutterstock.com

These types of questions better show that you are someone who wants to contribute to the organization and is eager to learn what the ideal candidate for the position you are interviewing for looks like.

After the Interview

Before we wrap up how to effectively interview for a job, don't forget that the impression you make on the interviewer doesn't end when the interview ends. There's one very important thing you should do *after* the interview. Don't forget to thank the interviewer. I believe in this so strongly that I would even say that the interview isn't over until you've sent that thank you. A recent Career-Builder survey (2016) showed that 22% of employers are less likely to hire a candidate who failed to send a thank you note and that 57% of job-seekers don't send thank you notes after an interview. Be the candidate that takes time to either send a hand written note or an email thanking the interviewer for taking time out of their schedule to meet with you. This can also be a great opportunity to tell the interviewer how excited you are for the employment opportunity as well as reiterate why you think you are a good fit for the position. By sending a word of thanks, you are demonstrating to the employer that you are someone who is appreciative and conscientious of the time they have taken with you. By doing so, you will stand out from the other interviewees who don't send a thank you.

© Studio KIWI/Shutterstock.com

Summary

Knowing how to prepare yourself before the interview by doing a thorough self-analysis and researching the employer will help you be more strategic in your job hunt and impress the interviewer. Setting a strong first impression, and knowing how to strategically answer common employment interview questions will help you have success during the interview. Sending a word of thanks will help you stand out from the rest of the applicants who don't. Interviewing skills are a critical to our competent communication skills and I hope you have garnered a few tips to confidently and effectively conduct yourself during your next employment interview.

Vocabulary Words

Behavioral question	First impression	Self-analysis
Elevator speech	Selection interview	

References

Bolles, R.N. (2018). *What color is your parachute?: A practical manual for job-hunters and career-changers*. New York, NY: Ten Speed Press.

Business Dictionary. Retrieved from http://www.businessdictionary.com/definition/behavioral-interview.html

CareerBuilder (2016). *CareerBuilder survey reveals five common job seeker pitfalls that will hinder any career search*. Retrieved from www.careerbuilder.com/share/aboutus/pressreleasesdetail.aspx?ed=12/31/2016&id=pr960&sd=7/28/2016.

Collamer, N. (2013). *The perfect elevator speech to land a job*. Forbes. Retrieved from https://www.forbes.com/sites/nextavenue/2013/02/04/the-perfect-elevator-pitch-to-land-a-job/#53ff4f751b1d

Demarais, A., & White, V. (2004). *First impressions. New York, NY: Bantam Books.*

Higgins, M. (2014). *Using the star technique to shine at job interviews: a how-to guide*. Retrieved from https://www.theguardian.com/careers/careers-blog/star-technique-competency-based-interview

Spodek, J. (2014). *Context, action, result (CAR): Answering interview questions and describing experience effectively*. Retrieved from http://joshuaspodek.com/context-action-result-car-answering-interview-questions-describing-experience-effectively

Stewart, C., & Cash, W. (2014). *Interviewing: Principles and practices*. New York, NY: McGraw-Hill Education.

Additional Reading

Strengthsfinder 2.0. by T. Rath

Maslow's Hierarchy in Relationships and Persuasion

By Rhonda Gallagher, M.S.

C

You know there are difficulties associated with relationships, but you also know that we get something from them, or we wouldn't keep engaging in them. So what do we get? According to Maslow's Hierarchy of Needs (Maslow, 1943), some things are more necessary for survival and health than others, or it might be more accurate to say that some needs are more pressing than others. Once you understand that, the appeal of human interaction becomes more readily apparent. Abraham Maslow identified a priority of needs. The bottom level is physiological needs such as food, and water that help us not to starve, freeze, or die of thirst, that sort of thing. The next level up is safety and security, which means once we have met basic physiological needs, we start to consider eliminating risk. We need to know we have a safe place to stay, that others will not injure us, and so on. The next level up is love and belonging. Belonging to a group is closely connected to safety in primitive situations, but even in more cosmopolitan settings, we want to be included and loved. We need friends and family. After the love and belonging needs are met, a person can begin to develop a sense of his/her own worth, his/her self-esteem. It is as if we need to know we matter to someone else before we can believe that we matter at all. The pinnacle of the hierarchy is self-actualization, which refers to our desire to be fulfilled. Creativity, spontaneity, morality, and just becoming a better person are all included in self-actualization, and we come to those things when our lower needs are being met. Taking a look at the graphic of Maslow's

Maslow's hierarchy of needs

Hierarchy, some of the things in any group of needs may seem less pressing than others. For instance, among safety and security needs, employment is listed. Some people never have employment, but because other resources are secure, it is not a need for them. Not every need at each level has to be met before one can move up to the next level. Try to think of the dividers between levels as a little bit porous. We can start to move up to the next level when most of the needs in a group have been met.

It is also useful to realize that the basic human needs represented in Maslow's Hierarchy can help us make emotional appeals (*pathos*) in a persuasive speech. Our basic needs can help demonstrate the benefits or detriments of any course of action. For instance, if you are persuading an audience to give blood, you can point out to them that they might be in an accident and need blood in medical treatment (physiological needs). You might also show them that the presence of a well-stocked blood bank provides for the needs of a community, making the inhabitants feel safer. If you point out to them that they would feel terrible losing someone they loved because there was no blood available, you'd be using love and belonging. If you could show them that they would feel better about themselves if they donated to help someone else, you would be accessing the need for self-esteem, and if you point out that giving blood is service to others and makes the world a better place, you are using self-actualization. These types of appeal are used often.

Reference

Maslow, A. H. (1970). *Motivation and personality* (2nd ed.). New York: Harper & Row.

Good Communicators Are Media Savvy

By Rhonda Gallagher, M.S.

© Ekaterina_Molchanova/Shutterstock.com

Media is both wondrous and suspect, terrifying and terrific! It is powerful by its very nature because images speak so deeply to our subconscious mind. It's also dangerous because people often fail to apply critical thinking to what they see in media. So, let's define it and discuss it. First, the definition.

Technically, **media** is any technology that carries a message from one person or group of people to another. But realistically, we usually mean mass media when we talk about it, so for our purposes let's say that **mass media** are any technologies that carry a message from an individual or group to a "large, unseen and anonymous audience" (Dobkin & Pace, 2003). Examples of mass media include multiple sources on the Internet (YouTube, Facebook, Twitter, Netflix, Spotify, etc.), television, radio, books, magazine, conventional CDs, and DVDs to name a few. The creators of media are usually gearing their message toward a **target audience**, which is the group for whom the message is intended. Often, advertisers pay for the production of media in order to provide a way to advertise their products, so the target audience becomes the people most likely to buy the product. For instance, Frito-Lay pays to host the Fiesta Bowl on TV in hopes that chip-eaters will buy their products. Football fans notoriously eat a lot of snack food, so it makes sense to advertise to them. According to Mark Savage (BBC News.com) a single episode of "The Big Bang Theory" costs a tidy four million dollars, so your average media producer isn't going to spend that kind of money just for the fun of it. They have to make money; the return on the investment must be enough to justify the cost. This leads us to a major thing you need to keep in mind when you are consuming mass media. Now this is important, so pay attention:

© Jacob Lund/Shutterstock.com

Media is an industry and the object of the game is to make money.

A media maker's job is to make money by attracting viewers, and if what we as viewers want is not entirely truthful about life or society, they are just doing their jobs. They are giving us what we asked for. They are just entertaining us. You see, media performs multiple functions, and one of them is to entertain. So, what are those other functions? I'm so glad you asked!

Media
any technology that carries a message

Mass media
technologies that carry a message from an individual or group to a large, unseen, and anonymous audience

Target audience
group for whom the message is intended

Audience gratification
media function that gives the audience what it wants

Agenda setting
choices media producers make about which stories are produced

What Media Does . . .

Media has some basic functions. The first is audience gratification (Dobkin & Pace, 2003). That means they give us what we want, whether that is keeping us up with the news, giving us information we might need, or keeping us entertained. Now, this is the media function that most of us think about when we fire up our computers to catch the latest episode of our favorite show on Hulu or plop down our $12 at the movie counter. But there are others.

A second function is agenda setting (McCombs & Shaw, 1972). Agenda setting involves the choices media producers, often news producers, make about which stories get produced. Obviously, not every event that happens in the world can get covered on the evening news. Somebody has to decide which stories get told and which do not. That's the job of the news director. She may decide based on what she thinks the audience is interested in, or (and this is what is so relevant to our discussion) there may be an issue she thinks is absolutely critical for the public to know. Whatever story gets told, it will generate discussion among people, and when that happens, an agenda has been set that affects what we talk about and also what we think about. That, in turn, often drives public policy and may lead to the change the news director wants to see. (Remember, these news directors are acting out of what they perceive to be the public good, whether you agree with them or not. If you think the wrong stories are getting told, you might need to go into media yourself and make the changes you want to see!)

Cultivation theory
theory that consuming the same media can cause people to have a more shared worldview

A third function is creating a shared worldview. Gerbner, Gross, Morgan, and Signorielli (1998) coined the term cultivation theory to describe what takes place when people consume the same media, which then shapes their worldview. That media will promote a worldview that is shared regardless of culture or individual differences. Political change in repressive regimes is possible largely because of the presence of the Internet, which exposes people to other ways of thinking. Many dissidents have incorporated into their worldview the idea of self-governance that they witnessed on the Internet, and regardless of race, religion, or culture, they began to share the idea that democracy and self-determination was a good thing. That's how cultivation of worldview works (Gerbner, Gross, Morgan, & Signorielli, 1994).

Why Can't We All Just Get Along?

Now, based on that last paragraph, you might think that people all over the world having exposure to the same ideas is a good thing, and it can be. An example would be the Red campaign that swept the Internet a few years ago, leading to massive funding for AIDS research and worldwide changes in perceptions of the disease. But there's an interesting idea that you might not have considered. We get to pick the media we consume, and we don't all pick the same things. If you do a little self-examination here, you'll admit that you are likely to pick or attend to media that agrees with and reinforce the worldview you hold. That's called selective exposure. Furthermore, even if you are exposed to other ideas, you are likely to remember those that (you guessed it!) agree with and reinforce your existing worldview. That's called selective retention. So, rather than gaining a broader understanding of the world through media, we just keep holding the same views (Wicks, 1996; Klapper, 1960). Even if we hold very extreme opinions, we can connect with a bunch of people via the Internet who hold the same views and reinforce our beliefs. We can even begin to believe that the majority of "reasonable people" in the world agree with us when, in reality, the people who hold the same opinions as us may make up a tiny fraction of the world's population. In effect, all this media may not be serving to unite humankind at all, but rather divide it. I don't know about you, but I find this idea very sobering.

Selective exposure
picking media to consume that conforms to one's worldview

Selective retention
tendency of consumers to remember media that supports one's existing worldview

Third-Person Effect
theory that consumers believe others to be more affected by media than they are

I'm Not Affected, No, Not Me!

If you read all this and think that the media has no effect on you, then (Surprise!) you have proven one of the most profound effects of mass media on individuals. It's called third-person effect (Salwen & Dupagne, 1999). Basically, it just means that we think other people are more affected by media they consume than we are. "Violent video games make people aggressive, but they don't affect me." Sound familiar? Most of us tend to think we are better than others, and the rules don't really apply to us. We allow ourselves to think there are extenuating circumstances in our case. We will say the rules are good—really good!—but we think we're

© bys/Shutterstock.com

the exception, so a different set of rules applies to us. (Does the phrase self-serving bias ring a bell?) For many of us, this is the origin of sin. We think the rules are good, just not good for us. Think about that for a minute. Are you as immune as you think you are? Really?

Another effect is the mean world syndrome (Signoreilli & Morgan, 1990), which hypothesizes that because media shows violence at a radically higher proportion than it appears in real life (about ten times higher), we tend to think that the world is much more dangerous than it is and that makes us more suspicious and fearful. Do you have a grandmother who watches lots of TV and also has six different locks on her doors? Now you know why.

Ethical Implications

We need to remember that media is an area in which the consumer has the responsibility for self-policing. It's easy to say that "someone" should be certain that violent games or sexually explicit materials don't get into the hands of children, but the bottom line here is that we have to be that someone. We must protect ourselves and those who depend on us. We must also realize that different viewpoints have to be available because there are places in the world where people don't think like we do.

Summary

Mass media carry messages from the message creator to a large, unseen, and anonymous audience. The purpose of the media industry is to make money, and the consumer must be aware of his media consumption. Media functions include audience gratification, agenda setting, and cultivation of worldview. Consumers must be aware of the tendency toward selective exposure, selective retention, third-person effect, and mean-world syndrome.

Vocabulary Words

Agenda setting	Media	Target audience
Audience gratification	Mean World Syndrome	Third Person Effect
Cultivation theory	Selective exposure	
Mass media	Selective retention	

References

Dobkin, B. A., & Pace, R. C. (2003). *Communication in a changing world*. New York: McGraw-Hill.

Gerbner, G., Gross, L., Morgan, M., & Signorielli, N. (1994). Growing up with television: The cultivation perspective. In J. Bryant & D. Zillman (Eds.), *Media effects: Advances in theory and research* (pp. 17–42). Hillsdale, NJ: Erlbaum.

Gerbner, G. (1998). Cultivation analysis: An overview. *Mass Communication & Society, 1*, 175–194.

Klapper, J. T. (1960). *The effects of mass communication*. New York: Free Press.

McCombs, M., & Shaw, D. (1972). The agenda setting function of mass media. *Public Opinion Quarterly, 36*, 176–187.

Salwen, M. B., & Dupagne, M. (1999). The third person effect: Perceptions of media's influence and immoral consequences. *Communication Research, 26*, 523–550.

Savage, M. (2014, August 5). More bucks for your Big Bang Theory: What justifies a $1m pay packet. *BBC News*. Retrieved from http://www.bbc.com/news/entertainment-arts-28658258

Signorielli, N., & Morgan, M. (1990). *Cultivation analysis: New directions in media effects research*. Newbury Park, CA: Sage.

Wicks, R. H. (1996). Joseph Klapper and the effects of mass communication: A retrospective. *Journal of Broadcasting and Mass Communication, 40*, 563–570.

Glossary

Acceptance speech - speech given by the honoree at a formal event to thank a group for an award they have given to the speaker

Accommodation - give in or sacrifice partially or completely to the other party

Active listeners - people who participate in listening by keeping attention focused, creating memory aids, and structuring the information received

Adaptors - gestures that help us feel better

Adrenaline - a hormone secreted by the adrenal glands, especially in conditions of stress, increasing rates of blood circulation, breathing, and carbohydrate metabolism, causing a noticeable increase in strength and performance, as well as heightened awareness, in stressful times

Agenda setting - choices media producers make about which stories are produced

Ambiguity - uncertainty of meaning

Analogy - an idea that we understand that helps us with one we don't yet understand

Anchor - one's strongest belief about the topic

Arbitrary - the characteristic of words that states the sounds of the words are random and do not affect the meaning

Artifactics - objects that reveal something about someone

Attention - intentional effort to capture specific sensory information

Attractiveness bias - the tendency to ascribe better motives for actions to attractive people than we would to less attractive people in the same circumstances

Attribution - drawing a conclusion about why we or someone else has acted in a particular way

Audience analysis - process of figuring out what the audience knows, thinks, and feels in order to adapt your topic, content, visuals, and delivery to meet their needs

Audience gratification - media function that gives the audience what it wants

Authoritarian leadership - leadership style characterized by directive activity without group input

Autonomy vs. connection - tension between wanting to be independent and staying connected to others

Avoidance - to evade conflict through silence or removing oneself from the situation

Avoiding - the couple begins to actively avoid each other

Award presentation - A speech given for awarding an honor to someone

Behavioral question - an interview question that focuses on past behavior for purposes of assessment of suitability for a position

Bibliography - the list of sources you used to gather material for the speech.

Blame - identify the source of the problem

Bonding - relationship stage marked by a formal commitment that makes it more difficult to dissolve the relationship

Breadth - how many different topics you can discuss with someone

Bullying - using nonverbal and/or verbal communication to control, threaten, or intimidate others

Call to action speech - persuasive speech that requires the audience to actually do something

Channel - the sensory medium that carries the message

Charisma - likability

Chronemics - messages sent by the way time is structured and used

Circumscribing - an unresolved conflict has started a rift between the partners

Civility - treating others decently

Closed family communication style - a communication style where predictability, structure, consistency and tradition are valued

Closed-ended question - question geared to solicit answers of one or two words

Closure - the ability of the brain to supply missing parts from a picture or situation

Co-culture - a culture that exists inside a larger culture

Coaching - leadership stage in which the leader will not direct the staff member, but rather analyze their weaknesses and offer correction

Code - tells us how we can or cannot communicate in a given cultural setting

Code-switching - adapting our communication style to the culture of the people with whom we are interacting

Cognitive dissonance - the internal turmoil we feel when our actions don't conform to our beliefs

Coherence - all parts of the story hold together and make sense together

Cohesion - all group members are in unity and going in the same direction to reach an expected goal

Collaborating - individuals attempt to have both parties reach consensus

Collectivist cultures - cultures that value the good of the group over the good of the individual

Commemorative speech - speech given at a special event to honor a particular person, group, or event.

Communication - the process of creating and sharing one's thoughts, emotions, or concepts with another person

Communication apprehension - the fear or anxiety associated with either real or anticipated communication with another person or persons

Communicators - people who communicate

Competing - you are more concerned with being right than getting the right answer for the situation

Compromise - achieved when each person gives up something in order to come to an acceptable solution

Concision - brevity

Conclusion - the inescapable judgement resulting from the connecting of the premises

Concrete - the characteristic of words that refer to an actual instance or a specific thing

Confirm - react to your persona as if it is true

Conflict - a state of disagreement, hostility, discord, or argument that can exist between people when they believe their needs, beliefs, or characteristics are irreconcilable

Construct - a single category in which we hold memory

Constructivism - theory that we create categories in our heads for like things, and we go to those categories to find information we need

Contempt - insulting a person through name-calling, sarcasm, hostility, mockery, sneering, eye-rolling, etc.

Context - the setting where the communication takes place

Context clues - hints at the true meaning of the conversation that can be found in the setting of the communication

Control messages - designed for the purpose of exerting control over the child

Cost - necessary expenditure of resources to address the problem

Credibility - believability

Criticism - attacking someone's personality, character, or style in an attempt to make the person wrong rather than their argument wrong

Cultivation Theory - theory that consuming the same media can cause people to have a more shared worldview

Cultural artifacts - tangible expressions of a culture

Culture - shared beliefs, values, symbols, and knowledge of group history

Cure - an acceptable solution

Decoding - the process of turning a symbol back into meaning

Defensiveness - playing the victim in an attempt to divert an attack or perceived attack

Delegating - leadership stage in which the leader recognizes that the follower has the ability and the motivation to complete the tasks at hand and does not provide any support or direction

Democratic leader - leader who delegates decision-making to the group itself

Demographics - basic, quantifiable information you know about the audience

Depth - the level of relationship that allows a person to talk about more personal and sensitive information

Derived credibility - credibility built during the speech based on appearance, presentation skills, and quality of evidence

Development leaders - leaders who motivate people by nurturing the strengths and weaknesses of their followers

Dialectical tensions - the tension that arises between opposing relational needs

Differentiating - stage in a relationship where the couple discovers significant differences between themselves

Directing - leadership stage in which the leader makes most of the decisions for the staff member

Disconfirm - failing to notice the presentation of a persona at all

Disruptive roles - characteristics that individuals use to disrupt the agenda of the group by prioritizing their own needs and agendas in a group

Double-barreled questions - questions that include two or more questions asked at the same time.

Doublespeak - an ambiguity used to protect or benefit the speaker, another person, or an organization to purposely deceive the listener

Elevator speech - a 30 second speech that summarizes your character, skills, and suitability for a position

Emblems - culturally recognized gestures that have a direct interpretation into a few words

Emotional intelligence - the ability to recognize, understand, use, and control our emotions and those of others

Empathetic listening - listening for the purpose of lending emotional support to another person

Empathy - putting yourself into someone else's shoes and thinking about what they feel

Encoding - process of choosing symbols to represent the message

Enduring credibility - credibility a speaker gets from the audience's previous experiences with that speaker

Entertainment speaking - speaking to help the audience relax and have fun

Ethnocentrism - the belief that one's own culture is superior to all others

Ethos - credibility established with the audience

Eulogy - speech to show honor for the deceased at a funeral

Euphemisms - ambiguities used to protect or benefit the listener, another person, or an organization

Evaluation - deciding what you think about what you've heard

Example - one item in a large group that enables the audience to better understand the larger group

Exclusivity - the belief that your partner will not be involved with another person while your relationship lasts

Experimentation - stage when one of the parties may move the conversation onto more risky information

Expert opinion - what an expert thinks about a condition, situation, or experience

Explanation - telling the audience about a process, how or why something is the way it is, or how something works or doesn't work

Expression vs. privacy - tension regarding sharing personal information

External attribution - assuming a person's actions may be driven by external forces influencing them to behave as they do

Eye messages - messages sent with our eyes

Facework - presenting a particular side of yourself to people based on the setting

Facial expression - the use of the face to send messages

Facts - supporting bits of information that are established knowledge

Fallacy - a mistake in logical reasoning

Feedback - a response to a message

Feminine cultures - cultures that value collaboration and nurturance

Fidelity - something is consistent with the way the world as we know it works

Figurative analogy - analogy that tells us how something seems or feels to help us understand

Filters - the pre-existing patterns in our minds that cause us to notice some things and not others

First impression - what a person thinks of you when they first meet you

Follow-up questions - questions that come up in your own mind during the conversation in response to what you hear the interviewee saying

Forensics - the study of public speaking

Forming stage - stage of group growth that is characterized by shallow, formal interactions

Framing - the manipulation of perceptions by highlighting certain aspects

Fundamental attribution error - the tendency to assume the cause of any negative behavior by another person is internal rather than external

General speech purpose - the big goal of the speech

Generalized other - the composite projection of social values and approved behaviors that we believe others use to judge us

Gestures - the way a person uses their hands and body to add meaning to a message

Goal incompatibility - one of the most common causes of conflict, both people wanting something different

Groupthink - desire for unanimity that takes precedence over the need to seek out all possible answers

Haptics - the use of physical touch to send or receive a message

Harm - convince people that a problem is significant enough to require action

Hearing - the physical process of sound being relayed to the brain along the auditory nerve

Hedges - additions such as "kind of" to lessen the impact of an utterance

High context - a communication situation or relationship in which there are numerous nonverbal cues to which you must adhere

High context culture - culture in which a great deal of the meaning is found in the context

I-statements - begin with I and enable the speakers to be assertive without making accusations

Identity - the perception you have of yourself as a member of a group

Illustrations - stories that demonstrate an idea by showing how it played out in someone's life

Illustrator - a gesture that shows the meaning of the words either through supplementing or reiterating a verbal message

Immediacy behaviors - verbal and nonverbal behaviors that a speaker uses to build closeness and connection with audience members to promote a sense of closeness and likability

Implicit Personality Theory - group of theories which collectively state that we associate certain characteristics together

Inclusive language - language that avoids expressions that highlight how a person or group is different

Individualistic cultures - cultures that place the emphasis on the individual

Informational interview - a conversation in which one person asks questions of another person in order to gain information

Informative speaking - speaking to give information to the audience

Initial credibility - credibility you get from knowledge of personal experience

Initiating - when people meet for the first time and make small talk

Inspirational speech - speech to encourage a group not to give up in adversity

Integration - stage when the relationship has become special, and the couple may be unhappy when they are separated

Intensifying - relationship stage when you really start to get to know the other party

Interference - anything that prevents or distorts the transfer of the meaning

Internal attribution - assuming a person acts as they do because it reflects who they are

Internal summary - transitions that provide the audience with a recap of each point that has been covered so far and prepares them for the next point

Interpersonal communication - communication that happens between people in a relationship

Interpretation - understanding what you have heard

Interview - a conversation with a purpose

Intrapersonal communication - communication within yourself

Introduction - speech to introduce another speaker

Jargon - the vocabulary of a particular group, profession, or trade

Johari window - an instrument for measuring a person's degree of self-awareness

Laissez-faire leader - leadership style that does not give direction or leadership structure but provides a hands-off approach to leading the group

Latitude of acceptance - what we believe

Latitude of non-commitment - what we haven't formed a definite opinion on yet

Latitude of rejection - things we are convinced are wrong

Leadership - ability to direct others toward a common goal

Leading question - question that reveals to the interviewee how the interviewer wants them to answer by the way it's worded

Leakage - when things slip out nonverbally that we didn't intend to share

Line-of-terror - that imaginary line a speaker is afraid to move past. It's typically the line that is represented by the front of the podium

Linguistic Relativity Hypothesis - theory that the words we learn from those who rear us transmit the mindset of our culture and that affects how we see the world

Listening - an active mental process that involves perceiving sound interpreting it, and responding to it

Listening cues - behaviors that let the speaker know that the listener is actually listening and engaged

Listening for fun - engaging in listening for enjoyment's sake

Listening for information - applying attentive listening for the purpose of learning something

Listening for judgment - listening to make a decision about the truth or value of something

Literal analogy - analogy that compares things in concrete ways

Loaded question - a question that is worded as a closed-ended question and causes the interviewee to be unable to answer without saying something bad about him/herself

Logos - logical organization of information throughout the speech

Low context - communication situations in which the interaction is governed by clearly expressed expectations

Low context cultures - cultures that require direct communication and communicators expect to have information stated aloud

Main points - the most important ideas that the audience needs to know

Maintenance role - characteristics that individuals use to focus on people and maintain good relationships

Major premise - establishes a generalization

Masculine cultures - cultures that tend to be competitive, focused on accomplishment, and materialistic

Mass media - publicly published forms of communication that are not addressed to individuals

Mass media - technologies that carry a message from an individual or group to a large, unseen, and anonymous audience

Mean-world Syndrome - the tendency of consumers of media to assume the world to be more dangerous than it is

Media - any technology that carries a message

Mediated communication - communication that takes place between two communicators who are separated from each other that utilizes some form of technology

Message - the idea one communicator wants to give to another communicator

Micro expressions - facial expressions that happen so fast most of us don't catch them

Mindlessness - doing and saying things without really thinking about them

Minor premise - establishes a specific case

Missional leaders - leaders who lead through an emphasis on the mission and vision or goal of the group

Monochronic time orientation - cultural view of time as linear

Monroe's Motivated Sequence - an organizational pattern with five steps that is used for calling an audience to action

Narrative Paradigm Theory - humans look for stories and patterns in events in an effort to make sense of life

Neutral question - question that does not reveal any interviewer bias and lets the interviewee respond however they choose

Nonverbal communication - all messages that are not sent by words

Norming stage - stage of group growth when conflict has been resolved and some progress is made

Novelty - the quality of being really unusual

Occasion analysis - process of considering the purpose of the gathering, the timing of the speech, the mood of the audience, and the social rules that govern interaction in public speaking communication

Open family communication style - a communication style is more open, flexibility is important, and authentic interaction and responsiveness are valued

Open-ended questions - questions that allow the interviewee to determine the amount and depth of information they want to give

Organization - the brain's process of identifying what the sensory information is

Organizational pattern - the structured order of the main points, or the Roman numerals of a speech

Outline - a visual representation of how speech ideas relate to each other

Parallel sentence structure - sentence arrangement in which each sentence follows the order of the first, and the sentences sound as much alike as possible

Passive listeners - people who do not take responsibility for listening

Pathos - emotional appeals

Pauses - a temporary stop or rest within the speech used deliberately by the speaker to emphasize a point or catch a breath

Perception - the process by which we gather information from our surroundings

Perception check - asking another to be certain that one is right in interpreting an event or situation

Perceptual constancy - our tendency to interpret the same symbols in the same way over time

Perceptual constancy - the tendency to perceive something the same way over time

Performing stage - stage of group growth that strong, cohesive groups move to where synergy develops and more work is accomplished together than individually

Personal construct - your personal interpretation of a particular construct based on your personal observations and experience

Personal relevance - personal connection

Perspective taking - process of seeing an issue from the other person's point of view

Persuasive speaking - speaking to make the audience believe or do something

Persuasive speech - a speech that helps someone change their mind about the way they think or act

Pitch - the highness or lowness of one's voice, comprising the natural range of highs and lows in which the voice operates

Plagiarism - using someone else's words or original ideas without giving them credit

Polychronic time orientation - cultural view of time as overlapping experiences to be coordinated

Positional leadership - leaders who rely on their title or position to utilize any type of authority

Positive imagery - a technique used to evoke positive mental images, feelings, and thoughts for one's public speaking skills through the use of positive mental images and positive words

Power distance - the perceived gap in respect and power between the people who govern and those who are governed

Preview - listing the main points to be covered

Priming - the process by which the brain follows constructs recently used to organize new information

Proofs - methods used to persuade people using logic, emotion, or ethics

Proposition of fact - gives the justification for the audience to accept that a statement is true

Proposition of policy - gives the justification for a plan to change procedures for doing something

Proposition of value - gives the justification for how a viewpoint is good or bad and centers on what the speaker thinks about an issue

Prototype - a collection of informational bits that make up a culturally recognized type of person, object, or event

Proxemics - the way that we use space to send a message

Pseudolistening - pretending to listen

Public communication - public speaking

Public speaking - the act of one speaker addressing a large group of people in person

Purpose statement - what the speaker is trying to do

Racism - believing one's race to be superior to all others

Random family communication style - a communication style where spontaneity, happiness, and individuality are valued

Rapport - getting the audience to identify with you

Rapport talk - the feminine speaking style that is intended to create connection between the parties engaging in the communication

Rate - how fast or how slow one speaks during a speech

Receiver - the person who receives the message

Reflected appraisals - our perceptions about the messages others send us about ourselves

Regulator - a gesture that stops or changes the flow of conversation

Reject - react as if your persona is not true

Relaxation exercises - the deliberate use of muscle relaxation and deep breathing that helps one relax and combat symptoms of anxiety before a speech

Remembering - being able to retrieve information from your memory bank

Report talk - the masculine speaking style in Western culture that is focused on sharing information

Response - your reaction to what you have heard

Response speech - speech given by the honoree at a dedication, inauguration, or graduation in response to the recognition

Role-taking - trying on a new persona to see if it fits you

Sarcasm - intentionally saying one message with the words while sending a contradictory message with the tone of voice

Scent - the nonverbal messages sent by smell

Script - a pattern for expected behavior

Selection - the step in the perceptual process in which you focus your attention on one form of sensory stimuli

Selection interview - an interview in which an organization chooses a candidate to receive a job, internship, or award

Selective exposure - picking media to consume that conforms to one's worldview

Selective retention - tendency of consumers to remember media that supports their existing worldview

Self-analysis - a self-inventory of one's talents and skills

Self-awareness - what you know about yourself

Self-concept - the stable image you have of yourself over time

Self-disclosure - revealing personal information about yourself to another

Self-fulfilling prophecies - statements about our future behavior that we hear and subconsciously make come true

Self-leadership - the development of your own leadership style and following it

Self-monitoring - trying to see one's own actions as others would see them

Self-perception - how you judge yourself based on your own standards

Self-serving bias - the tendency to give ourselves credit for the best of motives, but when others in the same situation act in the same way, we assume bad things about their reasons

Semantic interference - a psychological distraction that comes from your emotional reaction to a symbol that has been used in your presence

Sender - the person sending a message to someone else

Servant leaders - leadership style that focuses on serving first before leading

Similarity bias - assuming that a person who is like you in one way will be like you in other ways

Situational anxiety - anxiety caused by factors present in a specific speaking situation

Situational leadership - leadership style that adapts to match the needs of the group members

Small group communication - three to seven participants that meet for some specific reason

Small groups - 3 or more people who work together interdependently to get something done

Social comparison - learning about ourselves by comparing ourselves to other people

Social Judgment Theory - the range of attitude that explain why the more invested people are in an idea, the harder it is to persuade them to change their minds

Social learning - paying attention to specific actions or behaviors if we are trying to learn something

Social Penetration Theory - a theory that says that we reveal information about ourselves in layers

Socialization - is the process of teaching children how to behave in their social group

Speaking aids - items you show to or play for the audience in order to build their understanding or retention

Special occasion speaking - speaking done at a special occasion

Special occasion speech - Speech prepared for a specific, special kind of occasion

Specific speech purpose - what you hope to accomplish in the speech

Speech to convince - persuasive speech to get the audience to believe something different than they already believe

Speech to reinforce - persuasive speech to reinforce the audience's beliefs or behaviors

Speeches that describe - speeches that tell what something is like

Speeches that explain - speeches that tell how a process works or why a thing happened as does

Speeches to demonstrate - "how to" speeches

Speeches to narrate - speeches that tell a story

Stability vs. change - tension between our desire for things to remain relatively constant, expected, and with no surprises and our need to have new experiences, variety, and change

Stagnating - relationship stage where the couple doesn't want to go on like they have been, but they don't want to break up, either

Statistics - facts in number form

Stereotypes - predictions about how people will behave based on the expected characteristics of the group they belong to

Stonewalling - ignoring the other person's argument completely, the silent treatment, muttering to yourself, changing the subject, leaving the situation, ignoring texts and sending calls straight to voicemail

Storming stage - stage of group growth that occurs when conflict is introduced

Sub-points - the ideas that support the main ideas

Support messages - designed to help the child feel more comfortable and secure

Supporting - leadership stage in which the leader watches as the follower makes decisions and offers support when necessary, but allows the follower to choose what needs to be done and how it needs to be done

Supporting material - bits of information that help the audience understand the ideas the speaker is trying to share

Syllogism - a way of logically connecting two related ideas to reach a judgement

Symbol - something that represents something else

Systems Theory of Family - theory that says that a family is a complex entity unto itself with its own kind of dynamics

Tag questions - invitations for affirmation such as, "don't you think?" at the end of a statement

Target audience - group for whom the message is intended

Task role - characteristics that individuals use to make sure that the group goal is achieved

Terminating - one of the partners wants to terminate the relationship

Territory - the space we claim

Third-Person Effect - theory that consumers believe others to be more affected by media than they are

Toast - brief speech in preparation for drinking a beverage to honor a person or event

Trait anxiety - internal anxieties an individual brings to the speaking situation, usually stemming from feelings of inadequacy

Transitions - the sentences that connect main points to each other

Uncertainty avoidance - the degree to which a culture can tolerate uncertainty

Verbal code - composed of the words one speaks when giving a speech

Visual code - a nonverbal code that comprises anything an audience member sees regarding the actual components of a speaker's delivery such as their facial expressions, movement, gestures, and visual aids

Vividness - discrete and remarkable mental images

Vocal code - a nonverbal code composed of a speaker's tone of voice, which includes vocal expression, rate, pitch, and volume

Vocal fillers - sounds like "uh" and "um"

Vocalics - the meaning that comes from the way the words are said rather than the meaning of the words

Workplace harassment - a form of bullying in which the bully is usually in a position of official power over the victim

You-statements - shift the blame to the listener

Index

NOTE: Page references in *italics* refer to figures.

A

acceptance
    latitude of, 270
    self-acceptance, 29–30
    speeches, 283
accommodation, 160
active listeners, 70
adaptors, 56
adrenaline, 245–246
advertising, 297
advice, 75–76
agenda setting, 298
age of audience, 197
ambiguity, 131–134, *132*
American Psychological Association (APA), 228, 238
analogy, 227, *228*
anchor, 270
answering questions, 290–292
anxiety
    overcoming, 251–253, *253*
    public speaking issues of, 246–253, *248*
apologizing, 102, 161
arbitrary (arbitrariness), 135–136
arguing, fairness in, 99–100
Aristotle, 272–274
artifactics, 60
Art of Conversation, The (Tippett), 142
asking questions, 292–293
attention
    listening and, 70, 73, 76–77
    speech writing and, 234

attentiveness, 123
attitude of audience, 196
attractiveness
    attractiveness bias, 192
    perception of, *193*
attribution
    considerate communicators and, 191–193
    defined, 43
audience. *see also* public speaking
    attitude of, 196
    audience analysis, 196–197
    audience gratification, 298
    connecting with audience for persuasion, 266–267
        (*see also* persuasion)
    demographics of, 197–198
    expectations of, 197
    eye contact with, 255
    listening by, 83
    public speaking anxiety and, 250
    public speaking as service to, 194, 206
    speeches and knowledge of, *194,* 194–195
    target audience, 297–298
    writing introductions and conclusions for,
        233–237 (*see also* speeches; speech
        organization)
authenticity, 76
authoritarian leadership, 177
authority in unequal relationships, 162–163
autonomy *versus* connection, 152
avoidance, 160
avoiding, 98
awareness, 67

B

balancing power, 158
barriers, to listening, 79–81
Barry, Dave, 133
Berman, Sanford, 135, 138
behavioral question, 291
bibliography, 238
Blanchard, Ken, 178
bonding, 96
boundaries, conflict and, 157
breadth, 92
bull in a china shop (group member type), 175, *175*
bullying
    defined, 56
    workplace harassment as, 56–57
Burgoon, J. K., 56
Bush, Barbara, 133

C

call to action speech, 195
cause/effect, 277
change
    changeable words, *134,* 134–135
    in relationships, 99
    stability *versus* change, 153
channels, 8–9
Chapman, Gary, *97*
charisma, 235
choice, of words, *136*
Christian belief. *see also* ethics
    communication overview and, 1–2
    confident communicating, 244–246, 250–253, *253*
    conflict and, 163–164
    considerate communication and, 189
    culture and, 110, 114, 124
    gender and culture, 118
    groups and leadership, 170–171, 175
    interpersonal communication and, 89, 90
    listening and, 75, 84
    organization and, 219
    overview, xi
    perception and, 36, 46
    persuasion and, 268, 278
    self-awareness and, 17–18, 28–31
    words and civility, 142–144
chronemics, 60–61
chronological organizational pattern (speeches), 224, *224*
circumscribing, 97
citation, 228
civility, 13, 142–144
clarification, 73
closed family communication style, 101

close-ended questions, 212
closure, 41
clothing, 254
coaching
    leadership and, 178
    nonverbal communication and, 53
co-culture, 4, 111
code, 110
code-switching, 111
cognitive dissonance, 80
coherence
    in listening, 85
    perception and, 81
collaborating, 160
collectivist culture, 114, 232
commemorative speeches, 283–284
commitment
    leadership and, 179
    in relationships, 100
communication, 1–13. *see also* confident communicating;
        considerate communicators; culture;
        gender; groups; information; interpersonal
        communication; listening; nonverbal
        communication; organization; perception;
        persuasion; problem solving; self-awareness;
        speeches; words
    defined, 2
    elements of, 5–12
    ethical implications of, 12–13
    frame of reference in, 7
    principles of, 2–5
    study of, 1–2
communication apprehension, 246
communicators, 5–7
community, building, 181
comparative advantage, 278
comparison organizational pattern (speeches), 225, *225*
competing, 159
complaining, 123
compliments, 123
compromise, 160
concision, 140
conclusion
    of premise, 275
    to speech, 233–237
concrete (concreteness of words), 132
confidence, 243–262
confident communicating
    adrenaline for, 245–246
    anxiety issues, 246, *248*
    delivery of speeches, 253–254
    ethical implications of, 261
    nonverbal communication for public speaking, 255

general speech purpose, 207
gestures, 57, 123, 254
goals
    goal incompatibility, 150
    setting reasonable goals, 30
Golden Rule, 189
Gottman, John, 154
Greenleaf, Robert, 179
group affiliation, 198
groups, 169–185
    addressing (*see* audience; public speaking)
    ethical implications of, 184
    functioning of, 171–174
    group conflict, 171–174 (*see also* conflict)
    groupthink in, 158, 182–183, *183*
    leadership of, 175–184 (*see also* leadership)
    members of, 174–175, *175*
    order of, 170–171
    overview, 169–170
    phases of interaction in, 171

H

Hall, Edward, 59
Hall, Jeff, *93*
haptics, 62–63, 124
harassment
    bullying, 56
    workplace harassment, 56–57
Harrison, R. P., 52
healing, leadership and, 180
hearing, 69, 70
hedges, 141
Hierarchy of Needs (Maslow), 295–296
high context
    conflict and, 151
    high context culture, 112–113
Hormone Health Network, 246

I

ideal (group member type), 175, *175*
identity, self-awareness and, 18, 26–28, *27*
illustrations, 230
illustrator (gesture), 55
imagery, 252, *253*
immediacy behaviors, 254
implicit personality theory, 45
inclusion, 142–143, *143*
individualistic culture, 114, 232
inflection, 62
information
    informative organizational patterns for speeches,
        224–226, *224–226*

informative speaking, 206–207
informed speaking, 208
listening for, 72–73
research for speeches, 209–213, *213*
informational interviews, 211–213, *213*
initial credibility, 235
initiating, 95
inspirational speeches, 283–284
integration, 96
intensifying, 96, 122
interaction phases in groups, 171
interactivity, 8
interest, listening and, 77
interference
    listening and, 79–81
    overview of interference in communication, 6, 9–10
internal attribution, 191
internal interference, 10
internal summary, 233
Internet, for research, 210–211
interpersonal communication, 89–105
    characteristics of, 90–91
    defined, 12, 89–90
    ethical implications of, 103–104
    family relationships and, 100–102, *102*
    friendship and, 92–94, *93*
    Hierarchy of Needs (Maslow), 295–296
    overview, 90–91
    romantic relationships and, 94–100, *95, 97*
    self-disclosure for, 91–92
    social penetration theory, 92
interpretation
    listening and, 70
    perception and, 42–43
interrupting, 122
interviewers (group member type), 174, *175*
interviewing
    employment, 287–294
    informational interviews, 211–213, *213*
    interview, defined, 211
    selection, 287
intimate touch, 62
intimate zone, 59
intrapersonal communication, 11
introduction, to speeches, 233–237
introduction speeches, 283–284
I-statements, 140, 161
"it" factor, 254

J

jargon, 143
JoEllen (blogger), 161

N

name power, 136–138
narrate, speeches that, 207
narrative organizational pattern (speeches), 225, *226*
narrative paradigm theory, 44–45
nervousness, about public speaking. *see* anxiety
neutral questions, 212
Noller, P., 100, 102
non-commitment, latitude of, 270
nonverbal communication, 51–64
    artifactics, 60
    channels of, 8
    chronemics, 60–61
    culture and nonverbal differences, 123–124
    defined, 52
    ethical implications of, 63–64
    eye messages, 57–58
    facial expression, *58,* 58–59
    functions of, 54–57
    gender differences in, 120–123
    gestures, 57
    haptics, 62–63
    in interviews, 212–213
    overview, 51–52
    principles, 52–54
    proxemics, *59,* 59–60
    for public speaking, 255
    scent, 61
    symbols of, 2–3
    vocalics, 61–62
norming stage, of groups, 172
note-taking, 77, 213
novelty, 37

O

Obama, Barack, *142*
occasion analysis, 198–199
Ogden, C. K., 130
open-ended questions, 212
open family communication style, 101
open mind, listening and, 77
organization. *see also* speech organization
    listening for structure, 73
    order of groups, 170
    organizational pattern for speeches, 214, 223–226, *224–226*
    organizational patterns of persuasion, 277–279
    perception and, 39–42
outline of speech, 214, 220, *220. see also* speech organization

P

pain, listening and, 75–76
parallel sentence structure, 223
paraphrasing, 228
parenting, 101–102, *102*
passive listeners, 70
pathos, 273
pauses, 259
peers, friendship between, 93
perception, 36–46
    considerate communicators and, 190
    ethical implications of, 45–46
    filtering, 43–44
    identity and, 18
    implications of, 43–45
    implicit personality theory, 45
    interpretation and, 42–43
    listening and, 70
    narrative paradigm theory, 44–45
    organization and, 39–42
    overview, 36
    priming, 44
    process of, 36–43
    selection and, 37–39
    self-concept, 44
    self-perception, 22
perception check, 193
perceptual constancy, 41
performing stage, of groups, 172
personal relevance
    personal experience in public speaking, 213
    self-awareness and, 37
personal zone, 59
perspective taking, 193
persuasion, 265–280
    Aristotle on proofs, 272–274
    connecting with audience for, 266–267
    credibility for, *272*
    critical thought for, 269–270
    ethical implications of, 279
    fallacies and, 274–275, *275*
    goals of, 268
    Hierarchy of Needs (Maslow), 295–296
    organizational patterns of, 277–279
    overview, 265–266
    persuasive speech, defined, 267
    propositions for, 276–277
    quick-slow-quick thinking concept, 268, *268*
    Social Judgment Theory, 270–272, *271*
    uses of, 268–269
persuasive speaking, 208

pitch, 61–62, 259
plagiarism
 avoiding, with citation, 228
 defined, 213–214
 speech writing and, 232
podium, line-of-terror and, 255
policy, proposition of, 277
politeness, 102, 122, 132–133
politeness touch, 63
polychronic time orientation, 113
positional leadership, 177
positive imagery, 252, *253*
posture, 256
power
 of closing statements, 236
 conflict and balancing power, 158
 conflict in unequal relationships, 162–163
 power distance, 114–115
 power talk, 140–141, *141*
 of words, 136–138, *139, 141*
PowerPoint, 231, 260
preparation, for public speaking, 250
presentation programs, 231, 260
preview (speech), 236
priming, 44
privacy, expression *versus,* 153–154
problem solving, 149–166
 conflict and, 154–157
 conflict and apologizing, 161
 conflict as beneficial, 157–159
 conflict in unequal relationships, 162–163
 conflict management, 159–160
 cultural differences and, 121–122
 dialectical tension of, 152–154
 ethical implications of, 164–165
 group conflict, 159–160
 I-statements and, 161
 overview, 149–151
 problem-solution persuasion pattern, 278
 understanding context for, 151–152
professional touch, 63
proofs, 272–274
prototypes, 39
proxemics, *59,* 59–60, 123
pseudolistening, 81
public communication, 12
public speaking, 205–215. *see also* confident
 communicating; speech organization
 ambiguity of, 133–134
 audience and, 194–195, *194*
 defined, 205
 ethical implications of, 215
 informed speaking, 208

 note-taking and, 213
 organizational pattern for speeches, 214
 outlining, 214
 purpose of speeches, 207–208
 research for, 209–213, *213*
 as service, 194–195, 206
 setting for, 198–199
 topics for, 197
 types of speeches, 195, 206–207
public zone, 59
purposeful movement, 255–256
purpose of speech, 221–222
purpose statement, 236

Q

questions
 answering, 290–293
 asking, 75, 292–293
 behavioral,291
 clarifying, 73
 gender and verbal communication, 122
 neutral questions for interviews, 212
 promoting civility with, 142–144
 questions for interviews, 211–213
 tag questions, 140
quick-slow-quick thinking concept, 268, *268*

R

race. *see also* culture
 of audience, 198
 racism, 117
random family communication style, 101
rapport, 234
rapport talk, 122–123
rate (of speech), 61–62, 259
Raushenbush, Paul Brandeis, 142
receivers, 5
receiving, 2
reflected appraisals, 19–21
regulator, 55
reinforce, speech to, 195
rejection, 20
rejection, latitude of, 270
relaxation exercises, 249
remembering, listening and, 71–73
report talk, 121–122
research
 for public speaking, 209, 209–213, *213*
 supporting material for speeches, 226–232, *228,*
  229, 232
response, listening and, 71
Rheingold, Harold, *132*
Richards, I. A., 130

risks, taking, 244
role-taking, 22
romantic relationships
    characteristics of, 94
    interpersonal communication in, 94–100, *95, 97*
    maintaining, 98–100
    relationship development and disintegration stages, 95–100, *95*
    showing love in, *97*
Roosevelt, Theodore, 129, 130
rudeness, 83

S

Sapir, E., 111
sarcasm, 55
Savage, Mark, 297
scent, 61
scripts, 41
selection, perception and, 37–39
selection interview, 287
selective exposure, 299
selective retention, 299
self-analysis, 288
self-awareness, 17–31
    defined, 18
    emotional intelligence for, 25
    ethics and, 30–31
    experience and, 23
    identity and, 18, 26–28, *27*
    improving, 29
    measuring, 23–25
    overview, 17
    reflected appraisals for, 19–21
    role-taking and, 22
    self-fulfilling prophecies and, 20
    self-perception and, 22
    social comparison and, 21
self-concept, 18, 44
self-disclosure, 29, 91–92, 99
self-fulfilling prophecies, 20
self-leadership, 176
self-monitoring, 24
self-perception, 22
self-serving bias, 192
semantic interference
    defined, 10
    in listening, 79
senders, 5
Servant as Leader, The (Greenleaf), 179
servant leaders, 179–181
setting, for public speaking, 198–199
silence, 78–79
similarity bias, 191

situational anxiety, 247–250, *248*
situational leadership, 178–179
Smalley, G., 139
small group communication, 12
Smarter Faster Better (Duhigg), 176
social comparison, 21
social identity, 27–28
Social Judgment Theory, 270–272, *271*
social learning, 38
social penetration theory, 92
social zone, 59
socioeconomic status (SES) of audience, 197
Socrates, 17
space (proxemics), *59,* 59–60, 123
spatial organizational pattern (speeches), 224, *224*
speaking aids, 231, 260
special occasion speaking, 208
special occasion speeches, 283–285
specificity, 8
specific speech purpose, 221–222
speeches. *see also* public speaking; speech organization
    elevator speech, 291
    listening to, 83
    outlining, 214
    for special occasions, 283–285
    speeches that describe, 207
    speeches that explain, 207
    speeches to demonstrate, 207
    speeches to narrate, 207
    types of, overview, 195
speech organization, 219–240
    bibliography, 238
    ethical implications of, 239
    introduction and conclusion, 233–237
    magic line concept, *226*
    main points of speech, 222–223
    organizational pattern, 223–226, *224–226*
    outline of speech, overview, 220, *220*
    overview, 219–220
    purpose of speech, 221–222
    supporting material for, 226–232, *228, 229, 232*
    title of speech, 237–238
    topic selection, 195–196
    transitions, 232–233
speech to convince, 195
speech to reinforce, 195
stability *versus* change, 153
stagnating, 98
statistics, 229–230
stereotypes, 117
    perception and, 39
    self-awareness and, 28
stonewalling, 154, 156–157

storming stage, of groups, 172
storytelling, perception and, 81–82
sub-points (of speech), 222–223
Successfully Speaking (Wilner), 254
Superbosses (Finkelstein), 177
Superman, 21
supporting, by leaders, 179
supporting material (speeches), 226–232, *228, 229, 232*
support messages, 102, *102*
survival, building history of, 159
syllogism, 275
symbols, 2–3, 130–131, *131, 132*
Systems Theory of Family, 100

T

tag questions, 140
Tannen, Deborah, 124, 151
target audience, 297–298
task role, 158
technology, as communication channel, 8
terminating, 98
territory, 59
That's Not What I Meant! (Tannen), 151
They Have a Word for It (Rheingold), *132*
third-person effect, 299
Thomas, Kenneth W., 159
Thomas-Kilmann conflict mode instrument, 159
time
    chronemics in nonverbal communication, 60–61
    monochronic *versus* polychronic time orientation, 113
    for understanding and judging, 77
Tingley, Judith, 118
Tippett, Krista, 142
title of speech, 237–238
toast (speeches), 283–284
topic
    audience and, 197
    for public speaking, 197
    selection of, 195–196
    topical organizational pattern in speeches, 225, *226*
touch (haptics), 62–63, 124
Toulmin, Stephen, 277
Townsend, John, 89
trait anxiety, 247, 251
transitions, in speech organization, 232–233
Trent, J., 139
triangle of meaning, 130–131, *131*
truthfulness, 99

Tuckman, B. W., 171
turtle (group member type), 174–175, *175*

U

uncertainty avoidance, 116
unconscious messages, of nonverbal communication, 53
unequal relationships, conflict in, 162–163

V

value, proposition of, 276
values, self-awareness and, 24
Vangelisti, A. L., 95
Vaughn, Dianne, 98
Vaux, Bert, *136*
verbal code, 253
verbal communication. *see also* words
    channels of,8
    effects of nonverbal communication on, 55–57
    gender differences in, 118
    symbols of, 2–3
visual aids
    for public speaking, 260
    for speeches, 231
visual code, 254
visualization, 252, *253*
vividness, 139
vocal code, 253
vocal fillers, 61
vocalics, 61–62, 123, 258–260
volume, 62, 258
voluntary nature, of romantic relationships, 94

W

wardrobe, 250
Whorf, B., 111
Wilner, Lynda Katz, 254
words, 129–145
    ambiguity of, *132*, 132–134
    as arbitrary, 135–136
    as changeable, *134*, 134–135
    ethical implications of, 142–144, *143*
    nonverbal communication compared to language, 52
    overview, 129
    power of, 136–142, *139, 140*
    as symbols, 130–131, *131, 132*
    word choice, *136*
workplace harassment, 56–57
worldview, shared, 299